FAMILY COMMUNICATION
COHESION *and* CHANGE

SIXTH EDITION

Kathleen M. Galvin
Northwestern University

Carma L. Bylund
University of Iowa

Bernard J. Brommel
Northeastern Illinois University

PEARSON

Boston   New York   San Francisco
Mexico City   Montreal   Toronto   London   Madrid   Munich   Paris
Hong Kong   Singapore   Tokyo   Cape Town   Sydney

Executive Editor: Karon Bowers
Editorial Assistant: Jennifer Trebby
Marketing Manager: Mandee Eckersley
Production Editor: Michelle Limoges
Compositor: TKM Productions
Composition and Prepress Buyer: Linda Cox
Manufacturing Buyer: JoAnne Sweeney
Photo Researcher: Katharine S. Cook
Cover Designer: Joel Gendron

For related titles and support materials, visit our online catalog at www.ablongman.com.

Library of Congress Cataloging-in-Publication Data
Galvin, Kathleen M.
    Family communication : cohesion and change / Kathleen Galvin,
Carma Bylund, Bernard Brommel.—6th ed.
        p. cm.
    Includes bibliographical references and index.
    ISBN 0-205-37886-2
    1. Communication in the family—United States.   2. Interpersonal
communication—United States.   I. Bylund, Carma.   II. Brommel, Bernard J.
III. Title.

HQ734.G19   2003
306.87—dc21   2003043799

Printed in the United States of America

10 9 8 7 6 5 4 3 2 1   07 06 05 04 03

To my family: the Galvins, Wilkinsons, Nicholsens, Sullivans, and Lofinks, plus the special friends I consider as my family.   *KMG*

To the many people I am privileged to call family, especially Greg and Thurman.   *CLB*

To my 6 children, 15 grandchildren, and friends that are also family. Thanks to my clients who have provided many valuable insights.   *BJB*

CONTENTS

PREFACE

I t is with a deep sense of excitement and appreciation that we introduce the sixth edition of *Family Communication: Cohesion and Change*. When we wrote the first edition more than two decades ago, it was the first textbook to examine the family from a communication perspective. Very few classes addressed the topic and few communication scholars researched the issues. All that has changed. Today, most colleges and universities offer courses or units on the topic; many communication scholars have developed research programs focused on particular aspects of family interaction.

Historically, family interactions received scholarly attention from family therapists who addressed problem issues and from sociologists who addressed large group issues. In recent decades, communication scholars turned their attention to interactions within a diverse range of functional families. Current thinking places strong emphasis on theories and perspectives that reflect multiple research methods and celebrate the diversity of family experiences in terms of structure and culture. As growing numbers of communication scholars, as individuals and in research teams, study specific aspects of family interaction, their findings have increasingly filled pages of this text.

Our basic premise is that communication processes serve to create as well as reflect families. Relying on symbolic interaction and systems theories, we consider the communication processes within the family and how they affect, and are affected by, individual actions as well as movements in larger social systems. Our focus remains descriptive rather than prescriptive. We build on a framework that includes primary family functions—regulating cohesion and adaptability—and secondary family functions—developing appropriate family images, themes, boundaries, and biosocial beliefs. Throughout the book, we present first-person examples (names and identifying data have been changed) that complement specific content and ground the material in real-life experience.

The first three chapters establish the theoretical foundation of the text. Chapter 1 presents basic communication and family concepts as well as an overview of rapidly changing family demographics. Chapter 2 details our framework for analyzing family communication—an integration of primary and secondary family functions—that provide a template for exploring family interaction patterns. Chapter 3 establishes the systems perspective, which undergirds this text, explores the contributions of symbolic interaction and social construction theory to understanding family meanings, and details the ongoing contributions of dialectical theory to family communication. Chapter 4 explores how family meanings develop and emphasizes the power of multigenerational patterns. Chapter 5 examines relational maintenance through an examination of symbolic processes of rituals, currencies, and narratives, and Chapter 6 addresses the critical concept of family intimacy. Family roles and types are detailed in Chapter 7. Chapter 8, new to this edition, covers power and decision making, with emphasis on the critical role of interpersonal influence in family choices. Chapters 9 through 11 explore communication issues related to basic family interaction, including conflict, developmental stages, and management of unpredictable crises. Chapter 12 discusses the overlooked area of family contest, most specifically the physical and psychological realities of home. Finally, the last chapter examines various perspectives on well-functioning families and strategies for improving family communication.

With each edition, we attempt to reflect the patterned, yet constantly evolving, experience of family life and to incorporate the rapidly expanding research on families in general and family interaction patterns, more specifically. In this sixth edition, we continue to address critical issues of family diversity in terms of structure and ethnicity. In addition, we emphasize the growing research on the dark side of family life, including abuse, jealousy, and unpredictable stresses. Building on the fifth edition, we articulate explicitly our underlying theoretical structures, with special attention to social construction and dialectical theory. We continue to expand the work on family meanings and influence, and to emphasize family health issues as sites of communication. In researching each subsequent edition, we find a greater wealth of scholarship devoted to family communication, per se; this serves to expand and deepen our treatment of many issues.

We are grateful to Karon Bowers for her strong guidance and to Jennifer Trebby for her responsiveness, flexibility, and practical advice. We are indebted to the Allyn and Bacon editorial staff. Many persons contributed to the scholarly updating of the sixth edition. We received valuable feedback from Guy Bachman, Arizona State University; Karla Kay Jensen, Nebraska Wesleyan University; Sherilyn Marrow, University of North Colorado; and Teresa Sabourin, University of Cincinnati. Thank you, too, to reviewers of earlier editions: Vincent L. Bloom, California

State University–Fresno; Douglas L. Kelley, Arizona State University West; Teresa Sabourin, University of Cincinnati; Glen Stamp, Ball State University; Marlene von Friederichs-Fitzwater, California State University–Sacramento; and Gail G. Whitchurch, Indiana University–Purdue University at Indianapolis. We are most grateful to these colleagues. Our students and clients continue to provide insightful commentaries and useful examples. Jennifer Hollingsworth, Kathleen O'Connor, Danielle Uhlarik, Lesley Christensen, and Denise Scheive provided excellent research and editorial support, and Emily Bylund provided valuable bibliographic assistance.

Our family lives have changed significantly in the past two decades— a process that continues to teach us about family development and unpredictable stresses. To our growing number of family members, we express our continued gratitude for their patience, support, and unwitting contributions to our teaching and writing.

Finally, this book continues to reflect our own commitment to teaching family communication. Unlike most other academic courses, students bring extensive personal insight and experience to our classes. From them, and through our own research and clinical practice, we continue to learn about how families interact and what it means to be a member of a family system.

We hope you will find the exploration of family communication to be a meaningful and thought-provoking academic experience.

Kathleen M. Galvin
Carma L. Bylund
Bernard J. Brommel

INTRODUCTION *to* *the* FAMILY

Families, whether biological or chosen, are what give most people's lives their shape. They produce enormous pain and joy and all the emotions in between for their members. . . . I would never argue that families are great, only that they are human.

Mary Pipher, *The Shelter of Each Other*

We are born into a family, mature in a family, form new families, and leave our families upon death. Family life is a universal human experience. Yet, no two people share the exact same experience, partly because of the unique communication patterns in each family system. Because the family is such a powerful influence on our lives, we need to examine family relationships to understand ourselves better as members of one of the most complex and important parts of society. Family communication patterns serve to construct as well as reflect familial experience. In short, we create our families just as we are created by these families.

As you read this book, you will examine a subject in which you have some expertise, because you have spent your life in some type or types of family arrangements. Yet, because you have lived in only one or a small number of family structures, your experience is limited compared to the range of potential family experiences. Your reading should expand your understanding of many families' communication patterns and highlight similarities and differences from your experiences.

This book presents a framework for examining communication within families. By the end of the text, you should be able to apply this model to an unknown family and analyze it as a communication system. We also hope that you will apply what you learn about communication dynamics to your own family or family experiences.

Throughout this book, you will find some material written in the first person and set off from the text. These selections, some direct quotes and some reconstructions provided by friends, students, and clients, illustrate many of the concepts discussed in the text. These statements should enable you to understand the concepts more completely. Some comments will remind you specifically of your own family experiences, whereas others will seem quite different from your background. Yet, as the following portrays, there are different ways to live a family life.

I guess you could say I've had three "moms" and two and a half "dads." My parents divorced when my twin brother and I were about 3 years old. My dad remarried and, after two more sons, got divorced again. Then he remarried and now I have a baby sister young enough to be my daughter. My mom remarried and got divorced again when we were about 7. The "half-father" that we had was a man who lived with us for 10 years who recently moved out on my mother's request. The reason my brother and I are still sane is because our mom and dad have always remained friends. We were never treated like pawns in the middle of a battle.

As family members, teachers, and family therapists, we hold certain basic beliefs that undergird the words on the following pages. Our backgrounds have given us particular perspectives that affect how we view families and their communication. Our perspectives may be very similar to or quite different from yours. Because our backgrounds influence our thinking and writing, we wish to share these beliefs with you to establish a context for understanding.

1. There are many ways to be a family. Family life is as diverse as the types of persons who create families. There are varied types of families and numerous ways to relate within each family type. Families are human systems created by ordinary people; the "perfect" family does not exist. Each family must struggle to create its own identity as it experiences good times and stressful times. All families are influenced by the larger context in which they exist.

2. Communication serves to constitute as well as reflect family relationships. It is through talk that persons define their identities and negotiate their relationships with each other and the rest of the world. This talk also serves to indicate the state of family relationships.

3. Communication is the process by which family members create and share their meanings with each other. Members develop a relational culture, or a shared universe, that may be viewed as a unique communication system.

4. Families are part of multigenerational communication patterns. Family members are influenced by the patterns of previous generations as they create their own patterns, which will influence generations to come. The family serves as each person's first communication classroom.

5. Families provide members with ways to make sense out of the world. Families socialize members to their underlying values and beliefs about significant life issues, such as gender, health, and religion, to name a few.

6. Families reflect ethnic communication patterns. Family members are influenced by their cultural backgrounds that affect lifestyle and behavior. A family's ethnic heritage may set norms for communication that influence generations unless they are consciously altered.

7. Well-functioning families work at managing their communication patterns because developing and maintaining relationships takes effort. Such families develop the capacity to adapt, to share intimacy, and to manage conflict. They are self-aware; they value the goal of effective communication.

This text will not present prescriptive solutions for family problems; rather, it will introduce you to the diverse world of families and their complex communication patterns and it will develop your observational and analytical skills. We hope your increased understanding of family communication will be accompanied by an increased appreciation for complexities and change inherent in this area of study. We also hope you will find the area of family communication as fascinating and challenging as we do. As an introduction to the family, this chapter will discuss definitional issues and family status. The next section establishes an understanding of the concept of the family that will be used throughout the rest of the book.

FAMILIES: DEFINITIONAL ISSUES

What comes to your mind when you hear the word *family?* What do you mean by the term? Although *family* is a word used frequently, reaching agreement on its meaning is much more difficult than you might suspect. In the following section, you will see the variations implied in the simple term *family*.

Family Types

Essentially, there is no single, widely agreed-upon definition of the term *family*. Families have been viewed according to blood ties and legal ties, described as networks of persons who live together over periods of time, and defined as groups of people who have ties of marriage and kinship to one another. In their attempt to identify the essence of family, Fitzpatrick and Badzinski (1985) suggest that the only universal family type is a small, kinship-structured group whose primary function is the nurturing socialization of newborn children. This position describes a *family realm,* which is created by the birth process and the establishment of ties across generations (Beutler, Burr, Bahr, & Herrin, 1988), the core aspect being the "biological, emotional, social and developmental processes that are inherent in procreation and the nurturing of dependent children." This definition includes both intergenerational issues and multiple family forms.

The media culture appears to have a singular, idealized view of the family, vividly depicted in media holiday advertising—a middle-class, blood-related family with smiling parents and grandparents, eating a traditional turkey dinner. In reality, this image represents only one family form, and a life experienced by a small segment of people.

The American family does not exist. Family historian Harevan (1982) expresses her concern with this idealized family, claiming that U.S. society always has contained "great diversities in family types and family behavior that were associated with the recurring entrance of new immigrant groups into American society. Ethnic, racial, cultural class differences have also resulted in diversity in family behavior" (p. 461). Another family historian, Coontz (1992), believes that most Americans move in and out of a variety of family experiences across their lifetimes. In other words, "Families change their size and shape throughout their histories . . . but throughout these changes we recognize them still as families, and as whole ones at that" (Stewart, Copeland, Chester, Malley, & Barenbaum, 1997, pp. 245–246).

Families of today are defining themselves, for themselves, through their interactions. At the same time, longevity, legal flexibility, personal choice, ethnicity, gender, geographic distance, and reproductive technology are impacting traditional biological and legal conceptions of family. Society has passed the point of seeing the "traditional versus nontraditional" family categories as functional. Fitzpatrick (1998) argues that society needs to "employ definitions of the family that depend on how families define themselves rather than definitions based on genetic and sociological criteria" (p. 45). This point of view asserts that "families are constituted by the very communication processes one seeks to study as being 'within a family'" (Steier, 1989, p. 15). Many scholars are concerned with how family members define themselves as families—in other words, how they use communication to define their family for themselves. This *constitutive* approach to creating family challenges the conception of one dominant form of family life.

Today, a family may be viewed more broadly as a group of people with a past history, a present reality, and a future expectation of interconnected mutually influencing relationships. Members often (but not necessarily) are bound together by heredity, legal marital ties, adoption, or committed, voluntaristic ties. Wamboldt and Reiss (1989) developed a process definition of the family as "a group of intimates who generate a sense of home and group identity; complete with strong ties of loyalty and emotion, and experience history and future" (p. 728). In her essay on redefining families, Minow (1998) argues that it is not important whether a group fits a formal legal definition; instead what is important is "whether the group of people function as a family: do they share affection and resources, think of one another as family members, and present themselves as such to neighbors and others?" (p. 8). Clearly, these definitions emphasize the personal, voluntarily connected relationships among family members instead of relying solely on blood ties or legal agreements as the basis for a family. In a study that asked "What constitutes a family?" respondents provided a range of beliefs. Whereas 98 percent agreed that "a married couple living with their children" is definitely a family, only 20 percent saw "two gay men committed to each other and

Two-parent biological families are no longer the most common family form.

living together" as a family. Other answers ranged between these poles (What Constitutes a Family, 1992).

As we talk about families in this book, we will take a broad, inclusive view. Therefore, if the members consider themselves to be a family, we accept their self-definition. Generally, we will refer to family as *networks of people who share their lives over long periods of time bound by ties of marriage, blood, or commitment, legal or otherwise, who consider themselves as family and who share a significant history and anticipated future of functioning in a family relationship.* Such a definition encompasses countless variations of family forms and numerous types of interaction patterns.

In contemporary society, family diversity abounds. One indication of the complexities of today's families may be found in a review of current literature, which includes such categories as large, extended, blood-related groups; formal and informal communal groups; stepfamilies; single-parent families; and gay and lesbian partnerships. These families reflect multiple cultural and socioeconomic situations.

We, your authors, represent three very different family experiences. One grew up in New York City as an only child of Irish immigrants. After her parents died, she acquired an adoptive Norwegian-German family with three siblings. Currently she is married and a parent to 3 young adult children, one of whom was adopted from Korea. Another is the oldest of 7 children and grew up in a university town in Missouri. Her first marriage ended in divorce. She is currently married and the mother of an energetic toddler. The final one grew up on an Iowa farm in a German-Irish family of 9 children, married, fathered 6 children, divorced, and is now the grandfather of 12. He is retired from teaching and maintains a private family counseling practice. Although blood relatives are important to each of us, we all have friends who are considered to be family members.

You may have grown up in a small family, or a large four-generation household. Your brothers and sisters may be blood related, step, or adopted. Some of you may be single parents, stepparents, or foster parents. And some of you may have experienced one committed marriage, whereas others may have experienced divorce, death, and remarriage or a committed partnership. No simple pattern exists.

My family consisted of a mother and brother only, but lacked a father. Due to this fact, my mother brought us together ideologically with a strong focus on being one as a group, but lacking strength when separated. Her comments strongly suggest this when, in time of crisis, we always said, "As long as we pull together and believe in one another, we'll be okay." Physical proximity also played a role in this togetherness through attending church together on Sundays, and trying to speak to our mother at least once a day. Due to the fact that she worked 13-hour days, she normally arrived home after we had fallen asleep.

This reality creates a problem for texts such as this one. We wish to represent the multiple ways families are formed, yet almost all the research still refers to discrete categories for practical purposes. In the following pages we will note some of the traditional categories when talking about families because that is how the research is written. However, we recognize that actual families represent overlapping structural forms. Our category system encompasses the following styles of family formation: the two-parent biological family, single-parent family, blended family, extended or integrational family, and committed partners. These are not discrete categories; many families may belong to more than one.

A *two-parent biological family* consists of parents and the children who are from the union of these parents. Thus, blood ties and the original marriage bond characterize this type. Although traditionally thought of as "typical," this type of family no longer represents the most common family form.

A *single-parent family* consists of one parent and one or more children. This formation may include an unmarried man or woman and his or her offspring; a man or a woman who lost his or her partner through death, divorce, or desertion, and the children of that union; a single parent and his or her adopted or foster children. When two parents are still involved in child care, the term *primary parent* may be used. For some children, the experience in a single-parent system is temporary until the parent remarries; however, over one-third of custodial mothers will not remarry and the number of solo mothers continues to increase. Finally, some single-parent families are headed by a widowed parent or an adoptive parent.

Although the term *single parent* is commonly used, we will alternate the term with *primary parent* occasionally, recognizing Walsh's (1993) point that "single parent" describes one parent carrying out all parental obligations while ongoing involvement with the other parent is precluded. This occurs most frequently in cases of death and abandonment. When two parents take some, usually unequal, responsibility for children, the custodial parent is referred to as the primary parent. Both adults may be referred to as co-parents. The term *solo mother* refers to a mother rearing her children from birth without the support and assistance of the father (Gringlas & Weinraub, 1995).

The *blended family* consists of two adults and their children, all of whom may not be from the union of their relationship. Most are families blended through remarriage; a situation that brings two previous systems into new family ties. You may have witnessed the common pattern in which a two-parent biological family becomes a single-parent family for a period of time, after which certain members become part of a stepfamily. Families may also be blended through the addition of adopted or foster children.

The stepfamily has been compared to a challenging and complex chess game, a delicate and intricate spider's web, a second chance, and a time bomb. No matter what the analogy, the stepfamily is a complex, growing, and little-understood segment of American family life. Characteristics of stepfamilies include (Pasley, 1997; Papernow, 1993; Galvin, 1993; Bray & Kelly, 1998):

- Some or all members bring past family history from a relationship that has changed or ended. These members carry with them a sense of loss.
- The couple does not begin as a dyad but, rather, the parent-child relationship predates the partnership bond.
- One or two biological parents (living or dead) influence the stepfamily.
- The family has a complex extended family network and children may function as members of two households.
- No legal relationship automatically exists between the stepparent and stepchild.
- Many of these family relationships began as "not-so-freely-chosen" or involuntary relationships.

Although most stepfamilies are formed after the dissolution of a parent's first marriage, we can also include single parents marrying or gay and lesbian stepfamilies.

Adoption creates another type of blended family—a family "that is *connected* to another family, the birth family, and often to different cultures and to different ethnic and national groups as well" (Bartholet, 1993, p. 186). This legally constructed family "does not signal the absolute end of one family and the beginning of another, nor does it sever the psychological tie to an earlier family" (Reitz & Watson, 1992, p. 11). We think of it as expanding family boundaries for everyone.

Constructing families through adoption is a centuries-old process, evolving from a responsibility managed within family bloodlines to practices of matching personal characteristics, such as ethnicity or religion, to an open style of connections crossing religious, racial, and international lines. In contrast to earlier practices, in recent decades an increasing number of adoptions are transnational, are transracial, pertain to older children or children with disabilities, and involve single parents or gay male and lesbian parents (March & Miall, 2000). Many adoptions are "open," reflecting direct long-term connections between birth mothers and adoptive parents, creating new types of extended families.

Although an *extended (or intergenerational) family* traditionally refers to that group of relatives living within a nearby geographic area, it may be more narrowly understood as the addition of blood relatives, other than the parents, to the everyday life of a child unit. For example, this may take a cross-generational form, including grandparents who live with a parent-child system or who take on exclusive parenting roles for grandchildren. Given increasing longevity, more families will include four and five generations of relatives who may maintain active contact, as the following indicates.

I grew up in an extended family. My great-grandparents were the dominant figures. Most of us lived with our grandparents at one time or another. There were six different households in the neighborhood I grew up in. My great-grandmother, referred to as "Mother," babysat for all the kids while our parents were at work.

There are also people who were informally adopted in my family. My mother and one of my cousins were raised by their grandmother, even though their parents did not live there. In my family no one is considered half or step. You are a member of the family, and that is that.

The *voluntaristic* family involves a pair or a group of people, some or all of whom are unrelated biologically or legally, who share a commitment to each other, may live together, and consider themselves to be a family. These relationships are sometimes called *fictive kin*. Formal examples of these family types are found in communal situations such as a kibbutz or in a religious organization. Other extended families are informally formed around friendship or common interests or commitments. Two neighboring families may share so many experiences that, over time, both sets of children and parents begin to talk of each other as "part of the family."

Committed partners may include married couples without children, cohabiting heterosexual couples, and some gay male and lesbian partners. Committed partners may form their own familial unit as an outgrowth of their original families. Although their numbers are small, some married couples choose to remain child-free, whereas others remain childless due to infertility. Homosexual partners are included in this category, as long as the partners consider each other as family. They may also be parents through previous relationships, adoption, or use of reproductive technology.

Committed partners continue to serve as children to the previous generation and as siblings and extended family members to other generations, while at the same time providing loyalty and affection to one another. Most people experience family life in an evolutionary manner, moving through different family forms over time, experiencing changes due to aging and unpredictable stresses.

In addition, most persons experience life with one or more biological, adopted, or step siblings, the longest-lasting family relationships due to age similarity. Sibling relationships are significant sources of information on communication patterns.

Because I have very close relationships with my two brothers and my sister, we know which buttons to push when we go home as adults. I find myself adding words back to my vocabulary that haven't been there in years, words such as jerk, brat, and stupid. It is amazing how when I am with my family, we all revert to roles that we were in when we were children. Since I am the oldest, I find myself wanting to take charge.

It is important to distinguish between two types of family experiences: current families and families-of-origin. Families in combination beget families through the evolutionary cycles of coming together and separating. Each person may experience life in different families starting with his or her family-of-origin. *Family-of-origin* refers to the family or families in which a person is raised. Pioneering family therapist Virginia Satir (1988) stresses the importance of the family-of-origin as the blueprint for people making, stating, "Blueprints vary from family to family. I believe some blueprints result in nurturing families, some result in troubled ones" (p. 210). Multigenerational patterns, those of more than two generations, are considered as part of the blueprint (Hoopes, 1987). As you will discover, family-of-origin and multigenerational experiences are crucial in the development of communication patterns in current families.

FAMILIES: CURRENT STATUS

Demographic Trends

The composition and shape of the contemporary family is constantly changing. In order to understand family interaction fully, it is necessary to examine the current status of family life in the United States. No matter how old you are, you have lived long enough to witness major changes in your family or in the families around you—changes that reflect an evolving national picture. American families continue to reflect greater racial and ethnic diversity with each passing decade, and many families face increasing economic stress or poverty. Although there are numerous similarities in family communication patterns across large groups, differences in family forms, composition, and culture affect members' interactions. As you read about the current trends, try to imagine their implications for family communication. Although research figures shift constantly and various sources provide slightly different numerical data, the overall point is clear: The American family continues to undergo dramatic changes in the twenty-first century, as indicated by the following trends (Current Population Reports, 1998; Simmons & O'Neill, 2001).

- Americans continue to marry.

  Married couples account for 51.7 percent of U.S. households— 23.5 percent of which have children under age 18 (Simmons & O'Neill, 2001). Current trends indicate that first marriages are taking place later in life. For example, the median age for women at first marriage was 21 in 1975, 23 in 1985, 24 in 1994, and 25 in 1997. For men, it was 26.5 in 1992 and 26.7 in 1997, the highest since 1900. Approximately half of women marry before age 25; most of the rest marry before age 30. Men marry at slightly older ages. The average length of a first marriage ending in divorce ranged from 7.3 years in 1975 to 6.9 years in 1980; the number went back up to an average of 7.2 years in 1997. Often, one partner is remarrying while the other is marrying for the first time (National Center for Health Statistics, 2001).

- The divorce rate is stabilizing.

  Recently, the divorce rate dropped slightly after a significant rise from 1960 to 1990: 43 percent of first marriages break up in the first 15 years (National Center for Health Statistics, 2001). These divorce rate figures also reflect the longevity of people in today's society. In earlier times, when more people died at a younger age, many unsatisfactory marriages were ended by death rather than divorce—a situation that historian Lawrence Stone refers to as a functional substitute for death (Coontz, 1992).

- Remarriage rates, although high, are dropping.

  The majority of divorced individuals form new partnerships through remarriage. About five out of six men and three out of four women eventually remarry after a first divorce. The mean length of time between divorce and remarriage is four years; 30 percent remarry within a year (Coleman, Ganong, & Fine, 2000). Multiple remarriages are becoming more common. In 1997, 43 percent of weddings involved one partner marrying for the second time; in one of seven weddings, one partner is marrying for the third time. The divorce rate has hovered around 60 percent for second marriages, although remarriages of persons over age 40 tend to be more stable than first marriages (Wu & Penning, 1997).

- Age and parenting responsibility affect remarriage.

    Childless divorced women under 30 years old are most likely to remarry, followed by divorced women with children under age 30. Older women are the least likely to remarry. The incidence of re-divorce continues to rise as individuals remarry more often. For older divorced men and women, the rates of cohabitation are increasing.

- Stepfamilies continue to increase through remarriage and cohabitation.

    The stepfamily remains a vital family form, although census figures are difficult to use because of variations in custodial arrangements. One out of every three Americans is now a step-parent, a stepchild, a stepsibling, or some other member of a step-family (Larson, 1992). Researchers have estimated that 35 percent of all U.S. children will be part of a stepfamily before adulthood (Ganong & Coleman, 1994). Most children in remarried house-holds live with their biological mother and stepfather. Many step-families, approximately 25 percent, are formed by cohabiting couples, since cohabiting couples are more likely to enter a new union involving children than are remarrying couples (Bumpass, Raley, & Sweet, 1995; Coleman, Ganong, & Fine, 2000).

- The number of single-parent families continues to increase.

    Americans are witnessing the continuing rise of single-parent or primary parents systems. In the 1990s, 60 percent of youth were expected to live with only one parent sometime before reaching age 18. In 2000, 22 percent of children lived with only their mothers and 4 percent lived with only their fathers (Simmons & O'Neill, 2001). Throughout the past decade, U.S. women under age 30 who become pregnant for the first time were more likely to be un-married than married. In 1997, 41 percent of mother-child families included a never-married mother. Yet, today the number of births to unmarried teenagers has declined slightly and some single par-ents marry after bearing children. These figures vary by ethnicity. In 2000, 77 percent of white non-Hispanic children lived with two parents, compared to 38 percent of African American children and 65 percent of children of Hispanic origin.

- Families continue to be constructed through adoption.

    Although the government stopped collecting adoption records from 1975 to 1990, some experts estimate the number of adoptees at 2 to 4 percent of the population, or some 5 to 10 million individuals (Carp, 1998). Slightly more than half are adopted by relatives or stepparents (Brodzinsky, Smith, & Brodzinsky, 1998). Adoption may include "related" and "nonrelated" children. The past decades have witnessed a significant increase in transnational and transracial adoption.

- Some families are constructed or expanded through scientific technologies.

  Although the numbers are small, some individuals and couples are achieving parenthood through anonymous or known donor insemination due to lifestyle choice or infertility. Although success rates remain low for infertile individuals, multiple attempts and constant scientific advances are making this possibility more viable (Rosenbaum, 1995). Assisted reproductive technology has produced over 300,000 babies since 1977 (Parke, 2002). This is a process shrouded in secrecy for most families (Imber-Black, 1998).

- More adult children are living at home.

  Adult children are remaining at home until an older age and children are more likely to return after departures from the parental home (Mitchell & Gee, 1996). The latter are often referred to as *boomerang kids*. In 1997, 22 million adult children were living with one or both parents and increasing. One-third of Generation X returns home at some point in their early adulthood (Cetron & Davies, 2001). Although reasons vary, common explanations for this change include economic pressures, cultural norms, and returning young divorced mothers with small children.

- The number of cohabiting partners is growing rapidly.

  Unmarried partners comprise 5.2 percent of U.S. households. Conventionally, such households are defined as heterosexual couples who live together as intimate partners with or without children present. Rates of cohabitation are increasing: "By 1997 there were approximately 4.1 million cohabiting couples, an increase of 46 percent since 1990" (Selzer, 2000). For never-married young adults it is frequently a stage before marriage, but for others it is an end in itself. Cohabitation is frequently perceived as less of an investment in the relationship due to the lack of a formal ceremony and legal complications (DeMaris, 2001). Yet, cohabiters today are more likely to bear children than in previous times—a reality that involves commitment and legal ties.

- Families of lesbians and gay males are increasing.

  Census figures on gay and lesbian couples or families are not available. Blumstein and Schwartz (1983) suggest that, until the 1970s, gay males and lesbians were a fairly invisible part of the

U.S. population. Survey data from the 1990s found that 40 to 60 percent of gay men and 45 to 80 percent of lesbians were in steady romantic relationships (Patterson, 2000). Currently, an increasing number of gay men and lesbians have formed committed partnerships, consider themselves to be family, and are finding varying levels of legal and institutional recognition of their unions as a family type. Laird (1993) uses the terms *gay male family* and *lesbian family* to refer to same-sex couples and to families with children headed by a lesbian or gay couple or solo parent. Some researchers have reported that there are between 1.5 and 2 million lesbian mothers and gay fathers of 14 million children (Coleman, 1992; West & Turner, 1995).

- Extended families continue to flourish.

  Close to 4 million U.S. households are multigenerational. Many other families are surrounded by relatives in nearby neighborhoods or communities. As American families become more culturally diverse, the extended family has reemerged in importance. The African American tradition of extended kin, as well as the values of recent Asian immigrants reinforce the central importance of biological or fictive kin (Sudarkasa, 1998; Kibria, 1998).

- Families increasingly represent four and five generations.

  Individuals continue to live longer. People born in 1998 have life expectancies linked to place of birth as follows: for Western Europe, 78 years; North America, 76; Latin America, 69; Asia, 65; Sub-Saharan Africa, 49 (World Population Profile, U.S. Census Bureau, 1998). Gender differences do exist, however. U.S. men born in 1995 have a life expectancy of 72.6 years, whereas women have an expectancy of 78.9 years.

  The longevity results in an increase in four- and five-generation households. Increasing numbers of children are living in grandparent-headed households with or without a parent. In addition, more middle-aged persons are taking on caregiver roles for elderly parents and grandparents. Considering that most people marry first during their twenties, a continuous marriage might well be expected to last 45-plus years. The number of married couples without children at home continues to rise as people live longer and as women bear a smaller number of children in the early years of marriage. On a somber note, widowhood has become an expectant life event for older married women, since more than two-thirds who die at age 85 or older are females. Connections to siblings are becoming a central family concern for older persons.

These family descriptors do not fully capture the voluntaristic family commitments made by individuals or groups that are not recorded in census or related data. You can imagine how family interactions might differ given these trends. Some family forms tend to encourage secrets or avoidance of family composition; others tend to require consistent renegotiation of members' roles. Some families encourage members to talk about their lives with outsiders, whereas others discourage such openness. Many current families continue to engage in role negotiation.

Economic Issues

All these changes are intertwined with economic and cultural realities. Working mothers are commonplace today. Two-income couples are becoming the norm (Cetron & Davies, 2001). A dual income is seen as necessary, if not desirable, by most couples. Waite and Gallagher (2000) note that in most married couples with minor children, the husband is employed full time and half the time the wife has paid employment. Although the amount of time employed mothers spend with their children (3.2 hours a day) has remained constant over 20 years, the time employed fathers spend with their children has increased to 2.3 hours per workday. Yet, 70 percent of all parents feel they do not spend enough time with their children (Families and Work Institute, 1998). In many cases, dual-earner couples with children are working in shifts for economic or personal reasons. Such arrangements tend to strengthen parent-child bonds but limit couple contact significantly (Lawlor, 1998). Over 70 percent of single mothers are working and most have little choice but to work. Due to these changes, the United States is witnessing a phenomenon of *latchkey children*. These children return from school hours before a parent returns from work and are expected to contribute to the successful running of the household. Young children may spend many of their waking hours with babysitters or in day-care centers, encountering their parents only a few hours a day. Increasing numbers of counselors are concerned that the pressures of work, long hours, and downsizing have created enormous stress for families (Bielski, 1996). In their research on negative spillover between work and family, Grzywacz, Almeida, and McDonald (2002) conclude that negative stress from work-family overlap begins in young adulthood and continues through midlife.

Another economic reality that impacts directly on family life is poverty. Children have now replaced seniors as the poorest segment of the population; at the turn of the century, 16 percent of children under age 18 lived in poverty (America's Children, 2002). One-third of the homeless are families with children—a figure that is rising rapidly. Although a large number of poor families contain two parents, the female single-parent family is five times more likely to live in poverty than the two-parent family (Coontz & Folbre, 2002). In addition, there is an increasing gap between rich and middle-class families because decaying wage and job structures have resulted in income redistribution (Coontz,

The stresses of poverty increase family tensions.

1996). Economic pressures add significant stress to the lives of poor family members, and this stress affects the ways family members relate to each other. Although there is financial concern in families in which both parents work, only 8 percent of such families are poor compared to 42 percent of single-mother families. In good economic times, there are positive effects of male and female earnings and employment on marital quality, stability, and children's lives in general (White & Rogers, 2002). Through the turn of the century, older workers maintained solid incomes and many retired later (Cetron & Davies, 2001). The recent economic downturn has affected family members of all ages.

Ethnic Issues

No examination of family status is complete without a discussion of the effect of ethnicity on family functioning. Within the past decades, several forces have combined to bring ethnic issues to the attention of family scholars. First, the overall ethnic composition of U.S. families is changing as the number of African American, Hispanic American, and Asian American families increases. Second, scholars are recognizing the long-term effect of ethnic heritage on family functioning. Finally, there is an unequal impact of poverty across racial and ethnic groups.

American society represents a rapidly changing and diverse set of ethnic and cultural groups. In 1990, the U.S. population was 76 percent Anglo, 12 percent African American, 9 percent Latino, and 3 percent Asian. In 2000, 64 percent of U.S. children were white, non-Hispanic; 16 percent were black, non-Hispanic; 4 percent were Asian/Pacific Islander; and 1 percent were American Indian/Alaska Native. The Hispanic child population has increased very quickly, growing from 9 percent in 1990 to 16 percent in 2000. By 2020, more than one in five U.S. children may be of Hispanic origin.

There is considerable difference in family structure by race. Marriage remains much less common among African Americans than whites, leading to a higher proportion of births to unmarried black women (70 percent) than to unmarried white women (25 percent). The proportion of births to unmarried Hispanic women was 43 percent (Blau, Ferber, & Winkler, 1997). Families of varying ethnic/cultural backgrounds differ in size. White married couples had an average of 3.20 children, compared with blacks at 3.59 and Hispanics at 4.17. Female-householder families, with no spouse present, followed a similar pattern: for whites, 2.86; for blacks, 3.31; and for Hispanics, 3.43 people (Current Population Reports, 1998). Hispanic families are growing at the highest rate. Currently, Hispanics represent the largest minority group with children younger than age 18. Traditionally, these families report strong grandparent and extended family ties. Rates of marriage, divorce, and remarriage vary according to ethnic background (Heaton & Jacobson, 1994).

Current census data indicate the number of foreign-born residents and children of immigrants has reached the highest level in history—56 million people, who represent 20 percent of the population. Over 25 percent of foreign-born residents are from Mexico. Families with children vary greatly by ethnicity. "The proportion of married couples with children under 18 ranged from 35 percent for residents born in Europe to 73.4 percent for those from Latin America" (Scott, 2002, p. A18). As a result of immigration, many family members in the United States do not speak English at home or have difficulty speaking English. Approximately 17 percent of school-aged children do not speak English at home. The majority of these children are of Hispanic or Asian origin.

In general, classification systems are becoming less useful as people marry and adapt across cultures. In the future, categorization of family race/ethnicity will have to change as intermarriage, adoption, and cohabitation increase the population of mixed-ethnicity families. In 2000, interracial couples accounted for 1.9 percent of married couples and 4.3 percent of unmarried couples (Simmons & O'Neill, 2001). The number of African American and white interracial married couples has almost dou-

Increasingly, single women or lesbian partners are having or adopting children.

bled in the past two decades. Over 4 percent of U.S. children are of mixed race, and that figure is rapidly rising.

Although generalizations about cultural groups must always be accompanied by an indication of their many exceptions, a consideration of family ethnicity provides one more perspective from which to examine communication patterns. This perspective will receive increased attention because, by the middle of the twenty-first century, Americans of European ancestry will be in the minority. This shift will influence underlying assumptions about how families work.

It is important to consider ethnicity in families because, contrary to popular myth, Americans have not become homogenized in a "melting pot"; instead, various cultural/ethnic heritages are maintained across generations. In her overview of studies in family ethnicity, McGoldrick (1993) points to the increasing evidence that ethnic values and identification are retained for many generations after immigration and play a significant role in family life and personal development throughout the life cycle. She maintains that second-, third-, and even fourth-generation Americans reflect their original cultural heritage in lifestyle and behavior.

My parents' marriage reflected an uneasy blend of Italian and Norwegian cultures. My mother included her Italian relatives in on many issues my father considered private. He was overwhelmed by her family's style of arguing and making up and would retreat to the porch during big celebrations. I came to realize that cultural tension was reflected in many of their differences, including their child-rearing patterns. I carry pieces of those conflicting patterns within me today.

Ethnicity may affect family life through its traditions, celebrations, occupations, values, and problem-solving strategies. There are strong variations across cultures and familial issues, such as age at first marriage, single parenthood, older marriages, changing marital partners, and male-female roles (Dilworth-Anderson & McAdoo, 1988; McGoldrick, 1993). The definition of the concept *family* may differ across ethnic groups. For example, whereas the majority "white Anglo-Saxon" definition focuses on the intact nuclear unit, African American families focus on a wide kinship network, and Italians function with a large, intergenerational, tightly knit family that includes godparents and old friends. The Chinese are likely to include all ancestors and descendants in the concept of family. Each of these views has an impact on communication within the family.

It is important to remember that families are more likely to be poor if they are of African American or Hispanic American background. This is due to the influence of factors such as inequalities in educational and employment opportunities, lower parent educational attainment, younger parental ages, more single-parent families, larger family sizes, less steady employment, and less frequent child support by absent parents (Zill & Nord, 1994). Pressures that plague higher percentages of certain ethnic groups, unemployment, low wages, and poverty discourage or erode marriage, further confounding economic well-being (Coontz & Folbre, 2002).

Changes in family forms accompanied by economic and cultural variations have implications for the ways family members communicate with each other. For example, the rise of two-career families alters the amount of time parents and children are in direct contact. Economic stress frequently results in escalating family stress. The high divorce rate increases the chances that family members of all ages will undergo major transitions, including changes in their communication patterns. The growth in single-parent systems and dual-career couples increases a child's interpersonal contact with a network of extended family or professional caregivers. Most children in stepfamilies function within two different family systems, each with its own communication patterns. The family is no longer taken for granted as having one fixed form. As U.S. families reflect greater ethnic diversity, family life will be characterized by a wider range of communication patterns.

Functional Families

At this point, it is important to forecast the families we will discuss in the upcoming chapters. Historically, most literature on family interaction has focused on dysfunctional or pathological families. Early studies examined families with a severely troubled member with a disability—a trend that was followed by attempts to characterize "normal" families. As you may imagine from the previous description of the definitions and the status of families, there is little agreement on what is "normal." In recent years, attention has shifted to understanding the workings of the well-functioning, or "normal," family.

The following four perspectives on so-called normal families represent the evolution of related thinking (Walsh, 1993, pp. 5–7):

1. *Normal Families as Asymptomatic Family Functioning.* This approach implies there are no major symptoms of psychopathology among family members.
2. *Normal Families as Average.* This approach identifies families that appear typical or seem to fit common patterns.
3. *Normal Families as Optimal.* This approach stresses positive or ideal characteristics often based on members' accomplishments.
4. *Normal Family Processes.* This approach stresses a systems perspective focusing on adaptation over the life cycle and adaptation to stresses and contexts.

The first three perspectives quickly prove limiting or unworkable because of the static nature of the definition. The transitional perspective provides a sense of variation and adaptation that capture the dynamic nature of family experience.

Studies of well-functioning families highlight the tremendous diversity of families that appear to be functioning adequately at a particular point in time (Kantor & Lehr, 1976; Reiss, 1981; Olson, McCubbin, & Associates, 1983; Fitzpatrick, 1988; Walsh, 1993; Wallerstein & Blakeslee, 1995; Carter & McGoldrick, 1999).

In this text, we will focus on communication within functional families, because this constitutes the primary experience for most of you. This book will attempt to dispel two myths: (1) there is one right way to be a family and (2) there is one right way to communicate within a family. Throughout the following pages, you will encounter a wide variety of descriptions of family life and communication behavior. Our purpose is to help increase your understanding of the dynamics of family communication, not to suggest solutions to family problems. Hence, we will take a descriptive, rather than a prescriptive, approach.

We hope there is some personal, rather than just academic, gain from reading these pages. Most of you come from families that have their share of pain and problems as well as joy and comfort. It is our hope that you will gain a new insight into the people with whom you share your lives. As you go through this text, think about your own family and other real or fictional families with which you are familiar. We hope you choose to apply what you learn to your own family, although it may be difficult at times. The words of one of our students describe this process better than we can:

Analyzing my own family has not been an easy process. As I began, my entire soul cried out, "How do I begin to unravel the web of rules, roles, and strategies that make up our system?" I do not claim to have all possible answers; certainly my opinions and attitudes are different from those of the others in my family. I also do not claim to have the answers to all our problems. But I have tried to provide answers to my own confusion and to provide some synthesis to the change and crises that I have experienced. And I have grown from the process.

Conclusion

This chapter provides an overview of what it means to be a family and illustrates the diversity of family life. Basic beliefs about families and communication were shared and there was an examination of family definitions and ethnic consideration of the family as a system. The current status of the American family was examined, touching on issues of trends in marriage, divorce, and remarriage; the rise of dual-career couples and single-parent systems; increased life expectancy; economic pressures; and cultural diversity. Finally, issues related to "normal" family functioning were examined, indicating this text would be descriptive rather than prescriptive in its approach.

In Review

1. At this point in your personal and academic life, what is your definition of a family?
2. To what extent do you agree with the family categories described earlier? Describe how you would alter these categories, giving reasons for your choices.
3. Using a real or literary example, demonstrate the basic systems concept by describing how a change in one member of a family affected the other members.
4. Identify the family systems of four friends and describe them in terms of category types as well as socioeconomic and ethnic status. If possible, elaborate on how these factors appear to have affected members' interactions.
5. At this point in your personal and academic life, how would you describe a well-functioning family?

FRAMEWORK
for FAMILY
COMMUNICATION

2

In their mutual interaction, the family members develop more or less adequate under-standing of one another collaborating in the effort to establish consensus and to negotiate uncertainty. The family's life together is an endless process of movement in and around consensual understanding, from attachment to conflict to withdrawal — and over again. Separateness and connectedness are the underlying conditions of a family's life, and its common talk is to give form to both.

Robert D. Hess and Gerald Handel, *Family Worlds*

Families repeat themselves within and across generations. Members become caught up in predictable and often unexamined life patterns that are created, in part, through their interactions with others. This text explores the family as a communication system, concentrating on processes by which communication patterns serve to create and reflect family relationships. Within the framework of shared cultural communication patterns, each family has the capacity to develop its own communication codes based on the experiences of individual members as well as collective family experience. Individuals develop their communication skills within the family context, learning both the general cultural language and the specific familial communication patterns. Since most people take their own backgrounds for granted, you may not be aware of the context your family provided for learning communication. For example, as a child, you learned acceptable ways of expressing intimacy and conflict, how to relate to other family members, how to make decisions, and how to share information inside and outside the family boundaries. Other families may have taught their members different lessons. A fundamental position that undergirds a communication perspective on families holds that families are defined primarily through their interaction rather than through their structure (Whitchurch & Dickson, 1999). In other words, "Through their communicative practices, parties construct their social reality of who their family is and the meanings that organize it" (Baxter & Braithwaite, 2002, p. 94). Such a belief views communication as constitutive of the family and places communication at the core of family experience.

In order to understand the family as an interactive system, you need to explore key communication concepts and how they can be applied to the family. You also need to see how family communication may be viewed through theory lenses, including systems, symbolic interaction, and dialectical theories, because these form the theoretical bases on which this approach is constructed.

This chapter will (1) provide an overview of the communication process, including the development of interpersonal meaning; (2) present a set of primary and secondary family functions that influence communication; and (3) establish a framework for examining family communication.

THE COMMUNICATION PROCESS

<u>*Communication*</u> may be viewed as a *symbolic, transactional process of creating* and *sharing meanings.* Saying that communication is *symbolic* means that symbols are used to create meaning and messages. Words or verbal behavior are the most commonly used symbols, but the whole range of nonverbal behavior—including facial expressions, eye contact, gestures, movement, posture, appearance, and spatial distance—is also used symbolically. Symbols may represent things, feelings, or ideas. Families may use kisses, special food, teasing, and poems as symbols of love, and silence and distance as examples of anger. Although symbols allow you to share your thoughts on the widest range of possible subjects, the symbols must be mutually understood for the meanings to be shared. For example, if family members do not agree on what activities are "fun," how much is "a lot" of money, or how to express and recognize anger, confusion will result. If meanings are not mutually shared, messages may not be understood, resulting in the following type of misunderstanding.

In my first marriage, my wife and I often discovered that we had very different meanings for the same words. For example, we agreed we wanted a "large" family but I meant three children and she meant seven or eight.

I thought "regular" sex meant once a day and she thought it meant once a week. I thought spending a "lot of money" meant spending over $300; she thought it meant spending over $50. In my second marriage, we talk very frequently about what our words mean so we don't have so many disagreements.

To say that communication is *transactional* means that when people communicate, they have a mutual impact on each other. In short, you participate in communication; thus, in relationships, participants are both affecting and being affected by the others simultaneously. It does not matter how much more talking one person appears to do; the mutual impact remains the same. The focus is placed on the relationship, not on the individual participants. Participation in an intimate relationship transforms fundamental reality definitions for both partners and in so doing transforms the partners themselves (Stephen & Enholm, 1987). Joint actions of partners contribute to the development of private relational realities that are dependent on the uniqueness of the pair acting together. Siblings may create patterns of teasing that allow them to feel connected, but no one else could joke that way without creating tension. Essentially, family members are engaging in symbolic interaction or creating joint meanings within the relationships.

A transactional view of communication and a systems perspective of the family complement each other, because both focus on relationships. Within these views, relationships take precedence over individuals (Petronio & Braithwaite, 1993). A communication perspective focuses on the interaction between two or more persons. Accordingly, from a systems perspective it is nonproductive to analyze each individual separately. Each individual communicates within an interpersonal context, and each communication act reflects the nature of those relationships. As two people interact, each creates a context for the other and relates to the other within that context. For example, you may perceive a brother-in-law as distant and relate to him in a very polite but restrained manner. In turn, he may perceive your politeness as formal and relate to you in an even more reserved manner. A similar situation is demonstrated here.

My father and brother had a very difficult relationship with each other for many years, although both of them had an excellent relationship with everyone else in the family. Dan saw Dad as repressive and demanding, although I would characterize him as serious and concerned. Dad saw Dan as careless and uncommitted, although no one else saw him that way. Whenever they tried to talk to each other, each responded to the person he created, and it was a continual battle.

In the previous example, knowing Dan or his father separately does not account for their conflictual behavior when they are together. Both influence the other's interaction. Both create a context for the other and relate within the context. It is as if one says to the other, "You are sensitive," or "You are repressive," or "You are shiftless," and "that's how I will relate to you." The content and style of messages vary according to how each person sees himself or herself and how each predicts the other individual will react. As well as taking the environment or context into account, the transactional view stresses the importance of the communicators' perceptions and actions in determining the outcome of interactions.

Thus, the relationship *patterns*, not one or another specific act, become the focal point. One's perception of another and one's subsequent behavior can actually change the behavior of the other person. A mother who constantly praises her son for his thoughtfulness and sensitivity and notices the good things in his efforts may change her son's perception of himself and his subsequent behavior with her and other people. On the other hand, a husband who constantly complains about his wife's parenting behavior may lower her self-esteem and change her subsequent behavior toward him and the children. Thus, in relationships, each person (1) creates a context for the other, (2) simultaneously creates and interprets messages, and, therefore, (3) simultaneously affects and is affected by the other.

To say that communication is a *process* implies that it is continuously changing. Communication is not static; it does not switch on and off; rather, it develops over time. Process implies change. Relationships, no matter how committed, change continuously, and communication both affects and reflects these changes. The passage of time brings with it predictable and unpredictable crises, which take their toll on family regularity and stability. Yet, everyday moods, minor pleasures, or irritations may shift the communication patterns on a day-to-day basis.

As each day passes, family members subtly renegotiate their relationships. Today, you may be in a bad mood and people respond to that. Tomorrow, adaptations may need to be made around your brother's great report card. Next week, a major job change may affect all your relationships. Over time, families change as they pass through stages of growth; members are born, age, leave, and die, and their communication patterns impact and reflect these developments in family life.

As indicated earlier, communication may be viewed as a symbolic, transactional process of creating and sharing meanings. Communication serves to create a family's social reality. Successful communication depends on the member's shared reality, or sets of meanings (Bochner & Eisenberg, 1987).

Meanings and Messages

How often do people in close and committed relationships find themselves saying, "That's not what I mean" or "What do you mean by that?" According to Stephen (1986), even in the most mundane interchanges, participants' messages imply their visions of the nature of social and physical reality as well as their values, beliefs, and attitudes. These are referred to as their *meanings*. Communication involves the negotiation of shared meanings; if meanings are not held in common, confusion or misunderstanding is likely to occur. A primary task of families is "meaning making," or the "cocreation of meanings." In their classic work, Berger and Kellner (1964) capture the sense of creating meanings within a marriage, suggesting, "Each partner's definition of reality must be continually correlated with the definitions of the other" (p. 224). Such correlation requires regular communication. As indicated earlier, symbolic interaction is one lens through which family communication will be viewed. This theory is concerned with meaning and holds communication to be central to the process of creating a family's social reality.

Worldviews reflect one's fundamental beliefs about issues, such as the nature of change and the nature of human beings; in other words, these are the unspoken presuppositions a person brings to every encounter.

My mother and stepfather clash regularly because deep down, they hold very different beliefs about human beings. My stepfather believes people are always out for themselves and is generally suspicious. My mother trusts everyone and sees only the good in people. Over the past five years each has come a little closer but it's hard to alter such fundamental worldviews.

The meaning-making tasks of family members serve to create a relational culture or worldview that characterizes the family system.

Development of Meanings   How does a person develop a set of meanings? Basically, your views of the world result from your perceptual filter systems. For example, imagine each person has lenses, or filters, through which he or she views the world. Everyone views the world within the context of age, race, gender, religion, and culture. In addition, someone's view of reality will be affected by sibling position and family history with

Family members negotiate meanings in a variety of family activities.

its myths, party lines, and traditions across generations (Lerner, 1989). These and other factors combine uniquely for each individual and impact how that person perceives and interacts with the world in general, and more specifically with the surrounding family system. Although this sounds like a very individualistic process, remember the transactional perspective. Each communicator constantly affects and is affected by the other; thus, perceptions are cocreated within the context of a relational system and are constantly influenced by that system.

Meanings emerge as information passes through a person's filter system. The physical state based on human sensory systems—sight, hearing, touch, taste, and smell—constitutes the first set of filters. Perceptions are also filtered through the social system or the way a person uses language, a person's accepted ways of viewing things, his or her family cultural and class status, and all the socially agreed-upon conventions that characterize parts of his or her world. Eventually, a person shares common meanings for certain verbal and nonverbal symbols with those around him or her. A person may share some very general experiences with many people and much more specific experiences with a smaller group of individuals. For example, with some acquaintances, a person may share only general experiences, such as cultural background, including language, geographic area, customs, beliefs, and attitudes. With others, they may also share the specific and narrow experiences of living together in the house on 6945 Osceola Street and learning to understand each other's idiosyncracies.

Social experiences frame your world. The language you speak limits and shapes your meanings. For example, the current pressure to find new language to discuss stepfamilies reflects a belief that "step" terms are generally negative. Stepmothers, in particular, face negative images of themselves due to the historically "wicked" word association. Proponents of change believe perceptions of stepfamilies will be altered by the use of language such as "remarried," "reconstituted," or "blended." Current terminology limits easy discussion of certain new family relationships, such as "my stepmother's sister" or "my half brother's grandfather on his mother's side." Yet, although language may limit meanings, people are capable of broadening such perspectives by learning new terminology and opening themselves to new experiences.

Thus, the overall culture affects perceptions and meaning, but the immediate groups to which one belongs exert a strong influence on an individual's perceptual set. The family group provides contextual meaning and influences the way meaning is given to sensory data. If giving a handmade gift is considered a special sign of caring, a knitted scarf may be valued, whereas an expensive necklace may not. Being a member of the Thurman family, a flight attendant, a square dance caller, or a church elder provides context for giving meaning to the world for the individual and for a small segment of people who surround that person. Although physical and social systems provide the basic general filters, specific constraints and experiences influence an individual's meanings. Individual constraints refer to the interpretations you create for your meanings based on your own personal histories. Although some of you may have similar histories, each person develops a unique way of dealing with sensory information, and therefore an individual way of seeing the world and relating to others in it. This concept is captured in the expression, "No two children grow up in the same family."

Two members of the Thurman family may share being flight attendants, square dance callers, and church elders, yet they will respond differently to many situations. For example, many brothers and sisters disagree on the kind of family life they experienced together. One declares, "I had a very happy childhood" versus a sibling's statement, "I would never want to go through those years again." For each of you, specific events and people affect your meanings. Aunt Mary may have influenced your view of the world but not your sister's. Each experiences "family" differently, as indicated in the following example.

In our house, my sister Diane was considered the "problem child." As far as experts can determine, her emotional difficulties stemmed from an unknown trauma when she was age 3, when they suggest she was rejected by my parents at a time when she needed love. The reality was that Diane functioned as a scapegoat for all of us. Although Diane and I are very close in age, we had different experiences in our family because of the way she perceived the family and was perceived by its members.

Over time, communication or the symbolic transactional process permits individuals to negotiate shared meanings. When people relate to each other, they establish a process whereby they attribute meanings to their interactions. According to Breunlin, Schwartz, and Kune-Karrer (1997), "People may not see the same meanings, but meanings do become coordinated, so that meaning for one family member elicits complementary meanings for other family members" (p. 52). After each encounter with a person or situation, one becomes better able to deal with similar situations, and one's behavior takes on certain patterns. The greater the repetition, the greater the probability of the assigned meaning.

Enduring relationships are characterized by agreements between members as to the meaning of things. These persons develop a relationship worldview reflecting the members' symbolic interdependence (Stephen, 1986). Often, people in families develop this worldview even though it may include agreements not to discuss certain topics.

Over time, you become comfortable with the symbols, mainly because you are able to interpret them on all levels and feel that you really understand them. As a child, when you heard your mother yell "Jonathan" or "Kyung Chu," you were able to tell from her tone of voice just what to expect. Today, you hear your younger sister say, "I just hate that Ernie Masters" and know that she has just found a new boyfriend. Meanings are negotiated and renegotiated over time as children move into adolescence, as adults witness the death or decline of their parents and grandparents, and as world events force people to reevaluate their values and life cultures.

Levels of Meaning and Metacommunication Communication of meaning occurs on two levels: the content level and the relationship level. The content level contains the information, whereas the relationship level indicates how the information should be interpreted or understood. The relationship level is more likely to involve nonverbal messages. When your mother says, "When are you going to pick up those clothes?" she is asking an informational question, but there may be another level of meaning. It is up to you to determine if, by her tone of voice, she is really questioning at what time of day you will remove the dirty socks and jeans, or if she is telling you to remove them in the next 30 seconds. Relational pairs develop their own interpretation of symbols. When a father puts his arm on his daughter's shoulder, it may mean "I support you" or "Slow down, relax." Usually the daughter will understand the intended message, although she may misread the symbolic gesture and interpret it as "Let me take care of it."

Metacommunication occurs when people communicate about their communication—for example, when they give verbal and nonverbal instructions about how their messages should be understood. Such remarks as "I was only kidding," "This is important," or "Talking about this makes me uncomfortable" are signals to another on how to make certain comments, as are facial expressions, gestures, or vocal tones. On a deeper level, many family members have spent countless hours talking about the way they fight or the way they express affection. Metacommunication serves an important function within families, because it allows members to state their needs, clarify confusion, and plan new and more constructive ways of relating to one another. As you will recognize, meanings serve a central function in all family communication processes.

Dialectical Tensions

Significant relationships are not easily formed and maintained. Similarly, patterns of meaning are not developed quickly and then set in stone. Most long-term intimate relationships are built on a history of struggle, as well as pleasure, and a continued interplay between opposing tendencies. Baxter and Montgomery (1996) refer to this tension as "relational dialectics." *Dialectic* implies opposition, polarity, and interconnection. *Relational dialectics* refers to the "both/and" quality of relationships or the need for partners to simultaneously experience independence and connection or openness and privacy. From this perspective, "social life exists in and through people's communication practices, by which people give voice to multiple (perhaps even infinite) opposing tendencies" (p. 4).

How close can people get without interfering with each other? How much closeness do people need? How can individuals live together without hurting each other too much? How do people establish their ties and simultaneously relate to others? These questions are indicators of the tensions all relationships face. They reflect *dialectical tensions* and are managed through communication. As people come together in relationships, they encounter tensions and struggles in managing the relationship. Dialectics recognizes the tension between partners as they negotiate and renegotiate what it means to be in a functioning relationship.

Communication scholars identify a range of possible interactional dialectic tensions, including autonomy–connection, openness–closedness, and predictability–novelty (Baxter, 1990) as well as freedom to be independent–freedom to be dependent, affection–instrumentality, judgment–acceptance, and expressiveness–protectiveness (Rawlins, 1992). The primary dialectical concerns of autonomy–connection and predictability–

novelty will be developed as part of the underlying framework for examining families.

The ways in which people exchange messages influence the form and content of their relationships. Communication among family members shapes the structure of the family system and provides a family with its own set of meanings. Although we have used many family examples in describing the communication process, we have not explored the role of communication within the family. The following section examines the role communication plays in forming, maintaining, and changing family systems as families perform core functions.

COMMUNICATION PATTERNS AND FAMILY FUNCTIONS

When coming into contact with other families, you notice how their communication differs from that of the families with which you have lived. Everyday ways of relating, making decisions, sharing feelings, and handling conflict will vary from your own personal experiences. Each family's unique message system provides the means of dealing with the major functions that give shape to family life. In other words, communication provides form and content to a family's life as members engage in family-related functions. A function is simply something a system must do to avoid a breakdown. We will examine two primary family functions and four supporting functions that affect and are affected by communication and taken together form a family's collective identity.

Primary Functions

In their attempt to integrate the numerous concepts related to marital and family interaction, researchers Olson, Sprenkle, and Russell have developed what is known as the circumplex model of marital and family systems (Olson, Sprenkle, & Russell, 1979; Olson, Russell, & Sprenkle, 1983; Lavee & Olson, 1991; Olson, 2000). This model bridges family theory, research, and practice. Two central dimensions of family behavior are at the core of the model: *family cohesion* and *family adaptability*. Each of these dimensions is divided into four levels matched on a grid to create 16 possible combinations. The four types in the center of the grid are called *balance;* the four extremes are seen as *dysfunctional*. The theorists suggest moderate scores represent reasonable functioning, whereas the extreme scores represent family dysfunction.

Over the past years, the model evolved to include three dimensions: (1) cohesion, (2) adaptability, and (3) communication. The two central dimensions remain family cohesion and family adaptability, which are perceived as the intersecting lines of an axis. The third dimension is *family communication,* a facilitating dimension that enables couples and families to move along the cohesion and adaptability dimensions, but because it is a facilitating dimension, it is not included in the model diagram.

Questions have been raised about the entire use of the concept of adaptability (Beavers & Voeller, 1983) and the use of supporting research scales and the curvilinear nature of cohesion (Farrell & Barnes, 1993). Although we do not rely on the full circumplex model, we do adapt the dimensions of cohesion and adaptability as primary family functions.

In this text, the concepts of cohesion and change form a background against which to view communication within various types of families. From this perspective, two primary family functions involve: (1) establishing a pattern of *cohesion,* or separateness and connectedness, and (2) establishing a pattern of *adaptability,* or change. These functions vary with regularity as families experience the tensions inherent in a relational life.

Cohesion   From the moment you were born, you have been learning how to handle distance or closeness within your family system. You were taught directly or subtly how to be connected to, or separated from, other family members. In other words, every family attempts to deal with the extent to which closeness is encouraged or discouraged. *Cohesion* is defined as the emotional bonding that family members have toward each other and include concepts of "emotional bonding, boundaries, coalitions, time, space, friends, decision-making, interests and recreation" (Olson, 2000, p. 145).

Although different terminology is used, the issue of cohesion has been identified by scholars from various fields as central to the understanding of family life (Pistole, 1994). Family researchers Kantor and Lehr (1976) view "distance regulation" as a major family function; family therapist Minuchin (1967) talks about "enmeshed and disengaged" families; sociologists Hess and Handel (1959) describe the family's need to establish a pattern of separateness and connectedness. There are four levels of cohesion ranging from extremely low cohesion to extremely high cohesion. These levels are (Carnes, 1989):

Disengaged. Family members maintain extreme separateness and little family belonging or loyalty.

Separated. Family members experience emotional independence with some joint involvement and belonging.

Connected. Family members strive for emotional closeness, loyalty, and joint involvement with some individuality.

Enmeshed. Family members experience extreme closeness, loyalty, and almost no individuality.

It is through communication that family members are able to develop and maintain or change their patterns of cohesion. A father may decide that it is inappropriate to continue the physical closeness he has experienced with his daughter now that she has become a teenager, and he may limit his touching or playful roughhousing. These nonverbal messages may be confusing or hurtful to his daughter. She may become angry, find new ways of being close, develop more outside friendships, or attempt to force her father back into the old patterns. A husband may demand more intimacy from his wife as he ages. He asks for more serious conversation, makes more sexual advances, or shares more of his feelings. His wife may ignore this new behavior or increase her intimate behaviors. Balanced families generally are found at separated or connected levels and tend to be more functional.

Families with extremely high cohesion are often referred to as *enmeshed;* members are so intensely bonded and overinvolved that individuals experience little autonomy or fulfillment of personal needs and goals. Total loyalty is expected. Family members appear fused or joined so tightly that personal identities do not develop appropriately; thus, members are highly interdependent. Enmeshed persons do not experience life as individuals, as indicated by the following example.

My mother and I are the same person. She was always protective of me, knew everything about me, told me how to act, and how to answer questions. None of this was done in a bad way or had detrimental effects, but the reality is that she was and still is somewhat overbearing. If someone asked me a question, I typically answered, "Please direct all questions to my mother. She knows what to say."

Disengaged refers to families at the other end of the continuum in which members experience extreme emotional separateness; each member has high autonomy and individuality. Individual interests predominate.

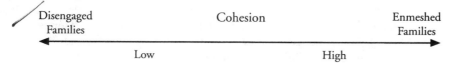

Throughout this book, we will look at ways families deal with issues of coming together or staying apart and how they use communication in an attempt to manage their separateness and togetherness. Families do not remain permanently at one point on the cohesion continuum. Members do not come together and stay the same, as is evident from the previous examples. Because there are widely varying cultural norms for moderate or extremes of cohesion, what seems balanced for one family may be quite distant for another. For example, Latino families may find balanced cohesion at a point that is too high for families with a northern European background.

Adaptability When you think of the changes in your own family over the past 5 or 10 years, you may be amazed at how different the system and its members are at this point. A family experiences changes as it goes through its own developmental stages and deals with stresses that arise in everyday life, such as adapting to an illness or a job transfer of one of its members. Even everyday living involves relational tensions with which family members struggle.

Flexibility is defined as the amount of change in a family's leadership, role relationships, and relations by rules. It includes concepts of "leadership (control, discipline), negotiation, styles, role relationships and relationship rules" (Olson, 2000, p. 147). *Family flexibility,* also referred to as *adaptability,* focuses on how family systems manage stability and change. We will continue to use the terms *adaptability* and *flexibility* interchangeably.

There are four levels of adaptability ranging from extremely low adaptability to extremely high adaptability (Thomas & Olson, 1994). These can be described as (Carnes, 1989):

Rigid. Family members operate under autocratic decision-making styles and strict roles and rules.

Structured. Family members experience authoritarian and some equalitarian leadership and stable roles and rules.

Flexible. Family members experience negotiation and decision making and easily changed rules and roles.

Chaotic. Family members have nonexistent leadership, confused decision making, and varied rules and roles.

Each human system has both stability-promoting processes (morphostasis, or form maintaining) and change-promoting processes (morphogenesis, or form creating). Such systems need periods of stability and change in order to function. Families that regularly experience extensive change may be considered chaotic. Due to total unpredictability and stress, they have little opportunity to develop relationships and establish common meanings. On the other extreme, rigidity characterizes families that repress change and growth. Balanced families are generally found at structured or connected levels.

Rigid Families	Adaptability	Chaotic Families
←———————		———————→
Low		High

Questions have been raised about the view of extreme flexibility as chaos, and therefore seen in a negative light, as opposed to seeing it as desirable (Lee, C., 1988). Although most scholars consider an excess or a paucity of change to be dysfunctional, they see the ability of a system to change its structure as generally necessary and desirable. Again, issues of ethnicity and socioeconomic status impact a family's experience of change. For example, families that deal with poverty and rely on social welfare agencies often experience life as more chaotic than those for whom a solid economic situation makes it easier to manage outside stresses.

Family systems constantly restructure themselves as they pass through predictable developmental stages. Marriage, pregnancy, birth, parenting, and the return to the original couple all represent major familial changes. Likewise, when positive or negative stresses arise involving such issues as money, illness, or divorce, families must adapt. Finally, family systems must adapt both structurally and functionally to the demands of other social institutions as well as to the needs of their own members, as evidenced here.

My son and daughter-in-law adopted an older child and had to adapt their communication patterns to accommodate her. Although lying was forbidden in their family when they adopted Shirley, they had to reassess this position, because she had learned to lie for most of her life. My son and daughter-in-law had to learn to be more tolerant of this behavior, particularly when she first joined the family, or they would have had to send her back to the agency.

Communication is central to the adaptive function of a family. Any effective adaptation relies on shared meanings gained through the family message system. Through communication, families make it clear to their members how much adaptation is allowed while regulating the adaptive behaviors of their members and the system as a whole. Olson and his colleagues hypothesize that where there is a balance between change and stability within families, there will be more mutually assertive communication styles, shared leadership, successful negotiation, role sharing, and open rule making and sharing. The functions of cohesion and adaptability combine to create the two major functions family members continuously manage.

Applying the work of Olson and his colleagues (1979, 1983), you can visualize the mutual interaction of adaptability and cohesion within families by placing them on an axis (Figure 2.1a). By adding the extremes of cohesion (disengagement and enmeshment) and adaptability (rigidity and chaos), you can picture where more or less functional families would appear on the axis (Figure 2.1b).

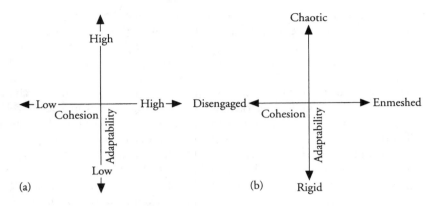

FIGURE 2.1   Family Cohesion–Adaptability Axes

The central area represents balanced or moderate levels of adaptability and cohesion, seen as a highly workable communication pattern for individual and family development, although there may be instances when a different pattern could aid a family through a particular developmental point or through a crisis. The outside areas represent the extremes of cohesion and adaptability, less workable for consistent long-term communication pattens. Research by Farrell and Barnes (1993) begins to question the curvilinear nature of cohesion.

Most well-functioning families are found short of the extremes, except when they are under high levels of stress. In those situations, placement at the extreme may serve a purpose. This concept, based on the work of Lavee and Olson (1991), will be developed in Chapter 11. If a family member dies, for example, a highly cohesive communication pattern may be critical for mourning purposes. At the time of a family death, members may find themselves at point Y (Figure 2.2a). Such a family may be experiencing extreme closeness among remaining members but chaos in terms of dealing with the changes in roles or in everyday activities.

As another example, a family with an acting-out teenager may find itself shifting from point X to point Z on the axis, as the adolescent demands greater freedom and less connectedness from the family and forces changes on the system (Figure 2.2b).

The situation in the following quotation may be graphed as three moves (Figure 2.2c).

As a small child I lived in an active alcoholic family in which people kept pretty much to themselves. We did not talk about the problems caused by our parents' drinking and we acted as if things were fine. Yet we were very rigid be-

cause we never could bring anyone into the house, and we never let outsiders know about the drinking. My older sister always took care of me if there was a problem, while my older brother locked himself in his room. Thus, we were at point A. When my parents finally went into treatment, the house was crazy in a different way for a while, since no one knew exactly how to act, but we did get closer and we were all forced to discuss what was going on. I guess we got closer and almost too flexible or unpredictable (point B). Now, five years later, I'm the only child left at home and my sober parents and I have a relatively close and flexible relationship (point C).

If you think about stages in your family life, you should be able to envision how the family shifted from one point to another on the cohesion–adaptability axis.

Families at different stages of development seem to function better in different areas of the model. For example, young couples without babies function best in either the upper right or lower left quadrants. Families with adolescents function best in the central, or balanced, area; older couples relate best in the lower right quadrant. Adolescents function best when they have average cohesion, being neither enmeshed with parents or disengaged, and when their adaptability is midway between rigidity and chaos. Obviously, these results indicate adolescents' need for a family system without threats or rigid rules. Older couples function best when cohesion is high but adaptability is low—more rigid. Possible explanations for these findings will become clearer in the chapters on developmental changes. Although results may differ for families from particular backgrounds or ethnic origins, these findings support maintaining a flexible attitude toward well-family functioning.

When viewing a whole system, there may be certain members who would be graphed in a different place if they were to be pictured individ-

FIGURE 2.2 Application of Family Cohesion–Adaptability

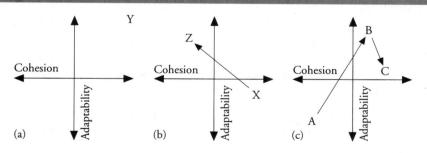

ually. These models attempt to represent the group on the axes. Throughout the text, the cohesion–change framework will be used as a backdrop for understanding family communication.

Finally, Olson (2000) suggests balanced families will display more positive communication skills. Such families are more likely to find ways to negotiate, express affection, address conflicts, and provide appropriate support than families on the more extreme ends of either continuum.

Dialectical Interplay   From a dialectical perspective, cohesion and adaptability may be viewed as both family functions and dialectical tensions due to their importance and inescapable presence within the family. In discussing the cohesion function, Sabourin (1992) suggests:

> The dialectical perspective is useful in explaining how difficult achieving balance can be. It is a contradiction to need both autonomy and connection with others. . . . The dialectical perspective incorporates both. . . . Hence some families emphasize togetherness at the expense of developing personal identities. (p. 5)

Most families find they struggle over time with the issues of closeness and distance both between members and between the family system and outside persons or groups. The following quote from a young wife captures this dialectical tension.

> On the one hand it is like, sure, I can go on my own. And on the other hand, I want him to go with me. . . . I want to do things with him, and I think it is okay if he doesn't want to go and then it actually upsets me a lot if he doesn't go. (Hoppe-Nagao & Ting-Toomey, 2002, p. 146)

Although the issues related to cohesion and adaptability/change are viewed as the primary functions, these functions do not provide a complete picture. There are additional family functions—supporting functions—that contribute to the understanding of family interaction.

Supporting Functions

In conjunction with cohesion and adaptability, four supporting functions give shape to family life. Hess and Handel (1959) identify five processes, or family functions, that interact with the development of a family's message system. Because one of these processes relates to cohesion, we will list only the remaining four. The supporting family functions include:

1. Establishing a satisfactory congruence of images.
2. Evolving modes of interaction into central family themes.

3. Establishing the boundaries of the family's world of experience.

4. Dealing with significant biosocial issues of family life, such as gender, age, power, and roles. (p. 4)

Each of these processes interacts with a family's point on the cohesion–adaptability axis and influences a family's communication pattern. Each process is based on principles of symbolic interaction, since their underlying thread is the role of subjective meanings (LaRossa & Reitzes, 1993).

Family Images   Relationship patterns can be viewed as metaphors, which allow people to understand one element in terms of another. We can also talk about root metaphors, which assume a connection between a way of talking about the world and a major analogy or metaphor. A simple metaphor may be, "My sister is a butterfly. You can never get her to settle down." A root metaphor for a family would capture an overarching image of life in that family. Identifying small and simple metaphors is relatively easy; identifying an overarching root metaphor usually takes a good deal of thought and analysis.

If you had to create a mental image or a metaphor for your family, what would it be? Do you see your family as a nest, a broken wagon wheel, a corporation, a spaceship, or a schoolroom? Every family operates as an image-making or metaphor-creating entity. These metaphors "reflect the world view of the family as they represent the family's collective experience" (Pawlowski, 1996a, p. 7). Each member develops images of what the family unit and other family members are like; these images affect his or her patterns of interaction with the others. Patterns of the marital relationship, which often cannot be communicated through literal language, are explained metaphorically. An image of one's family embodies what is expected from it, what is given to it, and how important it is (Hess & Handel, 1959). Thus, the image has both realistic and idealized components that reflect both the imagined and the imaginer.

The following root metaphor conveys a good deal of information about this two-parent family with four adolescent children.

My family is like a Navy fleet. In the center are my parents, both upon the carrier. My mother is the executive officer (XO). The XO is the bad guy who runs the ship, keeps things in order, and intercepts messes before they reach the commanding officer. My father is the commanding office (CO). He decides the general direction the family heads but is more concerned with navigating than maintaining everyday life on board. My siblings and I are the small ships in the group. We can go off but must return to refuel. I am the cruiser and have more responsibilities and provide services, such as information. Jon and

Stephanie are both destroyers, who are freer to range around. Michael is the airplane who sits on top of the mother ship. He has a short range and endurance away from the carrier. The destroyers like to intimidate him but would never really fire on him. We all know our places and positions and defend each other from any threat. We are close, but not too close. We all follow orders from the CO but spend much of our lives interacting more easily with the XO.

A less complex example follows.

My family is a team, with my dad as a player-coach. We all work together for the survival of our team, and we all contribute. Each one of us has strengths and weaknesses, yet there is always that force driving us to achieve more together. As the player-coach, my dad has the responsibility of overseeing our performances.

A family's conception of itself affects its orientation to areas such as cooperation versus competition and reaching out versus withdrawal; it also affects communication. Verbal and nonverbal behaviors of the family members are, in part, determined by this imagistic view of their relationship with each other and with the external environment. One dual-career couple described their family as a "seesaw," saying, "We are able to balance each other well and be flexible in allowing the kids to move between us. But if a crisis hits and we have to move in new patterns, such as sideways, we run into problems." In a survey of male and female college students, Thilborger (1998) reports female metaphors for their family-of-origin emphasize team/group, nature, and healing/nourishment. Male metaphors emphasize nature, particularly animals, and foundational things such as brick walls or concrete structures.

If you think about metaphors within interactive systems of interaction, individual behaviors and relationships may be seen as metaphors. One set of siblings may be seen as "two peas in a pod"; another set may be "oil and water." If the persons involved hold very different images of their relationship to each other, the differences will be reflected in communication patterns. If two people's images of each other are congruent and consistent for a period of time, a predictable pattern of communication may emerge in which both are comfortable. For example, if a mother sees her son as a helpless and dependent creature, she may exhibit many protective behaviors, such as keeping bad news from him. If the son's image of his mother is as a protector, the congruence of the images will allow harmonious communication; but if the child sees his mother as a jailer, conflict may emerge. If one child sees the mother as a jailer and the other sees her as an angel, the lack of consistent images held by family members may result in strong alliances among those with congruent images. A husband and wife are likely to experience conflict if they hold conflicting root metaphors. For example, one sees the family as a "nest" involving nurturing, emotion, and protection, and the other sees it as a corporation involving a strong power structure and good organization. Yet, since complete consensus is improbable and change inevitable, the patterns will never become totally predictable. In an interpretation of his grandmother's role in the family, Trujillo (1998) develops images of his grandmother as the giver, server, and body, acknowledging that other family members may have seen her differently. Yet, as one would imagine, the greater the level of congruence, the more effective the communication within the family. The family metaphor acts as a perceptual filter, an indicator of a family's collective identity, and serves as an impetus for future thought and action.

Some families have the theme "Working together keeps us together."

Family Themes   As well as having images for the family and for every member, each family shares themes—or takes positions in relationship to the outer world that affect every aspect of its functioning. A *theme* may be viewed as a pattern of feelings, motives, fantasies, and conventionalized understandings grouped around a particular locus of concern, which has a particular form in the personalities of individual members (Hess & Handel, 1959).

Themes represent a fundamental view of reality and a way of dealing with this view. Through its theme, a family responds to the questions, Who are we? What do we do about it? and How do we invest our energies? Themes may represent a family's attempt to deal with dialectical tensions by "taking a stand." For example, themes may emerge from predictable areas of contraction, such as independence–dependence, openness–closedness, and predictability–novelty. Sample theme issues that some families value include physical security, strength, dependability, inclusion, and separation. To demonstrate the viability of themes in a family, we view them as statements that actualize the values and collective identity:

The Nielsens play to win.

We have responsibility for those less fortunate than us.

You can sleep when you die.

If God gives much, much is expected in return.

You can depend only on your family.

You can always depend on your family.

The Garcias never quit.

You can always do better.

Seize the moment.

Be happy with what you have.

Take a chance.

Money is basic to life.

Respect La Via Vecchia (the old way).

The Logans welcome challenges.

We are survivors.

Do unto others as best you can.

We do not raise homing pigeons.

Themes relate directly to family actions, thereby allowing one to surmise a family's themes by watching its actions. Living according to a theme necessitates the development of various patterns of behavior, which affect how members interact with the outside world, how they interact with each other, and how they develop personally. For example, a family with the theme "We have responsibility for those less fortunate than us" might be a flexible system open to helping nonfamily members. The family might give to charity, raise foster children, or work with the homeless. Yet, it may be difficult for family members to accept help from an outside source because of its caregiving theme. Members may tend to put themselves second when they deal with outside problems. Following the classic line of the shoemaker's children without shoes, a mother who lives according to this theme may spend hours working at an adolescent drop-in center and be unaware of the problems her own teenage children are experiencing. Young members may grow up learning to minimize their problems and may not have much experience expressing painful feelings. Family themes undergird everyday life, as the following portrays.

I grew up with family themes of "Be a good sport," "You have to learn some lessons the hard way," and "No one can tell you; you have to experience it for yourself." For example, when we play sports, such as a family tennis match, the winners win gracefully and the losers lose gracefully. There are no bad sports. Also, if one of us disobeys our parents' advice and a problem results, they don't get too angry. Rather, they justify it by saying that we are naturally stubborn and have to learn the hard way.

Family themes may be complex and subtle, involving worldviews that are not immediately obvious. It is important to identify a family's main theme(s) in order to fully understand the meanings and communication behavior of its members.

Boundaries As well as developing images and themes, families create boundaries. The *boundary* of a system is what separates it from its environment. In short, the boundary defines the system as an entity by allowing it to create a permeable separation between its interior elements and its environment (Broderick, 1993; Constantine, 1986). One can imagine boundaries as physical or psychological limits that regulate access to people, places, ideas, and values. Anything inside the boundary has system's properties; anything outside is part of the environment. All families establish some boundaries as they restrict their members from encountering certain physical and psychological forces. Most frequently, family boundaries regulate access to people, places, ideas, and values.

In her communication privacy management theory, Petronio (2002) develops an understanding of how people manage private information through a boundaries metaphor, arguing, "Regulating boundary openness and closedness contributes to balancing the publicness or privacy of indi-

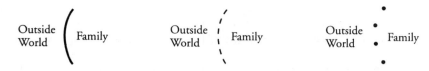

FIGURE 2.3   External Boundaries

viduals. The regulation process is fundamentally communicative in nature" (p. 8).

Some family boundaries are highly permeable, or flexible, and allow movement across them. These open boundaries allow resources such as information or energy to enter from the environment (Breunlin, Schwartz, & Kune-Karrer, 1997). Others resist movement and are rigid and inflexible (Figure 2.3). Finally, others are so invisible or diffuse that they are almost nonexistent.

External boundaries distinguish family members from the rest of the world, whereas internal boundaries help keep family members appropriately placed in relationship to each other. Let's look first at how external boundaries function.

Certain families permit or encourage their children to make many different kinds of friends, explore alternative religious ideas, and have access to new ideas through the media; such permeable boundaries permit new people, new ideas, and new values to enter the family. Some families retain rigid control of their children's activities to prevent them from coming into contact with what the family considers "undesirable." Or the family may expect members to carry the family boundaries within them, as does the grandfather in this example.

The family does not end at the front step. My grandfather says, "When you are a Cammostro, you represent the entire family (your aunts, uncles, cousins, grandparents, and your heritage), so never make a fool of yourself." This means that one must be at one's best whenever in public and never tell family stories or secrets.

Extremes of such behavior result in the creation of rigid boundaries around the family system.

Finally, some families provide no sense of identity for members and no control of their contact with people, places, ideas, or values. Members of this type of system experience little sense of "family," since there appears to be no collective identity. Rigid boundaries are often formed around secrets known to and guarded by members (Vangelisti & Caughlin, 1997).

Families are not always able to control their own boundaries. Outside agencies, such as schools, may require families to share private information or to follow rules, such as wearing a uniform, in order for children to be enrolled. Families formed through transracial/transnational adoption may confront invasive questions or comments from strangers because of the visual dissimilarity of members (Galvin & Wilkinson, 2000).

Family boundaries will vary according to the personalities of the members, the types of experiences to which members are exposed, and the freedom each member has to create his or her own value system. Although the family unit system may set strong boundaries, a strong, self-assured person may challenge rigid or stereotyped positions on certain issues and reject the traditional boundaries set for him or her. An intensely emotional or sensitive child may comprehend things never imagined by other family members. This child may push far beyond the geographic limits or aspirational labels held by other family members. Beavers (1982) suggests optimal family members can switch hit, flexibly identifying with the larger world at times and yet maintaining individual boundaries.

Functional families establish internal boundaries to protect members' self-identities and the identity of generational groups. If the boundaries between individuals are diffuse, or nonexistent, members may experience psychological problems, such as overinvolvement, codependency, or a loss of physical boundaries, such as occurs in incest. If the internal boundaries are too rigid and strong, members will feel disengaged and out of touch. Imber-Black (1998) suggests a patterned "family dance" occurs when members maneuver around the internal boundaries surrounding individual or subgroup secrets.

Most families experience boundaries between generations, which establish subsystems of generational hierarchy. Generations establish their boundaries based on behaviors appropriate for that subsystem (Wood & Talmon, 1983). For example, parents usually provide nurturance and control for their children. It is unusual for children to extensively nurture or control their parents unless the parents have become aged and ill. In two-parent families, the marital subsystem represents a critical entity in the functioning of family life. In most families, husbands and wives share unique information and give each other special emotional and physical support. Children are not allowed to share in all aspects of the marital dyad. Sometimes even adult children can be separated from the marital relationship.

My parents had used illnesses not only as intra-family secrets but also as punishment. My father had surgery at one time and needed to stay at the hospital for a short visit. My mother and father decided to keep this a secret and not tell anyone, even their children. When we figured it out and called to check in on my parents to see how they were, my father became angry that no one came to see him at the hospital and then refused to speak with us for awhile. All five of us children knew that if we were not told about any of their illnesses, we were considered outsiders.

Many types of conflict may arise if the system's interpersonal boundaries, particularly the marital boundaries, are too permeable and children or others are expected to fulfill part of the spousal role. For example, troubled families, such as those with a severely depressed spouse, may experience shifts in the marital boundary. If a depressed husband cannot provide the interpersonal support needed by his wife, she may co-opt one of the children into the marital subsystem by expecting the child to act as an adult confidant and to provide emotional support. When boundaries are inappropriately crossed, roles become confused and pain may result for all members.

Internal boundary inclusion may differ across cultural groups. Given the high degree of interdependence among extended family members in many American ethnic cultures, the nuclear household may have less rigid boundaries, as members are part of multiple households with strong emotional ties and mutual assistance (Sillars, 1995).

Sometimes boundary issues are played out across a series of generations. A daughter whose mother invaded her life may determine not to act in the same way toward her children, and actually distance herself from them. Her children, in turn, may resolve to develop closeness with their offspring and end up invading their children's lives.

Interpersonally testing or forcing boundaries may involve deep emotional conflicts, which could be resolved through the increased growth of all family members or by the severing of bonds with specific members who eventually leave the system. Each of you has experienced resisting boundaries or having persons challenge your system's boundaries with positive or negative results. Eventually, your family relationships may have become stronger or certain relationships may have suffered. Thus, the physical and psychological boundaries set by each family strongly influence the kinds of interpersonal communication that can occur within the system.

Biosocial Issues   All families operate in a larger sphere that provides conventional ways of coping with biosocial issues, but each family creates its own answers within the larger framework. Hess and Handel (1959) identify the following biosocial issues: male and female identity, authority and power, shaping and influencing children, and children's rights. In short, the family is a primary source of gender identity (Wood, 1997).

All people are faced with gender identity issues while growing up and/or while forming their own family systems and raising children. Gender identity and physical development issues affect styles of interaction and vice versa. A family that assigns responsibilities based on a member's gender operates differently than one that uses interest or preference as the basis for assigning responsibilities. If physical stature automatically determines duties and privileges, the interaction will be different than in a setting where physical development is only one factor among many by which privileges are awarded and duties are assigned to males and females.

Gender differences in families remain, although sometimes they are subtle and surprising. In their study of parental attitudes and infidelity, Fenigstein and Peltz (2002) found that both mothers and fathers regarded sexual infidelity as more distressing when committed by a daughter-in-law than by a son-in-law. In contrast, they found emotional infidelity was more distressing when it involved a son-in-law. Such traditional gender beliefs are often unrecognized but operational.

Gender experiences vary across cultural groups. For example, in Hispanic and African American families, collectivistic values affect gendered family roles (Gaines, 1995). The cultural perspective is displayed in the following quote.

My mother has characteristics of both the Korean attitude and the Western point of view toward women. She fulfills the Korean view of what a woman should be by being the primary nurturer of the family. She is the parent who drove us to piano lessons and took care of us when we were sick. Of the parental unit, she is the one that we would like to talk to first when we have a relational problem. In addition to being the nurturer of the family, she also meets the Western view that women should have careers. She is an equal financial contributor to our family. This makes us relate to her even more.

Other value decisions in the social sphere relate to the use of power within the family structure. To what extent are leadership, decision-making, and authority issues resolved according to traditional gender and role configurations? Families negotiate the use of power within the system, and members may find themselves in the renegotiation process for much of their lives. The social sphere also involves attitudinal issues related to roles and responsibilities that may be exemplified in parent-child relationships. Parent-child interaction reflects their mutually held attitudes. If a parent sees a child as a responsibility to be dispensed with at a given age, the interactions will be immensely different than if the parental attitude reflects a prolonged responsibility for his or her off-spring, perhaps far beyond the years of adolescence. The extent to which a child is permitted privacy, physical or psychological, also reflects a biosocial orientation.

Age, gender, and power interact in complex ways within family systems, and women may fall between the male parent and the child in some structures (Hare-Mustin, 1989). Thus, the parents versus child hierarchy may be too simple a concept when dealing with power.

For the first 11 years of life, my stepson, Travis, was raised in a household that catered to his every need. He was encouraged both to be dependent and to remain a little boy in many ways. His mother, Martha, could not have more children, so she doted on him as her only child. Before he died, Martha's first husband treated her and Travis as people who needed to be taken care of. When I married Martha, my two daughters came to live with us. They had been raised to be self-sufficient and independent. I have found myself becoming very impatient with Travis and pushing him to act like my children. As a result, Martha and I have had many fights over the children's responsibilities.

The development of images, themes, boundaries, and responses to biosocial issues interacts with the functions of cohesion and adaptability. Flexible families will experience greater variety in images, themes, boundaries, and responses to biosocial issues than will rigid ones. These responses also affect the family's acceptable level of cohesion. For example, a family with fixed boundaries and themes related to total family dependence will develop extremely high cohesion in contrast to the family with themes of service or independence coupled with flexible boundaries. This entire process rests with the communication behaviors of the family members. Communication, then, is the means by which families establish their patterns of cohesion and adaptability, based at least partially on their interactions in the development of images, themes, boundaries, and responses to biosocial issues.

A FRAMEWORK FOR EXAMINING FAMILY COMMUNICATION

There are numerous approaches to analyzing the family as a system, such as looking at a family as an economic, political, or biological system. Because concern lies with the interaction within and around the family, this text centers on the communication aspects of the family system. The following is a framework for examining family communication:

> **The family is a system constituted, defined, and managed through its communication. Family members regulate cohesion and adaptability to develop a collective identity through the flow of patterned, meaningful messages within a network of evolving interdependent relationships located within a defined cultural context.**

Each segment should be examined:

> **The family is a system constituted, defined, and managed through its communication.**

The family may be viewed as a set of people and the relationships among them that, together, form a complex whole; changes in one part result in changes in other parts of the system. In short, family members are inextricably tied to each other, and each member and the family as a whole reflect changes in the system. Communication—the symbolic, transactional process by which meanings are exchanged—is the means by which families are constituted and regulated.

> **Family members regulate cohesion and adaptability to develop a collective identity . . .**

Communication facilitates a family's movement on the cohesion–adaptability axis (Figure 2.1). The way in which people exchange messages influences the form and content of their relationships. Communication and families have a mutual impact on each other. The collective identity is formed through the congruence of the primary and secondary functions.

> **. . . through the flow of patterned, meaningful messages within a network . . .**

Family members cocreate their meanings and their relational culture. Based on families-of-origin and other environmental sources, each family develops its own set of meanings that become predictable, since family members interact with one another in the same manner over and over again. Such message patterns move through boundaries, define the relationships along specific networks, and determine who interacts with whom.

> **. . . of evolving interdependent relationships . . .**

Family life is not static; both predictable, or developmental, changes and unpredictable changes, or crises, alter the system. Family relationships evolve over time as members join and leave the system and become closer or farther apart from each other. Family members struggle with dialectical tensions and boundary management. Yet, due to the family's systemic nature, members remain interdependent, or joined, as they deal with relational issues of intimacy, conflict roles, power, and decision making.

. . . located within a defined cultural context.

Normality may be viewed as transactional or process oriented. This perspective emphasizes attention to adaptation over the life cycle and adaptation to various contexts. Thus, issues of developmental stages and reaction to change combine with contextual issues such as ethnicity, gender, and socioeconomic status to create a "culture" within which families operate. Norms and expectations vary greatly across groups of families, but may remain relatively similar for families within a given cultural context. Finally, the spatial context within which a family lives its everyday life affects its functioning.

Throughout the following chapters, we will examine the concepts mentioned in this framework in order to demonstrate the powerful role communication plays in family life.

When you really think about it, family life is extremely complex and most of us just go through the motions everyday without any reflection. I usually take for granted that most families are similar to mine. However, the more I look carefully at other family systems, the more aware I am of the differences. Perhaps families are like snowflakes, no two are ever exactly alike.

It seems appropriate to close this chapter with Handel and Whitchurch's (1994) statement, which captures the crucial nature of family interaction:

> A family creates and maintains itself through its interaction, that is, through social interaction both inside and outside the family, members define their relationships to one another, and to the world beyond the family as they establish individual identities as well as a collective family identity. (p. 1)

Conclusion

This chapter described the process of communication and proposed a connection between communication patterns and family functions. Communication was developed as a symbolic transactional process. Systems theory and symbolic interactionism were established as the critical underlying theories used to understand family communication. The importance of meaning-making and managing dialectical tensions was addressed. The primary functions discussed are cohesion and adaptability, and the supporting functions include family images, themes, boundaries, and biosocial issues. The chapter concluded with a framework for analyzing family interaction.

In Review

1. Using your own family or a fictional family, identify three areas of "meaning" that would have to be explained to an outsider who was going to be a houseguest for a month. For example, what would have to be explained for the houseguest to understand how this family views the world?
2. Describe a recurring interaction pattern in a real or fictional family in terms of the predictable verbal and nonverbal messages. Provide a statement of the effect of this interaction pattern on the persons involved or on the family as a whole.
3. Give three examples of behavior that might characterize an enmeshed family and three examples of behavior that might characterize a disengaged family.
4. Using a real or fictional family, give an example of how the family moved from one point on the adaptability–cohesion grid to another point due to changes in their lives.
5. How might one of the following themes be carried out in family communication patterns? What image, boundaries, and biosocial issues might support that theme?

Themes

- You can always depend on your family.
- We are survivors.
- Use your gifts.
- Take one step at a time.
- You only live once.
- There's always tomorrow.

FAMILY THEORIES

3

We live our lives like chips in a kaleidoscope, always part of patterns that are larger than ourselves and somehow more than the sum of their parts.

Salvador Minuchin, *Family Kaleidoscope*

There are many ways to make sense out of how a family functions, particularly how communication undergirds every aspect of family life. As you move through this chapter, you will encounter research from scholars in multiple fields who hold different assumptions about family dynamics. Although we cannot address all related theories, we wish to introduce some key theories and terminology that influence multiple family communication scholars. Specifically, we will focus on systems theory, symbolic interaction, social construction theory, and dialectical theory. Within the discussion you will encounter new terms and references to related theories. These theories and concepts will help you develop your own frameworks for analyzing family interaction.

When individuals come together to form relationships, what is created is larger and more complex than the sum of the individuals; they create a system. When individuals form families, they also create family systems built on their interaction patterns. Taking a systems perspective provides valuable insights into a family's communication patterns. Because communication is a symbolic, transactional process of sharing meanings, focus must be placed on family relationships, not just on individual members. In order to understand the communication patterns of family members, the overall communication context—the family system—must be examined.

The following personal statement provides insight into how a family operates systematically and reflects the complexity of the task of examining families from a systems perspective.

Family life is incredibly subtle and complex. Everything seems tied to everything else, and it's very difficult to sort out what is going on. For example, when our oldest daughter, Marcy, contracted spinal meningitis, the whole family reflected the strain. My second daughter and I fought more, while my husband tended to withdraw into himself, which brought me closer to my son. In their own ways, the three children became closer while our marriage became more distant. As Marcy's recovery progressed, there were more changes, which affected how we relate now, two years later. That one event highlighted the difficulty of sorting out what is really going on within our family.

Everyday family behavior patterns are often subtle, almost invisible, buried in apparent predictability, yet powerful in their effects. Individuals get caught up, often unconsciously, in their family patterns. Unless you view individuals within their primary context, you may never be able to make sense of their behavior.

THE SYSTEMS PERSPECTIVE

Very simply stated, a *system* is a set of components that interrelate with one another to form a whole. Due to the interconnections, if one component of the system changes, the others will change in response, which in turn affects the initial component. Therefore, a change in one part of the system affects every part of the system.

Families do not exist in a vacuum; they live within a time period, culture, community, and many other influential factors, such as religion, economic status, or geographical locations that impact them directly. This larger context, or ecosystem, affects a family's life course. From a systems perspective, "decontexted individuals do not exist" (Minuchin, 1984, p. 2). Persons are considered as part of an overall context, not as individuals. To grasp this concept, imagine a picture in which the people are in the background and their relationships are depicted in the foreground. The patterns of interaction take precedence over the individuals. Communication is central to understanding family systems.

When two individuals come together in a relationship, something is created that is different from, larger and more complex than those two individuals apart—a system. The most important fea-

> ture of such a relationship is communication. Relationships are
> established, maintained, and changed by communicated interac-
> tion among members. (Duncan & Rock, 1993, p. 48)

A family systems perspective should aid you in analyzing family interaction, predicting future interactions, and creating meaningful changes
within a family.

We will apply the following system characteristics to families: interdependence, wholeness, patterns/self-regulation, interactive complexity/
punctuation, openness, complex relationships, and equifinality (Watzlawick, Beavin, & Jackson, 1967; Whitchurch & Constantine, 1993; Bochner
& Eisenberg, 1987; White & Klein, 2002; Littlejohn, 2002). The following
summary of systems theory's impact will preview the concepts and help
guide your reading of these characteristics.

> Systems theory has taught us to see our own and other family
> members' behavior as interrelated, to locate predictable patterns
> of interaction that seem to exert more power over the family than
> do any individual family members themselves, to see problems in
> terms of relationship struggles rather than the "fault" of one per-
> son who is "scapegoated" and "blamed" for others' pain. Most of
> all, systems theory has helped us to pay attention to our interde-
> pendence. (Yerby, 1995, pp. 339–340)

An individual's behavior becomes more comprehensible when
viewed within the context of the human system within which he or she
functions and within the broader context in which the family is situated
(Cowan & Cowan, 1997).

Interdependence

How does one come to see oneself as an integral part of a larger whole?
Such a vision includes

> observing ourselves as components of an unfolding process
> rooted in the past and intertwined with larger living systems in
> the present. It is as mind boggling as gazing into the evening sky
> and trying to comprehend one's place in the vastness of the uni-
> verse. (Noone, 1989, p. 2)

Within any system, the parts are so interrelated as to be dependent on
each other for their functioning. Thus, this relatedness, or interdependence, is critical in describing a system.

Within a system, the parts and the relationship between them form
the whole; changes in one part will result in changes in the others. This is
true in families, also. Satir (1988) describes a family as a mobile. Picture a

mobile that hangs over a child's crib, with people instead of elephants or sailboats on it. As events touch one member of the family, other members reverberate in relationship to the change in the affected member. Thus, if a family member loses a job, flunks out of school, wins the state basketball championship, marries, or becomes ill, such an event affects the entire family system, depending on each person's current relationship with that individual. In addition, because family members are human beings, not elephants or sailboats on a mobile, they can "pull their own strings," or make their own moves. At some point, a family member may choose to withdraw from the family and, by pulling away, forces other members into closer relationships. Thus, as members move toward or away from each other, all members are affected.

Current thinkers support an evolutionary model of family systems that incorporates the possibility of spontaneous or kaleidoscopic change (Hoffman, 1990; Bochner & Eisenberg, 1987). No matter what kind of change a family is experiencing, all members are affected due to their interdependence.

You may be able to pinpoint events in your own family that have influenced all members in an identifiable way. Sometimes troublesome behaviors are acceptable, because that individual serves to keep the family relatively balanced by taking the focus off a more threatening problem. Parents may use, or focus on, an acting-out child to keep the marriage together; or children may use their parents' overprotectiveness to keep them safely close to home. A behavior that seems problematic to the outside world may serve an important function within the family system. The following example describes this exact process as 7-year-old Judy exhibits temper tantrums and obnoxious misbehavior:

> When specifically does Judy act up and act out? From what I can piece together, this occurs when her father's distance and her mother's anxious focus on Judy reach intolerable proportions. And what is the outcome of Judy's trouble-making and tantrums? Distant Dad is roped back into the family (and is helped to become more angry than depressed), and the parents are able to pull together, temporarily united by their shared concern for their child. Judy's behavior is, in part, an attempt to solve a problem in the family. (Lerner, 1989, p. 3)

In summary, then, in a family systems perspective, the behavior of each family member is related to and dependent on the behavior of the others. In addition, within-family relationships such as the marital relationship or the parent-child relationships affect each other (O'Connor, Hetherington, & Clingempeel, 1997).

Wholeness

A family systems approach assumes the whole is greater than the sum of its parts. A commonplace illustration is the cake that comes out of the oven, quite unlike its components of flour, oil, eggs, chocolate squares, and milk. A nonsystemic approach to families would look at individual members and "sum up" their personalities and attributes to describe the entire family. In contrast, the systems model reflects an integration of parts; overall family images and themes reflect this holistic quality. Families exhibit characteristics that reflect individuals and the interplay of family members. The characteristics exhibited are assumed by others to characterize the family and each member. The parts, or members, are understood in the context of that whole.

The Boyer family, for example, may be characterized as humorous, religious, warm, and strong, yet these adjectives do not necessarily apply to each family member. Thus, certain group characteristics may not reflect those of each individual. You may hear whole families referred to as "brainy," "artistic," "aggressive," "industrious," or "money-hungry," yet you know at least one member who does not fit the label.

In an ongoing human system, the components, or the people, have importance; but once these parts become interrelated, these properties

Families are characterized frequently by activities members share.

take on a life greater than their individual existences. Wholeness is characteristic of a system because there are

> behaviors of the system that do not derive from the component parts themselves when considered in isolation. Rather, these emerge from their specific arrangement in a particular system and from the transactions among parts made possible only by that arrangement. These are called *emergents* or *emergent properties* because they emerge only at the systemic level. (Whitchurch & Constantine, 1993, p. 329)

Communication patterns between or among family members emerge as a result of this "wholeness." Conflict or affection may become an inherent part of communication between various members. A certain cue may trigger patterns of behavior without members' awareness. A delightful example follows.

Something wonderful and funny happens when my sister and I get together. We tend to play off each other and can finish each other's sentences, pick up the same references at the same time, and create a dynamic energy that leaves other people out. We don't do it on purpose. Rather, we just seem to "click" with each other and off we go!

Patterns/Self-Regulation

Human beings learn to coordinate their actions in order to create patterns together that could not be created individually. Although coordination of actions varies dramatically across family systems, each system develops communication patterns that make life somewhat predictable and manageable.

Over time, you have learned to live within a family interaction system that is highly reciprocal, patterned, and repetitive. Interaction patterns provide a window for assessing communication behaviors within a system, because they provide the context for understanding specific or isolated behaviors. For example, taken as an isolated action, it may be hard to interpret an act such as Mike hitting his brother, Charles. Yet, if this act is viewed as part of a contextual pattern, it may make sense. If parental disagreements and Mike's aggressive acts are related, you may discover patterns, such as the parents stop fighting with each other when they focus on Mike's angry actions or Charles's tears. Or, Mike is scared by his parents' anger and takes his feelings out on his brother. The following example describes how family members unwittingly can get stuck in a pattern.

> My older sister, Susan (a typical firstborn), managed her anxiety by overfunctioning, and I (a typical youngest) managed my anxiety by underfunctioning. Over time our position became polarized and rigidly entrenched. The more my sister overfunctioned the more I underfunctioned, and vice versa. (Lerner, 1989, p. 28)

Communication rules are a very special type of relationship pattern. Rules are relationship agreements that prescribe and limit a family member's behavior over time; they are capable of creating regularity out of chaos. Ongoing communication generates rules and is regulated by rules. Every human system needs rules and regularity in order to function efficiently over time, yet rules themselves are not totally stable. Rules will be discussed in detail in Chapter 4.

Human systems attempt to maintain levels of constancy within an overall defined range of acceptable behavior. From a somewhat mechanistic viewpoint, a system needs to maintain some type of standard by noting deviations from the norm and correcting them if they become too significant. The function of maintaining stability in a system is called *calibration*. Calibration implies monitoring and correcting a scale. In the case of a family system, it implies checking and, if necessary, correcting the scale of acceptable behaviors. On occasion, the changes happen too dramatically for a family to exert any control. But everyday life is filled with opportunities to maintain or alter family patterns. Although systems can be compared to mechanical operations, Hoffman (1990) argues against this, suggesting that human systems are not mechanical and are capable of evolving.

Systems generate maintenance and change-promoting feedback processes. *Maintenance* feedback processes imply constancy or maintaining the standard while minimizing change. *Change-promoting* feedback processes result in recalibration of the system at a different level. You can visualize this process in the following ways. Figure 3.1a represents a system in which maintenance feedback prevents change from occurring. For example, this may happen when a teenager swears at a parent for the first

FIGURE 3.1   Feedback Systems

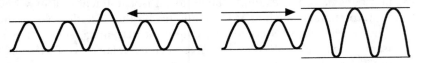

a. Maintenance Feedback
(no change)

b. Change-Promoting Feedback
(change occurs)

time, yet the rules themselves are not totally stable. The parent may threaten, "You swear at me again and I'll ground you for six months," or the parent appeals to the family values, "We show each other respect even in disagreement." If the teenager becomes frightened by the threat, or apologetic for breaking the family value system, swearing may not occur again. In another example, if one partner indicates a desire for sexual experimentation but the other refuses, the system will be maintained at the original level of sexual intimacy, at least for a while.

Figure 3.1b represents a system in which change-promoting feedback occurs. For example, if a wife cannot stop her husband's initial use of physical force, hitting may become part of their long-term conflict pattern. In another example, if the partner agrees to some sexual experimentation and both partners find pleasure in it, the system may develop a wider range of sexual expression.

Change-promoting feedback processes enable the system to grow, create, innovate, and change, whereas maintenance feedback processes attempt to maintain the status quo. In the following situation, change-promoting feedback processes operate as a father responds to his son's attempts to reach greater physical closeness.

As an adult, I became very aware of the limited physical contact I had with my father. Although he would hug my sister, he never touched the boys, with the exception of a handshake. I determined that I wanted a greater physical closeness with him and consciously set out to change our ways of relating to each other. The first time I hugged my father was when I returned from a trip and I walked in and put my arms around him. I was nervous and tentative; he was startled and stiff, but he didn't resist. Over time I continued to greet him with hugs until we reached the point at which both of us could extend our arms to each other. I can now see my brothers developing a greater physical closeness to him also.

When a family's communication rules have been developed over time, the family is calibrated, or "set," to regulate its behavior in conformity to the rules. If one or more family members challenges the rules, the family may be recalibrated in accordance with the new ones.

An unwritten family rule may be that a seriously ill 14-year-old is not allowed to hear the truth regarding his condition. If anyone should suggest that he has a blood disease, maintenance feedback in the form of a nonverbal sign or a change of subject may keep him relatively uninformed. The family is "set" not to discuss the issue with him. Yet, the rules may be changed and the system recalibrated through a variety of change-promoting feedback mechanisms. If the young man guesses the severity of his illness, he may confront one or more family members and insist on the truth. Once the truth has been told, he cannot return to his previous naive state, and the system will recognize that his illness is known. Another source of positive feedback may be a doctor who suggests that the young man's condition be discussed with him and may require the family to do so. Human systems must change and evolve in order to survive. Families constantly restructure themselves to cope with developmental stages and unpredictable crises. Change is a predictable part of the human experience.

Early family theorists viewed the family as a system attempting to maintain stability. Yet, current thinking about family systems views the concept of calibration as mechanistic and narrow. The ongoing dialectical struggles of human beings keep a system in some level of flux. In addition, human systems are capable of sudden leaps to new integrations, reflecting a new evolutionary state (Hoffman, 1990). In other words, sometimes families also experience change through leaps—as random and unpredictable forces propel members into new forms and experiences. The traditional calibration model needs to be modified and placed within an evolutionary framework, in an attempt to recognize both types of change.

Interactive Complexity/Punctuation

A systems perspective implies a move away from thinking about cause and effect to thinking about relationship patterns within contexts. Simply put, cause and effect are interchangeable. When you function as a member of an ongoing family system, each of your actions serves as both a response to a previous action and a stimulus for a future action. The term *interactive complexity* implies that each act triggers new behavior as well as responds to previous behaviors, rendering pointless any attemps to assign cause and effect. In most families, patterns of behavior develop and take on a life of their own. Thus, it is fruitless to assign a cause or blame to one person or action, because the behaviors are intertwined. Family problems are seen in light of patterns of behavior in which all members have a part; one member is not to blame. One person does not carry the problems. This approach has been labeled an *illness-free* lens through which to view relationships (Duncan & Rock, 1993).

In order to make sense of the world, human beings tend to "punctuate" sequencing of behavior. *Punctuation* refers to the interruption of the sequence of behavior at intervals in order to give it meaning. Punctuation suggests that "things started here." Interactions, like sentences, must be punctuated, or grouped syntactically, to make sense or create meaning. Yet, punctuation may also serve as a trap, forcing people into thought patterns that assign cause and blame to individuals instead of focusing on the problematic pattern.

Confusion occurs when people punctuate behavioral sequences differently, thereby assigning varied meanings to the behaviors. A son might say, "Our trouble started when my mother became depressed," whereas the mother might indicate that the family problems started when her son began running away from home. Punctuating the cycle according to the son's interpretation implies placing blame on the mother and suggests that "fixing" her would solve the problem. If the cycle is punctuated according to the mother, the son would be at fault for running away and if he is "fixed," the family troubles would end. This cycle could go on indefinitely. It is fruitless to try to locate the "cause" because, even if it could be found, the current pattern is what must be addressed, not an individual's past actions. Sometimes family members will "scapegoat" one person, suggesting he or she is responsible for all the problems and removing themselves from any responsibility. Working from the idea of circular causality within the system, it seems less important to try to punctuate the system and assign a beginning point than it does to look at the act as a sequence of patterns and try to understand this ongoing process. In Figure 3.2, you can imagine the different interpretations that could emerge depending on how the cycle is punctuated.

A classic example of punctuation is found in the "nag-withdraw cycle," which demonstrates the pointless nature of looking for cause and effect: "He withdraws because she nags" versus "She nags because he withdraws" (Dell, 1982, p. 26). An example of such a cycle is found in this analysis of Eugene O'Neill's play, *Long Day's Journey into Night:*

> The family members watch the mother closely, which makes her visibly nervous, which makes them watch her closely . . . until the circle winds into a spiral leading to the return of her addiction, which they all fear. The above description could also have begun: the mother is visibly nervous, which makes the family watch her closely. (Bavelas & Segal, 1982, p. 104)

FIGURE 3.2 Circular Causality within a System

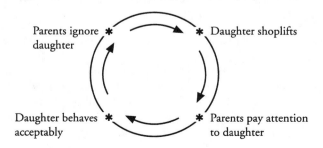

Openness

Just as there are no decontexted individuals, so, too, there are no decontexted families. Human systems include individuals, families, communities, and societies that form nested layers. Human systems are open systems that permit interchange with surrounding environments; information flows back and forth across that boundary (Broderick, 1993). Human systems need interchange with other people, ideas, and institutions in order to remain physically and psychologically functional. Family members maintain an almost continuous interchange, not only within the system but across the family boundary to the larger ecosystem. Family systems with closed boundaries develop extremely rigid family patterns.

Each family operates within the larger ecosystem, which includes legal, educational, political, health, and economic systems, as well as extended family and friendship systems. As a small child, you may have depended entirely on your family for all your immediate needs, but as you grew older, you needed to interact with nonfamily members in order to function in society. Such interchange with and adaptation to the environment is critical.

Family boundary strength depends partially on how the family views the "outside world." A family's immediate environment may be experienced as harsh or threatening, such as when children can be shot walking to school, or supportive and nurturing, such as when neighbors create a kinship network of support. Individual circumstances, such as that described in the next example, may force a family into active contact with institutions in their environment.

As the parent of a hard-of-hearing child, I am constantly managing our family's boundaries and dealing with outside systems. We deal regularly with the medical community in terms of advances that might affect Melissa's condition. The school system and I monitor which classes we should mainstream Melissa into each year. I need to keep up with legal changes to ensure that our child's rights are protected in terms of access to special programs. Finally, I am constantly aware of the effect of extended family and friends who reach out to support us.

Few families can insulate children totally, because schools and media expose them to a range of values and beliefs, some of which may be contrary to those held by the family. Television, the Internet, and music open worlds to children that parents may not even comprehend. Family systems rules include guidelines for maintaining and regulating relationships within the environment, but, in this rapidly changing world, families may not be able to keep pace with the technological advances.

Complex Relationships

Systems embedded in systems create a highly complex set of structures and interaction patterns and may be understood as members in relation to each other. Historically, the critical underlying concept of family organization was hierarchy, yet recent scholars argue there are other ways to understand system structures than just looking at hierarchy (Broderick, 1993).

A traditional hierarchical view establishes parents as more powerful than children. In almost all cultures, authority, respect, and power go to the older generation, often to the males of that generation. Appropriate boundaries separate generations; when generational boundaries are blurred, confusion results, such as in the following case.

After my father moved out, I found myself playing surrogate Dad to three younger sisters who needed a lot of support. I moved into the role very easily since it seemed to take pressure off my mother who was severely depressed for almost three years. At the time, I just did it. Now I wish I had not given up my adolescence so easily.

Families are not hierarchically structured in any stable fashion, yet how family members are positioned on vertical dimensions is a productive issue to explore. Structural issues include subsystems and dynamics of power and privilege (Broderick, 1993).

Given today's diverse family forms, the traditional hierarchical structures cannot account for the multiple family experiences. Immigrant families in the United States face dramatic structural changes as young members gain power by being the only English speakers. They control their parents' relationships to the schools and larger community. Certain responsible children find themselves as caregivers to a parent or grandparent who is physically or psychologically unable to manage.

In her book, *The Spirit Catches You and You Fall Down,* Anne Fadiman (1997) depicts the culture clash between Hmong refugees and U.S. culture. She describes the "role loss" that occurs as the family power structure turns upside down because the children gain English language proficiency and education while the parents and grandparents struggle to survive in such a different culture. This creates significant power shifts and hierarchical reversals that create sadness and conflict.

The complexity of the family system may be seen through the multiple subsystems that contribute to the whole family's functioning. For example, an extended family may include many smaller family units, which in turn contain subsystems. Each family system contains interpersonal systems and individual, or psychobiological, subsystems. As noted in the discussion of wholeness, knowing the family attributes does not necessarily equal knowing the specific members or their relationships.

Every family contains interpersonal subsystems, made up of two or three persons and the relationships between or among them. Typical subsystems include partners, parents and children, and siblings. Even a three-person system becomes complicated by the interpersonal subsystems within it. A mother, daughter, and grandson triad represents three such subsystems—the mother and daughter, the daughter and her son, and the grandmother and grandson. Thus, each of the subsystems has to be considered in order to understand the functioning of the whole. Each subsystem has its own roles, boundaries, and unique characteristics.

In most cases, interpersonal subsystems change membership over time. Yet, certain subsystems may become so strong or tight that particular members feel either overwhelmed, powerless, or left out. Relationships at different levels of the system may impact each other. For instance, spousal abuse may be the way that partners have managed unresolved issues in their family of origin; a parent and child conflict may preserve a marital bond (Yerby, 1995).

Coalitions develop when individuals align in joint action against others. For example, in a family with a gambling parent, the children and the nongambling parent may form a tight group as a means of coping with the gambler's unpredictable behavior. The coalition may develop strategies for hiding money, supporting the others in arguments, or lying to those outside the system.

Family triangles, characterized by two insiders and one outsider, represent a powerful type of coalition. Under stress, two-person relationships may become unstable, so they will draw in a third to stabilize their relationship (McGoldrick & Gerson, 1985). Under stress, the insiders try to rope in the outsider to reduce the stress between them. When tensions are low, the outsider may feel isolated. Many stepfamilies struggle with these issues in early years. By observing family triangles, you will see the absurdity of assigning causes or blame to particular events, since everyone plays a part, as noted below.

I grew up in a house where my dad could not keep a job. My mother and oldest brother formed a tight relationship against him, and sometimes against everyone else. They agreed on everything and my brother became my mother's protector. Even when Dad was employed, he could not break up that coalition, and I think that was one of the reasons they got a divorce. My brother discouraged my mom from ever trusting Dad again.

Triangles often result in frustration and unhappiness for the "third" person. This is especially difficult when the triangle cuts across generations, thereby violating the appropriate boundaries, such as when a parent is aligned with a child against the other parent.

The family therapy literature identifies three powerful triangles in two-parent families: the child as scapegoat, the child as mediator, and the perverse triangle (Broderick, 1993). A couple can triangulate a child into a scapegoat position by deflecting their marital tension onto the parent-child relationship, thereby labeling the child as the source of all family problems. A child may unwittingly learn to act out when his or her parents fight, thus deflecting their anger and keeping them together. Or a child may be cast in the role of mediator or counselor between two warring parents, a commonplace situation in divorcing families. A coalition may form between a child and one parent whereby the child is enmeshed with one parent and cut off from the other, creating a perverse triangle. As family systems grow in size, the complexity of the interpersonal subsystems develops accordingly.

To further complicate the issue, each family system reflects the individual, or psychobiological, system of each member as well as cultural norms that may privilege one type of subsystem over another. No matter how much three sisters may resemble one another, for example, each is a psychobiological entity who functions partially in an independent manner. In addition, outside factors such as their culture and socioeconomic level may strongly influence how women are treated in families.

Equifinality

How do you know a family is resilient? Happy? Healthy? Wealthy? Spiritual? An open, adaptive family system demonstrates *equifinality*, which means that "a particular final state may be accomplished in different ways and from different starting points" (Littlejohn, 2002, p. 41). There are many ways to reach the same result. For example, two families may believe they achieve success based on a particular income, education, and relationship level, but appear very different to an observer. Or, two families may have a theme of "Family members are supportive." Yet, one family may interpret the theme to mean emotional support, whereas the other may view it as an economic issue. The families may differ in their definition of need for support and their demands for assistance. In short, there are as many possible ways of reaching a goal as there are families striving for that goal.

This may appear as a linear process of setting a goal and striving toward it, but in reality it is more unpredictable. Hence, a family attempting to reach security in one way may find themselves experiencing it in an entirely unpredicted yet satisfactory way after six months or six years.

Communication and the Systems Perspective

When the components of a system are actually people in relationships with other people, a key attribute of the system is communication (Bavelas & Segal, 1982). Family systems are constituted by the communication process—it is communication that creates, maintains, and changes the system's reality. Humans act on the social reality they construct through their communication. Individuals in family systems behave according to the meanings they assign to each other, the family, and aspects of the environment. In most families there may be some differences but there is frequently an awareness of congruence in how members see the world. Communication messages may be viewed as interwoven patterns of interaction that stretch through a family's history rather than as singular events. Each message is simultaneously a response to someone else's message (real or anticipated) and a stimulus for future responses (Yerby, Buerkel-Rothfuss, & Bochner, 1990).

Limitations of the Systems Perspective

Although it is a well-known theory, particularly among family scholars and family therapists, decades of thinking and research have revealed limitations, which include gender and individual concerns and contextual issues.

Gender Issues   Systems theory has been criticized for ignoring the historical inequality between males and females in families, referred to as the "denial of gender" (Goldner, 1989). Certain feminist theorists argue that the implicit patriarchal nature of family life goes unchallenged, and an assumed equality of marital power is misleading and destructive. Some argue the systems view privileges male values (Hare-Mustin, 1994). A commonly cited problem area that overlaps gender and individual concerns relates to abusive families in which a systems perspective removes any individual level of responsibility for problems. As the extreme, this suggests that a victim shares equal responsibility for the abuse. The concept of circular causality and mutual influence can mask the responsibility of a man and the vulnerability of a woman in a physically abusive relationship (Hoffman, 1990). Greater attention to gender concerns could strengthen the systems perspective.

Individual Concerns Systems theory tends to overlook individual, or psychobiological, issues. Historically, the growing information about genetic components of disease was largely ignored and responsibility for problems was placed equally on the members of a troubled relationship. This resulted in inappropriate responsibility being assigned to family members for actions of individuals suffering from actual illness or having biological predispositions to certain disorders such as schizophrenia, manic depression, or anxiety (Broderick, 1993). For example, a genetic predisposition may contribute to an individual member's alcoholism, which impacts not only the individual but the entire family system. Neurobiological structures underlying temperament traits and individual differences are greatly affected by genetic inheritance (McCroskey, 1997). The assumption of shared or equal responsibility can be devastating to family members who are frustrated by the problems, as indicated next.

My brother's hyperactivity was not understood in the 1970s and my parents were blamed for his inattention and the mishaps he had (i.e., getting into the medicine cabinet and drinking a bottle of Dimetapp). His behavior problems were not just a product of the system, and the implication that my parents were involved in causing his problem was devastating to them. The doctors, teachers, and school counselors all made my mother feel like a bad parent.

Currently, theorists argue that systems approaches can be aided by individual approaches that recognize biological components of the problem (Beatty, McCroskey, & Heisel, 1998).

Contextual Issues Critics argue that there is no culturally contextual version of family process, although a number of efforts in this direction are underway. Until the 1980s, little thought had been given to ethnic and class variations in families and to their implications for understanding family interaction, such as in the areas of gender and power (Markowitz, 1994). Yerby (1995) suggests cultural differences in boundaries may not be recognized by those looking at patterns by focusing only on the nuclear family.

Throughout this text you will encounter examples of cultural impact on family functioning. These limitations, real as they are, also represent the signs of maturity of the approach. We believe a systems approach provides a valuable perspective from which to analyze family interaction. Although this chapter has dealt with a systems perspective primarily in an abstract manner, this view may be applied to everyday family functioning in concrete ways.

> Becoming aware of their system usually opens the way for family members to become searchers and to stop berating themselves and others when things go wrong. People can ask "how" questions instead of "why" questions. Generally speaking, "how" questions lead to information and understanding, and "whys" imply blame and so produce defensiveness. (Satir, 1988, p. 136)

Taking a systems perspective has very real consequences. For example, an elementary school teacher who holds a family systems perspective may try routinely to discover if an acting-out student's classroom behavior may be a symptom of a problem in his or her family life, or if his or her unacceptable behavior in class, such as exaggerated clowning, could serve a particular function in the family system. Therapists holding such a perspective would seek to meet and/or learn about the client's family to enable them to put the individual's behavior in context.

When viewed from this perspective, the focus shifts from an individual member's behavior to the family as a whole, with its interdependent relationships and patterns, which affect cohesion and adaptability. Looking at the family as a whole brings conceptions of interpersonal communication into greater congruence with the interactional complexity of family life. This perspective allows one to analyze specific behavior patterns in terms of the interpersonal context in which they occur and to understand their meaning in light of the entire family system.

SYMBOLIC INTERACTION

Symbolic interaction, a meaning-centered theory, assumes that (1) humans think about and act according to the meanings they attribute to their actions and context and (2) humans are motivated to create meanings to help them make sense of the world. Klein and White (1996) capture this in the following quote:

> A 3-year-old may show no interest in a particular toy doll. But when an older sibling plays with the doll, it suddenly takes on new interactional and situational meaning. Now, the doll is desired. The meaning of the toy is constructed by the situation interaction of the two siblings. (p. 92)

Symbolic interactionism focuses on the connection between symbols, or shared meanings and interactions, or verbal and nonverbal communication (LaRossa & Reitzes, 1993, p. 135). This approach views families as social groups; interaction fosters the development of self- and group identity. In summarizing key points of symbolic interactionism, the following assumptions reflect the importance of meaning for human behavior:

1. Human beings act toward things on the basis of the meanings that the things have for them.
2. Meaning arises out of the process of interaction between people.
3. Meanings are handled in and modified through an interpretive process used by the person in dealing with things he or she encounters. (LaRossa & Reitzes, p. 143)

Essentially, symbolic interaction requires paying attention to how events and things are interpreted by the actors (White & Klein, 2002). For all humans, meaning is negotiated through the use of language. This meaning-making process may be voluntary or involuntary, explicit or implicit, but it is always tied to language and discourse.

According to social interaction theorists, individuals and small groups are influenced by larger cultural and societal processes, and interpretation processes may be similar across groups who share similar contexts. Thus, ethnicity, gender, religion, and socioeconomic status would influence the interpretation process.

The importance of symbolic interaction from a family perspective is critical for both (1) defining families and (2) making sense out of family interaction. From this perspective, "a family is defined through its communication—both verbal and nonverbal—rather than solely through biological or legal kinship" (Whitchurch & Dickson, 1999, p. 687). Thus, it is through the process of interacting together as family that people establish a boundary between insiders and outsiders, thereby creating their family.

Interaction among family members and the interpretation of that interaction serves as the source of meanings for each member. Partners or siblings frequently do not label the same events as fights, apologies, or invitations. How often have you heard someone say, "I apologized to you" and the other reply, "I never got an apology from you." Finally, you hear, "I did so apologize. I took you to dinner." The issue revolves around one partner's assumption that "taking someone to dinner" means "apologizing." Holiday wars erupt regularly in some families because the gifts did not carry the meaning a recipient desired (for example, "A crockpot is not a birthday present!" or "All this gift certificate means is he did not want to take time to shop"). Enduring relationships are characterized by agreements between members as to the meaning of things. These persons develop a relationship worldview reflecting the members' symbolic interdependence (Stephen, 1986).

Social constructionism, considered an extension or branch of symbolic interaction, suggests that persons co-construct their social realities through conversation (West & Turner, 2000). Social construction is unique in its intense focus on how meanings are created and negotiated _situa-_

tionally by actors, rather than significantly influenced by social norms or expectations. Essentially, each partnership, marriage, or family is seen as having its own created world. Social constructionists are convinced that "the events and objects of the social world are *made* rather than *found*" (Griffin, 1997, p. 70).

Families are seen as constructing their realities, whether it's the personal definition of "family" or a highly unique understanding of what things or events "mean." According to Klein and White (1996), "The private understandings constructed by family members are based on their shared history, perspective, and interpretation of events. Dating and marriage are viewed as a process by which separate individuals 'fuse' into a common living arrangement and worldview" (p. 107). In their classic work, Berger and Kellner (1964) capture the sense of creating meanings within a marriage, saying, "Each partner's definition of reality must be continually correlated with the definitions of the other" (p. 224). Such correlation depends on communication. Therefore, in order to form a marital system, a couple must negotiate a set of common meanings through interaction and mutual accommodation so that, eventually, the meanings for one are linked through conjoint action with the meanings of the other.

Finally, families are meaning-generating systems since all social systems are created by their communication. In her discussion of the relationship between systems theory and social construction, Yerby (1995) maintains:

> The assertion that families are linguistically constructed and co-constructed reflects the social constructionist view that families are meaning-generating systems and that meaning is generated through the conversation or dialogue between and among participants in a social system. The assumption is that all social systems are defined by their communication. (p. 357)

In ongoing relationships, such as families, members eventually gain the ability to recognize shared meanings and to negotiate joint understandings through their interactions. Or, they break apart or struggle constantly with the lack of shared meanings on critical issues. One learns that the reason a partner's belief that "having a third beer" implies a drinking problem is because her father became drunk after more than two beers, or that a stepfather's anger about "wasting money" reflects his past need to watch every penny. Although most family members co-construct shared meanings, perfect agreement is never the outcome. Of course, as individuals form new families, or families merge through remarriage, whole new negotiation processes are set in motion.

Communication—the symbolic, transactional process of sharing meanings—undergirds and illuminates the structure of kinship relationships. The form and content of family messages combine to create a family's view of itself and the world. Members of family systems, through their interdependence and mutual influence, create meanings based on their interaction patterns. Meanings are formed as persons interpret what they perceive and construct a sense of reality. These meanings are created through communication. These selected tenets of symbolic interaction and social construction will guide your thinking about the importance of families as meaning-making systems.

DIALECTICAL THEORY

Family relationships are not static—they are constantly in process as a grandparent and grandchild negotiate how much authority the older person has or as siblings move back and forth between sharing and keeping secrets. A dialectical perspective highlights the continual tensions that relationships must manage. Dialectical theory "asserts that in any relationship there are inherent tensions between contradictory impulses of dialectics" (Wood, 2000, p. 179). "Looked at dialectically relationships are defined and shaped over time by the ways in which partners manage contradictions" (Littlejohn, 2002, p. 238). Relationships are shaped and maintained by the ways members manage contradictions. Sometimes this is referred to as the "me-we pull," or a desire to be with one's partner or sibling at the same time one wants independence (Baxter & Montgomery, 1996). Dialectical tensions are reflected in questions such as: How close can we get without interfering with each other? How much spontaneity can we incorporate into our lives? How can we live together without hurting each other too much? These questions are indicators of the tensions in all relationships. A dialectical approach focuses on competing and opposite possibilities that exist in a relationship (Brown, Werner, & Altman, 1994). It recognizes the tension between members of a family as they negotiate and renegotiate what it means to be in a functioning relationship.

Communication scholars identify a range of possible dialectical tensions, including autonomy–connection, openness–closedness, and predictability–novelty (Baxter, 1990). A common struggle in almost all relationships revolves around issues of closeness and distance, sometimes called autonomy and connection, as you saw in the cohesion axis in Chapter 2. An adolescent may wish to be independent yet connected to her parents. The openness–closedness tension refers to family members' conflicting needs to be open and expressive as well as private. Finally, the predictability–novelty tension is reflected in partners' struggles regarding a desire for constancy, ritual, and familiarity as well as a competing need for excitement and change. A dialectical approach does not mean that a relationship experiences struggle or tension every moment or even every day. Although at critical times, struggles may be in the forefront of the relationship, there are more times when the dialectical tensions remain in the background. In other words, "dialectics may work backstage in a relationship beyond partners' mindful awareness or ability to identify and describe them, but still contributing a sense of unsettledness or instability in the relationship" (Montgomery, 1992, p. 206).

Within stepfamilies there is often a strong pull in competing directions. The main dialectical dilemma is to manage the voluntary marital relationship and the involuntary stepparent-stepchild relationship (Cissna, Cox, & Bochner, 1990). Between step-relations there is a tension between getting close and staying distant in order to remain loyal to a biological parent or child.

It's been six years and I still can't reach some stability with my stepdaughter. Just when we seem to have made progress and are getting closer, we take four steps backward. One day she asks my advice on how to talk to her Dad and a week later she makes fun of me in front of him. Or she tells me how worried she is about her boyfriend, and the next time I ask about him, she says it's none of my business.

Although dialectical tensions are ongoing, partners or family members make efforts to manage them through the following main strategies: (1) selection, (2) separation, (3) neutralization, and (4) reframing (Baxter, 1990). *Selection* implies making a choice between the opposites. An older couple may choose intense togetherness to the exclusion of individual friends or interests. *Separation* involves denying the interdependence of the contrasting elements by uncoupling or separating them. To do this, partners may use cyclic alteration when family members choose one of the opposites at particular times, alternating with the other. A mother and daughter may set aside time for each other and time to spend with individual friends. Or family members may use topic segmentation, whereby certain issues or activities are defined as belonging to one end of the spectrum. For example, partners may define caring for an aging parent as a joint activity or define opera as an individual interest. *Neutralization* implies diluting the intensity of the contrasting poles. A parent and child may modify their personal sharing to keep from being closed off from each other or enmeshed. *Reframing* is characterized by a transformation of the elements along different dimensions of meaning so the apparent contradictions are not viewed as opposites. The partner who stops viewing autonomy as the opposite of connection but now sees it as a way to develop closeness has reframed the tension. A sports-oriented father may reframe his son's interest in music instead of athletics as providing a new way to connect as equals. A dialectical approach recognizes that relationships develop and deteriorate, but it stresses the ongoing struggles characteristic of the overall life of a relationship.

Clearly, dialectical tensions forcefully impact family life. According to Sabourin (1992), "The qualities of dialectical tensions—contradiction, interconnection, and change—are inherent in the family's interaction" (p. 91). Communication is the process by which family members cope with these relational paradoxes.

It is important to note that whole families experience dialectical tensions across family boundaries as they negotiate with institutions, such as schools or courts, as well as extended family members or friends. They face contradictions such as inclusion–exclusion, conventionality–uniqueness, and revelation–concealment. Members may argue or negotiate about "family time" or the constant inclusion of friends and neighbors at all family events. They may encounter being viewed as "weird" by community members on the basis of areas such as religious expression, artistic interests, and so on, and try to balance that perception with contributions to schools or the community. A drug arrest or truancy charges may raise issues of family privacy versus an extended family norm of revealing problems.

A FINAL NOTE

A final theory often cited in family communication research is *developmental theory*, which addresses changes across the life span of individuals as well as families. A variation on traditional developmental stage theory is the life-course approach that focuses on the significance of a factor such as the timing of personal life decisions or how a family is situated in social and historical time. Because this theoretical approach is developed in detail in Chapter 10, it will not be discussed here.

These family theories do not operate separately. The constant underlying dialectical tensions that confront every familial relationship affect each system's communication patterns, complexities, and interconnections. Meaning-making involves addressing dialectical struggles and creating system alliances to argue for one point of view. And, as you will see later, as families change over time through personal development or facing crises, family systems and family meanings are recreated.

Conclusion

This chapter described three main theories that undergird family interaction. It established that a family system consists of members, relationships among them, family attributes, and an environment in which the family functions. The following systems characteristics were applied to family life: interdependence, wholeness, patterns/self-regulation, interactional complexity/punctuation, openness, complex relationships, and equifinality. The importance of communication to family process was established, and certain limitations and implications of systems theory were noted. Symbolic interaction and social construction were described as meaning-making processes, which create and reflect family patterns and understandings. Finally, the ongoing processes of managing dialectical tensions both within a family and between a family and the ecosystem were explored.

In Review

1. Using Satir's mobile image, describe how a change in one member of a real or fictional family affected the other family members.
2. Using a real or fictional family, describe its calibrated level of conflict in terms of acceptable behaviors. Describe attempts to change this calibrated level in terms of the maintenance or change-promoting feedback process.
3. How would holding a family systems perspective affect your work as one of the following: doctor, religious leader, school counselor, office manager, novelist?
4. Cite an example of a family circumstance that would demonstrate a limitation of family systems theory.

COMMUNICATION PATTERNS *and* *the* CREATION *of* FAMILY MEANINGS

We are never the first in our family to wrestle with a problem, although it may feel that way. All of us inherit the unsolved problems of our past; and whatever we are struggling with has its legacy in the struggles of prior generations.

Harriet Lerner, *The Dance of Anger*

Every family creates its own identity. Two families may share the same ethnic background, uphold similar values and goals, and have members of similar ages and abilities, but they will not have identical experiences. The interaction of your family members creates an overall experience of family life that cannot be re-created by any other family. This uniqueness reflects the family meanings developed through patterned interactions. Eventually, each family develops what is called a *relational culture,* or a *jointly constructed worldview*. This view of reality influences all parts of a family's everyday existence and its effects are felt across generations.

The previous chapter examined the family from various perspectives; this chapter centers on the meaning-making function of families. It is through communication that family members construct and manage their everyday lives, and hence their collective identity. In order to understand the significant role that meaning plays in the development of family relationships, this chapter will look at (1) the formation of a family's relational culture through communication and (2) the development of those meanings through four sources of communication patterns: family-of-origin influences, communication rules, family secrets, and family networks. The next chapter will focus on relational maintenance, family rituals, celebrations, narratives, and relational currencies. Throughout both these chapters you will see how everyday experiences, patterned and spontaneous, contribute to a family's collective sense of identity and meaning. The selected tenets of social interactionism will guide your thinking about the importance of families as meaning-making systems constructing their reality through communication.

RELATIONAL CULTURES

Each of you learns to interpret and evaluate behaviors within your family system and to create a set of meanings that may not be understood by an outsider. Each family system creates a worldview that organizes shared beliefs and meanings. All members may not invest equally in the worldview, but this view of reality undergirds a family's communication patterns.

Communication is not only a simple interchange among people; it also shapes and alters the structure of the family system and the individuals in it. Communication serves to create a relational culture, a privately transacted system of understandings that coordinate attitudes, actions, and identities of participants in a relationship. It is based on a jointly constructed worldview. According to Wood (2000), *relational culture* includes "processes, structures, and practices that create, express, and sustain personal relationships and the identities of partners" (p. 77). Relational cultures are created out of communication, maintained and altered in communication, and dissolved through communication. Just as friends and romantic pairs form relational cultures, family members also form powerful familial relational cultures with long-lasting effects.

Consider the behaviors of a couple as they begin to form a family system. Each young couple must undergo a process of mutual accommodation through which the partners develop a set of patterned transactions— "ways in which each spouse triggers and monitors the behavior of the other and is, in turn, influenced by the previous behavioral sequence. These transactional patterns form an invisible web of complementary demands that regulate many family situations" (Minuchin, 1974, p. 17). To form a marital system, couples must negotiate a set of common meanings. This negotiation process is both subtle and complex; some couples never effectively accomplish this task. A couple who succeeded is described here.

My parents see each other as intelligent, attractive, loving, and genuine. They don't respond well to each other when it is obvious that the other partner is trying to avoid conflict. They openly discuss problems relating to their personal relationship, inner feelings, and children because they desire to grow together through the good times and the bad times. My parents are a highly interdependent couple that value being together and experiencing life as a couple, yet they enjoy their separate careers and friends outside of the home. Both believe they need each other plus their independence to make themselves spiritually whole.

A couple strives to create mutually meaningful language. General similarities in their physical and social processes assure some generalized common meanings. However, the intent of some behaviors, if not discussed, may be misinterpreted; yet, these behaviors and their interpretations will become part of the couple's meaning pattern. Usually, the more similar their backgrounds, the less negotiation is needed. With the entire realm of verbal and nonverbal behavior available, they have to negotiate a set of common meanings that reflect their physical, social, and individual processes for viewing the world. When behaviors are interpreted in the same way or interpretations are discussed and clarified, similar meanings emerge, and communication becomes clearer.

Often it is assumed that words are the key to developing a relational culture, yet in an attempt to distinguish between distressed and nondistressed couples, research concluded that nonverbal behavior was an important key. In his early work, Gottman (1979) found that distressed couples were more likely to "express their feelings about a problem, to mind read, and to disagree, all with negative nonverbal behavior" (pp. 467–468).

After decades of marital research, Gottman (1999) reports that contemptuous facial expressions are powerfully corrosive. He states that "a certain number of contemptuous facial expressions by husbands was predictive of their wives' infectious illnesses over the next four years" (p. 46). Gottman refers to contempt as "the sulfuric acid of love" (p. 47). Related research indicates that premarital patterns of aggression strongly predicted marital aggression (O'Leary, Malone, & Tyree, 1994). When families add members, the relational culture becomes more complex.

As a family system evolves, the communication among members affects the continuously adapting form of the structure. Over a period of time, family members come to have certain meanings within each relationship. In their classic work, Hess and Handel (1959) suggest that interpersonal ties reflect these meanings because "the closeness between any two members, for example, or the distance between a group of three closely joined members and a fourth who is apart, derives from the interlocking meanings which obtain among them" (pp. 18–19). This can be seen in the following example.

Our communication patterns tend to separate family members from each other, although Mom and Amy are really joined against Dad. Here's a typical example of the family in action:

MOM: *Sam, let's go to the zoo. The kids would love to see the animals.*

DAD: *I'm tired of doing what the kids want. Let's just sit around the house.*

SISTER: *Damn, Dad, you never want to do anything that we like.*

MOM: *Amy, watch your language. Now, apologize to your father!*

SISTER: *No, he doesn't care about us.*

DAD: *That's correct. I don't care! (Very serious facial expression)*

SCOTT: *We always have these fights. Why do we bother being a family? (Scott storms to his room)*

By now we are so used to the "moves" that we hear the opening line and go through the predictable scene.

Coordinated meanings do not emerge early or quickly within relationships. Partners may struggle for years to gain similarity in interpreting and responding to each other's behaviors. Parents and children may live with serious misunderstandings and mistaken assumptions throughout most of their shared lives as a result of communication breakdowns. For example, if siblings sense parent favoritism, both may consciously avoid the subject, one may resist the other's attempt to explore the subject, or one may remain unaware of a difficulty that the other is reluctant to address directly.

A sense of self and family worldviews are analogous to symbolic blueprints that guide behavior (Brighton-Cleghorn, 1987). Family disorder occurs when great differences occur among individuals' worldviews, such that there is no longer a family set of common meanings.

COMMUNICATION PATTERNS THAT INFLUENCE FAMILY MEANINGS

Meanings emerge through the continuous interpretation of and response to messages. Over time, these interactions become predictable and form communication patterns or complex sets of "moves," which have been established through repetition and have become so automatic as to continue without conscious awareness. These patterns then serve to create meanings.

Communication patterns emerge from the reciprocally shared verbal and nonverbal messages, which become recurring and predictable within a family relationship. They serve to define the relationship and may be altered by forces within the ecosystem or the family system itself. To fully understand how these family meanings emerge from patterns, the following areas must be explored: (1) family-of-origin influences, (2) family communication rules, (3) family secrets, and (4) family communication networks.

Family-of-Origin Influences

"My son's a Kaplan, all right. He'll walk up and talk to anyone without a trace of shyness." "My family always fought by yelling at each other and then forgetting about it. My grandparents and my parents were great shouters. My wife doesn't understand this." These statements indicate family-of-origin influence on communication patterns in new family systems. *Family-of-origin* refers to the family or families in which a person is raised and is generally thought to be the earliest and most powerful source of influence on one's personality (Bochner & Eisenberg, 1987). Many of you still function primarily within your family-of-origin systems. Others of you have already formed new family systems.

The term *family-of-origin influences* refers to how current relational experiences reflect a unique combination of (1) multigenerational transmissions and (2) the ethnic heritages represented within the family-of-origin. Although the development of common meanings within a couple's relationship depends on the physical, social, and individual filters of each person, the multigenerational and ethnic background that each partner brings to a relationship is also a significant social influence. Many of you may desire a family life different from the one in which you grew up, yet you find yourself re-creating similar patterns in a new relationship. Parental socialization serves as a major factor in determining children's family-formation behavior (Dixson, 1995). People often work out marriages similar to that of their parents, not because of heredity, but because they are following a family pattern.

Multigenerational Transmissions   Families-of-origin may provide blueprints for the communication of future generations. Initially, communication is learned in the home, and, throughout life, the family setting provides a major testing ground for new communication skills or strategies. Each young person who leaves the family-of-origin to form a new system takes with him or her a set of conscious and unconscious ways of relating to people. For example, the idiosyncrasies and culturally based communication patterns of the current Watson family may be passed on to generations of children in combination with the patterns gained from in-laws'

Messages and meanings pass from one generation to the next.

families-of-origin. Most families develop "family words," which are only understood by a small circle, which can be traced back to a child or a grandparent, and which may be passed down from generation to generation (Dickson, 1988). These may cause great confusion or humor, as noted here:

My husband gets crazy with all the odd words my family uses, especially around children. I came from a family of 12 kids and there were always words someone couldn't say or codes for things. So I talk to our kids about "I-box" (ice cream), doing a "zipperino" (getting dressed), or "the throne" (toilet).

Just as simple language terms travel across the generations, more significant attitudes and rule-bound behaviors move from a family-of-origin to a newly emerging family system. The family-of-origin serves as the first communication classroom.

Wide differences in family-of-origin behaviors can lead to a communication breakdown in a couple's system. In the following example, a wife describes the differences in nonverbal communication in her family-of-origin from that of her husband.

It was not until I became closely involved with a second family that I became conscious of the fact that the amount and type of contact can differ greatly. Rarely, in Rob's home, will another person reach for someone else's hand, walk arm in arm, or kiss for no special reason. Hugs are reserved for comfort. When people filter into the den to watch television, one person will sit on the couch, the next on the floor, a third on a chair, and finally the last person is forced to sit on the couch. And always at the opposite end! Touching, in my home, was a natural, everyday occurrence. Usually, the family breakfast began with "good morning" hugs and kisses. After meals, we often would sit on our parents' laps rocking, talking, and just relaxing. While watching television, we usually congregated on and around someone else as we sat facing the set. Even as adults, no one ever hesitated to cuddle up next to someone else, run their hands through another person's hair, or start tickling whoever happens to be in reaching distance.

This example illustrates the extent to which each partner was raised differently and how that affects communication in the new system. When you consider your parent's marriage, or your own, you can find instances of this situation in which the rules or networks affect how and what communication occurs. Models of relationships can act as a guide for children's behavior and become central to their interpretation of others' behavior (Dixson, 1995). For instance, if you have lived in a stepfamily, you may have witnessed the stress involved in integrating your stepparent's family-of-origin influences into a system with communication patterns that already reflected two families-of-origin.

Frequently, family-of-origin patterns have been used to study abusive or harsh parenting. Recently, Chen and Kaplan (2001) examined the continuity of supportive parenting across generations and found positive patterns. The results of their longitudinal study report modest intergenerational continuity tied to factors such as interpersonal relations, social participation, and role modeling. This is consistent with Simons, Beaman, Conger, and Chao's (1993) findings on the connection between early experiences of supportive parenting to later adoption of similar parenting strategies. In this study, the effects of wives' parenting beliefs and degree of satisfaction with the child affected the husbands' quality of parenting, but not vice versa.

Scholarly interest in religion and families reveals that religious affiliation has obvious connections to gender roles and parenting styles, as well as family and work decisions (Smits, Ultee, & Lammers, 1996). In their meta-analytic review of links between religion, marriage, and parenting, Mahoney and colleagues (2001) report that there is some evidence for linking religiousness with greater use of adaptive communication skills, collaboration in handling disagreements, positivity in family relationships, and parental coping. These patterns may be transmitted across generations.

Although family-of-origin issues may be discussed as parent-to-child transmissions, greater emphasis has been placed on transmission across generations. In recent years family scholars and researchers have focused more directly on the effect of multigenerational systems, suggesting, "Evidence indicates a link between the parenting children receive and their subsequent behaviors" (Buerkel-Rothfuss, Fink, & Buerkel, 1995, p. 63). Following are the basic assumptions inherent in such an approach.

Multigenerational systems:

- Influence, and are influenced by, individuals who are born into them
- Are similar to, but more complex than, any multiperson ecosystem
- Are developmental in nature
- Contain patterns that are shared, transformed, and manifested through intergenerational transmission
- Impact two-parent families as the partners' heritages reflect cross-generational influences
- Contain issues that may appear only in certain contexts and may be at unconscious levels
- Have boundaries that are hierarchical in nature
- Develop functional and dysfunctional patterns based on the legacy of previous generations and here-and-now happenings (Hoopes, 1987, pp. 198–204).

As a way to envision some of these influences, consider Figure 4.1, a multigenerational system genogram that contains examples of powerful parent-child relationships, a theme of service as well as flexible boundaries. In reading the genogram, men are represented by squares, and women are represented by circles.

The power of multigenerational transmission is part of a puzzle that is unfolding. In the following passage, a young woman reflects on her painful experiences and insights.

I have come to learn that my problem of behavior was a reaction to my mother's alcoholism, and to her emotional distance during my infancy and childhood. Likewise, my mother's behaviors had a similar origin. Handicapped by her own mother's chronic depression, my mother never received the affirmation she needed and desired. Yet, having been reared by an alcoholic mother, my grandmother was in no better position to be an effective mother or role model for intimacy. With such unavailable models, the women in my family were perpetually unable to develop this essential capacity. Consequently, my own mother had to build our relationship from a faulty blueprint.

Such patterns are not usually so dramatic. According to Duck (1986), relationships that have major effects on people are of this perpetual but dormant kind: "They are part of the unchallenged and comfortable predictability of lives made up of routine, regular conversation, and assumptions that most of tomorrow will be based on the foundation of today" (p. 91). Yet, although patterns do move across generations, changes also occur. In their study of grandfather-father-son relational closeness patterns, Buerkel-Rothfuss, Fink, and Buerkel (1995) conclude, "Males use

FIGURE 4.1   Multigenerational System

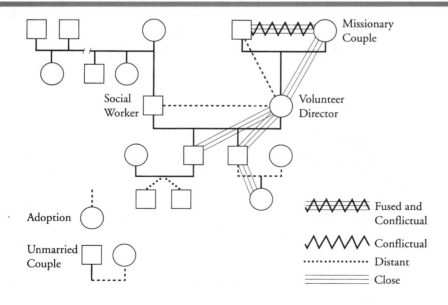

communication behaviors similar to those of their fathers and in many cases, their grandfathers, but father-son relationships may be evolving into a more positive form than they were in the 1940s and 1950s" (p. 80).

Some of the factors that may be used to examine multigenerational issues include the following: how gender roles are played out; how families deal with losses; how ethnic patterns affect interactions; how certain people are liked, such as through names of physical similarities; how themes are played out; how rigid or loose the boundaries are; and how members deal with conflict. These and other related issues are viewed across three or four generations to see how patterns are passed down, consciously or unconsciously. Yet, further research is needed on numerous topics, such as why some children adopt parental behaviors and others do not. This issue raises the question: Why do some children in problematic families continue the family tradition while others create well-functioning adult familial relationships? In his analysis of family psychosocial risk factors, Rutter (2002) states, "Some children seem to escape most serious ill effects (although that does not mean that they have been totally unaffected or unscarred) whereas others succumb to lasting psychopathology" (p. 335).

In their study of father and child pairs, Buerkel-Rothfuss, Fink, and Buerkel (1995) found the patterns quite varied. Although some seem to adopt behaviors in spite of good intentions not to, some rejected them. In addition, mutual influence must be better understood because parents and children interact and mutually influence each other; this occurs in a bidirectional manner as opposed to unidirectional manner (Saphir & Chaffee, 2002).

Current genetic studies will influence thinking in this area over the next decades. According to Taylor, Chatters, and Jackson (1993), many of the family problems, such as domestic violence and substance abuse, have recognized intergenerational components. Some of these issues are genetically linked.

Genetic Factors Booth, Carver, and Granger (2000) propose the importance of the following biological topics on family studies, suggesting direct links to family interaction: (1) behavioral endocrinology, (2) behavioral genetics, (3) evolutionary psychology, and (4) behavioral psychopharmacology. The impact of physiology, genetics, and evolution on interaction patterns gained attention in the past decade with renewed attention to biological contributions to individual communication practices and discussion of a communibiological paradigm (Beatty, McCroskey, & Valencic, 2001; Cappella, 1991). As noninvasive assessment of many biological processes becomes increasingly available to family research teams, such considerations will become commonplace. For example, an MRI, or magnetic resonance imaging, has the potential to reveal explanations for a disruptive child's inability to attend to parental directives, or a sibling's inability to track seemingly simple information. These are understandings that may alter future interaction patterns.

Although knowledge of the effects of complex sets of genes on behavior is limited, established lines of research are exploring passive, reactive, and active influences related to behaviors of parents and children. For example, a way in which genes influence environmental risk exposure is through their effects on children's behavior. Thus, adoptee studies have shown that the adoptive parents of children born to, but not reared by, antisocial parents are more likely to exhibit negative forms of control than are parents of children who lack that biological risk (Rutter, 2002). The mediation in this case comes about through the genetic effects on the children's disruptive behavior, which in turn influences their interactions with their adoptive parents who are rearing them. The implication of these and related findings is the necessity of designing future studies that can differentiate between genetic and environmental effects. For example, Schwartz and Liddle (2001) argue that, although genetic risks may predispose a child toward problem behaviors, conduct problems tend to be brought out by the interaction of difficult child temperament with poor and unskilled parenting. They believe that genetic factors are important to family researchers because the family is "both the source of the individuals' genetic material and the context in which they spend the majority of their early years" (p. 302).

The importance of a family-of-origin is summarized well by Kramer (1985) in her depiction of its influence on a child's view of the world.

> [The child] observes the environment he inhabits, partakes of its ambiance. He forms values and beliefs, develops assumptions about how marriages and families are and should be, and learns about life cycles, including how to handle the changes of maturation and of aging and death. He learns about power and control and about the consequences of emotions, both his own and others. He is schooled in patterns of communication: what role to take in triangles; how to handle secrets; how to respond to pressure. (p. 9)

Such a description captures the power of a child's family experiences to influence his or her entire life.

Ethnicity The role of ethnicity in multigenerational patterns often is overlooked, yet its influence can be powerful, since ethnic values and identification are retained for many generations after immigration (Mc-Goldrick, 1994). Ethnicity describes people by their supposed common ancestry, language, and cultural ancestry. Yet, after declaring the term *Asian American* contains more than two dozen subgroups, Coontz (1999) argues that ethnicity is a product not just of the traditions brought by immigrants but of the particular immigrant group's class origins and occupational skills interacting with the historically or regionally specific jobs, housing stock, and political conditions they meet (p. xvi). Broad labels create greater stereotypes.

Ethnic family issues may be reflected in issues such as age, gender, roles, expressiveness, birth order, separation, or individuation (McGoldrick, 1993). In their examination of Italian families, Giordano and McGoldrick (1996) highlight the families' cultural enjoyment of celebrating, loving, and fighting and their orientation toward social skills, including cleverness, charm, and graciousness. These behaviors exist within an orientation to values that places heavy emphasis on how actions affect the family, especially its honor. In addition, Italian families function within a network of significant other relatives, *gumbares* (old friends), and godparents from whom mutual support is expected. This orientation stresses parental role distinction, with the father as the undisputed head of the family and mother as the heart, or the family's emotional sustenance.

This generalization about the Italian heritage comes into sharp contrast with descriptions of Scandinavian family patterns, which generally stress the importance of emotional control and the avoidance of open confrontation (Erickson & Simon, 1996). Within the Norwegian family, words are likely to be used sparingly; inner weaknesses are kept secret; aggression is channeled into teasing, ignoring, or silence. In terms of male-female roles, the man serves as head of the family and exacts discipline, while the woman is the communication center establishing the social network among kin. The marriage of persons reflecting these two ethnic backgrounds has the potential for misunderstanding unless differences are addressed. Strong conflicts may develop as each plays out behaviors appropriate to his or her family-of-origin. Such differences may never be resolved because of the strength of the family pattern, or compromises may be necessary as the whole family is influenced by social forces.

African American families emphasize extended kinship bonds, African roots, strong three-generation systems, religion, and spirituality (Hines & Boyd-Franklin, 1996). African American parent-child interaction patterns involve parents as cultural advisors, coaches, and participants, given unique needs of racial socialization (Socha, Bromley, & Kelly, 1995). Specifically, African American parents exhibit the "imperative mode" of content as a protective authority (Daniel & Daniel, 1999). Parents also prepare children for dealing with the problems of racial insults (Ferguson, 1999).

A family's ethnic heritage may dictate norms for communication, which are maintained for generations. For example, an emphasis on keeping things "in the family," the acceptability of discussing certain subjects, or the way in which such subjects are discussed may pass from generation to generation, reflecting individual and cultural influences. An examination of communication patterns through three generations of an extended Irish American family revealed great similarities across generations in terms of culturally predictable communication patterns (Galvin, in press). Respondents from each generation reported their variations on the theme of privacy, saying: "What you see and hear in this house goes no further; don't advertise your business. Handle it on the q.t. This information doesn't leave this table." Whereas the Irish family sets strong boundaries, the following description of Arabic family life portrays a different picture.

Growing up in an Arab household, our immediate family and our extended family reflected the strong patriarchical influence and a theme of "family is family," which implied active support of many relatives. We lived by the Arabic proverb "A small house has enough room for one hundred people who love each other" and we shared joys, sorrows, money, and things among and across generations.

In addition, the acculturation patterns in the United States create tensions and conflicts for multigenerational immigrant families. For example, Chinese American child-rearing philosophies and practices differ with the degree of acculturation (Ho, 1989). Whereas traditional approaches reflect authoritarian methods—including firm discipline, the absence of praise, and limited verbal communication other than scolding or orders—Americanized Chinese parents create different communication patterns: "They use more verbal praise, talk and joke more with their children, and give them more freedom in decision making" (DeGenova & Rice, 2002, p. 61). Mexican American family interaction patterns reflect the powerful influence of intergenerational relationships, but certain differences emerge based on time of immigration. For example, immigrant mothers stress autonomy and responsibility, productive use of time, and strict obedience more than mothers of third-generation adolescents (DeGenova & Rice, 2002). In her study contrasting Mexican American and Euro-American households, Gangotena (1997) suggests that Mexican American families display the continued interdependence of all members as well as the values of sharing time in conversation, touching, and showing affection. As generations become more established in the United States, they reflect greater individuality and reduction in intensity of interdependence.

Although a growing number of studies address different ethnic patterns, few studies address ethnic patterns that occur as the result of remarriages and stepfamilies, or most transnational adoptions (particularly of older children), or transracial domestic adoption or foster care. Many adoptive and foster families face a bicultural socialization process. An early study (Kim, 1977) revealed that older Korean adoptees adjusted less well than those adopted at infancy. Simon and Alstein (1987) found that over 60 percent of transracially adopting parents described their children as identifying with both the racial backgrounds of their birth and those of their adoptive parents. In their study of American adoption of Chinese children, Tessler, Gamache, and Liu (1999) explain that even the term *bicultural socialization* implies different things, ranging from an emphasis on acceptance and inclusion of all ethnicities as "real" Americans, to emphasizing Chinese culture, to creating a Chinese and American perspective. All of these have communication implications for current and future family systems. The following quote from a Korean adoptee captures a sense of the identity issues.

> People would make assumptions about my Asian heritage and then try to guess it. After finally learning the answer is "Korean" they often asked, "Do you speak Korean?" That was met with my answer, "My parents are Irish so I didn't learn any Korean." Any of my general references to the fact that I was a member of an Irish family had the same effect. (Galvin & Wilkinson, 2000)

To date, much of this related research presumes family communication issues are similar across ethnic groups; unique issues have been overlooked or underrepresented. The attention placed on the "traditional" family has led some authors to proclaim, "The psychology of marriage as it exists is really a psychology of European American middle class marriage" (Flanagan et al., 2002, p. 109). Yet, "there is little research on identities and family communication among non-European American families that can be used to generate predictions for future research" (Gudykunst & Lee, 2001, p. 80). However, few would disagree that the unique family patterns and the ethnic heritage combine to create a powerful lineage that influences generations.

Family Communication Rules

When I was 15, my father had surgery on . . . to this day I don't know exactly what! My parents mentioned nothing until the day of the surgery when Mom told me, that, instead of riding the bus home from school, I would take a taxi with her to visit my Dad in the hospital. It wasn't my business to know, I guess, and it certainly wasn't my business to talk about it. I got the message loud and clear—never talk about your father's health.

The previous example reflects a common family pattern—the communication rule. Every family develops rules for interaction and transmits them to new members. As noted in Chapter 3, rules are relationship agreements that prescribe and limit a family's behavior over time. *Communication rules* are "shared understandings of what communication means and what behaviors are appropriate in various situations" (Wood, 1997, p. 98). A family acts as a rule-governed system; family members interact with each other in an organized, repetitive fashion, creating patterns that direct family life. Rules serve as generative mechanisms capable of creating regularity where none exists. In most cases, rules reflect patterns that have become "oughts" or "shoulds." *Relational rules* refer to the tendency of people in relationships to "develop rules unique to a specific interaction situation and to repeat them until they become reflected in patterns of behavior" (Yerby & Buerkel-Rothfuss, 1982, p. 3).

Because of their regularities, rules serve a powerful function in coordinating meanings between people (Cronen, Pearce, & Harris, 1979). Through rules, family members gain a sense of shared reality and mutual understanding. Cronen, Pearce, and Harris stress the need to coordinate joint meanings and how society relies on two types of rules, constitutive and regulative, to accomplish this coordination.

Constitutive rules define what counts as what in communication. They help people construct meanings. The family-of-origin is a primary source of such learning. "During the early years, families teach us what counts as affection (in some families, members kiss and hug; in other families, affection is not displayed overtly), how to deal with conflict (families differ in how openly and civilly they manage differences)" (Wood, 1998, p. 37). In the Rosaldo family, respect may be communicated by calling if one is late; in the Ryckoff family, saying "Yes sir" and "Yes ma'am" counts as respect. *Regulative* rules actually are rules for action that guide coordination. They indicate how communication operates, such as when and how to speak and what is acceptable, such as "Do not raise your voice in an argument," "Don't correct a family member in front of other people," or "Discuss financial worries in a calm, restrained tone."

West and Turner (2000) provide a marital example of constitutive and regulative rule interaction by describing how a couple married for 20 years responds when the wife discovers her husband's extramarital affair and enacts certain rules. "She decides on a venting session because the constitutive rule tells her that such an affair is wrong in their marriage. In turn, her husband must determine how to interpret the venting (constitutive rule) and must construct some sequence in response (regulative rule)" (p. 98). As the couple discusses the issue, they cocreate their social reality, which reveals each other's rules systems.

Development of Rules   You were raised in a world of rules, particularly communication rules, but how did you learn them? You learned some rules through conscious direction, but you learned most implicitly through redundancy, or repeated interactions.

Rules vary on a continuum of awareness, ranging from very direct, explicit, conscious relationship agreements that may have been clearly negotiated to the implicit, unspoken, unconscious rules emerging from repeated interactions. Whereas the former are rather straightforward, the latter are extremely complex and convoluted. In some families, particular rules are negotiated directly, such as "We will never go to bed without kissing goodnight" or "We will openly discuss sex with the children." But most rules develop as a result of multiple interactions. One person's behavior becomes capable of evoking a predictable response from the other person. Influential and invisible rules are so much a part of the family's way of life that they are not recognized or named, but they are enforced, as indicated in the following example.

When I bring up a subject that is "taboo," and we are around other people, my mother gives me the cold stare although she would deny it. When we are engaged in a one-on-one conversation, she ignores me or changes the subject. We've never talked about these topics or rules directly. I doubt we ever will.

Rules have great staying power. Kellogg (1990) suggests, "We follow the rules of our families, stay loyal to those rules, even though they didn't work for our family" (p. 90). Many rules reflect the partners' family-of-origin rules that, if not questioned, pass from generation to generation. Spouses from families with dissimilar rules experience greater struggles than those from similar families-of-origin. Some rules are tied to ethnic communication patterns.

Persons who form a system must be sensitive to the relational consequences of their acts. Consider the difficulties if two people bring to their marriage the following individual rules for behavior during a family argument:

Person 1: If one person expresses strong negative emotion, the other should consider it carefully and refrain from spontaneous response. This is considered thoughtful.

Person 2: If one person expresses strong negative emotion, the other should respond with emotional supportiveness. To avoid responding would indicate rejection.

You can imagine the process of rule negotiation that would have to occur in order for these two people to achieve a communication pattern with which both of them feel comfortable.

Ethnic backgrounds influence family rules. Chung (1992) contrasts the Asian environment-centered worldview to the Euro-American individual-centered worldview, suggesting communication implications for Asian families who value harmony: "Self-limits, shame, cooperation with the group, and embarrassment are natural products under this value system. Children are taught not to speak in front of elders and to apologize for disturbing the family" (p. 31). In contrast, members of Jewish families value direct verbal expressions of feelings (Rosen & Weltman, 1996). Each ethnic group reflects its own rules.

Analysis of any rule-bound system requires an understanding of the mutual influence pattern within which the rules function. Due to the transactional nature of communication, the mutual influence process will result in new relational patterns. This process has been described as follows:

> No matter how well one knows the rules of communicator A, one cannot predict the logic of his/her communication with B without knowing B's rules and how they will mesh. The responsibility for good and bad communication is thus transactive with neither A nor B alone deserving praise or blame. (Cronen, Pearce, & Harris, 1979, p. 36)

Once rules are established, changing them may be complicated and time consuming unless the family has a flexible adaptation process and can recognize the rule for what it is. When a family rule has been developed over time and members are accustomed to certain "acceptable" behaviors, the family tends to regulate its behavior in accordance with the rule.

Rules are maintained or changed through negative (maintenance) or positive (growth) feedback processes. Limits can be recalibrated unconsciously or consciously. For example, rules may be renegotiated as family members pass through certain developmental stages. This recalibration may not be a totally conscious process but one that evolves. On the other hand, rules may be openly negotiated or changed as the result of various factors, such as member dissatisfaction or feedback from outside sources. A teacher's suggestion to "encourage Patrick to stand up for his own opinions" may affect a parent's behavior.

Breaking the rules results in ambiguity as the system recalibrates itself to accept a wider variety of behavior. Old patterns shift. For example, one may hear, "I have broken the rule about not discussing sex with my mother by openly discussing my living arrangement." Some family rule changes reflect societal shifts. It is clear that family rules about sexual communication have changed over the past decades, although dissatisfaction is still common (Warren, 1995). Even though adoption used to be a highly secretive and rule-bound experience, the advent of open adoptions has made it a transparent, discussible experience (Fein, 1998).

Most rules exist within a hierarchy. The Parsons and the Coopers may each establish the rule "You do not swear." In the Parson family, it may be a critical concern, whereas the Coopers may see it as desirable. Once you learn the family rules, you then have to figure out the importance placed on each of them.

For years, you have lived with certain rules without discussing them, but they are adhered to as closely as if they were printed as a list of "shoulds" on your refrigerator door. As a family insider, you make subtle adjustments to context with ease and limited awareness. The power of patterns emerges as you adjust your language in front of an older relative or assess your partner's mood before discussing money.

Yet sometimes a member of a family system operates according to rules unknown to the others. A major source of conflict centers on the breaking of rules that one member of the pair may not even know exist (e.g., "Don't listen to my phone calls"). Such conflicts frequently arise when stepfamilies form. In their study of topic avoidance, Guerrero and Afifi (1995) suggest the familiy life cycle influences parent-child communication. For example, teenagers may exhibit verbal avoidance, thus unilaterally establishing a rule. The more conscious the rules, the greater the possibility of their coordination at appropriate times.

Importance of Rules   Rules are important because they support (1) family self-definition, (2) relational development, and (3) family satisfaction (Pearson, 1989). Through rule-bound interaction, families establish their primary and secondary family functions. Rules set the limits of cohesion and adaptability within a family. In some families, members learn that everything is to be kept within the family, intimate physical and verbal behavior is expected, and friends are to be kept at a distance. Rules help form a family's images, themes, boundaries, and positions on biosocial issues such as power and gender. These in turn guide further rule development. The interaction of rules and functions supports the development of self-definition.

When individuals come together to form relationships, they create an increasingly unique pattern of interaction. The higher the relational knowledge between partners, the greater their comfort and ability to predict interaction patterns. Rules provide a major means of coordinating meaning in such a developing relationship.

Finally, rules contribute to a family's sense of satisfaction. Rules provide stability in interactions and serve to socialize younger members. If every time a "hot" topic, such as family wealth, arose, a family had to discover each member's response to the subject, there would be constant confusion. Predictable communication patterns allow a family to carry on its functional day-to-day interactions smoothly.

Types of Communication Rules   Key questions provide a framework for looking at types of communication rules: What can be talked about?

How can it be talked about? And to whom can it be talked about? (Satir, 1988).

The first set of rules relates to what one is allowed to talk about. Can death, sex, salaries, drugs, and serious health problems be talked about in the family? Are there family skeletons or current relatives who are never mentioned? Most families have topics that are taboo either all the time or under certain circumstances. These become extremely clear, as explained by this young person.

At my father's house there are lots of unspoken rules that dictate unsafe topics of conversation. It's clear that I should never mention (1) my mother, (2) the way we used to celebrate holidays, (3) my need for money, (4) my mother, (5) old family vacations, (6) my mother's relatives, (7) (8) (9) (10) my mother!

Although topics may not be restricted, many families restrict the feelings that can be shared—especially negative feelings. Emotions such as anger, sadness, or rage may be avoided at all costs and denied whenever necessary.

Decision making often provides a fertile field for family rules. Does the system allow children to question parental decisions, or are they "the law," which cannot be challenged? The Shih children may hear such words as, "We're moving and that's final." Other families have rules that allow joint decision making through discussions, persuasion, or voting.

The next question is: How can you talk about it? Can you talk about things directly, really leveling about feelings on a particular issue, or must you sneak it in? For example, in a family with an alcoholic parent, the other members may say, "Mom's under the weather," but no one says, "Mom is an alcoholic." There is a tacit agreement never to deal with the real issue. Many couples have never drawn up a will, because partners cannot find a way to talk directly to each other about death. Thus, the "how" may involve allusions to the topic or euphemisms for certain subjects.

Strategy involves the timing of conversations, such as "Don't bother your father with that while he's eating," or the timing of discussion on a particular issue. It also involves selecting a place. Some families have a place, such as a kitchen table or the car, where the "real" talking gets done. Verbal and nonverbal strategies, including the issues of time and place, indicate how members may talk about things.

The final question is: With whom can you talk about it? Consider the following: "Don't you think Jenny is too young to hear about custody battles?" Often, the rules for "who" relate to the age of family members. For example, when children are small, they may not hear much about family finances, but as they grow older, they are brought into the discussion of the family's worth.

Sometimes unforeseen circumstances, such as death or divorce, move a child into a conversation circle that would have been denied otherwise. A 14-year-old in a single-parent family may discuss topics that only the other parent typically would have heard. Such shifts can make a younger person uncomfortable, as demonstrated here.

Lately, my father has taken to discussing his dating, and even his sex life with me. He seems to think this is a way for us to get closer, but I wish he could find a friend instead. My mother died only a year ago and it's hard for me to imagine Dad with other women.

Family myths or stories dictate the directions of many conversations. The message of "Don't tell so and so—she can't take it" sets up myths that may prevail for years. Consider statements such as "Don't tell your grandfather. He'll have a fit" or "Don't talk to your sister. She'll just get sad." No one ever attempts to see if Grandpa will be outraged or if Alice will cry—it is assumed, and communication proceeds accordingly.

Rules may specify how the family handles boundaries. Although family members may be able to talk freely, there may be restrictions of who can hear outside the family. West and Turner (1995) interviewed lesbian mothers and found communication outside the family was more stressful than inside when discussing family structure. Children appeared to establish their own restrictive rules for talking with friends.

In order to fully appreciate the "what," "how," and "who" of a family's communication rules, it is necessary to analyze the system to see which rules are enforced in what contexts. The following set of regulative communication rules, developed within one young woman's family, indicate the interpersonal nature of rules:

- Don't talk back to Dad unless he's in a good mood.
- When Mom is tired, don't discuss school problems.
- Tell the truth at all times, unless it involves a happy surprise.
- Do not fight with Mom about your appearance.
- Don't talk about the family's finances outside the family.
- Don't discuss sex.
- Don't talk to Dad about Grandma growing old.
- Don't mention that Mom and Dad are over 50.
- Share feelings with Mom.
- Don't talk about Granddad's two previous marriages.

- Never mention Aunt Bea's cancer.
- Tim's hearing problem is not to be discussed.
- Family deaths are discussed only in terms of religion.
- Mother's pregnancy at marriage is not admitted.

The author of these rules concluded that she had learned to distinguish among people and circumstances but had not experienced very direct open communication in her family.

The process of forming new systems through marriage or remarriage provides fertile ground for renegotiating existing rules. When forming a stepfamily, partners may involve each of their children in an extensive rule recalibration process.

Metarules In addition to ordinary rules, there are metarules, or rules about rules. As Laing (1972) aptly states, "There are rules against seeing the rules, and hence against seeing all the issues that arise from complying with or breaking them" (p. 106). When a couple does not make a will because of the difficulty of dealing with death, there may also be a rule that they not talk about their rules about ignoring death. Both pretend they are too busy or too poor to meet with a lawyer. The following thoughtful analysis of the rules in the previous young woman's family indicates this metalevel of rule-bound behavior.

The death of my brother has spawned an entire catalogue of rules. It is acceptable to discuss his death with outsiders to the family. There is a strong rule to not avoid mentioning him in conversation among family members where it would be appropriate. There seems to be a rule that has evolved over the past two years that it is all right for my mother, but not my father and I, to show grief in front of the family. My father and I have a sort of metarule that we ignore the rule about not showing grief to each other but both pretend (for each other's benefit, ostensibly, but probably more for ourselves) to not be affected by a grief-imposing situation. I have the feeling that these rules will change when I go home this summer and help my family disassemble my brother's room.

All family members live with powerful rule-bound patterns, giving little conscious attention to most of them. Yet, they give meaning to each relationship. As each child is born into the family, the family map changes and its rules and metarules evolve (Perlmutter, 1988). Therefore the birth of each child increases the communication complexity.

Secrets may establish strong subgroup boundaries.

Family Secrets

The issue of family secrets emerges as one considers the link between powerful family rules and taboo topics. Secrets involve information that is purposefully hidden or concealed by one or more family members (Bok, 1983). For example, a communication rule of alcoholic families, "Don't talk" is a way to maintain denial of the problem (Black, 1981). Although communication researchers have only recently examined this topic, other family scholars and practitioners have studied secrets, ranging from traditions and religious beliefs to incest and chemical dependency (Imber-Black, 1993).

Family secrets are critical communication concerns because "family relationships are shaped, in part, by what is shared and what is held secret by family members" (Vangelisti & Caughlin, 1997, p. 679). Making, keeping, and revealing secrets all shape a family's interaction patterns. What is considered a family secret may change over time. Whereas certain topics such as adoption, divorce, cancer, and mental illness are less stigmatized now, other issues such as AIDS or a sperm donor as a biological dad emerge (Imber-Black, 1998).

Secrets and Boundaries   Secrets create or reinforce boundaries—whether between the family and the outside world or around individuals or subsystems. In her Communication Privacy Management Theory, Petronio (2002) suggests control is a boundary issue because people believe private information is owned or co-owned with others and revealing private information may make one vulnerable.

Family secrets may be known to all family members but kept from the outside world (whole family secrets), known to subgroups of the family (intrafamily secrets), or known only to an individual family member (individual secrets). Although secrets are usually considered to have a negative valence, hiding something that would hurt or embarrass one or more members, some secrets have a positive valence, reinforcing cohesiveness and identity. Such secrets may include funny childhood stories, jokes that only family members would find humorous, or nicknames. Although secret keeping is a common family practice, sometimes maintaining powerful secrets can have negative physiological consequences for the secret bearer (Pennebaker, 1990). Having no secrets means having no boundaries, and the reality of difference may disappear (Imber-Black, 1998).

Types of Family Secrets

Secrets may be categorized in a variety of ways. Imber-Black (1998, pp. 13–19) concludes there are four types of family secrets: sweet, essential, toxic, and dangerous. *Sweet* secrets are created for the purpose of fun or surprise and are usually time limited. These may create a new and positive view of a person or relationship. This may be airline tickets to Disney World placed in a child's Christmas stocking or a surprise baby shower.

Essential secrets promote necessary boundaries that define a relationship. This may include talk about fears or insecurities, which enhance closeness and foster the development of self, relationships, and communities. For some partners, private, self-disclosing conversations are an integral part of their personal and relational growth. Sibling pairs may feel free to reveal deep concerns and fears with each other.

Toxic secrets poison family relationships; key family issues and stories remain untold and unavailable. According to Imber-Black (1998), maintaining such secrets may have chronic negative effects on problem solving, conversational repertoire, perceptions, and emotional well-being since "even when no one is in immediate physical or emotional danger, toxic secrets nonetheless sap energy, promote anxiety, burden those who know, and mystify those who don't know" (p. 13). The protected alcoholism of one member may shut down vital interaction among other family members and between these members and the outside world. Issues such as affairs, drug abuse, or bankruptcy inhibit interactions about other topics.

Dangerous secrets put people in immediate physical jeopardy or such severe emotional turmoil that their capacity to function is threatened. These may involve physical or sexual abuse or threats of suicide or harm to others.

Using a somewhat different approach, Vangelisti (1994b) categorizes types of secrets as (1) *taboos,* or skeletons in the closet, including marital abuse, substance abuse, and illegalities; (2) *rule violations,* such as premarital pregnancy, cohabitation, and disobedience; and (3) *conventional* secrets, or information that is private but not "wrong," such as death, religion, and personality conflicts. Clearly, her taboo category is somewhat similar to the toxic and dangerous secrets, whereas conventional secrets are similar to the essential category. No matter how they are categorized, secrets play an important role in a family's communication patterns.

Functions of Secrets   Given the commonplace nature of family secrets, a key question arises: What functions do secrets serve? In her early work on whole family secrets, Vangelisti (1994b) reports on six functions of such secrets:

1. *Bonding.* Individuals believe their family secrets increase cohesiveness among family members. The sister who intercepts her brother's bad report cards or absence notices strengthens the sibling bond. Most couples' sexual rituals remain private to them.

2. *Evaluation.* Family secrets serve to help members avoid negative judgment. Parents may hide a child's sexual preference from their friends to avoid negative evaluations of the family. Issues such as multiple divorces or prison terms may fit here.

3. *Maintenance.* These secrets help keep family members close and protect them from stressors. Religious practices or an unexpected inheritance may be kept a secret to prevent outside pressures. The "conspiracy of silence" that often accompanies adoption involves talking only about the "chosen child" but leaves unstated the losses underlying such family construction (Imber-Black, 1998). These represent attempts to prevent tension and sadness.

4. *Privacy.* Secrets are concealed because they were seen as personal and/or irrelevant to others. Family members may see income, plans for pregnancy, or payments for major purchases as none of anyone else's business.

5. *Defense.* Secrets keep information from outsiders who might use the information against family members. Dropping out of college or dealing with a certain illness may be kept inside the family so an outsider could not hurt the family. More enmeshed families do tend to rely on these secrets.

6. *Communication.* Secrets reflect a lack of open communication among family members. In families with low verbal interaction, certain topics may never surface because the family is not perceived as open or no one would know how to talk about it, such as in this example.

When one of us wants our space, we may go into our room, drive to the mall, or take a run by ourselves. In addition, none of us really share too much of our private lives with one another. Our friends, social lives, and romantic lives are rarely disclosed, and if they are, it is done humorously.

The functions of family secrets have direct links to revelation choices because "people who noted they were unlikely to reveal their family secrets more strongly endorsed functions associated with *evaluation, maintenance, privacy* and *defense*" (Vangelisti & Caughlin, 1997).

In their study of criteria for revealing family secrets, Vangelisti, Caughlin, and Timmerman (2000) identified 10 criteria linked to individuals' tendencies to reveal family secrets. Respondents who closely identified with their family secrets and saw them as intimate or as negative were more likely to support a number of the criteria, such as relational security and important reason. A respondent's relationship to the listener was linked to the criteria he or she chose.

Secrets and Family Change   Secrets are tied frequently to family change. Although the creation or dissolution of a secret can occur at any moment, many secrets are created or revealed at periods of intense relationship change, such as marriage, divorce, the birth of a child, leaving home, or death. Secrets constructed at such key developmental points may stop the natural enfolding process. "Relationships that would ordinarily change and grow become frozen in time, as the presence of a secret locks people in place" (Imber-Black, 1998, p. 10).

As noted earlier, multigenerational communication patterns frequently involve protecting secrets. In her study of three-generation families of Holocaust survivors, Chaitin (2002) found the *conspiracy of silence* continues to affect what the survivors and their descendants feel they can or cannot talk about. Families had to handle the theme of how to deal or avoid dealing with the Holocaust—a choice that had significant consequences. "On one hand, by not confronting the past, the grandchildren may be spared the difficulty of dealing with emotionally loaded issues. On the other hand, by avoiding the subject, the grandchildren may be distancing themselves from the topic, and perhaps from their grandparents as well" (p. 395).

Family secrets impact individuals and the system as a whole. According to Imber-Black (1998), "A secret may be silently and unknowingly passed from generation to generation, like a booby-trapped heirloom" (p. 4). A hidden suicide, abortion, or prison term can block or affect the communication patterns of future generations. A member may struggle with questions such as: Do I have the right or responsibility to keep this a secret? Who would be injured if I reveal this secret? What is the best time or place for talking about this?

Families with HIV members confront painful choices as members hesitate to reveal the illness for fear of rejection, isolation, and harassment by co-workers, acquaintances, friends, and other family members (Haas, 2002). Even revealing the secret within the family has great consequences and challenges. For example, reasons mothers disclosed their HIV status to their children included wanting to educate them, wanting the children to hear it from them, and wanting children to know before they became very ill. Yet, some mothers gave reasons for secrecy, which, in addition to age and maturity level, included not wanting children to have such an emotional burden, to experience rejection, and to fear losing their mother, as well as wanting children to recover from previous losses (Schrimshaw & Siegel, 2002).

Vangelisti and Caughlin (1997) suggest a link between relational satisfaction and secret keeping, saying, "Those who were unlikely to reveal their secrets were more satisfied with their family relationships than were those who were moderately or highly likely to disclose their secrets" (p. 694). In an essay on family secrets, Pogrebin (1992) discusses the impact of discovering her parents' lies about their marriage, saying, "I became an inveterate doubter, always peeling the onion trying to get at the truth behind the 'facts.' . . . I will never know how much it has damaged my capacity to trust" (p. 23). Family secrets, which are an outgrowth of family rules, have powerful effects on families. They also have ties to how information moves between and among family members, or the family communication networks.

Family Communication Networks

Family members establish patterned channels for transmitting information, which are called *family networks*. By definition, a *network* determines the interactive flow of messages among family members or significant others outside the family.

The basic idea of family networks is connectedness, or the interaction of members along relatively stable pathways of communication. Family members regulate the direction of message flow—up, down, or across the network. Horizontal communication occurs when the persons involved represent perceived equal status or power, as when siblings pass messages or when parents and children sit down and work out problems together. The communication is vertical when real or imagined power differences are reflected in the interaction.

Families develop communication networks to manage cohesion and deal with relational tasks, such as conveying instructions, maintaining secrets, organizing activities, regulating time, and sharing resources. High member adaptability implies a wide variety of network arrangements; low adaptability implies rigid networks.

Although two-generation networks are complicated, most current families involve multigenerational networks of even greater complexity. Such networks are highly complex, yet only key persons will relate regularly across generations.

Networks also play an integral part in maintaining the roles and rules operating within the family system. Thus, networks and rules operate with mutual influence—rules may dictate the use of certain networks; networks create certain rule patterns.

Types of Networks   By observing the flow of verbal exchanges between members of a family, one can learn who talks to whom about what. What is the flow of information? This processing of communication may be horizontal or vertical and take one of several forms: chain, Y, wheel, all-channel, or a combination of these. The choice of network types indicates much about family relationships.

There are four girls in our family, and we have a very set pattern for requesting things from our mother or father. Gina tells Angela, who tells Celeste; Celeste tells me, and I talk to Mom. Usually, things stop there, because she makes most of the decisions. If it is something really important, she will discuss it with Dad and tell me their decision. Then I relay the message down the line.

This preceding example describes an operating *chain* network in which persons talk along a series of links. It has a built-in hierarchy whereby messages proceed up through the links or down from an authority source. Quite often, a father or mother controls the chain network and passes out orders to children. For example, in male-dominated families, the father may control the flow of messages on vital family issues. Some chains are horizontal and used for efficiency, as indicated here.

My mother is the one who keeps the immediate family in touch with one another. My brother frequently travels with his job. Although he may be in four different states in one day, my mother will know exactly where he is and at what time. In the past eight years I have spoken to my brother less than a dozen times by telephone. However, my mother does it regularly.

There are times when the chain has definite advantages. All busy families tend to rely on a chain network. However, chains can also keep certain family members separated. If Wei-Lin always avoids dealing with her stepfather, communicating all her desires or concerns through her mother, she and he will remain distant. In a chain network, a two-way exchange of information may occur between all persons except those on either end, who have only one member with whom to communicate.

In the Y network, the key person channels messages from one person on a chain to one or more other family members. In blended families with a new stepparent, the biological parent may consciously or unconsciously set up a Y network, separating the stepparent from the children. An inverted Y might involve a domineering grandmother who rules her daughter who deals with her children.

The *wheel* network depends on one family member at the hub or center to channel all messages to other members, a position that carries with it power or control. This central figure can filter and adapt messages positively or negatively or enforce the rules about how to communicate within the family. Because only one person communicates with all the others, this person becomes critical to the ongoing family functioning and may experience high dominance. The central family member in the wheel network can be severely taxed or exhausted. In some families, the central member can be quite effective in holding a family together.

My mother was the hub of the wheel in our family. When we were children, we expected her to settle our problems with other family members. She always knew what everyone was doing and how they felt. When we left home, each of us always let Mom know what we were doing. Mom digested the family news and relayed the information about what each of us was doing. For several years after her death, we children had little contact. Now, seven years later, we have formed a new subsystem in which four of us stay in contact with each other. One sister, Mary Alice, is the new hub.

Messages in chain, Y, and wheel networks are filtered, so they may become distorted as they pass from one person to another. A family member can selectively change parts of a message. This may help defuse some family conflicts, but misinformation could escalate others.

The *all-channel* network provides two-way exchange between or among all family members. Communication flows in all directions. This network provides for direct interaction and maximum feedback. No family member serves as a "go-between," and each participates freely in the process of sharing information or deciding issues. Although this network allows equal participation, it can be the most disorganized and chaotic, since messages flow in all directions.

Variations of these networks occur under certain circumstances. The ends of the chain may link, forming a circle; chains may lead toward the central figure in the wheel. Most families use a variety of networks as they progress through daily life. Special issues arise that may cause a family to change the usual network patterns—for example, a family may operate primarily in chain and wheel networks, but when vacations are planned, the network becomes all-channel. Multigenerational networks may add more variations when they are operational.

Subgroups and coalitions directly affect the family networks. The two people on one end of the chain may become very close and support each other in all situations. The key person in the Y formation may conspire with another member to keep certain information from the others. Some family members may never relate directly. Often, the family rules about "who one may talk to" determine the access. If you learn never to raise sensitive topics with your mother, for instance, your family may develop a strong Y network in which only her partner talks to her about such topics, and only when absolutely necessary. Toxic secrets may remain between two people indefinitely.

Most functional families have the capacity to use more than one network pattern, shifting to meet the needs of a particular situation. As children grow up and increasingly take over the direction of their own lives, adaptive families often move from the chain or wheel network to the all-channel. The wheel and chain networks facilitate order and discipline but may no longer be needed when children become autonomous. Parents may signal their recognition of these changes by permitting more issues to be discussed via an all-channel network. When parents enter later life stages, they may lose their central places in a network. The loss of a member can send the system into chaos, since entire systems may fragment. After a divorce, family members must establish new networks, often involving additional members, in order to maintain certain types of contact.

Extended Networks Because each family functions within the larger ecosystem, it becomes involved in a wide variety of formal and informal kinship and nonfamily networks. Significant others outside the family may have an influence on the communication patterns within it if the boundaries are permeable. A *significant other* is a person who has an intimate relationship with one or more of the family members. As open adoption becomes the norm for U.S. families, extended networks of adoptive and birth relatives are creating those new networks (Fein, 1998). In these cases, the birth family is considered extended family (Silber & Dorner, 1990). Significant others may include godparents, very close friends, and a child's partner. In long-term defined relationships such a person's place in a network may become predictable and clear. A parent's long-term partner must be included in decisions about vacations and holidays; a godmother must be consulted about the wedding plans of her godchild. A family member with ties to a significant other outside the family may very well make decisions within the network influenced by this relationship.

Extended networks provide social support and serve to alleviate stress and encourage well-being during life transitions and crises (Gottlieb, 1994). Families experiencing divorce or remarriage report a high need for friendship and community support (Simons, Whitbeck, Beaman, & Conger, 1994). In some cases, former spouses retain strong ties through co-parenting and friendship, creating an extended workable network (Masheter, 1997) as indicated in this experience.

At my grandfather's funeral, Ann and Ruth, Uncle Kenneth's first and second wives, were in the kitchen preparing dinner. Because they were involved in the ritualistic task of preparing a meal, their societal roles were not important. There was no tension or animosity between them. Another factor easing the tension between the stepfamilies was the sense that everyone was together for a greater cause—to help my grandmother by being there for her.

Large extended family networks are common among immigrant and second-generation Americans of many ethnic backgrounds. In their study of the networks of three-generation African American families, Taylor, Chatters, and Jackson (1993) found that two-thirds of their respondents reported interacting with family members at least once a week or nearly everyday. The parent generation reported highest interaction followed by the grandparent and child interactions.

Not all networks have positive consequences. In their study of spousal participation in networks, Burger and Milardo (1995) found a gender effect. For husbands, involvement with kin had a positive effect on the marriage, but wives with many kin in the network reported higher marital conflict and greater ambivalence concerning the marriage.

Thus, networks serve a very important function within families. They determine who talks to whom, who is included or excluded, who gets full or partial information, and who controls certain information. Yet, the rules for what, how, and to whom to communicate exist within each style of network.

Conclusion

This chapter explored how a family develops its own identity by creating a relational culture. It also examined the importance of coordinated meanings between family members and how those meanings are developed through repeated interpretation and evaluation.

Family systems need patterns to provide order and predictability for their members, such as (1) family-of-origin influences, including multigenerational transmissions and ethnic/cultural heritages; (2) communication rules; (3) family secrets; and (4) communication networks. Each contributes to unique family meanings and each factor influences the others. As you will see throughout the book, patterns serve as the skeletal structure for family life, both reflecting and determining relationships.

In Review

1. To what extent does the family-of-origin influence the communication patterns of future generations? Give examples.
2. What communication patterns have been passed down from your family-of-origin that you believe reflect key multigenerational transmissions?
3. Describe three incidents in a real or fictional family's development that demonstrate specific communication rules by which the members live.
4. Identify a family secret in a real or fictional family. Discuss the type of secret, how it was managed communicatively, and the effect of the secret on family members.
5. Using a real or fictional family, describe how the most frequently used communication networks have changed over time due to developmental changes or family crises.
6. Draw a three-generation representation (genogram) of a real or fictional family, and indicate and explain the coalitions among certain family members. See Figure 4.1 for a model. Indicate the effect of these coalitions on other family members.

SYMBOLIC MEANINGS *and* RELATIONAL MAINTENANCE: FAMILY RITUALS, CURRENCIES, *and* STORIES

5

Ruth, one of my dearest friends, has been married for more than fifty-five years. I once asked her to what she attributed her long marriage to Bob. She smiled and calmly said, "The knowledge that some decades are harder than others."

Randy Fujishin, *Gifts from the Heart*

Every family lives its own unique symbolic world, yet also participates in a larger world of shared symbolic activity. Family meanings are formed and relationships maintained through symbolic activity such as rituals and narratives. Just as message structures such as family-of-origin patterns, rules, and networks serve to create and reflect family ties, symbolic activities do the same. Family members create symbols to make sense of their lives or to continue their connections; this is a communicative process.

As you explore a symbolic frame for understanding families, the following assumptions are helpful. From this perspective, (1) what is most important about a family event or situation is not *what* happened but *what it means;* (2) the same event or situation may have many different meanings depending on who is engaged in the sense-making process; and (3) faced with uncertainty, humans create symbols to increase predictability as well as a sense of order and meaning. As human systems, families strive to create symbolically a sense of connection and control for their members. Symbolic activity helps family members make sense of their lives. Thompson and Dickson (1995) argue that rituals function as communication events, that their symbolizing function undergirds "sense making." This sense making takes on several forms, including (1) remembering, which includes recalling and storytelling; (2) belonging or creating identity; (3) educating members or socializing new members to the family; (4) transitioning, or accepting the family's changes; and (5) providing continuity or creating some stability (pp. 30–36). Although they only discuss rituals, these sense-making forms may be applied to relational currencies and narratives as well.

This chapter focuses on the research on maintaining marital and family relationships as well as on the role of specific symbolic practices such as family rituals, relational currencies, and narratives that serve to construct and convey messages of identity, connection, and caring.

RELATIONAL MAINTENANCE

Much of the time, family relationships just *are!* We live them rather than analyze them. The ordinary, routine behaviors of life carry us through each day, usually in a patterned and often unreflective way. And, as the opening quote attests, there are good times and tough times. We *communicatively maintain* families through our everyday interactions, but, on occasion, we stop and carefully analyze an interaction, respond to an unpredictable crisis, strategically plan a message, or seriously consider the role of family members in our lives.

This chapter introduces relational maintenance, and the next chapter will explore intimacy or deeper levels of attachment. These are interwoven issues, separated by degree rather than by category; therefore, you should find some continuity between the chapters. Whereas relational maintenance involves family routines and patterns, intimacy includes relational intensity and rejuvenation.

Consider all the types of things we maintain—cars, computers, gardens, homes, and much more. Adults schedule health checkups for themselves and family members; they make regular efforts to keep life running smoothly. This sounds mechanistic but it has relevance for significant relationships because, on some level, relationships are maintained through a combination of everyday routines and strategic behaviors. The routine may be functional behavior, such as picking up a child after school or discussing the day after work. The strategic behavior may be more obviously nurturing, such as pleasing a partner on a birthday or apologizing after a fight. Maintenance addresses "garden variety" activities, not managing major crises (Canary, Stafford, & Semic, 2002).

Exactly what does *relational maintenance* mean? It is that "huge area where relationships continue to exist between the point of their initial development and their possible decline" (Duck, 1994, p. 45). Essentially, it involves the "everyday stuff" of relational life. Relational maintenance involves keeping a relationship (1) in existence, (2) in a state of connectedness, (3) in satisfactory condition, and (4) in repair (Dindia & Canary,

1993). Relational maintenance ranges from romantic weekends and family vacations, to dealing with problems as they occur and apologizing for mistakes.

How is relational maintenance accomplished? Although more may be involved, "talk is the essence of relational maintenance" because it presents "symbolic evidence to the partners that the two of them share an appreciation of the relationship and approach important experiences in similar ways" (Duck, 1994, p. 45). Talk may involve metacommunication, such as discussing individual needs, negotiating new behaviors, or forgiving another. Often, it includes specific behaviors, or "actions and activities used to sustain desired relational definitions" (Canary & Stafford, 1994). Why does this everyday relational maintenance matter? The answer is, "People in relationships characterized by high levels of maintenance tend to stay together longer and be more satisfied" (Guerrero, Andersen, & Afifi, 2001, p. 229).

Relational maintenance differs across marital, partnership, and family forms because issues are different for adults than they are for parents and children, or siblings. Marriage or partnerships involve voluntary, adult relationships, whereas parent-child or sibling relationships are essentially involuntary, although many develop voluntary ties. Most adults recognize relationships need attention and nurturing, implying focused attention. Adults choose whether to put forth such effort; children have not reached levels of emotional maturity to understand the concept of "maintaining" or "working at" a relationship. Most studies of relational maintenance focus on marriages or other adult partnerships.

Marital Maintenance

"Maintaining high levels of satisfaction and love in marriage is problematic" (Vangelisti & Huston, 1994, p. 179). This blunt statement reflects the folk wisdom of "Over time, romance moves into reality." Although most partners experience periods of great intimacy, everyday life intrudes with demands and routines. One characteristic of enduring marriages is the ability to change over time. Most relationships do not escape health concerns, money worries, and work pressures; there may be children as well as older parents who need care. Marriages and partnerships frequently become caught up in the demands of everyday life, or just "getting through" days, weeks, or years.

Marital maintenance has received the most extensive research attention. In their study of the first two years of marriage, Vangelisti and Huston (1994) suggest, "Although most spouses start with extraordinarily high levels of satisfaction and love these feelings dwindle as time passes" (p. 179). Partners develop routines and become more aware of their spouses' flaws. By the second year, couples face relational reality, including disenchantment. The authors conclude, "Couples who are able to maintain strongly positive feelings toward each other over this period of adjustment may be in a particularly advantageous position to maintain their relationship over the longer haul" (p. 179).

Sometimes the term *relational resilience* is used to depict efforts at active relational maintenance. Marital resilience implies a process in which people purposefully engage in *maintenance strategies*—activities to repair, sustain, and thereby continue relationships in the ways they want them to be (Canary & Stafford, 1994, p. 395). Maintenance strategies help promote relational resilience since they prevent relationships from decaying and help repair troubled relationships. Stafford and Canary (1991) identify the following five maintenance strategies that contribute to relational maintenance:

1. *Positivity.* Includes acting polite and cheerful; giving compliments; being nice, courteous, and upbeat when talking; and avoiding criticism. There is a sense of pleasure in being involved with one another.

2. *Openness.* Includes explicitly discussing the relationship and sharing thoughts and feelings about relational goals and how the relationship is going. The smaller the number of taboo or off-limit topics, the greater the openness.

3. *Assurances.* Includes expressions of love and commitment, implying the partners are faithful to their commitment and the relationship has a future. Messages are designed to stress one's desire to remain in the relationship.

4. *Social Networks.* Includes spending time with and including family and friends in activities as well as sharing interconnected networks. Relationships that experience social support can be more stable because others are there to help.

5. *Sharing Tasks.* Involves engaging in household chores and other responsibilities, and often performing one's "fair share" of the work.

The importance and intensity of these strategies vary. For example, assurances tend to endure over time, so the need for constant assurance is not as great as the need for positivity. Assurances, related to comforting tactics, include emotional advice and assuring the other about the future of the relationship. Married couples tend to use more networking than other relational types.

These five strategies are tied to relational characteristics of (1) liking; (2) commitment, or a desire to continue the relationship indefinitely; and (3) control mutuality, or agreement on who has the right to influence the other. Each relational characteristic is considered necessary for a stable long-term marriage. Partners' association between the five strategies and liking, commitment, and control tend to decline over time, so the strategies need to be used regularly. In particular, partners express preferences for continual positive reactions from their partners, even when a partner feels tired or otherwise negative. The crucial nature of positivity is supported by the "5 to 1 magic ratio" of positivity to negativity, characteristic of stable marriages (Gottman, 1994b). In one of the only longitudinal examinations of marital maintenance, Weigel and Ballard-Reisch (2001) found that maintenance behaviors are used to sustain desired relational definitions and that effective use of such behaviors should predict future marital satisfaction. They also reaffirmed the importance of positivity, assurances, and similar social networks. It should not be surprising that among challenges to relational maintenance, in-laws play a role. Bryant, Conger, and Meehan (2001) note a potentially causal role of quality of in-law relationship and marital success, suggesting that parents-in-law are influential far beyond the early years of marriage.

Other Family Ties

Persons in various family roles or structures face similar, as well as different, relational maintenance challenges. In contrast to marital relationships, in which adults choose to remain connected, children under age 18 have few options other than to remain with their parent or parental figure. In addition, most children are not mature enough to be equal contributors to the quality of a parent-child relationship; parents are more powerful forces in determining the quality of family relationships.

Little is known about young sibling relational maintenance practices. In an attempt to examine the five relational maintenance behaviors noted, Myers and colleagues (2001) examined the involuntary sibling relationship. They found that although siblings are involuntarily linked, most have a commitment to the relationship beyond obligatory ties. In their study of 257 persons, ranging in age from 18 to 91, siblings reported using sharing tasks most frequently and openness least frequently. Such tasks may include participating in family events, helping each other, sharing duties, and spending time together (p. 27). They also found sibling use of all five behaviors is related to liking the other sibling. Sibling liking is predicted by use of positivity and networks. In addition, supportive and nurturing behaviors on the part of a parent or even an older sibling reduce the influence of negative life events on children's social adjustment (Conger & Conger, 2002). It could also be argued that sibling alliances help maintain relationships because, as the opposite of sibling rivalry, they represent a combination of efforts (Nicholson, 1999).

Maintenance of gay and lesbian partnerships involves many of the marital patterns discussed here but the lifestyle includes additional stresses (Haas & Stafford, 1998). There is a desire to live and work in environments supportive of the relationship, to be "out" in the social network, to be able to introduce the other person as one's partner, and to spend time with others who accept these relationships. When there are differences between partners about "coming out" to network members, problems can emerge (Patterson, 2000, p. 1054).

Long-distance partnerships require special attention in terms of maintenance (Rohlfing, 1995). Ongoing ties are dependent on staying in touch through mediated communication, often resulting in avoidance of difficult topics. In addition, partners report they are likely to be on their "best behavior" when they are together, which gives an unreal sense to the relationship. The pressure to have "good" times when together results in the use of more positivity and avoidance of painful or problematic topics; challenging topics may be avoided in order to preserve harmony.

Families that have experienced divorce and remarriage encounter significant complexities in maintaining relational ties. Adult siblings frequently confront the challenge of keeping connected across many miles while raising their own children. Single parents confront intense pressure to provide nurturing and functional support to their children.

Occasionally, external factors support family maintenance. To be realistic about it, some relationships continue, perhaps in a stagnant state, due to barriers to dissolving them (Attridge, 1994). In the case of marriages, these include external barriers, such as money, or the financial cost of ending a long-term marriage; legal complications, such as the effort involved in getting a divorce; and social barriers, or the networks of people who would be upset or negatively affected by a relational breakup. Certain sibling or extended family relationships may be maintained primarily through sharing rituals, such as holiday dinners, or attending life passage events, such as weddings or graduations. Although many behaviors support relational maintenance, certain strategies promote it by encouraging positivity, openness, assurances, social networks, and task sharing.

RITUALS

Rituals contain a variety of meanings and messages in patterned and emotionally powerful forms; they serve to remind members of who they are and they reflect a family's relational culture, as demonstrated here:

> My mom and I have a ritual of taking long late-night walks together . . . whenever I come home, I can count on a walk usually every other night. We generally walk late, after we have done our own things during the day and family things in the evening. It is our chance to talk together without interruption. We tend to share our deepest secrets at this time. (Koppen, 1997, p. 11)

> Whoever goes in and brushes their teeth first always puts toothpaste on the other's toothbrush. . . . If we're upset with one an-

other we might set the tube next to the brush, not put paste on it. This is sort of a sign of "How ya feeling today about one another?" (Bruess & Pearson, 1997, p. 35)

Repetition of actions and words carries great meaning, eventually developing into ongoing family rituals. *Family ritual* is "a symbolic form of communication that, owing to the satisfaction that family members experience through its repetition, is acted out in a systematic fashion over time" (Wolin & Bennett, 1984, p. 401). The special meanings and their repetitive nature contribute significantly to the establishment and preservation of a family's identity or relational culture. Rituals are not just pleasurable routine events; rather, rituals serve central ongoing maintenance and relational functions (Bruess & Pearson, 1997). They may cluster around occasions such as dinnertime, errands, vacations, or religious celebrations, or rites of passage such as birthdays, graduations, weddings, or funerals. Sometimes rituals form around less pleasurable events such as conflicts, discipline, or teasing.

Family rituals range from those tied to the overall culture to those known only to two or three members. Wolin and Bennett (1984) categorize rituals in the following manner:

1. Family celebrations, often tied to cultural norms, may include the ways holidays are celebrated or certain events are recognized.
2. Family traditions, reflecting the unique family occasions, may reflect patterns passed down by family-of-origin members.
3. Patterned family interactions reflecting everyday connections emerge out of increasingly patterned interactions usually developed implicitly.

Because culturally oriented holiday rituals are so well known and family-of-origin patterns have been explored in the previous chapter, we will focus on the more unique, everyday couple and family rituals.

Couple Rituals

Expressions of affection, code words for secrets, and repetitive daily or weekly experiences are signs of a developing relational culture. Research by communication scholars examines the role of rituals within marriages or partnerships (Dainton, Stafford, & McNeilis, 1992; Braithwaite & Baxter, 1995; Pearson, 1992). Bruess has extensively researched couple rituals, and based on her interview research, she reports on the following types (Bruess & Pearson, 1995, 1997, pp. 33–41).

Couple Time These are the most frequently reported types of rituals, divided into three subcategories: enjoyable activities, togetherness rituals, and escape episodes. *Enjoyable activities* are illustrated by the couple who reports "playing volleyball every Tuesday" or watching foreign films. *Togetherness* refers to times when couples simply spend time being together, such as walks after dinner. *Escape episodes* include rituals specifically designed to satisfy couples' needs to be alone. Escape rituals, which provide "shared time," provide couples with a way to create boundaries around themselves.

Idiosyncratic/Symbolic   These rituals are divided into favorites, private codes, play rituals, and celebration rituals. *Favorites* include couples' favorite, often symbolic, places to go, things to eat, items to purchase or give, and activities to do. For example, one woman reports:

> His favorite cake is wicky-wacky chocolate. It's a chocolate-out-of-scratch cake, an old family recipe . . . so when I really, really, really, really like him, and he's really, really, really, really made me happy, I bake him a wicky-wacky cake. He knows I'm really happy with him when he gets a wicky-wacky cake. (Bruess & Pearson, 1997, p. 35)

Private codes include the repeated, idiosyncratic use of jointly developed words, symbols, means, or gestures for communicating. These have a unique and special meaning. *Play rituals* represent intimate fun in the form of couples' kidding, teasing, silliness, and/or playful bantering. Finally, *celebrations* represent the shared manner couples develop for celebrating or acknowledging special holidays, birthdays, anniversaries, or other special events. Most involve established rules or guidelines for appropriateness. One couple may celebrate every month's anniversary; another may have elaborate birthday surprise rituals.

Daily Routines/Tasks   These involve accomplishing everyday, mundane activities, tasks, and chores, and shared daily patterns. For instance, one partner will cook and the other cleans up.

Intimacy Expressions   These are rituals that involve physical, symbolic, and verbal expressions of love, fondness, affection, or sexual attraction. They are linked to the currencies described later in this chapter.

Communication   This ritual encompasses couple talk time, including the specific times and means couples develop for talking, sharing, or getting in touch with each other. Rituals in this category include debriefing, conversations, chronicling, regular phone calls, or e-mails.

Patterns/Habits/Mannerisms   These rituals involve interactional, territorial, and/or situational patterns or habits couples develop. For example, partners may always sleep on the same side of the bed or sit in the same chairs to watch television.

Spiritual These rituals serve couples' religious needs and include rituals of prayer or attending spiritual worship. Partners may pray together before meals or attend worship services together.

Such rituals are common and pervasive in established relational partnerships; they serve to maintain the partners' relationships and to signal coupleness to the outside world.

An infrequent couple ritual involves the renewal of marriage vows. After interviewing couples who participated in such a ritual, Braithwaite and Baxter (1995) suggest that couples use this ceremonial event to "weave together their past, their present and their future commitments to one another" (p. 193). The ritual serves to maintain rather than repair the relationship, while communicating commitment to each other and the partners' larger network of family and friends. In another study of individuals engaged in a renewal ritual, the authors found the experience allowed married couples to weave together two different idealizations of marriage—the public marriage, experienced with a community, and the private marriage of two expressive people (Baxter & Braithwaite, 2002). Countless couple rituals exist, but often their meaning and power is overlooked.

Intergenerational Rituals

Rituals serve as a way to bond family members of all ages across generations, providing a sense of family identity and a linkage. Sometimes grandparents and grandchildren have their own rituals. Rituals frequently involve parents and children. In an attempt to apply Bruess's categories to parent-child relations, Koppen (1997) looked at mother-daughter rituals. She reports, "Although mothers and daughters share an involuntary relationship unlike that of married couples, the rituals shared by many mother-daughter pairs are relatively similar in form and type to those enacted in marital relationships" (p. 3). The following is one example:

> When my mom and I lived alone, we ate cold niblets from the can and had cereal for dinner repeatedly. But later she got married and he only likes hot corn, served on the table, etc. So, whenever he goes away or misses dinner, we revert back to our old ways, all the while making jokes about it and bonding. It evolved into a bonding event for "the girls" because it was a reminder of the past and it only involved us. (p. 10)

Frequently, grandparents and grandchildren develop their own rituals, which provide them with special connections. These may include phone calls, e-mails, sleep-overs, special meals, everyday care, or a trip, as indicated by this grandchild.

Ever since I was about 5, my grandfather has taken me on a trout fishing weekend in the mountains. He rents a cabin at a fishing camp and we pack lots of food and all our gear. We spend most of the day in the streams and cook on a grill every night. Then we sit and stare at the stars and talk about life—usually this is really about me. Over the years, the conversations have changed from my baseball games to my career plans, but generally he asks and listens. He does not give much advice. Hopefully these will go on for a long time.

As families change, rituals are dropped or altered since "people are inventing new families to live by as well as with. The old images and rituals are changing even as new ones are coming into being" (Gillis, 1996, p. 226). This is a time of much family transition as indicated by divorce-recognition greeting cards and divorce ceremonies as well as gay-male and lesbian commitment ceremonies as the evidence of ritual adaptation.

The extent to which religious beliefs impact family interaction remains remarkably understudied. Given that 95 percent of married couples and parents report having a religious affiliation (Mahoney et al., 2001), this seems a critical and fruitful area for extensive consideration. Most family researchers do not address religion; yet, such beliefs create a taken-for-granted subtext for interaction patterns, especially tied to gender roles and parenting.

The blended family represents a group that struggles with the role of rituals and stories in their development. According to Baxter, Braithwaite, and Nicholson (1999), the challenge is selectively to embrace certain of the old family features so that both old and new family structures can be legitimated. Successful family rituals in the blended family "hold both sides" of the contradiction between old and new family systems. Their study of stepfamily rituals reveals that some unsuccessful rituals carried from the old family were perceived to threaten the new one, such as mother and biological children visiting a family friend for the weekend or the family going to an "old" favorite restaurant. They conclude that ritual practices help well-functioning stepparents and stepchildren accept the historical roots of their blended family. It reflects the different ritualized experiences that members brought to the blended family from their previous families as well as new unique ones generated in the stepfamily. In general, stepfamily research indicates a need for adaptive responses to

Holiday dinners usually involve sharing certain family stories.

old ritualized behaviors and a need for new rituals that bond the stepfamily (Whiteside, 1989).

Family Ceremonials and Celebrations

Ceremonials and major special events include several rites or rituals (Trice & Beyer, 1984). Family ceremonials may include weddings, graduations, and funerals, as these are major rites of passage events celebrated in U.S. culture. Such ceremonials involve much preparation. "The whole family goes through the passage at nodal events in the life cycle, and the passage often begins months before and ends months after the ceremony" (Friedman, 1998, p. 124). In addition, major annual events such as Thanksgiving or the Fourth of July involve ritualized celebrations in most families. In their study of Thanksgiving rituals, Benoit and associates (1996) identify "chronicling" as the most frequently occurring verbal behavior. *Chronicling* refers to "talk about present events or those of the recent past, in which the communicator updates others by providing information about his or her life" (p. 22). Grandparents and older relatives are likely to elicit this from children; the extended kinship network participates also. Thompson and Dickson (1995) suggest that the stages of major rituals are preparing, gathering, and terminating; they carry significant symbolism for all members involved and contribute to their sense making.

Negative Rituals

Although most of the writing and research on family or couple rituals reflects members' attempts to connect and convey caring in a positive manner, negative rituals are experienced in some families. Carnes (1989), an expert in sexual addiction, identifies rituals that are deliberately negative in nature, saying, "An addict may routinely pick a fight with his or her spouse and then sexually binge in self-righteous anger" (p. 63). A partner may obsessively engage in work rituals to gain distance and avoid relational contact. Children in alcoholic families may ritualistically water down the liquor bottles. Even ordinary circumstances may foster negative rituals; when a younger child mispronounces a word, an older sibling may launch into a list of the child's other verbal mistakes, or when one spouse watches televised sports, the other may complain loudly about being deserted. Incest or partner abuse may also become ritualized. Incest reflects a destructive ritual played out in families. Partner abuse in some families is ritualized. Negative rituals are difficult to identify because persons are not likely to self-report their negative experiences (Bruess, 1997).

In today's fast-paced, frantic lifestyles, some family members try to reduce rituals in order to save time and hassle, or to establish rituals such as checking workplace e-mails each evening from home. Others attempt to maintain such patterns and to create new ones that can be incorporated into the family's everyday life. The latter choice will serve its members well.

Rituals create a sense of order, continuity, and predictability, linking participants to one another as well as groups that may be absent, even to ancestors and future family members (Myerhoff, 1984).

RELATIONAL CURRENCIES

Since as early as I remember, affection has been displayed openly in my household. I remember as a young child sitting on my father's lap every Sunday to read the comic strips with him. I always hugged my father and mother, and still do. "I love you" is still the last thing said by my parents and by me when we talk on the telephone.

One partner may cook beef stew to please the other, or a grandfather may rock a grandchild for an hour while telling his childhood stories. Both of these instances represent an attempt to share affection, but the meaning depends on a shared perception.

Communication behaviors that carry meaning about the affection or caring dimension of human relationships can be viewed as *relational currency* (Villard & Whipple, 1976) or a vocabulary of loving behaviors (Wilkinson, 1999). The currencies can be seen as a symbolic exchange process. As partners share currencies, they will form agreements about their meanings and either strengthen or limit their relationship worldview (Stephen, 1984). Many currencies arise from family-of-origin patterns because if you think of family as your "first communication classroom you will realize how much you learned about how to share or withhold affection before you could even carry on a conversation" (Wilkinson, 1999).

Types of Currencies

Certain currencies make a direct statement. The act is the message—for example, a hug can mean "I'm glad to see you" or "I'm sorry you are leaving." Usually, the sender's intent is clear and easily interpreted. Other currencies permit a greater range of interpretation. After a family quarrel, does the arrival of flowers mean "I'm sorry" or "I still love you even if we don't agree on one issue"? There are many possible relational currencies. The list that follows and is shown in Figure 5.1 presents some of the common ways family members share affection; you may mentally add to this list. Each of these currencies represents one way of sharing affection. The use of each currency must be considered within the contexts of gender, ethnicity, class, and developmental stage.

Positive Verbal Statements   Such statements include oral and written messages indicating love, caring, praise, or support. In some households people express affection easily, saying, "I love you" directly and frequently. Other families view such directness as unacceptable, preferring to save such words for unusual situations. Within families, age, gender, and roles affect this currency.

Self-Disclosure   Self-disclosure is a type of self-revealing, or taking a risk and voluntarily telling another things about yourself that the other is un-

FIGURE 5.1   Sample Relational Currencies

Positive verbal statements	Gifts
Self-disclosure	Money
Listening	Food
Facial expressions	Favors
Touch	Service
Sexuality	Time together
Aggression	Access rights

likely to discover from other sources. Although self-disclosure can be manipulative, generally it serves as a means of deepening understanding between people. As a currency, self-disclosure is intentionally used to show caring and commitment in a relationship. This currency is discussed later in Chapter 6.

Listening Listening carries a message of involvement with, and attention to, another person. Empathic listening requires focused energy and practice. Having a partner who listens and is understanding is very important for relational satisfaction (Prager & Buhrmester, 1998). Listening may be taken for granted and the effort discounted unless the speaker is sensitive to the listener's careful attention.

Facial Expressions Affect displays are spontaneous indications of affection best characterized as "love in that 'eyes lighting up' sense" (Malone & Malone, 1987, p. 14). These nonverbal displays of affect indicate joy at being in the other's presence.

Touch This is the language of physical intimacy. Positive physical contact carries a range of messages about friendship, concern, love, comfort, or sexual interest. Touch, a very powerful currency, varies greatly across genders and cultures, so it may be easily misinterpreted.

Sexuality For adult partners, sexuality provides a unique opportunity for intimacy. The discourse around intercourse, as well as the act itself, combine to create a powerful currency. Sexuality as communication is discussed in detail later in Chapter 6.

Aggression Aggressive actions, usually thought to be incompatible with affection, may serve as the primary emotional connection between members of certain families. Persons frightened of expressing intimacy directly may use verbal or physical aggression as a sign of caring. Children find teasing or poking as a way to connect to a sibling. When adults do not know how to express intimacy in positive ways, they may use bickering, sarcasm, or belittling as their means of contact. Some conflictual partners maintain their contact through screaming and name-calling, which serve as currencies.

Gifts Presents are symbols of affection that may be complicated by issues of cost, appropriateness, and reciprocity. "Gifts become containers for the being of the donor" (Csikszentmihalyi & Rochberg-Halton, 1981, p. 37). The process of identifying, selecting, and presenting the gift serves as part of the currency.

Money The exchange of dollars represents an exchange of relational currencies. Money must be given or loaned as a sign of affection and not as a family or spousal obligation for it to serve as a currency.

Food A symbol of nurturing in many cultures, food has emerged as an important currency in romantic and immediate family relationships. Preparing and serving special food for a loved one serve as major signs of affection in many relationships.

Favors Performing helpful acts for another are complicated by norms of reciprocity and equality. Favors, to be considered currencies, must be performed willingly rather than in response to a spousal or parental order. The underlying message may be missed if the effort of the favor is taken for granted.

Service Service implies a caring effort that has evolved into a habitual behavior. Driving the car pool to athletic events, making the coffee in the morning, or maintaining the checkbook may have begun as favors and moved into routines. Such services are frequently taken for granted, thus negating the underlying message of affection.

Time Being together, whether it is just "hanging out" or voluntarily accompanying a person on a trip or errand, carries the message "I want to be with you." Men, in particular, report great tension between their desire to spend time with their children and workplace pressures (Daly, 1996). This is a subtle currency with potential for being overlooked.

Access Rights Allowing another person to use or borrow things you value is a currency when the permission is intended as a sign of affection. It is the exclusive nature of the permission that is given only to persons one cares about that makes this a currency.

This list of currencies does not represent the "last word" on the subject. You may identify unnamed currencies that you exchange or that you have observed in family systems. For example, Fujishin (1998) suggests that "doing nothing" can be a loving and powerful message in certain relationships because it may "communicate trust in what your loved one is doing by not intervening, redirecting, evaluating, instructing, or correcting" (p. 103). Across various cultures, currencies may convey different meanings.

Meanings and Currencies

Satisfaction is tied to perceptions of currencies. Pipher (1996) captures this idea, saying, "Two of ten people spend their lives searching for one kind of love, when all around them there is love if only they would see" (p. 142). The meanings attached to relational currencies have a direct impact on relationship maintenance. Stephen (1984) proposes a framework in which interaction may be viewed as an exchange process of trading meanings. He suggests that when meanings are shared, rewards are experienced; when meanings are missed, costs are experienced. Therefore, over time, intimate partners will create common assumptions about the importance of currencies and develop high levels of symbolic interdependence.

Although currencies may be exchanged with the best intentions, accurate interpretation occurs only when both parties agree on the meaning of the act. Consider this example:

> Each of us tends to identify as *loving* those expressions of love that are similar to our own. I may express my love . . . by touching you, being wonderfully careless with you, or simply contentedly sitting near you without speaking. You may express an equally deep love feeling by buying me a gift, cooking the veal, working longer hours to bring us more monetary freedom, or simply fixing the broken faucet. These are obviously different ways of loving. (Malone & Malone, 1987, p. 74)

In this example, the question remains, does the contented silent partner know that a good dinner or a fixed faucet is an attempt to show love and vice versa? Perhaps you may see others as more loving if they express their love the way you do. Such similarity adds to a growing sense of symbolic interdependence and the strengthening of a relational culture. Misunderstanding may develop when two-family systems attempt to blend into a new one and create a set of mutually understood currencies.

Without common meanings for relational currencies, family members may feel hurt or rejected. One spouse may consider sex to be the ultimate currency in married life and place a high value on regular sexual relations. If the other partner holds similar views, the sexual currency will be appropriately exchanged. If not, these two people will have difficulty communicating affection. Such differences are very common.

Many currencies may become routine but at times can be strategic, which changes their meaning (Guerrero, Andersen, & Afifi, 2001). Holding hands while taking a walk may be routine touching, but reaching for another's hand after a fight may be strategic. Such a shift frequently reflects new attention to the currency, as noted in the following comment.

My mother and I often say "I love you" in a routine way. We take the phrase for granted. But, after a fight, or if something bad happens to one of us, we tend to look directly at each other and say, "I really do love you" just to make sure the message gets across.

		Other	
		Yes	*No*
Self	*Yes*	Both value the currency	You value the currency; other does not
	No	You do not value the currency; other does	Neither values the currency

FIGURE 5.2   Dyadic Value of Specific Relational Currency

One way to think about how meaning about currencies is shared between people is to consider the chart shown in Figure 5.2. As you look at Figure 5.2, think about a particular currency and a particular family member. In quadrant 1, both persons value the currency, which makes communication relatively direct. In quadrants 2 and 3, one party values the currency but the other does not, leading to disappointments and missed messages. In quadrant 4, neither person values the currency, thus the agreement helps avoid missed messages.

What happens if family members wish to share affection but seem unable to exchange the currencies desired by others? Villard and Whipple (1976) concluded that spouses with more similar affection exchange behaviors were more likely to report (1) high levels of perceived equity and (2) higher levels of relationship satisfaction, thus greater relationship reward. Interestingly, accuracy in predicting (i.e., understanding) how the other spouse used currencies did not raise satisfaction levels. For instance, just knowing that your husband sends love messages through flowers does not mean that you will be more positive toward this currency if you prefer intimate talks. Persons who were very accurate at predicting how their spouses would respond to certain currencies still reported low marital satisfaction levels if the couple was dissimilar in their affection behaviors. Unfortunately, this finding, coupled with the finding that wives are more likely to use intimate currencies, suggests that many marriages may face struggles. These differences can be opportunities for growth if partners can talk about them and grow through them.

When my wife went through a very bad time in her work, we bumped into our differences. My caring solution was to give advice, try to help more around the house, and leave some little gifts for her. These were not what was desired at the time. Cybele wanted someone to listen to her—empathic listening—not a bunch of suggestions. She wanted to be held. She needed verbal reassurance.

Fortunately, Cybele let her needs and wants be known, and in the midst of that self-disclosure, a crisis was turned into an opportunity for growth. Since that time I have worked to provide listening, compliments, and hugs, and the bond between us has grown stronger.

A family's levels of cohesion and adaptability interact with its communication of affection. Highly cohesive families may demand large amounts of affection displayed with regularity, whereas low-cohesion families may not provide enough affection for certain members. Families near the chaotic end of the adaptability continuum may change the type of currencies valued, whereas more rigid systems may require the consistent and exclusive use of a particular currency. Family themes may dictate the amount or type of currencies used. "The Hatfields will stick by each other through thick and thin" may require members to provide money for hard-pressed relatives. Boundaries may establish which members or outsiders may receive more personal types of affection.

Because the family system evolves constantly through dialectical struggles, personal meaning of currencies changes. Members may change their ways of sharing affection because of new experiences, pressures, or expectations. A lost job may result in fewer gifts but more sharing and favors within a family.

The process of sharing relational currencies significantly affects the intimacy attained by the family members. The more similar the exchange process, the higher the levels of relational satisfaction.

NARRATIVES

My father was in his early twenties when he came to the United States from Taiwan, leaving behind his parents, three brothers, and two sisters. His first job was as a waiter in a Chinese restaurant. During this time the only thing my father would spend pay on was bread and bologna to feed himself on days when he did not work.

He earned about $300 a month of which he sent $200 home to repay the money he borrowed for travel. He sent $50 to his family. He used the rest for chemistry books and English classes.

My father, who became a research chemist, has told this story many times because I think he was trying to instill in us the importance of working hard for your dreams and the importance of helping your family. I will tell my children about their grandfather's struggles so they understand the importance of hard work and sacrifice.

Such a story is a powerful example of how one creates family meanings. Wells (1986) writes:

> Constructing stories in the mind—or storying, as it has been called—is one of the most fundamental means of making meanings. When storying becomes overt and is given expression in words, the resulting stories are one of the most effective ways of making one's own interpretation of events and ideas available to others. (p. 194)

How often have you heard comments such as "Uncle Wayne, tell us how Mom drove the car into the lake" or "Ask my grandmother to tell you about the one-room school she went to when she grew up in Alabama." Stories give meaning to everyday life. "People grow up and walk around with their stories under their skin" (Stone, 1988, p. 6).

Every family develops stories that reflect its collective experience. Some stories are too painful to remember; others are the centerpiece of any family gathering. Some provide a sense of belonging; some provide continuity, while others are in a transition. According to Stone (1988),

> A family culture makes its norms known through daily life, but it also does so through family stories which underscore . . . the essentials, like the unspoken and unadmitted family policy on marriage or illness. Or suicide, or who the family saints and sinners are, or how much anger can be expressed and by whom. (p. 7)

Stories have a strong personal power. According to Yerby (1993), "From the narrative perspective one's sense of self is the story that a person has created about herself from the totality of her experiences" (p. 6). A person's story brings together parts of a self into a purposeful whole (McAdams, 1993). Personal stories may "fit" with family stories or may serve to separate a member from his or her family.

Stories, once voiced, take on a life of their own and collect meanings beyond the first telling. One story may be embellished to turn one member into a hero; another story may be cut short to save a member embarrassment. Each teller places a slightly different "spin" on the tale. Some stories are told only by a particular family member, whereas others tend to be told with overlapping voices. Each retelling makes this story more significant within the family's life. Stories shape life with powerful effects. They are not just reflections of life.

Family members' stories are connected to each other's stories. You may be recruited into your brother's story of a childhood prank; your partner may delight in retelling your Thanksgiving dinner disaster. Certain family members may find their images carved in stone by how they are depicted in the story.

Frequently, a story gains one meaning that seals off alternative explanations; Uncle Fred will always be a hero for scaring the robber by sneezing, for instance. Sometimes families revise an interpretation to create a slightly different view of the world. For example, a mother may reframe her son's actions as "cautious" rather than "scared," or a single aunt may be reframed as "courageous" rather than "foolish" for entering the Peace Corps at age 53.

Functions of Stories

Stories carry important messages to family members, thus serving the following key functions: (1) to remember, (2) to create belonging and reaffirm family identity, (3) to educate current members and socialize new ones, (4) to aid changes, (5) to provide stability by connecting generations, and (6) to entertain. Family stories encourage members to remember together the times when Jamal ran the car into a bus or when Aunt Debra won the state track meet. Such remembering connects siblings as they age by helping them recall certain key people or moments in their shared lives. Stories construct and reaffirm the members' identities representing part of a self-definition. Many identity stories remind members of what it means to be a Shih, a Joravsky, or a Washington. It may mean you are stubborn, resourceful, or entertaining. Membership may emphasize spirituality, service, cleverness, or physical endurance. Stories reaffirm a family's identity, often by reflecting family themes or images. Grandpa's fight to live after a war wound demonstrates that "Wilsons are tough."

Family stories tell members what is expected of them. Such stories contain moral lessons or practical lessons but there is an instructive intent. Frequently, stories are linked to themes such as "Do it right the first time" tied to a story of trying to cut corners and having to do it again or "Only your best is good enough" accompanied by stories of trials and failures eventually followed by a success.

In one study, themes typifying individuals' stories about their families were associated with family satisfaction. Stories reflecting themes such as care, togetherness, or adaptability were linked to satisfaction, whereas themes such as disregard, hostility, or chaos were negatively linked to feelings about the family (Vangelisti, Crumley, & Baker, 1999).

Stories socialize new members to the family system. The prospective in-law may hear all about the family's journey from Costa Rica to St. Louis or about eccentric family members. Stepfamily members socialize each other to past family experiences because they are a kind of glue that

Some family stories can be told only by one key member.

holds people together as they create their own stories and learn about each other through historical stories (Collins, 1997). A study of 115 couples revealed 96 percent occasionally talked to their small children about their childhood; 45 percent of preschool mothers and 38 percent of preschool fathers told childhood stories at least once a week (Fiese, Hooker, Kotary, Schagler, & Rimmer, 1995).

Family stories remind people about who they are and help them to see the good or bad times that contributed to current situations. Some families have disaster stories that include the coming of the floods, surviving the high water, the terrible weeks of cleanup, and the ways things have changed. Stories about how Aunt Jenna experienced so much pain from her cancer may ease the family's sense of loss after her death.

Stories create bridges connecting generations and create a sense of history that gives younger members a place in the world. Family stories also connect people to their cultures. An African American family, for instance, might use family stories to teach their children how to deal with racism (Bylund, in press). Members of Franco-American families tell *memere* stories that capture the cultural formation of their identity, including gender and nationalism, as well as the enchantment of Franco-American grandmothers (Langellier, 2002). Immigration stories frequently serve to bring family heroes and risk takers alive to younger generations.

Finally, family stories bring joy or laughter to members as they remember special times or embarrassing moments; they also may showcase the narrative talents of a particular member. Sometimes these storytelling times can be bittersweet as in the following comments.

Now that Mom is in a nursing home and Dad comes to visit, we get them to tell us stories about camping trips, birthdays, family moves, and other childhood events. Sometimes they will have very different versions of the same story, or each remembers various pieces, or one won't remember it at all. They joke and say that in old age they "have one brain between them." Together, we get from them a fuller picture of events in our lives.

Types of Stories

A family develops stories that represent its collective experience. These are frequently tied to primary and secondary family functions. Family stories often respond to questions such as the following:

- How did this family come to be?

    Most families tell some version of "creation" stories. These may be first meetings of adult partners, birth stories, the first stepsiblings' meetings, or adoption stories. Such stories tell about how family members came to be in the family and therefore how the family came to be. Often, they are accompanied by strong feelings statements, such as this one.

We arrived at the airport two hours before the plane from Seoul by way of San Francisco was due to arrive, because we were too excited to stay at home. We brought Grandma and Poppa and Uncle Allen and Aunt Mary. Your father kept walking up and down the concourse and we could not get him to sit down. He had your picture, which he showed to the airline attendant, and he started to tell all the people near the gate we were going to become parents when the plane arrived. Three other couples arrived and were waiting for their babies also. We were all beside ourselves trying to pass the time. Finally the plane arrived, 15 minutes late, and one by one all these business passengers came out. Finally it looked like there were no more people on board when a young woman carrying a baby came struggling down the ramp. She was followed by other young people with babies. When I saw the third baby I knew it was you and started to grab you as the woman carrying you said "Dobbs." You gave me the most beautiful smile and your dad and I started to cry and laugh. We had waited 2 1/2 years for that moment.

- Are parents really human?

Children love to hear stories in which parents struggle with issues of growing up or making decisions—stories that take a parent figure off a pedestal. There are usually humorous ones, such as when Dad fell off a motorcycle or when Mom "lost" her baby brother. Sometimes they are serious, such as the stories of a stepfather struggling with drug addiction as a young man. These stories may be told for the first time as a parent self-discloses his or her mistakes at the point a child is old enough to learn from such a story. The telling represents an attempt to try to prevent a child from making a similar mistake.

- How does a child become an adult in this family?

These are the narratives in which a child grows into adulthood by accomplishing some feat—beating a parent at a sport, earning more than a parent, or solving a problem in a very mature manner. Often, these are poignant because they signal a passage of time and, in some cases, a role reversal between parent and child. A middle-aged adult may tell of having to care for a parent whose recent fall left her unable to live alone.

- Will the family stand behind its members?

There is much to be learned from stories of family support, or lack of support, at stressful times. In some families you learn that when you leave the accepted path, you will be disowned or cut off. In other families you learn that time heals many wounds and you can always return to the family. These stories link to family themes and to levels of adaptability. There are important stories behind comments such as "No one ever mentions Aunt Ginny at family gatherings because she married outside our religion and Granddad disowned her." Such stories often center on an event and begin with "when," such as "When my uncle left the priesthood," or "When Deon got fired," or "When Linda was pregnant with Julia."

- How does the family handle adversity?

    When unpredictable crises arise, such as illness or job loss, does this family pull together or does the family split and force members out on their own? How does the family cope—through cunning or through hard work? Countless immigrant stories recount heroics of family members who battled against great odds to build a new life. Stories of family members facing illness, accidents, prejudice, or economic hardships may depict aggressive or passive responses. In the stories family members may fight against the stress or may be overcome by the pressure.

- What does it mean to be a (family name)?

    This is a question of collective identity. There may be a key story that serves to capture the essence or being a Pearcy or a Stone. Family stories carry powerful messages that influence family members' lives as they organize their lives by making decisions in accordance with the dominant narratives (Sluzki, 1992). These dominant narratives tell these members who they are in the world and how they should act.

Performing Family Stories

As you listen to family stories, you may wish to think about the performance element—who tells the stories, and when and where are they told?

Who Tells? Sometimes storytelling is a singular experience, but frequently stories are told by pairs or small groups, often in a patterned fashion. According to Dickson and Wood (1997), "coupleness" is part of the performance in the joint storytelling ritual. In her research on couple storytelling, Dickson (1995) identifies three types of couples according to their performance style of storytelling. *Connected* couples tell stories "as if they are jointly owned by both partners" (p. 36). Dialogue overlaps and partners confirm each other. *Functional separate* couples demonstrate respect, validation, and support while engaging in individual storytelling, often of unshared experiences. *Dysfunctional separate* couples exhibit contradiction, disagreement, and poor listening as each tells his or her stories. Couples who jointly tell more coherent and expressive stories are also more likely to have higher marital satisfaction, both at the time the story is told as well as two years later (Oppenheim et al., 1996).

Some parents and children develop patterns whereby, on cue, one disagrees, adds the punch line, or recruits the other into the narrative. One parent may perform the bedtime ritual and become skilled at recounting key family events. An older sibling may be asked to perform the "warning" stories about troubles with drugs or drinking. Only Uncle Allen, the family comedian, may be allowed to tell key childhood stories.

Family storytelling varies by gender. Females, especially mothers, maintain most of the family stories through telling them (Benoit, 1997). In fact, mothers have a tendency to introduce family stories as a way to control the topic and the timing of the stories (Ochs & Taylor, 1992). Females also hear more family stories and become more familiar with stories of previous generations. Mothers are more likely to function as family historians (Hall & Langellier, 1988). Mothers also tell stories with stronger "affiliation themes," whereas fathers tell stories with stronger "achievement" themes (Fiese et al., 1995).

When and Where? Stories appear in context. Although the traditional image of family storytelling compares images of holiday celebrations, many family stories are bedtime stories or stories told in response to a trigger situation, such as a bad grade or a disloyal friend. The holidays are classic contexts for family stories. In her study of Thanksgiving rituals, Benoit and associates (1996) suggest members "chronicle" or individually update others on the recent past events in their lives and share stories at the table. They report that grandparents and parent generations control the content of talk by encouraging chronicling from younger generations and by acting as narrators. Stories may be told at the table, in the car, at family parties, or in any meeting that elicits the recall. Wherever and whenever they are recounted, they carry the family meanings within them.

These stories function to develop family solidarity and to enact family structure. Parents and grandparents usually tell the stories; children are frequently the protagonists. This creates a sense of solidarity for all involved. Occasionally, the reason creates a tense or emotional situation. In their study of foster family narratives, Jacob and Borzi (1996) describe how two sets of husbands and wives display degrees of emotion when discussing their experience of deciding to become foster parents. Women display more emotion; men remained more passive until the end of the narrative when they were active and enthusiastic.

Storytelling is common at dinnertime but the style may differ by culture. Whereas American families tend to encourage children to tell stories about their day, Israeli families are more likely to divide storytelling between children and adults, allowing the children to collaborate on adult stories (Blum-Kulka, 1993).

The following story was written by a foster father for his first foster daughter.

Children in foster care often lose contact with their foster parents when they are reunited with their biological families or placed with an adoptive family. As a result they are often missing personal histories and stories of their child-

hood. There is no one around who can tell them what they were like or what they did for the period of time they were in foster care. I wrote the following letter to my former foster daughter, Sierra, hoping that one day she will have the opportunity to read it and fill in some missing pieces from her childhood.

I'll never forget the night you first came into our lives. It was about five-thirty in the evening. Middle of December. I was at the stove making dinner when the phone rang. It was a case manager from the social service agency. "We're looking for a foster home for a nineteen month old girl," she said. She told me about your case and why you were in foster care. "So are you interested in taking her in?" she asked. I put my hand over the receiver and turned to my partner, Tom. "They have a nineteen month old girl." I repeated everything I was just told about the case. "Do we want to take her in?" "Wow," Tom said. "Yeah, I think I want to do this," he replied. "What do you think?" he asked. "I think I want to do this too," I answered. We were feeling both excited and nervous at the same time. I got back on the phone. "Yes," I said. "We'll be happy to take her in." The case manager said, "That's great. Can you pick her up at eight o'clock?" I glanced at the clock. It was less than three hours away. I put my hand back over the receiver. "Can we pick her up in a couple hours?" I asked Tom. "Sure," he said. "We can do this," he reassured me. I got back on the phone. "No problem. We'll meet you at eight." I hung up the phone. And then panic set in. We had nothing for a girl your age. Nothing. No car seat. No crib. No high chair. I wasn't even sure I knew how to change a diaper. I remember calling some of our friends who were parents and asking them all kinds of questions. What can she eat? What do we need? The couple hours flew by and it was soon time for us to leave.

I remember driving in the snow and in the dark to pick you up at the social service agency. We walked through the front door into the lobby. There you were, this tiny little girl, all wrapped up in a big coat with your head peeking out from under the hood. We borrowed a car seat from the agency and put you in the back seat. We took your stuff, which was packed in plastic bags, and put it in the trunk. On the way home I kept glancing at you in the rear view mirror. You were beautiful. The first few days you called both me and Tom "Mamma." I never thought I would be a "Mamma." It was funny. We would be someplace like the grocery store and you would point to something and say, "Mamma, look!" And I could see the other shoppers turning their heads and staring at us. You could tell they were wondering why this little girl was calling this man "Mamma." So Tom and I talked it over and decided that I would be "Daddy" and he would be "Papa." That made you the very first one to call me "Daddy." And when you said, "I love you, Daddy" for the first time, my heart melted.

There were so many things to love about you. I really liked picking you up at daycare. No matter what you were doing or who you were playing with, you dropped everything when I walked into the room. You just got this big smile on your face. And then you would run over to me, and wrap your little arms around my legs. If I was working late and you were already home, you would come running up to me as I walked through the door, yelling, "Daddy! Daddy! Daddy!" There was nothing better to come home to. We had lots of fun together. We wrestled. And jumped up and down on the bed. And played goofy games. You loved playing "Ring Around the Rosie." You called it "Ashes." You wanted to play it again and again and again. "Ashes, Daddy. Ashes," you would say. You loved to be held and you wanted to be carried everywhere. I pretty quickly learned to do everything with one hand while I held you in my other arm. You told great stories. At night we would sit on the couch and you would sit on the little bench. Sometimes you would tell us stories about your friends and what happened at daycare. "Madison BUMP her head. Madison cry." Most of the time you would make things up. "And I was shopping. And a monster came. And it BIT me." "Where did it bite you, Sierra?" "It bit me RIGHT HERE," you would say, holding up your hand. Half the time your stories didn't make any sense but it was so much fun to just sit there and listen to you talk.

There were some nights you refused to fall asleep. So I would pick you up and carry you to the car. I acted like it was a big inconvenience and I didn't want to do it, but I secretly loved it. This was my time to be alone with you. Just Daddy and Sierra. After a while you learned the routine. "Go for a ride, Daddy?" you would ask. "I get your glasses, Daddy." I would wrap you in a blanket, grab your doll, and put you in the car seat. And we would drive around. Sometimes we were both quiet. We wouldn't say a word and just enjoyed being with each other. Sometimes we would talk. "Moon. Look at the moon, Daddy," you would say. Sometimes we would sing "You Are My Sunshine." That became our song. "Old McDonald Had a Farm" was another favorite. One night you sang, "Old McDonald had a farm. Eee Eye Eee Eye Ohh. And on his farm he had some trees. Eee Eye Eee Eye Ohh." And I thought to myself, "That's so sweet. He had some trees on his farm. That's pretty good." But then you continued, "Poopy diapers in the trees. Eee Eye Eee Eye Ohh." We cracked up laughing and it would be another twenty minutes before you would fall asleep. When you finally did close your eyes, I would drive back home. I would carry you into the house, with your little body pressed against mine, and put you in bed.

Then one day we got a phone call from the social service agency. You were going back to your mom. "Back home," they said. On one hand we were happy for you. Your mom loved you a lot and she worked really hard to get you back. We liked her and wanted her to succeed. Many of the kids in foster care never return to their biological families. You were one of the lucky ones. You got to go back. But it was gonna be so hard to say goodbye to you. You had been with us for nine months. 270 days. We were completely in love with you. And the thought of saying goodbye to you and never seeing you again really hurt.

We didn't know how to explain to you what was going to happen. You were only two. I wasn't even sure you remembered a time when you lived with your mom. We kept talking about her. And how much she loved you. And how much fun it was going to be to live with her. We completely spoiled you the last few days you were with us. We let you do pretty much anything you wanted to do. We stayed up late. We ate lots of ice cream. We cherished every moment we had with you. No matter what we were doing I caught myself thinking this would be the last time for us to do it together. The last trip to the grocery store. The last time making popcorn and watching videos. The last time getting you dressed in the morning. On your very last day with us I took you and the other kids out to eat. You were asleep when we got to the restaurant. I picked you up and carried you in. While the other kids ate, I closed my eyes and held you in my arms while you slept. "This is it," I said to myself. "The last time you'll be sleeping in my arms. The last time I'll hold you like this. Just the two of us. Sierra and Daddy. For the last time."

When we dropped you off at your mom's house that night she had a little party to welcome you back. There were relatives and friends there, and she had ordered a cake and bought balloons. Papa and I thought the best thing for us to do would be to slip out without saying goodbye. We thought it would be easier that way. Easier for you, easier for us, easier for your mom. But you saw us leaving. You ran to the door and you were crying. And you were calling our names. "Daddy! Papa!" And we had to get into the car and drive away. That was so hard. It was the most difficult thing I had to do in my entire life. I kept wondering what was going through your little head. If you had any way of understanding what was happening and why we were leaving you. It still hurts to think about that day.

I don't know if you'll remember us five years from now. Ten years from now. I don't really remember anything from my life when I was two years old. But I hope there's a part of us that will always be with you. Because there's a part of you that will always be with us. Since then we've had other foster kids. And we love them very much. And we even have the opportunity to adopt some of them. But you know what, Sierra? You were our first little girl. You were the first to call me "Daddy." You were the first to win my heart. And I'll never forget you.

You are my sunshine.
My only sunshine.
You made me happy when skies were gray.
You'll never know dear, how much I loved you.
Please don't take my sunshine away.

—Dennis Grady

Conclusion

This chapter explored relational maintenance, importance, and strategies, as well as the role of symbolic interaction in family relational development by examining rituals, relational currencies, and family narratives. The underlying patterns found in each of these symbolic areas undergird identity and relational development. Rituals, everyday and ceremonial, serve to join members to their history and to each other. Relational currencies provide symbolic ways of sharing affection if interpreted appropriately. Family narratives serve to link generations and reaffirm values and beliefs.

In Review

1. Consider an adult partnership you have observed and identify two relational maintenance strategies this pair uses. Give two examples of each.
2. Using a real or fictional family, describe the relational currencies most commonly used. Indicate any family-of-origin influences you see in the current pattern.
3. After reading the list of currencies, note a "missing" currency that you believe contributes to family connection.
4. Identify and describe the impact of a family story that you believe represents that family's collective identity.
5. Take a position on the value of the following: "Relational patterns must change or their message is lost over time."

INTIMACY *and* CLOSENESS *within* FAMILIES

The real wedding and the real vows don't happen on the day of the formal social occasion. There comes a time, usually some days after the proposal and acceptance . . . when there is a conversation between two people in love, when they are in earnest about what they've agreed to do. The conversation happens over several days—even weeks. . . . It's a conversation about promises, homes, family, children, possessions, jobs, dreams, rights, concessions, money, personal space, and all the problems that might arise from all those things. And what is promised at that time, in a disorganized, higgledy-piggledy way, is the making of a covenant. A covenant—an invisible bond of commitment.

Robert Fulghum, *It Was on Fire When I Lay Down on It*

What keeps partners in a close, trusting relationship for years? How do young people move from being "the kids" to creating a caring adult relationship with a parent? Why do siblings in one family drift apart, while members of another remain connected throughout a lifetime? Why do some voluntaristic family ties last for a lifetime? Family connections, sometimes solid and sometimes fragile, depend on members' communication and their management of dialectical tensions to sustain meaningful relationships.

Everyday life revolves around day-by-day patterns and routines. Functional communication supports such task-oriented interactions. Family members engage in communication that keeps the home running, children fed, clothes clean, and bills paid; such functional communication contributes to a low-level sense of connection. However, both men and women believe emotional communication is more important than task activities in the development of intimacy (Burleson et al., 1996).

As you saw in Chapter 5, families have the opportunity to provide their members with deeper communication experiences—including those that nurture the relationships involved. Nurturing communication carries messages of recognition and caring that indicate "I'm aware of you; I care about you" (Wilkinson, 1989). Nurturing communication contributes to intimacy among family members.

This chapter will focus on how communication influences the development of closeness and intimacy within a family's relational culture. It is a continuation of our discussion of relational maintenance, emphasizing the deepening and identifying of certain family ties. Although we will discuss parent-child closeness, there is less writing on parent-child intimacy because the concept of intimacy usually implies a voluntary involvement, such as between partners. Understanding intimacy within the family realm involves exploring (1) the development of marital and family intimacy, (2) the communication building blocks of intimacy, and (3) the barriers to intimacy.

DEVELOPMENT OF INTIMACY

Relational culture symbolizes strong, unique relational connection; it is the nucleus of intimacy (Wood, 1999). Persons, such as partners or family members, collaboratively create a unique relational culture that represents their understandings of each other and the world. Relational culture is fundamentally a product of communication—it arises out of communication, is maintained and altered in communication, and is dissolved through communication. It is within these relational cultures that intimacy and closeness develop consistent with the understandings of the members, their cultural backgrounds, and family-of-origin experiences.

The word *intimacy* comes from the term *intimus* meaning "inner." Most individuals have a sense of what intimacy means but multiple definitions exist. Some descriptions of intimacy suggest it is about persons seeking someone to reassure them that they are worth loving or a quest for a reflected sense of self. At the other end of the continuum are the definitions that address acceptance of existential separateness and rely on self-validated rather than other-validated intimacy (Schnarch, 1991). Although intimate relationships may be characterized by mutual devotion and committed love involving intellectual, emotional, and physical capacities (Spooner, 1982), intimacy also means that "we can be who we are in a relationship and allow the other person to do the same" (Lerner, 1989, p. 3). Guerrero and Andersen (2000) refer to intimacy as involving a cluster of interpersonal emotions including love, warmth, passion, and joy that are tied to intimate feelings. Clearly, these definitions reflect different understandings when persons in intimate relationships find themselves in the autonomy–connection dialectical struggle. Each family and each member develops a sense of the experience of intimacy.

Marital and family intimacy reflect many similarities. Feldman (1979) suggests that marital intimacy involves the following characteristics: (1) a close, familiar, and usually affectionate or loving personal relationship; (2) a detailed and deep knowledge and understanding from close personal connection or familiar experience; and (3) sexual relations (p. 70). Gottman (1994b) maintains contented couples exhibit a 5 to 1 ratio of positivity that includes displaying interest, affection, caring, acceptance, empathy, and joy. With the exception of sexual relations, these characteristics may be applied to all family relationships, understanding that intimacy is much different among siblings than between children and parents (Perlmutter, 1988). As noted earlier, marital or partnership intimacy has received the greatest research focus. Family intimacy involves interpersonal devotion along intellectual, emotional, and physical dimensions. This is demonstrated by shared knowledge and understanding as well as close loving relationships, both of which are reflective of developmental stages and culture. Such a concept of intimacy translates into reality through the communication patterns of families.

Marital and family intimacy reflect many similarities.

Yet, acceptable levels of family intimacy reflect the interaction of members as they deal with dialectical tensions. Intimacy embodies each member's past intimate experiences, current need for intimacy, perception of the other, and desire for increasing predictability within a relationship. The rule of reciprocity in intimacy is controversial. Schnarch (1991) argues that expectations of reciprocity promote unrealistic expectations of emotional fusion and is "alien to the acute experience of self and partner as related entities" (p. 116). Persons have varied levels of tolerance. When one member of a couple feels that the intimacy is becoming too great, he or she will initiate some type of conflictual behavior to decrease the amount of interpersonal closeness. The same concept may be applied to other family relationships. Each two-person subsystem sets its limits for acceptable intimacy. A small son and his mother may cuddle, tickle, kiss, and hug. A teenager and stepmother may discuss important events, hopes or dreams, and exchange kisses on occasion. A husband and wife develop limits for acceptable and unacceptable sexual intimacy as well as sharing feelings and showing affection. But these limits change over time. These acceptable limits of intimacy reflect the family's ways of showing affection and the depth of the particular relationship. In order to understand how closeness may be experienced, it is valuable to look at the characteristics of developed relationships. Such closeness may lead to intimacy.

RELATIONSHIP DEVELOPMENT AND INTIMACY

Developing a Relationship Culture

All developing intimate relationships reflect a history-building process. There are multiple perspectives on how this occurs, the most common of which involves developmental stage models. Such models apply to adults or older adolescents since they presume voluntary connections and a capability to make an effort. The stage models assume that all relationships exhibit points of initiation, maintenance, and possible dissolution (Wilmot, 1987). The issues raised by a dialectical perspective have called into question some of the assumptions of the stage model, which will be addressed later.

Stage Models Numerous scholars have proposed models of linear relationship development based on stages through which the partners move as they draw closer (Knapp & Vangelisti, 1996; Altman & Taylor, 1973; McWhirter & Mattison, 1984). Psychologists Altman and Taylor created a model called *social penetration,* which captures the stages of relational development. They hypothesize that interpersonal exchange gradually progresses from superficial, nonintimate areas to more intimate, deeper layers of the self. People assess interpersonal costs and rewards gained from interaction because future development of a relationship depends on their perception of this exchange.

Altman and Taylor (1973) propose a four-stage model of relational movement relying on the eight characteristics of a developed relationship discussed in the previous section. These stages are orientation, exploratory affective exchange, affective exchange, and stable exchange. The stages are connected to the growth of eight characteristics of developed relationships, which include *openness, efficiency* and *uniqueness* of exchange, and *richness,* or conveying a message in multiple ways. These four are interrelated, as are the next four: *substitutability,* or conveying messages in an alternative manner, if necessary; *pacing,* or coordinating interpersonal actions and talk; *spontaneity;* and *evaluation,* or sharing positive or negative judgments about each other and the relationship. The eight characteristics are reflected in the communication that occurs between the persons involved; each dimension becomes more apparent as the relationship moves through the early stages toward the highest point. (Relationships at the orientation stage do not display these characteristics; relationships at the stable exchange display them strongly.) Yet, even stable level relationships require extensive effort if they are to be maintained. Partners who share a stable relationship are very aware of each other's needs and changes. They are willing to work actively to maintain their relationship, as seen here.

After 26 years of marriage, my parents seem to have an incredibly close relationship that I haven't seen in other people. They often hold hands. They share common interests in music and theatre. They just can't get enough of each other but each has special friends and interests, which balances their intensity. Life hasn't been all that easy for them, either, yet each has helped the other cope.

According to Altman and Taylor, the stages can be reversed when considering the decline of a relationship. For example, a couple may reach the stable stage before the births of their children, but attending to the children may have taken so much time and energy that the couple's relationship moves to a lower level of connection.

Other models provide variations on the theme. In an extension of Altman and Taylor's work, Knapp and Vangelisti (2000) propose a model of interaction stages in relationships that details five coming-together and coming-apart stages. This model has a unique "bonding" stage, which occurs when the partners undergo a public ritual announcing to the world a contract of commitments. In essence, bonding is a way of gaining social or institutional support for the relationship. Although ritual events, such as weddings or baptisms, may be viewed as examples of partner or family bonding, it is more difficult to imagine traditionally accepted bonding experiences for homosexual pairs, stepchildren and stepparents, or long-term foster families. Commitment ceremonies have become more common for same-sex pairs, however. Recently, the *New York Times* announced that the paper would report such ceremonies—an acknowledgment of this growing trend ("Times Will Begin," 2002).

Dialectical Approaches   As you saw in Chapter 3, relational culture is not static—it is constantly in process; there is a need for constant reflection and redefinition. Theorists who question stage models believe they are linear and static, implying relationships remain in the same place for a long time. A dialectical perspective highlights the continual tensions that relationships must manage. Relationships are maintained by the ways partners manage competing needs and obligations, how they organize and coordinate their activities, the way they introduce novelty and pleasure into their relationship, and how they build a place in which to nurture the relationship (Werner & Baxter, 1994, p. 324). Sometimes this is referred to as the *me-we pull*, or a desire to be with the partner at the same time a person wants autonomy or independence (Baxter & Montgomery, 1996). Dialectical tensions raise the questions: How close can we get without interfering with each other? How much closeness do we need? How can we live together without hurting each other too much? These questions are indicators of the tensions all relationships face. A dialectical approach focuses on competing and opposite possibilities that exist in a relationship (Brown, Werner, & Altman, 1994). It recognizes the tension between partners as they negotiate and renegotiate what it means to be in a functioning relationship.

Communication scholars identify a range of possible dialectical tensions, including autonomy–connection, openness–closedness, and predictability–novelty (Baxter, 1990). This approach, noted earlier in Chapter 3, does not mean that every moment or every day a relationship experiences struggle or tension. Although at critical times, struggles may be in the forefront of the relationship, there are more times when the dialectical tensions serves as the background. In other words, "Dialectics may work backstage in a relationship beyond partners' mindful awareness or ability to identify and describe them, but still contributing a sense of unsettledness or instability in the relationship" (Montgomery, 1992, p. 206).

There are times when family members feel equal pressure to be open and closed. One husband captures this struggle, saying, "She wants to spend more time together, where I kind of want to go off and do my own thing with friends. And that is not bad, and I don't love her less. I mean I need my independence to just get away" (Baxter & Braithwaite, 2002, p. 146).

Dialectical struggles are especially complicated in new stepfamilies. The adults try to maintain a high level of closeness and connection with each other while dealing with the tensions created as children try to stay tightly connected to their biological parent and distant from their stepparent. Most stepfamily members can identify with the use of Baxter's (1990) four main strategies that were discussed in Chapter 3 (selection, separation, neutralization, and reframing). Imagine a custodial mother stepfamily in which the stepfather's children visit on alternate weekends. The adults might make a conscious decision to stay tightly connected, no matter what issue arises with the children, and to take time away from the family regularly in order to develop the marital relationship. Thus, partner connection is valued highly. In another stepfamily of a similar form, the parents may choose to spend individual time with their biological children, shifting back and forth on the adult autonomy-connection scale. Adults in stepfamilies make choices about how much to share with each other about their interactions with former spouses or how to manage the openness–closedness dialectic. Some partners agree to share every comment; others decide to limit such discussions because they evoke conflict. Many use the neutralization strategy of *selective sharing,* thus diluting the poles of total disclosure or secrecy. Some adults reframe an issue in order to reduce the tensions surrounding it. For example, if the woman is upset about how the children cling to their father for the first six to eight hours of their visit every weekend, she can interpret this as rejecting her. If such a belief causes anger after each weekend visit, the couple may learn to reframe the clinging time as a necessary intense period after which the husband and wife are free to reconnect because the children can be more independent for the rest of the weekend. Of course, in a stepfamily all the parent-child dynamics must be managed simultaneously, creating a highly intense situation, especially in the early years of family life.

In their marital study, Hoppe-Nagao and Ting-Toomey (2002) identify six specific communication strategies couples use to manage the openness–closedness tensions. These are topic selection, time alteration, withdrawal, probing, deception, and antisocial strategies such as arguing, crying, or giving the partner "a cold shoulder."

Although all humans seem to have intimacy needs—to be loved, held, touched, and nurtured—there may also be fear of intimacy: a fear of being controlled by another, loved and left by another, or possessed by another. Thus, the needs and fears become part of the struggle.

> Relationship development models assume voluntary involvement. There has been little careful study of nonvoluntary relationships, such as those experienced within some stepfamilies. Such relationships may begin with stages characteristic of deteriorating re-

lationships, such as low self-disclosure, conflict, and resentment. (Galvin & Cooper, 1990)

Finally, intimacy is tied to overall themes, images, and boundaries and biosocial issues. Family themes that stress verbal sharing, such as "There are no secrets in this family," may promote honest disclosure if a sense of support exists; if not, such themes may promote silences. Boundaries influence how much intimacy occurs in family subsystems and how intimacy may be developed with those outside the immediate family. Gender-related attitudes support or restrict the capacity of members to develop certain levels of intimacy. Knowledge about another family member is not sufficient to develop intimacy. Relational growth depends on communication about that knowledge (Duck, Miell, & Miell, 1984).

COMMUNICATION AS A FOUNDATION OF INTIMACY

The basis for all relationships lies in the members' abilities to share meanings through communication. Countless studies of enduring and/or healthy marriages or families emphasize the importance of communication as a hallmark of successful family relationships (Stinnett & DeFrain, 1985; Pearson, 1992; Covey, 1997). The terminology varies but similar factors emerge. Robinson and Blanton (1993) identify key characteristics of enduring marriages as intimacy balanced with autonomy, commitment, communication, congruence, and, in some cases, religious orientation. Pearson's study of lasting happy marriages discussed the importance of positive perceptions, commitment, understanding, and unconditional acceptance.

In this section we will examine six major factors that serve to undergird the development of communicated-related intimacy. These are talk, confirmation, self-disclosure, sexual communication, commitment, and forgiveness. We will also briefly address effort and sacrifice. Their function varies with the unique marital or family system, its ethnic heritage, and the maturity of its members. Because closeness is co-constructed in the ongoing management of both interdependence and independence, differences and struggles are inevitable.

Talk

There are direct and indirect messages that create and reflect investment in a relationship. Direct relational talk occurs when partners share with each other their feelings and desire to grow in the relationship: "I love you." "It's so great to have a sister to go through life with. We are a pair, no matter what." According to Duck and Pond (1989), not only do relationships "affect or influence talk, but also talk defines the relationship" (p. 26). Both direct communication and intentional metacommunication are essential to developing and maintaining intimacy (Schnarch, 1991). Talk creates its own rewards. For example, trust is inspired when both partners communicate that the relationship is a priority—something they want to invest in for their own benefit as well as their partner's benefit (Avery, 1989, p. 30). Talk serves as the underpinning for connection, as will be evident as different types of connecting talk is explored.

Confirmation

Confirming messages communicate recognition and acceptance of another human being—a fundamental precondition to intimacy. Sieburg (1973) provides four criteria for confirming messages. A confirming message (1) recognizes the other person's existence, (2) acknowledges the other's communication by responding relevantly to it, (3) reflects and accepts the other's self-experience, and (4) suggests a willingness to become involved with the other.

Confirming responses may be contrasted with two alternative responses: rejecting and disconfirming. Whereas *confirming responses* imply an acceptance of the other person, *rejecting responses* imply the other is wrong or unacceptable. Confirming messages do not necessarily imply one person agrees with the other, but responses such as "I see" display one's regard without expressing agreement (Canary, Cody, & Manusov, 2000). Rejecting messages might include such statements as "That's really dumb" or "Don't act like a 2-year-old." Disconfirming responses send the message "You don't exist"; they are a direct invalidation of the person. Disconfirming responses occur when a person is ignored, talked about as if he or she is invisible, excluded from a conversation, or excluded from physical contact (Stafford & Dainton, 1994).

When my sister remarried, she and her new husband tried to pretend they did not have her 12-year-old son, Wayne, living with them, because her new husband did not really want him. They would eat meals and forget to call him, plan trips and drop him with us at the last minute, and never check on his work in school. The kid was a nobody in that house. Finally, his father took him, and Wayne seems much happier now.

Confirming communication is characterized by recognition, dialogue, and acceptance, which indicate a willingness to be involved.

Recognition   Verbally, one may confirm another's existence by using the person's name, including him or her in conversation, or just acknowledging the individual's presence. Comments such as "I missed you" or "I'm glad to see you" serve to confirm another person's existence. Nonverbal confirmation is equally important in the recognition process. Touch, direct eye contact, and gestures also may serve to confirm another person within norms of ethnic culture.

Dialogue   Dialogue implies an interactive involvement between two people. Comments such as "Because I said so" and "You'll do it my way or not at all" do not reflect a dialogical attitude, whereas "What do you think?" or "I'm upset—can we talk about it?" open the door to dialogue and mutual exploration. Nonverbal dialogue occurs in families in which appropriate affectionate displays are mutually shared.

Acceptance   Acceptance gives a powerful sense of being all right. "When we feel acceptance, even though disagreed with, we do not feel tolerated; we feel loved" (Malone & Malone, 1987, p. 73). Acceptance avoids interpreting or judging one another. Rather, it lets one another be. This may involve allowing yourself to hear things you really do not want to hear or acknowledging that you understand another's perspective.

Confirming behavior often reflects cultural backgrounds and one's family-of-origin. Persons who grew up in a nonexpressive family may have trouble satisfying the reassurance and recognition needs of a spouse. Cultural differences in the use of eye contact or touch may create disconfirming feelings for one partner. Family intimacy develops from each member's sense of acceptance and care. If one "learns to love by being loved," then one learns to confirm by being confirmed.

Self-Disclosure

Self-disclosure is an important, complex, and difficult type of communication. In an original definition, *self-disclosure* is described as occurring when one person voluntarily tells another personal or private things about himself or herself that the other is unable to discern in a different manner (Pearce & Sharp, 1973). It involves risk on the part of the discloser and a willingness to accept such information or feelings on the part of the other. Historically, scholars assumed that the most powerful and profound awareness of oneself occurs with one's simultaneous opening up to another human (Malone & Malone, 1987). Such openness is experienced through sharing and receiving self-disclosure.

Trust, the essence of which is emotional safety, serves as the foundation for self-disclosure because "trust enables you to put your deepest feelings and fears in the palm of your partner's hand, knowing they will be handled with care" (Avery, 1989, p. 27). Self-disclosure, trust, and inti-

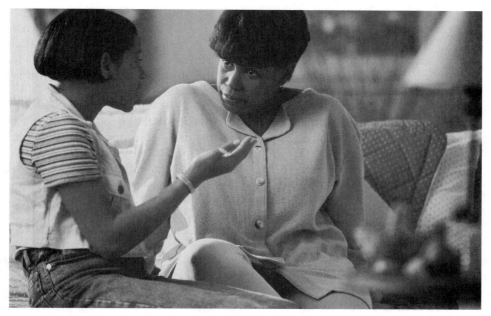

Parent-adolescent self-disclosure paves the way for strong adult relationships.

macy are frequently linked. High mutual self-disclosure is usually associated with voluntary relationships that have developed a strong relational culture and are characterized by trust, confirmation, and affection. Yet, high levels of negative self-disclosure may occur at points in such relationships, resulting in conflict and anger.

Traditionally, self-disclosure has been considered a skill for fostering intimate communication within families. Jourard (1971), an early researcher, describes the optimal marriage relationship as one "where each partner discloses himself without reserve" (p. 46). Many current marriage and family enrichment programs support self-disclosing behavior, as do popular texts on the subject of marital or parent-child interaction (Stafford & Dainton, 1994). Premarital counseling often focuses on revealing areas of feelings or information not yet shared by the couple.

Yet, some cautions about unrestrained self-disclosure need to be considered, since it can be destructive, manipulative, or at least a utopian premise (Wilder & Collins, 1994). Petronio (1991) suggests the process of boundary management is ongoing as partners decide which feelings and thoughts they are willing to share with each other, understanding the cost of greater sharing is personal vulnerability. Satisfaction and disclosure have a curvilinear relationship; that is, relational satisfaction is greatest at moderate levels of disclosure (Littlejohn, 1992, p. 273). Wood and Inman (1993) argue that verbal emotional disclosure is a more feminine style of relating, whereas the more masculine style may privilege sharing joint activities. Accordingly, women seem to receive more self-disclosures than do men (Pearson, West, & Turner, 1995). Therefore, selective, rather than total, self-disclosure contributes to intimacy development. Essentially, self-disclosure is coordinated through a boundary management process tied to partner or family rules (Petronio, 2000).

Variables in Self-Disclosure   Much of the research in self-disclosure has been conducted through questionnaires and self-reports collected from family members, usually adult partners. The actual self-disclosing behavior is not easily observed or measured. What family material exists focuses on marital couples or parent-child interactions; entire family systems have not received attention. Yet, even this limited research raises issues and implications for family relationships.

Some generalizations can be made about self-disclosure in family relationships, but much of the original research in the area is under review due to more sophisticated follow-up studies. Historically, self-disclosure has been viewed as a reciprocal process in which exchange is expected. In their study of self-disclosure in spouse or stranger interactions, Dindia, Fitzpatrick, and Kenny (1997) report that disclosure of highly intimate feelings is reciprocal regardless of the type of dyad, since "highly intimate disclosure appears to entrain communicators and demand a reciprocal response" (p. 408). Schnarch (1991) maintains that the reciprocity model of intimacy leads to an "I will if you will" strategy that "fosters a relative sense of adequacy rather than autonomous identity and self-worth," saying, "Self-disclosure based on the consolation that the partner has flaws involves a mental interpersonal tally system" (p. 118). This may limit partnership development.

Family Background   Family-of-origin, cultural heritage, and gender set expectations that influence self-disclosing behavior. Ethnic heritage may influence the amount and type of disclosure. For example, in many Asian families, the degree of intimacy is prescribed by position and status and relies heavily on nonverbal communication to share critical feelings and important messages (Chung, 1992). Whereas Jewish families exhibit verbal skill and a willingness to talk about trouble and feelings, Irish families may find themselves at a loss to describe inner feelings (Galvin, in press).

Spousal Relationships   Although the research on gender and disclosure is inconclusive, some studies find female pairs tend to be more disclosive than male pairs (Cline, 1989). Generally, women tend to be higher disclosers than men; they disclose more negative information, they provide less honest information, and they disclose more intimate information (Pearson, 1989). These differences may reflect socialization of females and males. Yet, some studies do not find that women self-disclose more than men (Dindia, Fitzpatrick, & Kenny, 1997).

Partner Relationships Marital self-disclosure studies reveal consistent findings across groups. According to Fitzpatrick (1987), self-report studies show a positive correlation between the self-disclosures of husbands and wives and between self-disclosure and marital satisfaction. Yet, a high disclosure of negative feelings is negatively related to marital satisfaction. In addition, dual-career couples appear to be more able to disclose to one another. Married men are less likely to disclose to friends than married women, although of married men and women who reported high self-disclosure within the marriage, only the women reported moderate to high disclosure to a friend (Tschann, 1988). Couples who insist on no secrets frequently discover such openness obliterates any sense of individuality (Imber-Black, 1998).

Parent-Child Relationships Parent-child disclosure has received some attention, revealing that self-disclosure does not involve all family members equally. Most mothers receive more self-disclosure than fathers (Waterman, 1979). Parents perceived as nurturing and supportive elicit more disclosure from children who find those encounters rewarding. College students are more likely to disclose more information more honestly to same-sex best friends than to either parent (Tardy, Hosman, & Bradac, 1981). In many families, parental primacy invasion occurs as parents and growing children struggle with autonomy and closeness—boundary conflicts (Petronio, 1994). Parental invasion may be met with secrecy or confrontation. Although one might imagine stepfamily members would report more secrets and single-parent family members would report fewer secrets, Caughlin and colleagues (2000) report the degree of openness, number of topics, and function of secrets was consistent across stepfamilies, single-parent families, and two parent biological families.

Such a brief review only highlights certain issues but indicates the complexity of a subject that some popular writers tend to treat simplistically as they encourage unrestrained, open communication in family relationships.

Satisfaction The positive effect of self-disclosure on intimate relationships has been described extensively. Clearly, shared and accepted personal information or feelings enhance intimacy in a relationship. In general, marital self-disclosure is rewarding because it signals to the listener the speaker's willingness to trust and share (Fitzpatrick, 1987, p. 585). Yet, such sharing and acceptance are not the norm. In fact, high self-disclosure is not necessarily linked with relational satisfaction, because it is clear that satisfied couples are more likely to engage in positive disclosure or sharing pleasant feelings. Unsatisfied couples tend to disclose more unpleasant feelings or negotiate messages. These studies highlight the value of "selective disclosure" (Sillars, Weisberg, Burggraf, & Wilson, 1987). It appears that the quantity of sharing fails to contribute to marital satisfaction. Partners who feel comfortable in sharing their emotions and talking about different issues in their marriage are more satisfied with marriage (Finkenauer & Hazam, 2000). In addition, Finkenhauer and Hazam find that both talking about conflictive issues and avoiding diffi- cult topics are related to marital satisfaction. This may reflect an individ- ual's cost-benefit analysis as to the centrality of the topic to relational maintenance.

The valence, or balances between the positive or negative nature of the message, relates directly to how comments will be received. Most people appreciate receiving positive self-disclosure. More frequently, self- disclosure is considered "dirty laundry," the misdeeds or negative feelings that are likely to cause pain for the listener. Some of the studies cited ear- lier report that higher self-disclosure levels are more characteristic of hap- pily married couples, but that unhappily married couples are higher in disclosure of a negative valence. Families characterized by pleasant self- disclosure content can experience intimacy more easily than those trying to discuss painful, negative-laden issues. For example, talking about a de- sire for continued sexual experimentation within a generally satisfactory relationship has much greater possibilities of leading to further intimacy than a revelation of severe sexual dissatisfaction.

As relationships move from being nonintimate to intimate, the initial high positive self-disclosure gains in importance. In order to handle this and remain satisfied with the relationship, both individuals must be char- acterized as high self-disclosers because of the amount of trust and risk involved. Intimate relationships are less likely to engage in high self- disclosure due to the amount of trust and risk involved (Pilkington & Richardson, 1988).

Because family life involves long-term growth and change, it would be ideal if members could handle the negative and positive aspects of each other's disclosures, permitting total honesty within a supportive con- text. Yet, many negative self-disclosures are necessarily painful, and each individual varies in a capacity to endure emotional pain. Thus, in many relationships, high levels of self-disclosure result in low levels of satisfac- tion. Research indicates partners may naturally cycle between being open and closed in their communication, meeting needs for separateness and togetherness (Montgomery, 1994).

The Practice of Self-Disclosure   If you think about family relationships in terms of these characteristics, you can see ways in which family systems tend to encourage or discourage self-disclosure. Considering the time it takes to do the functional things in families, you can understand that little time or energy may be available for self-disclosure. According to Mont- gomery (1994), "While self-disclosure may have significant impact in close relationships, it does not occur with great frequency even between the happiest of partners" (p. 78). Finding everyday time to talk sets a con- text for the occasional self-disclosure. Partners can lead parallel lives and may never get in the habit of sharing their lives with each other

(Schwartz, 1994). Vangelisti and Banski (1993) report that if couples hold *debriefing conversations* and talk about how their days went, they are more likely to experience marital satisfaction, because such conversations set the groundwork for discussing riskier topics. Hence, risk-taking communication is not likely to occur frequently within family life, but certain developmental or unpredictable stresses may trigger extensive amounts of personal discussion.

The self-disclosure process has an overlooked nonverbal component. A sequence of appropriate nonverbal signals occurring in the context of verbal disclosure also contribute significantly to mutual understanding. For example, nonverbal signals may tell a husband that his wife is surprised that he is unaware of her feelings about a topic (Duck, Miell, & Miell, 1984, p. 305). Duck and colleagues propose the term *intimation sequences* for these signals in which both partners intimate new levels of evolving awareness within a discussion. Parents may become skilled at reading a child's face and recognizing a desire or need to talk. Thus, verbal self-disclosure and nonverbal intimation sequences are bound together in face-to face interaction.

If high levels of disclosure occur mainly in dyads, how often does a parent of four children get time alone with each one of them? When do a stepparent and stepchild make time alone for themselves? Many family members never spend one-on-one time with each other, yet such time is important for openness to develop in their relationships.

Families create unique opportunities for self-disclosure. Joint living provides the potential for such interaction. Yet, this can take place only where positive social relationships, including trust, exist. Parents may break a child's trust unwittingly because they discussed the child's concern with another adult, not respecting the child's privacy. Unless disclosers indicate how private certain information is to them, another person may accidentally reveal that information to others and, as noted in the next quote, damage the relationship.

I have stopped discussing anything important with my mother because she cannot keep her mouth shut. She has told my aunt and some friends at work all about my relationship with my boyfriend, my use of birth control pills, and some of my health problems. Well, she doesn't have much to tell them now since she doesn't hear about my real concerns anymore.

In some involuntary family relationships, especially those involving stepfamilies, the bases of trust and liking may be missing, thereby reducing the likelihood of openness developing within the first five years (Galvin & Cooper, 1990).

One is likely to repeat self-disclosing if it is rewarded or met with a positive response. In a family that indicates satisfaction at knowing what the members are thinking or feeling, even if the information itself is not necessarily pleasant, continued self-disclosure is likely. If self-disclosure is met with rejecting or disconfirming messages, the level of sharing will drop significantly. Families with strong secrets may discourage self-disclosure in order to protect highly bounded areas.

Some people are dishonest or inaccurate in their disclosures (Berger & Bradac, 1982, p. 87). Although self-disclosure enhances intimacy development, it can be used to manipulate or control another family member. Partial or dishonest disclosures can undermine trust in a relationship. Sometimes young persons or immature adults engage in pseudo self-disclosure to gain something else from the relationship. In this process, they take advantage of the other. Unauthentic disclosures may be difficult to detect, but once discovered, they may interfere with future believability and mutual self-disclosure. In marriage, partners may be caught between desires for openness and protectiveness. A husband may be dismayed by his wife's weight gain, but he knows that bringing up his feelings would feed her low self-esteem.

Self-disclosure bears a direct relationship to family levels of cohesion and adaptation. An extremely cohesive family may resist negative self-disclosure because it would threaten the connectedness, particularly if the family has a low capacity for adaptation. For example, a highly cohesive family with a theme of "We can depend only on each other" would resist negative disclosures that might threaten security and cause internal conflict. Such a theme might be accompanied by rigid boundaries that would limit self-disclosures to outsiders.

Families with very low cohesion may tolerate negative self-disclosure but have difficulty with positive self-disclosure, which might lead to greater cohesion. Families with moderate to high adaptation and cohesion capacities may cope relatively well with the effects of high levels of positive or negative self-disclosure. Self-disclosure is a complicated process that may result in increased intimacy. In short, self-disclosure, or "sharing what's inside—even if what's inside isn't pretty—is the supreme act of faith in another" (Avery, 1989, p. 31).

Sexuality and Communication

How would you describe sexuality? As a series of isolated physical encounters? As an integral part of a growing relationship? Do you see marital sexuality as restricted to "being good in bed"? For most partners, sexuality within a marital relationship involves far more than just physical performance; it involves the partners' sexual identities, their history of sexual issues, their mutual perceptions of each others' needs, and the messages contained within sexual expression.

The quality of the sexual relationship affects, and is affected by, the other characteristics of intimacy—the affectionate/loving relationship and a deep, detailed mutual knowledge of the two partners. In their study of over 6,000 couples, Blumstein and Schwartz (1983) conclude that a good sex life is central to a good relationship. Schwartz (1994) reports the importance of equitable sexuality in peer marriages.

How would you describe sexuality within the family relationship? According to Maddock (1989), healthy sexuality reflects the balanced expression of sexuality in family structures that enhance the personal identity and sexual health of members and the system as a whole.

At both the marital and family level, sexual issues are linked directly to communication. In fact, "communication plays an important role in the development of intimate sexuality" (Troth & Peterson, 2000, p. 195). Sex communication implies "people exchanging verbal and nonverbal messages in a mutual effort to co-create meaning about sexual beliefs, attitudes, values, and/or behavior" (Warren, 2003). Sexuality, including sexual attitudes and behavior, may be viewed as a topic of communication, a form of communication, and a contributing factor to overall relational intimacy and satisfaction. Sprecher and McKinney (1994) suggest, "Sex is not only an act of communication or self-disclosure. Verbal and nonverbal communication is essential for the accomplishment of rewarding sexual episodes" (p. 206). Sheehy (1997) argues that it is important for partners and family members to talk about sex because sexuality is part of the essence of who we are, and not to talk about it sends messages that there is something wrong with it.

Although sexuality and intimacy may be experienced as disconnected or unrelated in certain relationships, we believe sexuality is directly related to intimacy in partner and family ties. In the following pages, sexuality will be explored in terms of socialization, parent-child communication, partner communication, and communication breakdowns.

Socialization and Sexuality The basis for a mutually intimate sexual relationship reflects each partner's orientation toward sexuality, particularly that which is learned in the family-of-origin. An individual's sexuality remains closely intertwined with his or her intrapersonal, interpersonal, and environmental systems—systems that interlock yet vary in importance according to an individual's age.

The sexual dimensions of family life are tied strongly to gender identities, boundaries, and developmental change. Much of your sexual conduct was originally learned, coded, and performed on the basis of biosocial beliefs regarding gender identity, learned in your family-of-origin. Parents possess a set of gender-specific ideas about males and females developed from their childhood experiences and from "typical" behaviors of girls or boys of similar ages to their children. In addition, strong ethnic influences convey expectations about what it means to be a man or woman. This identity is so strong that efforts to alter such socialization patterns must occur very early or they will have little impact. Your personal identities include sexual/gender identity as a core component, which influences later sexual experiences.

Parent-Child Communication   Many of today's adults grew up in a home atmosphere of sexual silence and now live in a world of open sexual discussion. Much of what you learned about sexuality took place within the rule-bound context of your family. In the earlier discussion of communication rules, you may recall that many sex-related rules are negative directives—"Do not . . . ." The extent to which a family encourages or discourages talk about issues such as pregnancy, birth control, masturbation, menstrual cycles, the initial sexual encounters of adolescents, and the sexual intimacy of the parents is related to communication and sexuality rules (Yerby, Buerkel-Rothfuss, & Bochner, 1990).

Sex communication within the family has become more open in the past decades due to greater societal openness, media references to sex, concerns about health issues, and greater parent comfort. Data are sometimes contradictory in this area, however. In 1986, Fisher found that college students and parents in high communication families have more similar sexual attitudes than those in low communicative families. Even in recent years, however, a low percentage of families (10 to 15 percent) still has any kind of ongoing discussions about sex (Warren, 1995).

Frequently, teenagers are more comfortable discussing sex than are their parents. A study of students' attitudes about parent-child discussions on sex-related topics reports that teenagers believe parents need to learn how to communicate supportively and empathically, even if there is disagreement (Bonnell & Caillovet, 1991). Often, family communication about sexual issues remains indirect, resulting in confusion, misinformation, or heightened curiosity, although close to 40 percent of parents say they are talking frequently with their children about sex (Family Chats, 1998). Many parents "recognize the importance of communication and want to communicate with their children but they lacked good sexual communication role models in their own lives and are unaware of how and when to initiate sexual conversations" (Hutchinson, 2002, p. 246).

The research of Warren and Neer relying heavily on their Family Sex Communication Quotient (FSCQ) instruments is summarized in the following points:

- *Satisfaction with family discussions about sex is dependent on the key factor of mutual dialogue.* Furthermore, children are most satisfied with patterns of family communication about sex when parents help them feel comfortable, or at least free, to initiate discussions. Thus, for best results, parents must move beyond the role of initiators and into the role of facilitators.

- *The ability to communicate supportively about sex revolves around an attitude of openness.* Teens want parents to talk with them, not at them, and to avoid preachy messages. Parents who want only to give their children instructions and commands are likely to have little success as communicators in this area.
- *For discussions to have the greatest impact, they should become part of the family patterns well before children reach age 16.* Many parents tend to put off talking about sex with their children; and the longer they wait, the harder it is to start. On the other hand, early initiation of discussion tends to facilitate more frequent discussion as well as children's perceptions that their parents are effective communicators.
- *Parent-child communication about sex that is frequent and that is regarded as effective tends to facilitate children's open discussion with dating partners.* The resonance effect is at work here, as children go on to model what they have encountered at home (Warren, 2003, p. 320; used with permission).

Families differ greatly in their approach to sexuality. Maddock (1989) has described communication behaviors of *sexually neglectful, sexually abusive,* and *sexually healthy families.* In some "sexually neglectful" families, sex is discussed little or not at all. If it must be addressed, sexual communication occurs on an abstract level so direct connection is not made between the topic and the personal experience of family members (p. 133).

My mother explained the act of sex in the most cold, mechanical, scientific, factual way she could. I was embarrassed and I couldn't look at her face after she finished. I know it was very difficult for her. Her mother had not told her anything at all, and she had let her get married and go on a honeymoon without any knowledge of what was going to happen. She made a point of saying throughout, "After marriage . . . ."

Messages like the previous example communicate an underlying attitude of anxiety or displeasure, but the direct issue remains hidden. Veiled messages often continue through adolescence and into adulthood. According to Satir (1988), many families use the rule:

> "Don't enjoy sex—yours or anyone else's—in any form." The common beginning for this rule is the denial of the genitals except as necessary nasty objects. "Keep them clean and out of sight and touch. Use them only when necessary and sparingly at that" (pp. 124–125).

In some families, the marital boundary remains so closed around the area of sexuality that children never see their parents as sexual beings—no playful jokes, hugging, or tickling occurs in view of the children. In such cases, children may not learn that sexual expression is central to marital intimacy or that men and women can express their sexuality in any direct affectionate way.

Yet, in other families, the marital boundary is so open that children encounter incestuous behaviors as they are co-opted into spousal roles. This "sexually abusive" family is typically a closed, rigid system with boundary confusion between individuals and generations. Communication reflects a perpetrator-victim interaction pattern, especially in cross-gender relationships, resulting in marital conflict and lack of emotional intimacy (Maddock, 1989, p. 134). Yet, in both the sexually neglectful and sexually abusive families, sexual attitudes and sexual behavior are seldom addressed directly.

According to Maddock (1989), sexually healthy families are characterized by (1) respect for both genders; (2) boundaries that are developmentally appropriate and support gender identities; (3) effective and flexible communication patterns that support intimacy, including appropriate erotic expression; and (4) a shared system of culturally relevant sexual values and meanings. Sheehy (1997) argues that children should see their parents teasing each other and enjoying each other because parents "can make jokes, they can communicate that sexuality is sacred, because actually sex is a lot of things. It's not just one thing. And I think kids need to know and see that."

Maddock (1989) suggests that sexually healthy families communicate effectively about sex "using language that can accurately cover sexual information, reflect feelings and attitudes of members, and facilitate decision making and problem solving regarding sexual issues" (p. 135). Sex education is accurate and set in a context of family values transmitted across generations. Talking about sexuality has been avoided by a great majority of parents (Roxema, 1986). After interviewing women in their thirties regarding their mother-daughter conversations about sex, Brock and Jennings (1993) report that memories were primarily of negative, nonverbal messages, and limited discussion focused on warnings and rules. The women wished for openness and discussions of feelings and choices. Interestingly, most of these women excused their mothers for their silence or discomfort, but indicated a desire to do better with their own children.

Parents appear to buffer adolescents from certain peer or environmental pressures on sexual activity. In her study of sexual risk communication, Hutchinson (2002) found that girls who talk to their mothers about sexual topics are more likely to have conservative sexual values and less likely to have initiated sex; girls who talk to parents about when to have sex are less influenced by peer behavior. She suggests that, although mothers are more likely to provide sexual information, fathers may provide daughters with a general understanding of men in heterosexual relationships. Hispanic-Latina women reported less parent-adolescent sexual risk communication than non-Hispanic peers.

You may have noticed that we have been discussing partners throughout this section in recognition of the multiple types of adult and young adult sexual partnerships that exist. Most of the research on sexual communication has been based on married or romantic heterosexual pairs. Yet, there are variations based on partnership type that are worth noting. According to Waite and Joyner (2001), society provides guidelines for marital sexual conduct that binds partners to a sexually exclusive contract, implies strong emotional connections and a lifetime commitment, barring divorce. The respondents were over 3,000 adults in varied types of relationships; the researchers found that for men and women, a sense of expected length of the relationship and sexual exclusivity are tied more to emotional satisfaction than to physical pleasure with sex. Thus, married couples would be reflected in this finding. They also found that "those who have sex frequently and couples in which the female partner has frequent orgasms report high levels of both emotional satisfaction and physical pleasure" (p. 263).

In their study of relationship quality for child-free lesbian couples and those with children, Koepke, Mare, and Moran (1992) found that both groups reported happy and solid relationships but that couples with children, who had been together longer, scored higher on relationship satisfaction and sexual relationship satisfaction. Lesbian couples are more likely to report fusion-related struggles as they attempt to develop high levels of cohesion (Laird, 1996). In some cases, fusion is blamed for diminishing sexual interest. In their classic study of American couples, Blumstein and Schwartz (1983) note that gay males have sex more often in the early years of their relationship, but after 10 years, they have sex far less frequently than do married couples. Lesbians have sex less frequently than other couple types, yet are likely to be sexually exclusive in their partnerships. In same-sex couples, it is the more emotionally expressive partner who initiates sex most frequently.

Discussing one's own homosexuality with a child raises particular issues. Father disclosure strategies may be direct, such as open discussion, or indirect, such as taking a child to gay social events (Bozett, 1987). Children who showed the greatest acceptance were gradually introduced to the subject of homosexuality through printed material, discussion, and meeting gay family friends before full parental disclosure. Today, some parent-child discussions include explanation of donor insemination. Following is a journal entry by Blumenthal (1990/91) describing one of her conversations with her 5-year-old son conceived through anonymous donor insemination:

March, 1989. At dinner tonight Jonathon asked me to explain again why we don't know who his seed daddy is. I first explained that I didn't know a man who wanted to be a seed daddy when I wanted to have him. I also told him that I didn't want anyone to ever try to take him away from me, so I thought it would be better to have an anonymous seed daddy. When I asked him, "Does that make you feel sad?" he said, "a little." I told him we could always talk about that; "I know."

Today, direct parent-child communication about sexuality is not only important for healthy family functioning but for the long-term physical health of family members. Pressing issues such as AIDS, sexually transmitted diseases, and a high percentage of unwanted pregnancies necessitate such discussions. Parents need to be able to address issues of safe sex practices and ways of talking about sex with their children.

In our family we did not discuss sexuality openly. When I left for college, my mother (totally unprovoked) told me that if I ever decided to go on birth control, I was never to tell her, and NOT to get it through our family doctor, but through the school health service. By doing so, she made sure she separated herself from ever discussing the topic—so much that she did not even ask me if I had ever thought of it. This is how much she wanted to avoid the subject.

The family represents the first but not the only source of sexual information. As children mature, they gain additional information about sexuality from peers, church, school, and the media. When you look back over your childhood and adolescence, what were your major sources of sexual information? What attitudes were communicated to you about your own sexuality?

Partner Communication   As an individual embarks on sexual experiences, personal background influences these encounters, as does the partner's sexual identity. Couples establish their own patterns of sexual activity early in the relationship, and these patterns typically continue (Sprecher & McKinney, 1994). Open communication becomes critical for both individuals, since a good sexual relationship depends on what is satisfying to each partner. A couple that cannot communicate effectively about many areas of their life will have difficulty developing effective communication about their sexual life. In short, "Communication in the bedroom starts in other rooms" (Schwartz, 1994, p. 74).

This sense of mutuality is enhanced by direct and honest communication between partners. Some understanding comes only through a combination of self-disclosure and sensitivity when spouses reveal their needs and desires while learning to give pleasure to the other. For some spouses, this involves working on "signal clarification" to minimize miscommunication. From another perspective, there is a distinction between monological and dialogical sex—the former being sexual experiences in which one or both partners "talk to themselves" or attempt to satisfy only personal needs. Dialogical sex is characterized by mutual concern and sharing of pleasure (Wilkinson, 1999).

Yet, many partners still find it difficult to talk about their sexual relationship. Adelman (1988) defines the *discourse of intercourse* as "sexual conversation which occurs between two people prior to, during, and after sex" (p. 1). She maintains that the vocabulary for sex talk is impoverished and thus ineffective in many relationships. Therefore, impoverished language and parental socialization may combine to restrict the adult sexual experiences, preventing husbands and wives from communicating freely about or through their sexual encounters.

Sexual discussions are rife with euphemisms (Bell, Buerkel-Rothfuss, & Gore, 1987), which may serve to romanticize or confuse the message. Euphemisms serve partners well when they promote the desired erotic reality but may serve to create disappointment or anger. Satisfied couples report their ability to directly discuss issues of feelings about sex, desired frequency of intercourse, who initiates sex, desired foreplay, sexual techniques, or positions. They avoid "mind reading," such as "If she really loved me, she'd know I would like . . ." or "If he really loved me, he would . . . ." This is a powerful trap. Hatfield and Rapson (1993) suggest that both men and women wished that their partners would tell them exactly what they wanted sexually. However, these same people were reluctant to tell their partners what they wanted. They kept expecting the partner to mind read. Schnarch (1991) believes that metacommunication is central to intimate sexual experience, saying, "Marital difficulties often lead to sexual difficulties (and vice versa) because of the difficulty of precluding metacommunication during sexual contact" (p. 98).

Because of their "taboos" regarding a discussion of sexual behavior, many couples rely solely on noverbal communication to gain mutual satisfaction. For some, this may be acceptable, but for others, unclear messages result in frustration, when partners misinterpret the degree or kind of sexual expression desired by the other. Much communication around sexuality is nonverbal; it may be more romantic but it also can create more confusion (Sheehy, 1997). Some partners report a fear of using any affectionate gesture because the other spouse always sees it as an invitation to intercourse; others say their partners never initiate any sexual activity, while the partners report being ignored or rebuffed at such attempts. Mutual satisfaction at any level of sexual involvement depends on open communication between spouses, yet intercourse, according to Lederer and Jackson (1968) is special "in that it requires a higher degree of collaborative communication than any other kind of behavior exchanged between the spouses" (p. 117).

The AIDS crisis brought about a new consciousness of the need for clear discourse about intercourse (Michall-Johnson & Bowen, 1989). The following vignette from an interview about safe sex talk (Adelman, 1988) illustrates the depth of the problem:

> She spoke openly about her sexual practices, describing in candid terms her preferences for foreplay and certain positions. When she had finished her graphic description I asked her, "So what do you say to your partner during sex?" She laughed nervously and replied, "Oh, now you're getting personal." (p. 1)

Given the dangers, partners can no longer remain silent about their sexual pasts. The need for safe sex talk and practice becomes more apparent daily. Thus, for couples engaged in an intimate relationship, open and direct communication about sexuality may deepen the intimacy and provide tremendous pleasure to both spouses.

Sexuality and Communication Breakdowns   Although sex as a form of communication has the potential for conveying messages of love and affection, many spouses use their sexual encounters to carry messages of anger, domination, disappointment, or self-rejection. Often, nonsexual conflicts are played out in the bedroom because one partner believes it is the only way to wage a war. Unexpressed anger may appear as a "headache," great tiredness, roughness, or violence during a sexual encounter.

As more information is gathered about sexuality over the life cycle, it becomes clear that sexual expectations are altered due to developmental changes and unpredictable stresses. Couples interviewed about the history of their sex lives report that they have experienced dramatic changes in sexual interest, depending on other pressures in their lives. Dual-career couples report a decline in time and desire for sexual activity. There are indications that sexuality may become more pleasurable in later life when a couple's child-rearing burdens cease. In their study of married couples over age 60, Marsiglio and Donnelly (1991) report 53 percent of all respondents and 24 percent of these over age 76 had sexual relations in the past month.

Based on his work in the area of sexual communication, Scoresby (1977) developed a chart indicating areas of sexual breakdown, including failure to talk openly, repeated lack of orgasm by females, lack of relaxation, one demanding the other to perform, excessive shyness or embarrassment, hurried and ungentle performance, and absence of frequent touching, embracing, and exchanges of intimacy.

Scoresby (1977) sees the following advantages of thinking of sex as communication: (1) an awareness of complexities and limitless potential (2) viewing the sexual relationship as a continuous process instead of as a series of isolated events (p. 46). Warren (2003) provides suggestions for effective family communication—start talking early, include both parents and sons and daughters in the conversation, and establish a supportive environment in which mutual dialogue can occur.

The area of sexuality and communication within the family realm has received less attention than other, less sensitive topics. Yet, because sexual standards, values, and relationships are negotiated among people through their interactions, the area of sexual communication is critical to the development of family and marital intimacy.

Commitment

"If you have to work at a relationship, there's something wrong with it. A relationship is either good or it's not." These words capture a naive but common belief about marital and family relationships. How often have you heard people argue that relationships should not require attention or effort? Yet it is only through commitment that a loving relationship remains a vital part of one's life.

Commitment implies intense singular energy directed toward sustaining a relationship. As such, it emphasizes one relationship and may limit other possibilities. "Commitment represents extended time orientation, and highly committed individuals should accordingly behave in ways that are consistent with this perspective, acting to ensure that their relationships endure and are healthy" (Rusbult, Drigotas, & Verette, 1994, p. 123).

Knapp and Taylor (1994) describe relational commitments as (1) want-to, (2) ought-to, and (3) have-to. Want-to commitment is based on personal choice and desire, usually rooted in positive feelings. Ought-to commitment stems from a sense of obligation based on a promise, a sense of guilt, or a fear of hurting another. Have-to commitment is based on the perception that there is no good alternative to maintaining membership in this relationship. Similarly, Johnson, Caughlin, and Huston (1999) identify three distinct types of commitment as personal, or wanting to stay in the relationship; moral, or feeling morally obligated to stay; and structural, or feeling constrained to stay regardless of the level of personal or moral commitment.

Another view of commitment includes personal dedication and constraints (Stanley, 1998). *Personal dedication* involves one's internal devotion to the relationship, whereas *constraint commitment* refers to factors that keep people in relationships regardless of devotion. The latter include religious beliefs, promises, children, finances, or social pressure. Frequently, partnerships and families are held together by a combination of these types of commitments. At good times, members *want-to* be connected; during rough times, members stick it out because they *ought-to.* Under difficult conditions, they may *have-to* stay together. Schnarch (1991) suggests that adult mature commitment in intimate relationships goes deeper than an equity model of reciprocity. In such relationships "the bittersweet awareness of immutable separateness heightens the salience of intimacy" (p. 118) because of the depth of the commitment.

Commitment is associated with higher relationship satisfaction and stability and with behaviors that maintain and enhance the quality of relationships (Flanagan et al., 2002).

There have been two times when James and I have remained together only because of outside forces—money was tight, no one else was an option or guilt at breaking a promise. That may not be bad for 17 years but they were low points and relatively brief. Thankfully.

Commitment may carry people through rocky feuds. In their study of marriage renewal rituals, Baxter and Braithwaite (2002) found that their couples viewed commitment as a "lifetime promise to stay in the marriage, not a fair-weather declaration to be abandoned when maintaining the relationship became effortful" (p. 103).

In her exploration of a marital life of commitment during a period of geographic separation, Diggs (2001) examines her own marriage to explore a 24-year African American marriage from inside the relationship. She captures the intensity of connection, the gender differences in emphasizing emotional versus physical presence, and concludes by suggesting that their commitment is characterized by "displays of love, and physical presence (emotional and instrumental), and dialoguing to find a connection (*I feel ya;* refocus on the person or values that keeps a couple together; and the awareness of levels or areas of unity)" (p. 25).

Intensity, repetition, explicitness, and codification support commitment talk (Knapp & Vangelisti, 2000). As described in the discussion of verbal relational currencies, certain phrases need to be repeated, and certain ideas needs to be emphasized or reaffirmed. Explicitness reduces misunderstanding: "I will stand behind you even if I don't agree," "We are brothers and that means I will support you." Such comments make the commitment quite clear. Codifying communication may be reflected in anything from love letters to a written agreement of rules for fighting to a marital contract. Commitment is not always easy; words may be hard to find and say. According to Knapp and Vangelisti, "The way we enact our commitment talk is at least as important, if not more so, than the content itself" (p. 298).

Effort and Sacrifice   Many factors compete for attention in your life. Meeting home, work, school, friendship, and community responsibilities take tremendous time and effort. The nurturing of marital or family relationships often gets the time and energy that is "left over," a minimal amount at best. In most cases, this limited attention spells relational disaster. Unless familial ties receive high priority, relationships will "go on automatic pilot" and eventually stagnate or deteriorate.

Because the family operates within larger systems including work and school, each system impacts the other. In describing the tensions between work and home obligations, Blumstein and Schwartz (1983) refer to the interaction between "where people put their emotional energy (home versus work) and their commitment to their relationship" (p. 173). In this era of dual-career couples and families, commuter marriages, and high technology and subsequent job loss or relocation, family intimacy can be lost in the shuffle.

Only a conscious and shared determination to focus on the relationship can keep marital and family ties high on one's list of priorities. Many couples and families seek out opportunities to enrich their lives, to reaffirm their connection to work on their relationships. According to Avery (1989), the way partners demonstrate their commitment is tied to communication.

> It can be willingness to do things for each other, spending time together, making personal sacrifices on the other's behalf, being consistent. Self-disclosure is part of it too, because sharing what's inside—even if what's inside isn't pretty—is the supreme act of faith in another. (p. 31)

Sacrifice implies giving up something in order to please another. It may involve a high level of effort and a shift away from self-interest. "Willingness to sacrifice for one's relationship is associated with strong commitment, high relational satisfaction, and longer relationships" (Flanagan et al., 2002). This may involve major efforts, such as giving up a vacation to stay with a sick grandparent, moving to support a partner's career, or working a second job to fund college tuitions. Commitment and sacrifice have an existential aspect of being there, which transcends unique communication skills and reciprocity. Thus, only conscious commitment and dedication to working at relationships, particularly through talk and effort, can preserve or heighten intimacy.

Forgiveness

What is the relational impact of saying "I forgive you"? And what might that statement really mean? Until recently, the concept of forgiveness primarily appeared in popular and religious writings on relationships. Yet, current work on repairing relationship includes an emphasis on forgiveness. Defining *forgiveness* is difficult because of multiple meanings. It may be viewed as "a transformation in which motivation to seek revenge and to avoid contact with the transgressor is limited" (Fincham & Beach,

2002, p. 240) but this does not reflect a relational focus. Essentially, all this definition implies is avoiding retaliation. Other definitions emphasize acknowledging the wrong but also changing one's heart to engage in positive attitudes or behaviors such as compassion, affection, generosity, and love. Kelley (2003) captures this intent, saying, "Forgiveness, at its best, is 'abandoning' the negative and 'fostering the positive'" (p. 224). Frequently, forgiveness implies an explicit renegotiation of the relationship that usually involves metacommunication.

Forgiveness appears directly related to family interactions given the long-term nature of family ties and the intensity of connections. According to Fincham and Beach (2002), "Paradoxically, those we love are the ones we are most likely to hurt and may not always be the ones with whom we communicate most effectively" (p. 239). In his study of close relationships, Kelley (1998) found that over 70 percent of respondents' motivations for forgiveness included love, restoring the relationship, and well-being of the other. He also found family members reported being less motivated to offer forgiveness because of love, restoring the relationships, or the other's behavior toward making up. He suggests that the obligatory nature of family relationships may create a sense of stability and resiliency. It seems self-evident that motivation and ability to discuss forgiveness depends on the severity of the transgressions; family reasons for forgiveness could range from an affair or violent act to an insult or sharing of another's secrets.

Not surprisingly, forgiveness and marital satisfaction are related. Fincham (2000; Fincham & Beach, 2002) found that marital unforgiveness may be especially associated with patterns of negative reciprocity because partners often hurt each other and initiate negative reciprocity patterns that work against intimacy. The authors also found unforgiveness to be related to partner psychological aggression, and that, for husbands, readiness to forgive is a strong predictor of wives' constructive communication. The current research on forgiveness indicates gender differences that need greater exploration.

Essentially, forgoing retaliation is unlikely to increase relational intimacy; only a proactive attempt to engage a family member in reconciliation has much chance for positively increasing constructive communication and intimacy.

BARRIERS TO INTIMACY

Building marital or familial intimacy can be difficult and risky. For many, it is more comfortable to maintain a number of pleasant or close relationships, none involving true intimacy, than to become intensely involved with a partner or child. Some family members establish barriers to relationship development to protect themselves from possible pain or loss.

General Fears

There are many reasons for a fear of intimacy, including the following four discussed by Feldman (1979, pp. 71–72): merger, exposure, attack, and abandonment. People may fear a *merger* with the loved one resulting in the loss of personal boundaries or identity. This occurs when the "sense of self" is poorly developed or when the "other" is very powerful. Comments such as "I'll disappear altogether" or "I have to fight to keep my identity" indicate struggles with merger. Individuals with low self-esteem fear interpersonal *exposure* and feel threatened by being revealed as weak, inadequate, or undesirable. Those who fear exposure avoid engaging in self-disclosure. Some individuals fear *attack* if their basic sense of trust is low. If you have self-disclosed to another and that person has turned against you, it will take a while before you can trust another person. These persons also choose to protect themselves by avoiding self-disclosure. The fear of *abandonment,* the feeling of being overwhelmed and helpless when the love object is gone, may affect those who have experienced excessive traumatic separations or broken relationships. Their way to prevent such helplessness is to remain distant. Once one has taken the risk to be intimate, rejection can be devastating, resulting in reluctance to be hurt again.

Jealousy

Although sometimes jealousy is seen as a sign of affection, when it becomes violent or obsessive, it creates a barrier to intimacy. *Jealousy* is an "aversive emotional experience characterized by feelings of anger, sadness, and fear induced by the threat or actual loss of a relationship with another person to a real or imagined rival" (DeSteno & Salovey, 1994, p. 220). In their study of 200 couples, Andersen, Eloy, Guerrero, and Spitzberg (1995) conclude that cognitive jealousy is negatively related to relational satisfaction; constantly mulling over jealous concerns heightens tension. The tension may result in active distancing, expression of negative affect, general avoidance/denial, and violent communication/threats. Jealousy tends to erode relational connections.

Although romantic jealousy is most closely associated with marital and partner relationships, one parent may be jealous of the other's connection to a child or to another family member. Siblings may be jealous of another's ties to a parent (Guerrero & Andersen, 1998). Frequently, family jealousy occurs when members fear they may lose something they value, such as the intensity of a particular relationship. Older siblings may resent the new baby for fear of losing the powerful connection to a parent, a teenager may reject a sibling's new "best friend" who interferes with family time, and an adult may experience animosity toward a partner's new teammate at work because of the perceived emotional connection. In their work on communicating favoritism to children, Lucchetti and Roghaar (2001) note its many negative consequences, including increased chance of sibling rivalry, lowered self-esteem for the less favored children, and perceptions of declining family support.

Deception

Given that trust appears as a hallmark of intimacy, deceiving another violates the understanding. Most people expect family and loved ones to be truthful as a sign of connection or relational commitment. Deception involves intentionally managing verbal and/or nonverbal messages so that another will believe or understand something in a way that the deceiver knows is false (Buller & Burgoon, 1994). The suspicion that a partner keeps information from the spouse is strongly associated with marital dissatisfaction (Finkenauer & Hazam, 2000).

Sometimes deceptions create accidental privacy dilemmas or predicaments where a member accidentally finds out information about someone in the family (Petronio, Jones, & Morr, 1999). This might include discovery of a parent's affair, a sibling's unrevealed adoption, or a grandparent's alcoholic relapse. Pogrebin (1992) describes the effect of discovering that her parents had been in a fictional marriage for 28 years and that she had two half-sisters, one of whom she thought was her full sister, and the other of whom had remained a secret. The impact of the deceptions turned her into a doubter with a damaged capacity for trust—factors that would affect intimacy in future relationships.

For most people, fear of intimacy is tied directly to issues of boundary management. Intimacy becomes confused with an unhealthy togetherness or extreme cohesion, resulting in a loss of personal boundaries and identity. In families with unclear boundaries, one person's business is everyone's business. Much communication occurs across family subsystem boundaries, and members may feel obligated to engage in high self-disclosure and even seek disclosure inappropriate to the subsystem. An adolescent may feel obligated to discuss dating behavior with a parent. Yet, the pressuring person requires the other to "be like me; be one with me," demonstrating the difficulty of negative self-disclosure. Members may demand constant confirmation to serve as a reassurance that they are cared for. Yet, intensive intimacy can smother, as this person relates.

My father thinks we all experience life as he does. He expects us to love and hate what he does. He assumes when he's cold, tired, or hungry, we are cold, tired, or hungry. He's like a whale swallowing little fish.

Sometimes adults are so afraid of sharing both good and bad things with each other that they establish a "united front" for themselves and displace any anger onto a child. Thus, the child serves as a scapegoat while the partners convince themselves that they are experiencing intimacy. Such false togetherness becomes a barrier to true marital intimacy while seriously harming the scapegoat child.

Within disengaged, or low-cohesive, families, individuals experience rigid boundaries, and the members may not receive necessary affection or support. Each person is a psychological subsystem with few links to the surrounding family members. Intimacy may be undeveloped in households where each family member is concerned solely with personal affairs, remains constantly busy, and spends extensive time away from home. Males and females believe that emotional communication is more important in the development of intimacy than are task-oriented efforts (Burleson, Kunkel, Samter, & Werking, 1996).

Moving Forward

Although many intimacy studies center on marital or parent-child relationships, multiple family types create valued intimate connections. When asked about their current relationship, lesbians and gay men report as much satisfaction with their relationships as do heterosexual couples; the great majority describe themselves as happy. The correlates of relationship quality for lesbian and gay couples include feelings of having equal power, perceiving many attractions and few alternatives to the relationship, endorsing few dysfunctional beliefs about the relationships, and engaging in shared decision making. A particular issue faced by such partnerships involves supportive networks. Certain gay and lesbian couples may find tremendous pressure to be "everything" to each other due to lack of family knowledge because one or both of the partners is not "out." In some cases, partners' expressions of affection are discouraged within the family or community network.

Intimacy in stepfamilies is exceptionally complex, particularly in the early years. Issues of loyalty, guilt, and loss compound the ability of stepchildren and stepparents to develop intimate ties. According to Papernow (1984), it is only at the later stages of stepfamily development, as the alliances recede, that the couple can experience their marriage as an intimate sanctuary. This is also the time when stepparent-stepchild relationships can be characterized by voluntary and deep personal interaction. Members often struggle with intimacy barriers such as favoritism or jealousy.

Single-parent families face different issues. Unmarried women with children may find more intimacy and support in their extended families, particularly in matriarchal systems, but many report difficulty in sustaining strong intimate adult relationships due to child-raising pressures. Some children, fearing the loss of parental intimacy, sabotage a parent's efforts to develop new romantic ties. Because they do not have a partner to share their problems, joys, and decision making, single parents need to function with strong adult communication networks.

One of the challenges of life is to learn how to be yourself while you are in a relationship with another person. In a truly intimate relationship, the "I" and the "we" coexist, to the joy of all persons. Lerner (1989) captures the link between the development of intimacy and communication. Her words serve as a fine conclusion to this chapter.

> "Being who we are" requires that we can talk openly about things that are important to us, that we take a clear position on where we stand on important emotional issues, and that we clarify the limits of what is acceptable and tolerable to us in a relationship. "Allowing the other person to do the same" means that we can stay emotionally connected to that other party who thinks, feels, and believes differently, without needing to change, convince, or fix the other.

Conclusion

This chapter explored the close relationship between intimacy and communication. It focused on specific communication behaviors that encourage intimacy within marital and family systems: confirmation, self-disclosure, sexual communication, and commitment effort. Confirming behaviors communicate acceptance of another person. Self-disclosure provides a means for mutual sharing of personal information and feelings. Sexuality serves as a means of communicating affection within a partner relationship. Family intimacy cannot be achieved unless members nurture their relationships through commitment. Because most people experience anxiety about intimacy, this is an ongoing and sometimes frustrating process. The barriers to intimacy may prevent certain relationships from developing their full potential.

Think about the kinds of interactions you see in the families around you. Is most of their communication strictly functional? Do you see attempts at intimacy through confirmation or self-disclosure? Are these people able to demonstrate an ability to touch each other comfortably?

All human beings long for intimacy, but it is a rare relationship in which the partners (spouses, parents and children, siblings) consciously strive for greater sharing over long periods of time. Such mutual commitment provides rewards known only to those in intimate relationships.

In Review

1. Create your own definition of *intimacy* and provide two examples of a marital and a family relationship characterized by intimate communication. Discuss some specific communication behaviors.

2. Describe some confirming behaviors that can become patterned into a family's way of life.
3. Under what circumstances, if any, would you recommend withholding complete self-disclosure in a marital and/or family relationship?
4. Discuss ways you have seen a family relationship overcome jealousy or deception.
5. Take a position on the following statement and defend it: If you have to work at a relationship, there's something wrong with it.

COMMUNICATION *and* FAMILY ROLES *and* TYPES

In other words, husband, wife, parent, child, grandparent, and grandchild are names of roles that people assume as they go through life. The roles describe two things: how one person is related to another, and how this particular role is lived out.

Virginia Satir, *The New Peoplemaking*

Current terminology about family roles includes words such as *dual-earner couples, latchkey children, Mommy tracker,* and *DINK (dual income, no kids),* all of which have family role implications. Today, there are no easy answers to what it means to be in a partner, parent, sibling, grandparent, or stepchild role. Tremendous variability is found in communication across families as members interact with each other, creating patterns of role relationships. In order to explore these complex role issues and their implications for communication, this chapter will discuss (1) role definition, (2) role functions, (3) role appropriation, and (4) couple and family typologies.

ROLE DEFINITION

Within families, roles are established, grown into, grown through, discussed, negotiated, worked on, and accepted or rejected. As family members mature or outside forces impact the family, roles emerge, shift, or disappear. The term *role* is so widely used that it can mean very different things to different persons. In order to understand role development, you need to consider first the definitions of *roles* and then examine role expectations and role performance.

Role theorists disagree on the definition of family roles (Minton & Paisley, 1996). This text defines *family roles* as recurring patterns of behavior developed through the interaction that family members use to fulfill family functions. From a communication perspective, these expectations develop within a family system and its members create a series of shared meanings about how roles should be enacted. This perspective contrasts with theories presenting a fixed, or unchanging, view of roles. For example, some theories maintain that family members hold specific expectations toward the occupant of a given social position, such as a father or grandmother.

Rather than take a fixed view of the position of a child or a parent in a family, we prefer an *interactive perspective,* emphasizing the emerging aspects of roles and their behavioral regularities developed out of social interaction. Family members develop roles through dialogue with each other reflecting the transactional nature of communication. Persons with labels such as "father" or "wife" struggle with dialectical tensions as they manage the reciprocal nature of roles. According to this interactive perspective, you cannot be a stepfather without a stepchild, or a wife without a husband; in fact, you cannot be a companionable father to a child who rejects you, or be a competitive wife to a man who avoids conflict. Family members exchange interrelated behaviors—action and reaction, question and answer, request and response (Montgomery, 1994). Today, roles are less tied to age, as age is no longer a predictor of life stage (Rubin, 2001). A 44-year-old female may parent three preschoolers; and an 18-year-old male may do the same. Over time, family members negotiate their mutual expectations of one another; they acquire role identifications and make an emotional investment in carrying out, for example, the roles of provider or nurturer. In addition, as circumstances change, members may have to give up roles, a process called *role relinquishment.*

Interactive role development reflects (1) the personality and background and role models of a person who occupies a social position, such as oldest son or stepmother; (2) the relationships in which a person interacts; (3) the changes as each family member moves through his or her life cycle; (4) the effects of role performance on the family system; and (5) the extent to which a person's social/psychological identity is defined and enhanced by a particular role. For example, a woman's behavior in the role of spouse may have been very different in her first marriage than in her second, due to her own personal growth and the actions of each husband.

Roles are inextricably bound to the communication process. Family roles are developed and maintained through communication. One learns how to assume his or her place within a family from the feedback provided by other family members, such as "I don't think we should argue in front of the children." Children are given direct instructions about being a son or daughter in a particular household. Adults tend to use their family-of-origin history as a base from which to negotiate particular mutual roles; children develop their communicative roles through a combination of their cognitive skills, family experiences, peer relationships, and societal norms and expectations. Young family members in immigrant families sometimes feel role tension when they sense that their parents' values differ from their desires to be Americanized.

Family roles and communication rules are strongly interrelated, for each contributes to the maintenance or change of the other. Rules may structure certain role relationships, whereas particular role relationships may foster the development of certain rules. For example, such rules as "Children should not hear about family finances" or "School problems are to be settled with Mother" reinforce the role of family members.

SPECIFIC ROLE FUNCTIONS (5)

The concept of the family as a mobile can be applied to roles using the McMaster Model of Family Functioning (Epstein, Bishop, & Baldwin, 1982). This model focuses on discovering how the family allocates responsibilities and handles accountability for them. It examines five essential family functions that serve as a basis for necessary family roles:

1. Providing for adult sexual fulfillment and gender modeling for children
2. Providing nurturing and emotional support
3. Providing for individual development
4. Providing kinship maintenance and family management
5. Providing basic resources (Epstein, Bishop, & Baldwin, 1982)

These family functions can be categorized as instrumental (providing the resources for the family), affective (support and nurturing, adult sexual needs), and mixed (life-skill development and system upkeep). When you look at Figure 7.1, imagine a mobile with the system's parts balanced by the multiple role functions operating within the family. These role functions become superimposed on the family system and its members.

(1) Providing for Gender Socialization and Sexual Needs

In a culture that provides multiple possibilities and few clear distinctions, men and women today can easily receive mixed messages. Men may hear that a woman wants a man who is expressive, gentle, nurturing, and vulnerable, yet also successful, prosperous, and capable. Women may receive similar conflicting messages regarding dependence and independence. Pelias (1996) speaks humorously of the expectations placed on men when he lists the following criteria: "be able to lift your own weight;

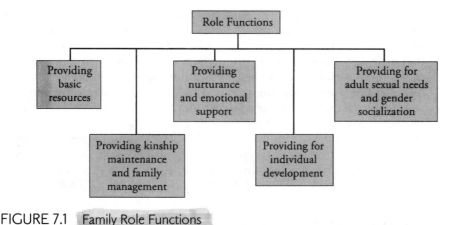

FIGURE 7.1   Family Role Functions

never be the last player chosen; make gobs of money; talk like a man, preferably one from Mars; rule the world; don't be afraid of the dark; know how to score; fix everything; and look down when kissing" (p. 3).

The process of learning what it means to be male or female begins at birth. Even as newborns, males and females are handled differently and may be provided with "sex-appropriate" toys. Studies of kindergarten children show that boys are keenly aware of what masculine behaviors are expected of them and restrict their interests and activities to avoid what might be judged feminine. Girls continue to develop feminine expectations gradually over five more years. Parents teach children about gender and physical appearance. Children learn what is "masculine" and what is "feminine" from parent comments about exercise, weight, appearance, and dress that is masculine or feminine. Certain religious or political groups and cultural traditions support strong male-female distinctions (Kraemer, 1991). Such gender-bound distinctions appear repressive to others.

The gender-based communication directives you received as a child come into play when you form your own family system and try to communicate effectively. For example, men are thought to disclose less about themselves than women and keep more secrets (DeVito, 1993). Compared to women, men relate more impersonally to others and see themselves as embodiments of their roles. Some men fear that talking about emotions reduces their competitive edge. If men accept a very restrictive definition of their nurturing communication, they may deprive themselves and their family members of desired intimacy. Vangelisti and Banski (1993) report that husbands' expressiveness and ability to self-disclose affect both husbands' and wives' relational satisfaction more than wives' ability to be open and expressive.

Wood and Inman (1993) challenge some of the research that finds women more effective in self-disclosure via more open, expressive communication, suggesting it privileges one type of intimacy. They indicate that male self-disclosure does not reduce stress as much as it does for females; men regard practical help, mutual assistance, and companionship as better benchmarks of caring. Wood (2001) captures the differences by suggesting that talk between women tends to be personal and disclosive, whereas men express closeness through action. These differences are carried out in family role behaviors. Mothers share more time with daughters in meal preparation and family care projects; fathers share more time with sons in doing home repairs, yard work, car upkeep, and shopping for these activities (Bryant & Zick, 1996). Same-sex couples, due to a lack of tradi-

unruience adut roles

Family
school
media

Sterotype -
rigid beliers
oversimplified &
over generalized about
the personality &
abilities of a person
based upon that
person's ... age/skin
color etc.

Role development involves observing and imitating role models.

tional marital role models, tend to negotiate each confict rather than rely on societal expectations or previous gender role models for their answers.

Today young adults live very different lives than many of their parents did, as this writer indicates here.

I recently received an e-mail from my son that reminded me of how his marriage is so different from ours. He wrote about his week as a "single parent" while his wife was in Los Angeles on business and how he survived the car pools and cooking. Their lifestyle amazes me, but I love to see Brian act as such a caring and active parent to their two sons.

Androgyny, or the capacity for either sex to be masculine and feminine in their behaviors, affects role performance and suggests that persons may be nurturing and assertive, strong and sensitive (Wood, 2001). Androgynous family members evaluate issues on their merits or demerits, without reference to the gender of the persons involved. The androgynous person is flexible, adaptive, and capable of being both instrumental (assertive, competent, forceful, and independent) and expressive (nurturing, warm, supportive, and compassionate) depending on the demands of the situation.

In general, androgynous married partners demonstrate more understanding of their spouses (Gunter & Gunter, 1990). They perceive emotional messages much more accurately and listen more empathetically (Invik & Fitzpatrick, 1982). Mott (1994) reports that parents who are less gender-typed in their own activities were less likely to gender-type activities for their children. This is especially true of single-parent mothers who need more kinds of help from their children (Brown & Mann, 1990).

Sometimes gender differences impact sexual communication. As indicated in the previous chapter, even in today's more open society, many communication breakdowns stem from an inability of couples to communicate honestly about their sexual relationship. Not only do couples have problems in their sexual communication with partners but they also have greater difficulties talking about sex with their children (Hutchinson & Cooney, 1998). Rules in their current system may inhibit adult discussion, which may result in frustration, anger, or confusion as noted in this example.

If there is anything I would wish for my daughter as she enters marriage, it would be the ability to talk to her husband about sex. It was unthinkable to me that men and women could really talk about what gave them pleasure in sexual activity. My husband and I spent years in troubled silence. It took an affair, a separation, and counseling for us to be able to begin to talk about our sexual life.

If a woman has inhibitions in being sexually assertive, it may prevent her from being active in meeting her needs, and it may block an empathic understanding of her needs. Thus, the circle of poor communication continues.

 Providing Nurturing and Support

In a family, members need mutual admiration, support, and reassurance. Transactionally, family happiness develops when each member meets the needs and expectations of the others. Children are socialized by parents and the community, which affects their future capability to be nurturing and supportive.

Nurturing Children This family function incorporates communication, since it is the chief process used to transmit parental caring, values, and a sense of community to the children. Through advice, directives, and answers to questions, children learn what parents and society expect of them. Until recently, mothers had greater amounts of contact with their children than fathers and were more likely to contribute to the nurturing process. Hochschild (1997) reports that women are opting for more overtime, having discovered "a great male secret" that the workplace is nurturing and it provides an escape from home pressures of needy kids, piles of unwashed clothes, and no leftovers in the refrigerator. Historically, children usually experienced their fathers as more distant, less empathic, and less caring, especially in verbal and nonverbal signs of love. However, some research indicates that "men's time in the family is increasing while women's is decreasing" (Pleck, 1992, p. 4). Perhaps these differences are due to the fact that men spend less time caring for children, regardless of their work schedules. One large study of men whose wives worked full time found that 75 percent of the women do the majority of the family chores (Kleiman, 1998). LaRossa (1998) cites evidence that men spend one-third the time that women do in one-on-one communication with children, and the same one-third ratio was found in a study of African American fathers (Ahmeduzzaman & Roopnarine, 1992).

Men are also less likely to be involved in nurturing children with special needs. Schock and colleagues (2002) report that fathers with children with mood disorders have more difficulty accepting the illness and are less likely to participate in therapy efforts. Mothers are more typically caregivers of children who have special needs.

Socialization for nurturing includes learning acceptable or unacceptable communication behaviors, such as yelling, lying, crying, hugging, directness, and silence. Nurturing messages vary across cultures; silence may be affirming in one and alienating in another. Sibling socialization is often overlooked, yet cross-cultural studies indicate the power of siblings in a child's learning of nurturing competence (Zukow, 1989).

In keeping with the bidirectional nature of family member influence, children can resist socialization messages. This frustrates parents, especially those in a rigid family system. Communication between parents can also become confused if the mother feels threatened when the father demonstrates to relatives and neighbors that he is capable of effective child care. It is important for children of either sex "to see their father share parenting responsibility so that society no longer idolizes motherhood and dismisses fatherhood" (Pickerd, 1998, p. 205). Likewise, the father can feel undermined in his providing role when the wife demonstrates her capabilities in a career and puts pressure on him to take more responsibility for the children (Zernike, 1998). Such struggles are communicated to children, leaving them confused.

The role of the father in the family after divorce, separation, or out-of-marriage birth is important. Maintaining supportive contact on significant child-related matters has beneficial consequences for the mother and children. Single fathers are more likely than married fathers to share breakfast, home activities, and outings with their children (Thomson, McLanahan, & Curtin, 1992).

Providing Support and Empathy   This function, sometimes called the therapeutic function, implies a willingness to listen to problems of another and provide emotional support. The listening must be empathic in order to give the other the understanding needed or the chance to ventilate pent-up feelings of rage, frustration, or exhaustion. This is a gift that may not be appreciated until a child becomes a parent.

My father's way is to be very calm and patient with his children. When he helped me with my homework, he would never leave until he knew I understood it completely. He would recall how hard it was to deal with math and science assignments. Now when I explain something, I try to see that my children understand because I remember the good feelings that I had when I finally understood my homework.

Empathy implies nonjudgmental understanding of what another family member is sharing. If the communication channels between family members encourage and permit the expression of open feelings, various individuals in the family can function therapeutically, which includes offering advice and questioning motives. Several important studies indicated not only how providing support and empathy is perceived by children, but how it affects them. Endres (1997) surmises that fathers create four special roles with daughters: the "Knight in Shining Armor" or dad on a pedestal; the "buddy" who sees his child as an equal and friend; the "authoritarian" who rules strictly and expects high standards of behavior; and the "shadow" who distances himself, avoiding activities with his daughter, especially communication. Daughters prefer the buddy type. A related study of father-son closeness reveals a tendency toward dissatisfaction with dads' communication skills, their resources to demonstrate empathy, and the amount of time that dads made available for communication (Fink, Buerkel-Rothfuss, & Buerkel, 1994). Another report examining mother-daughter communication from a dialectical perspective indicates that pronounced variation was on the autonomy–connection and openness–closedness dimensions (Pennington, 1997).

③ Providing for Individual Development

This role function includes those tasks that each individual must fulfill in order to become self-sufficient. Individuals must simultaneously seek to sustain a "sense of uniqueness from other relationships yet the sense of commonality with other relationships" (Baxter, 1990, p. 16). Family members who do not develop this role function can easily become dependent or enmeshed in the system. A "take care of me" attitude on the part of any member diminishes the wholeness and interdependence aspects of the family system.

Family members must facilitate each other's opportunities for self-discovery and talent development. Parents perform this function in their children's formative years, but from an early age, children influence one another's talents. Never underestimate how children in their play with one another develop the communication strategies they use in role situations. Peer group influence is receiving increased attention (Harris, 1998). In communication with children, it is very important that fathers bond with their children at an early age. Men who take family leaves when the children are young take a more active, involved role as the children grow older (Hochschild, 1997). In order to avoid enmeshment, family members need messages that support or encourage making individual choices. Recognition of members' ideas creates a context for valued independence.

4 Providing for Maintenance and Management

Kinship Maintenance One important maintenance function involves arranging kinship ties with the extended family network. Kinship involves sharing, participating in, and promoting the family's welfare as contacts are maintained with relatives and friends outside the family home. In short, it involves boundary management. The kinship maintenance function has direct implications for family communication because "kin-work" is the labor that enables families to endure over time (Stack & Burton, 1998). Whether one is included or excluded from family events or hears the latest family gossip signifies one's place within the family system. Kinship maintenance roles are shifting as more individual family members are using e-mail to stay in touch directly.

Holidays are a special time for kin-related family communication. In some families, particularly highly cohesive ones, attendance at get-togethers is mandatory, and only illness or great distances may be acceptable excuses. In some households, the events are painful, since "cut-off" members may be excluded, or members of low cohesive families may feel they are missing something. Stepfamilies must work to create their own rituals to provide members with a sense of identity. At holiday time, men and women share the tasks of calling, visiting, buying gifts, and attending events; women are more involved in sending cards.

Women do most of the communicating with relatives. Female partners do more of the relational maintenance; make greater use of the family kin network; and focus more energy on spending time both with friends and family (Ragsdale, 1996). Husbands maintain fewer kinship contacts with their relatives and actually have more contact with their wives' relatives (Stack & Burton, 1998). Stepfamily kinship ties are affected significantly by the attitudes of stepgrandparents; kinkeeping gender roles may change based on the new configurations (Crosbie-Burnett & McClintic, 2000). Almost all interactions with the kin are concentrated in three areas: visiting, recreation, and communication by letter, phone, e-mail, and instant messaging.

The single-parent and blended family systems encounter special kinship concerns. For example, in divorced families, there may be special problems in communication with the ex-spouse and his or her new family. One of the ex-partners may refuse to communicate with the other; children may become pawns and resent forced separations. On occasion, children lose active contact with an entire side of their family heritage.

Family networking also varies according to family-of-origin and ethnicity. For example, Puerto Rican men and women have equally strong relationships with their relatives. However, Puerto Rican men networked more with other persons outside their families, whereas the women formed their strongest relationship ties within families (Toro-Morn, 1998).

In Chicano cultures, godparents (compadrazgo) link families and communities through friends or authorities. Although often not relatives, godparents play key roles in religious activities, such as first communion, confirmation, and marriage. They also provide nurturing and financial aid when needed, as a moral obligation (Dill, 1998).

Because a family consists of persons who consider themselves to be a family, kinship ties often include extended family members bound together by caring, as noted here.

Since my immediate family is dead, and any other distant relatives on my husband's side or my side live thousands of miles away, we have worked at creating a local family. Over the years, we have developed close friends who serve as honorary aunts and uncles for the children. The highlight of our Christmas is our annual dinner when we all get together to decorate the tree and the children get to see Uncle Bernard or Aunt Lois within a family context. I feel closer to these people than I do to many of my blood relatives.

Such activities represent a special way to communicate the message that kinship is important. In this age in which families often live great distances from their kin or have few relatives, this idea has merit. When family members feel safe in sharing their problems, joys, and family celebrations, they reap the benefits of the kinship function.

Management of Daily Needs   Other role maintenance and management functions include decision making to facilitate housekeeping, child care, recreation, and taking care of family budgets, bills, income taxes, savings, and investments. Discussions about decision making occur in Chapter 8. Housekeeping and child-care aspects of family roles have been noted throughout previous sections. The changes in this area reflect active negotiation between partners, since most are creating a housekeeping system different from that in their families-of-origin. Changes in family structure through divorce creates a redefinition of roles tied to daily routines (Downs, Coleman, & Ganong, 2000).

Recreation management implies coordinating those things you do for relaxation, entertainment, or personal development. More husbands than wives value family recreation activities. Stereotypically, men have found a recreational niche in strong, masculine athletic behaviors (Townsend, 1998). Extremely cohesive families encourage much group activity, whereas low cohesion families may not. Parental behavior telegraphs to children what is appropriate recreational behavior, and conflicts may result if a child does not measure up. Most of you have heard parents yelling at a Little League umpire or at their 8-year-old batter who has struck out.

5 Providing Basic Resources

The current economic climate impacts families, forcing members to cope with economic pressures and stressful lifestyles. Traditionally, men were expected to be major providers in families, and laws and customs help to carry out these expectations. There have always been exceptions, especially African American women who are expected to have a job outside the house to contribute to the economic resources of the family (Caruthers, 1998). Today, as more couples share responsibility for providing resources, greater potential for shared power and decision making results.

Current literature on family roles often centers on terms that reflect the changing role of providing basic resources, such as *dual-career couples* and *dual-earner couples.* The type of career couple affects communication about roles. The term *dual-career couple* refers to a pair in which each pursues full-time career advancements. By contrast, in a *dual-earner couple,* both spouses work primarily for economic reasons. Researchers who study this area have described the merging of the roles as provider/worker and family member as "spillover." Although 25 years ago, spillover was conceptualized as how work demands spill over into family life (Kanter, 1977), today we think of spillover as bidirectional—family demands can also spillover into work life. Small and Riley's research (1990) enriches a perspective on the interface between work and family roles. They examined how work spillover affects four nonwork role contexts: the parent-child relationship, the couple or marital relationship, the use of leisure time for family activities, and the home management role. Barnett, Marshall, and Pleck's (1992) research on men's multiple roles and stress focuses on three key roles in men's lives: the job role, the marital role, and the parental role. The same roles and stresses exist in women's lives.

Managing the role identities of work and family can be viewed as a process of communication. Like the interactive perspective of roles explained earlier in the chapter, Golden (2002) suggests that couples create shared meanings of their roles as providers and caregivers through their communicative practices.

Stepfamilies often face conflicts when the stepparent may feel that he or she has lost control of resources that go toward the stepchildren. Single parents often feel that providing economic stability has become a primary role. Solo mothers tend to work longer hours and experience more stress and less emotional support than the other single parents (Gringlas & Weinraub, 1995).

Blumstein and Schwartz (1983) found that cohabiting couples regard money and work differently than do other couples. These varying perceptions influence the ways cohabiting couples negotiate differences and establish patterns and rules affecting their interaction. Cohabiting couples reported a stronger sense than married couples of each partner's contributing his or her share.

Cohabiting women view money as a way to achieve equality, and therefore they seek independence and want to avoid economic dependence. Cohabiting men expect economic equality more than married men. The cohabiting partner with the greater income determines more of the couple's recreational activities, including vacations. Cohabiting couples usually maintain separate checking accounts and when they do, they fight less about finances than do married couples.

These same researchers found that cohabitors believe that both partners should work and share housework. Yet, women do more of this work than men. Male cohabitors, more than married men, rank the relationship as more important than their job. Male cohabitors are also more competitive with their partners, although the partners' success or lack of it has less effect on the relationship. Cohabitors more frequently spend time on their own.

The Combined Functions

Each family combines the five role functions in unique ways. For example, in the Kondelis family, child rearing and child socialization may no longer be important functions, although recreation may be highly valued and organized by the husband/father. If finances permit, some housekeeping functions may be provided by a cleaning service, whereas providing may be done by both husband and wife. In the Rosenthal family, the single mother may engage primarily in the providing and therapeutic functions, partially delegating child care and socialization functions to the two older children. Recreation may be more individually oriented, while kinship functions may receive limited attention. In some single-parent, dual-career, or dual-earner families, children may be required to engage in a type or amount of activity such as sibling supervision or meal preparation, usually reserved for a spouse. For example, an older child may assume total child-care or housekeeping responsibilities in a busy dual-career household. In a single-parent system, children may be expected to provide therapeutic listening that might be expected of a spouse in a two-parent household.

ROLE APPROPRIATION

The key question remains: How do family members learn, demonstrate, adjust, or relinquish these role functions? The answer requires an understanding of the three aspects of role appropriation. *Role appropriations*

can be seen as a three-part overlapping process involving role expectation, role enactment, and role negotiation (Stamp, 1994). Issues of role conflict also emerge. Each of these will be explored in the following section.

Role Expectations

Society provides models and norms for how certain family roles should be assumed, thus creating role expectations. Look at any newsstand and you will see articles on how to be a good parent, grandparent, or stepparent. Television has provided many family role models through specials, situation comedies, or talk-show hosts. Advertising reinforces stereotypes of how family members should act.

Daily life within a community also serves as a source of role expectations. When you were growing up, the neighbors and your friends all knew who were the "good" mothers or the "bad" kids on the block or in the community. Religious leaders or school leaders set expectations for how family members should behave. Each of you has grown up with expectations of how people should function in family roles, just as this example shows.

My mother grew up on a ranch in the Great Uinta Basin in Utah. The women in her family were extremely strong and used to doing "men's work." Again, whatever had to be done would be done by whoever was available. It didn't matter whether one was a girl or boy—all hands were necessary and looked upon as being equal in her family.

Cultural groups convey beliefs about parenting or spousal roles, which are learned by members of their community. For example, in the Jewish tradition, the role of mother is associated with the transmission of culture and, as such, carries a particular significance and implies certain expectations. In a comparative study with Anglo children, Mexican American children described fathers significantly more as rule makers, but sensed both mothers and fathers as rule enforcers (Jaramillo & Zapata, 1987). In their study of middle-aged and older African American women, Blee and Tickamyer (1995) report a strong expectation of dual parenting and providing. Toro-Morn's (1998) study of Puerto Rican women in Chicago indicates that families reluctantly accept the mother working, hopefully temporarily. If she works, the home duties of cooking, cleaning, and child care also are hers to maintain.

In addition, role expectations also arise from significant others and complementary others. *Significant others* are those persons you view as important and who provide you with models from which you develop role expectations. A favorite teacher who combined a career with a family, or a close friend who succeeded as a trial attorney while she raised three children as a single parent may influence your role choices. Thus, part of learning roles occurs by observing and imitating *role models*, persons whose behavior serves as a guide for others (Golden, 1997).

Complementary others are those who fulfill reciprocal role functions that directly impact on your role. During early stages of romantic relationships, men and women spend long periods of time discussing their expectations for a future spouse. "I want my wife to be home with the children until they go to school" or "I need a husband who will help parent my children from my first marriage." A future stepparent may try to explore expectations with a future stepchild; a parent and college-aged child may discuss expectations for their interaction during summer vacations.

When one parent leaves the family system, the other parent may expect a child to fulfill an emotional role of confidant or a task role of household helper. "You're the man of the house now" typifies this lowering of boundaries between parent and child subsystems and often results in communication breakdowns. This may place great pressure on the child, alienate the child from other siblings, and eventually interfere with the normal process of separating from the family at the appropriate developmental point.

Dual-career families face constant role negotiation.

Additional expectations come from each person's self-understanding. You may find that you relied on a role model or you decided that with your skills or personality you would like to be a certain kind of partner or parent. Sometimes one's role expectations clash with those of significant others, as this man reports.

Colleen and I have arguments with our parents. They expect us to produce grandchildren, but neither of us wants the responsibility of children. It has taken each of us over a decade to finish our education by paying for it on our own and working full time. We love our dog, but that doesn't guarantee we would be nurturing parents!

Role expectations are influenced by an imaginative view of yourself—the way you like to think of yourself being and acting. A father may imagine himself telling his child about the facts of life. A teenager may imagine lecturing a younger sibling on drug use. Such imaginings are not just daydreams; they serve as a rehearsal for actual performance. No matter what you imagine, until you enact your role with others, you are dealing with role expectations.

Role Enactment

Role enactment, sometimes called *role performance,* is the actual interactive behavior that defines how the role is enacted. As with role expectations, role performance is influenced by the individual's capacity for enacting the role.

Persons in complementary or opposing roles have direct bearing on how you enact your role. Have you ever tried to reason with a parent who sulks, pamper an independent grandparent, or correct a willful child? However, if two complementary persons see things in similar ways, it enhances role performance. College students who believe that they should no longer have to answer for their evening whereabouts will be reinforced by parents who no longer ask. Thus, the way others assume their roles and comment on your role affects how you enact your role.

Additionally, your background influences your behavior. For example, if certain communication behaviors are not part of your repertoire, they cannot magically appear in a particular situation. A father may wish he could talk with his son instead of yelling at him or giving orders, but he may not know how to discuss controversial subjects with his child. Self-confidence in attempting to fulfill a role may affect behavior. A shy stepmother may not be able to express affection either verbally or nonverbally with her new stepchildren for many months. On occasion, people discover that they can function well in a role they did not expect or desire, as this woman discovered.

I was really furious when my husband quit his sales job to finish his degree. I didn't choose the role of provider and I didn't like being conscripted into it. But after a while, I got to feeling very professional and adult. Here I was supporting myself and a husband. I didn't know I had it in me.

When trying to enact both work and family roles, husbands' and wives' experiences may be somewhat different. Among a predominantly working-class sample, where husbands average about twice as many hours than their wives at work, women's sense of balance between their work and family roles was dependent on their gender ideology. Women who had a more traditional gender ideology perceived more balance in their roles than women who had a less traditional gender ideology, but men's gender ideology did not affect their sense of balance between work and family roles (Marks, Huston, Johnson, & MacDermid, 2001).

Choosing to enact one role may affect a person's ability to enact other roles as well. Hewlett (2002) studied how women who are highly educated and in the top 10 percent of earning power have enacted roles in their lives. At age 40, one-third of these women were childless, most not by choice. Instead, enacting the very demanding role of a consultant, lawyer, doctor, or other profession left these women with very little time to pursue relationships. In fact, Hewlett found that the more successful these women are in their careers, the less likely they are to have a partner or children. For male professionals, however, the opposite is true. The more successful they are in their careers, the more likely they are to be married with children.

Occasionally, there are no role models for a particular role. For example, gay men and lesbian partners may not have had a role model, as those in an older generation may have chosen invisibility.

Role Negotiation

As individuals confront their roles, they experience a process whereby, in conjunction with others, they structure their reality and give meaning to their lives. This is called *role negotiation*. In describing the move to parenthood, Stamp (1994) concludes that when couples become parents, "their ongoing conversation constructs, monitors, and modifies the new reality of their changed existence. Their new roles are appropriated into their overall identities" (p. 91). This critical use of conversation applies to assuming and maintaining any family role.

Once a role is assumed, the process of role enactment usually involves negotiation with those in related roles. This may involve reconstructing differences and exploring new ways to act regarding certain expectations. Stamp ties the openness–closedness dialectic to new parent role negotiation and emphasizes quality of commitment and provides no guarantee that the couple will experience greater marital satisfaction.

Frequently, role negotiation involves managing interpersonal conflict when members attempt to work out their roles. Individuals may know what is expected of them in a family, but not all members perform the expected behaviors. For example, a husband may relinquish the provider function by deciding to write "the great American novel" or by suffering a fall that prevents him from returning to work, or by being laid off. Consequently, his wife may be thrust into providing for the family, which results in potential conflict. When this happens, the organizational structure in the system changes; a new kind of interdependence must evolve. For instance, in career choices more men refuse to move to accommodate their wives. Seventy percent of women would pack up and move; only 14 percent said they would refuse. Thirty-four percent of the men said they would not move for a wife's career (Weldon, 1997a).

In a study of 90 low-income noncustodial fathers, half of whom had been imprisoned and half of whom had criminal histories, Edin, Nelson, and Paranal (2001) found that fathers with damaged family bonds before imprisonment used prison time as an opportunity to turn their lives around and reconnect to their children—a strong role re-negotiation.

Clearly, many areas of potential conflicts over roles are evident. When complementary or significant others have different expectations of the way a person should be performing a role, conflict occurs. A child or adolescent may expect far more nurturing from a parent and complain about the lack of emphasis on it. If the wife refuses to work outside the home, then the husband feels all the responsibility is unfairly his. Swanson (1992) writes of men being treated as "success objects" who must provide well for their families or else lose respect. In order to rearrange roles over time, negotiation is critical.

Such conflict over roles may happen when a divorced parent remarries, bringing a stepparent into the family system. Papernow (1984) describes a healthy stepparent role in this way:

> (a) The role does not usurp or compete with the biological parent of the same sex; (b) the role includes an intergenerational boundary between stepparent and child; (c) the role is sanctioned by the rest of the stepfamily, particularly the spouse; (d) the role incorporates the special qualities this stepparent brings to this family. (p. 361)

Role conflict also occurs when a family member is trying to enact more than one role at the same time that seem to be incompatible with each other or difficult to enact together. You have probably seen or experienced examples of role conflict in your family. For instance, a 14-year-old boy who finds out that his 17-year-old sister is sneaking out of the house at night might experience role conflict between his role as the dependable son that would tell his parents, and his role as a sibling who wants his sister's approval. Frequently, grandparents who, by necessity, assume parental roles experience role conflict. Most report viewing support groups as beneficial to this role (Smith, Savage-Stevens, & Fabian, 2002).

Hochschild's (1989) influential book on work-family issues introduced the idea of "the second shift," suggesting that married women work at taking care of house and children after putting in a full day's work on the job. In order to negotiate the role conflict that occurs from being both a provider and primary homemaker, Hochschild (1989) described how one woman would make her own meals, but not her husband's. Another woman gave up on keeping the house clean. Other families find more functional ways to negotiate these role conflicts.

Feelings for the other person may affect the extent to which conflict occurs. A parent may react differently to each child by basing his or her actions on the child's behavior. Conflict results when individuals struggle to maintain roles that are not appropriate to their ages or relationships.

As the oldest daughter, I ended up with a great number of responsibilities and feel as if I lost a part of my own childhood. My mother was an alcoholic and my father and I almost become the "adult partners" in the house. He expected me to take care of the younger kids and to fix meals when Mom was "drying out." I hated all the work I had to do and all the responsibility. He didn't even want me to get married because he didn't know how he would cope.

Sometimes family members build in time to discuss roles. Couples who take time to debrief and share work experiences greatly increase their relational satisfaction (Vangelisti & Banski, 1993). Certainly, increasing each partner's sense of worth would affect his or her role performance and lessen conflicts.

As you will see in later chapters, predictable and unpredictable life crises affect the roles you assume and how you function in them. Unforeseen circumstances may alter life in such a way that roles change drastically from those first planned or enacted. The next section explains how couples and families can be categorized into types depending on their role behavior.

COUPLE AND FAMILY TYPOLOGIES

Couple or family typologies represent another way to explore how roles develop through family interaction. Many family researchers and therapists believe family behavior and organization can be classified into various typologies, depending on the patterns of the interactions. Typologies are useful to researchers and students of family communication because they help bring order to phenomena studied in family communication. We will discuss three couple typologies and two family typologies.

Couple-Oriented Typologies

Fitzpatrick's Couple Types The most extensive work done in classifying couple types is found in Fitzpatrick's research (Fitzpatrick, Fallis, & Vance, 1982; Noller & Fitzpatrick, 1993; Fitzpatrick & Badzinski, 1994). In her early work, Fitzpatrick (1977, 1988) tested a large number of characteristics to find out which made a difference in maintaining couple relationships. She isolated eight significant factors that affect role enactment: (1) conflict avoidance, (2) assertiveness, (3) sharing, (4) the ideology of traditionalism, (5) the ideology of uncertainty and change, (6) temporal (time) regularity, (7) undifferentiated space, and (8) autonomy. All eight affect role enactment. Fitzpatrick designated three couple types called traditionals, separates, and independents. She also found six mixed couple types wherein the husband and wife described their relationship differently. She found that 20 percent are traditionals, 17 percent are separates, and 22 percent are independents (1988). Thus, about 60 percent can be classified as pure types and 40 percent as mixed.

Independent types accept uncertainty and change. They pay limited attention to schedules and traditional values. Independents represent the most autonomous of the types but do considerable sharing and negotiate autonomy. Independents are more likely to conflict and to support an androgynous, flexible sex role (Fitzpatrick, 1988).

Separates differ from independents in greater conflict avoidance, more differentiated space needs, fairly regular schedules, and less sharing. In relationships, separates maintain a distance from people, even their spouses. They experience little sense of togetherness or autonomy. Separates usually oppose an androgynous sexual orientation and tend to avoid conflict (Fitzpatrick, 1988).

Traditionals uphold a fairly conventional belief system and resist change or uncertainty because it threatens their routines. This leads to a high degree of interdependence and low autonomy. They will engage in conflict but would rather avoid it. Traditionals, like separates, demonstrate strong sex-typed roles and oppose an androgynous orientation (Fitzpatrick, 1988).

The other six mixed types (approximately 40 percent), which have the husband designated by the first term, are traditional/separate separate/traditional, independent/separate, separate/independent, traditional/independent, and independent/traditional (Fitzpatrick, 1988). These are not a category of "leftovers," but represent many different family systems (Fitzpatrick & Ritchie, 1994).

Which relational type experiences the greater satisfaction? Which couples are the most cohesive? The answers follow and have implications for role enactment. In their summary of the research, Fitzpatrick and Best (1979) reported that traditional couples were significantly higher than separate, independent, or mixed-type couples on consensus, cohesion, relational satisfaction, and expressing affection. Independents were lower on consensus, open affection to one another, and dyadic satisfaction. However, their lack of agreement on issues regarding dyadic interactions did not impair their cohesiveness. Separates were the least cohesive, but on relational issues appeared high on consensus. Separates demonstrated few expressions of affection toward their spouses and rated lower on dyadic satisfaction. In the separate/traditional category, couples had low consensus on a number of relational issues, but they were moderately cohesive. These couples claimed high satisfaction for their relationship and outwardly expressed much affection (Noller & Fitzpatrick, 1993).

Table 7.1 summarizes the ways in which couple types responded to a variety of relationship measures, including sex roles and gender perceptions. In predicting communication, you might expect that traditional families would demonstrate affection and sharing of the role functions discussed earlier in this chapter, with males and females remaining in defined positions. You could expect male dominance in attitudes and values regarding the providing, recreational, housekeeping, sex, and kinship functions, since the traditional type resists change. Because independents are more open to change, they might be more open to dual-career marriages and sharing the providing and housekeeping functions. Because independents value autonomy and avoid interdependence, individual partners may be freer in their role functions.

The potential for problems when communicating about role functions relates especially to the separates who have not resolved the interdependence/autonomy issue in their marriage. Fitzpatrick uses the label "emotionally divorced" for this type, because separates are least likely to express their feelings to their partners. Baxter (1991), in her explorations of dialectical theory, suggests that Fitzpatrick's traditionals privilege continuity over discontinuity, with independents privileging change over continuity, with separates somewhere in the middle.

Hochschild's Marital Ideology Role Types   Hochschild's research on working mothers revealed three types of marital roles for dual-career and dual-earner couples: traditional, egalitarian, and transitional.

TABLE 7.1   Couple Type Differences on Relational Measures

Couple Types	Marital Satisfaction	Cohesion	Consensus	Affectional Expression	Sex Roles	Psychological Gender States (Wives Only)
Traditionals	High	High	High	Moderately high	Conventional	Feminine
Independents	Low	Moderately high	Low	Low	Nonconventional	Sex-typed androgynous
Separates	Low	Low	Moderately high	Low	Conventional	Feminine sex-typed
Separates/ Traditionals	Moderately high	Moderately high	Moderately high	High	Conventional	Feminine sex-typed
Other mixed types	Moderately high	Low	Low	Moderately high	Depends on mixed type	Depends on mixed type

Women in *traditional* couples may work, but they see themselves primarily as mothers and community members and want their husbands to identify primarily with work. Husbands in traditional couples base their identities on their work and expect their wives to manage the home.

The *transitional* husband and wife see the husband's identity as the provider. The wife identifies with home management as a role, although she also wishes to identify with her work. Transitional husbands don't mind that their wives work, but also expect them to take most of the home responsibility.

In an *egalitarian* marriage, both partners wish to jointly share home responsibilities as well as take advantage of career opportunities. Power is to be shared and each partner strives to maintain a life balance between career and family, while supporting the other in this effort. The way egalitarians accomplish this may differ from couple to couple. Some might want the couple to place the most emphasis on the home or on work, whereas others expect both spouses to put joint emphasis on work and home.

As with Fitzpatrick's marital types, husbands and wives may be mixed in their types—for example, a traditionalist husband and a transitionalist wife. Hochschild (1989) also found that both husbands and wives may say one thing about their roles, yet act as if they feel another way. An example of this would be a husband who says he is egalitarian, but he expects his wife to stay home with the children each night while he goes out with his buddies because he earns more money than she does.

Hochschild's (1989) role types are not based on communication processes, yet understanding these types may be helpful when trying to understand marital communication. A dual-earner couple might argue frequently about who does the grocery shopping. To understand why they argue, it could be important to understand their gender ideology types. Perhaps the wife has an egalitarian ideology, believing that each spouse should take turns, but her transitionalist husband views grocery shopping as the wife's responsibility. Examining the couple's family-of-origin gender ideologies might also help to explain their behavior.

Gottman's Conflict Types   Gottman classifies his couple types according to the style of the conflict interactions. The couple types are validating, volatile, and conflict avoiders. He found that lasting marriages existed in all three types, if a "magic ratio" of five positive interactions to one negative interaction developed over time (1994a). In the *validating* type, partners respect one another's point of view on a variety of topics and, when they disagree, they try to work out a compromise. This type agrees on most basic issues of sex, money, religion, and children. When they disagree about roles, they listen to one another and refrain from shouting or "hitting below the belt." The *volatile* type of couple is comfortable with disagreement and lack of harmony. Any question over roles and who does what and when leads to open conflict. They don't fight fairly, but they fight often. It tends to energize the relationship. The third type, *conflict avoiders*, abhors negative messages and goes to any length to lessen potential conflicts. Partners placate and please one another rather than meet their own needs. They walk away from arguments, often giving family members the silent treatment. They are comfortable with standoffs, and uncomfortable with rage or protest. Gottman and colleagues (2002) capture the communication differences, suggesting that volatile couples are high on immediate persuasion attempts and low on listening or validation before persuading. Validating couples listen efficiently and reflect feelings before persuading. Conflict-avoidant couples avoid persuasive attempts.

Family Typologies

Family Communication Patterns   Although people often talk in general terms about the patterns of communication in a family, a typology based on specific types of family communication patterns also exists. This typology of family communication patterns is designed using two types of communication labeled conformity orientation and conversation orientation (Koerner & Fitzpatrick, 1997). Families may use one of these orientations or may be divided by members who use one while others prefer the opposite. A family high on *conformity* expresses similar values and attitudes that enhance harmony. A family low on conformity expresses more varied values, attitudes, and patterns of interaction. It upholds individuality and brings out the unique personalities of family members. Family members high on the use of *conversation* require an open family system so that individuals can speak their minds easily on a whole range of conflict issues with little fear of what they say. Families low on this dimension speak out less frequently on fewer conflict issues.

These family communication patterns also relate to Fitzpatrick's marital types discussed earlier in this chapter. A study that examined perceptions of both parents and one child found that in families with traditional, separate, and separate/traditional couples, the family members perceived that they were high on conformity orientation. In families with independent and traditional couples, the family members viewed themselves as having a high conversation orientation (Fitzpatrick & Ritchie, 1994).

Fitzpatrick and Ritchie (1994) describe four different kinds of families (consensual, pluralistic, protective, and laissez-faire) based on the family's use of either a conformity or conversation orientation in their interactions (see Figure 7.2). *Consensual families* are high in both conversation and conformity strategies with their communication characterized by pressure for agreement, although children are encouraged to express ideas and feelings. *Pluralistic families,* high in conversation orientation and low in conformity, have open communication and emotional supportiveness in their families. *Protective families* rank low on the use of a conversational approach and high on conformity dimensions. They stress upholding family rules and avoiding conflict. *Laissez-faire families,* low on both conformity and conversation dimensions, interact very little. In this kind of family, children may look outside the family for influence and support.

Differences also exist among family types in the motives parents have for talking to children. For example, in the two family types that are marked by a high conversation orientation (consensual and pluralistic), parents have relational motives for talking with their children, such as for pleasure or relaxation or to show affection. In the protective family types, parents are motivated to communicate with their children to seek control, although these parents also report affection as one reason they communicate with their children (Barbato et al., 2001).

It is important to think about family communication patterns and types from a transactional perspective, as family communication patterns are developed through interaction between family members. Communication from parents and adolescents affects both perceptions of family communication patterns (Saphir & Chaffee, 2002).

FIGURE 7.2   Family Types Based on Family Communication Patterns

	High Conversation Orientation	*Low Conversation Orientation*
High Conformity Orientation	Consensual	Protective
Low Conformity Orientation	Pluralistic	Laissez-faire

Closed, Open, and Random Types Kantor and Lehr's work, *Inside the Family* (1976), serves as the touchstone study of family types. As a means of dealing with the basic family issue of separateness and connectedness, or what Kantor and Lehr call "distance regulation," they developed a six-dimensional social space grid on which family communication takes place.

All communication represents efforts by family members to gain access to targets—that is, things or ideas members want or need. Specifically, family members use two sets of dimensions. One set reaches targets of (1) affect, (2) power, and (3) meaning through the way they regulate the other set, the access dimensions of (4) space, (5) time, and (6) energy. In carrying out the functions in any role, all family members have a target or goal of gaining some degree of affect, power, or meaning. *Affect* means achieving some kind of intimacy or connectedness with the members of the family and receiving some reward in the form of nurturing behavior in their verbal and nonverbal communication. *Power* implies that a member has the independence to select what he or she wants and the ability to get the desired money, skills, or goods. The third target is *meaning*. Each family member in the system seeks some philosophical rationale that offers reasons for what happens to them in the family and the outside world. When family members collectively find meaning in their interactions, cohesion develops.

Kantor and Lehr provide descriptions of the access dimensions (space, time, and energy) from an analogical as well as physical point of view. The *spatial* dimensions include the way a family handles its physical surroundings (exterior and interior) and the ways in which the members' communication regulates their psychological distance from each other. The *time* dimension includes a consideration of clock time and calendar time in order to understand a family's basic rhythmic patterns. The *energy* dimension deals with the storing and expending of physical and psychological energy. Each of these dimensions would affect role enactment because they regulate behavior. Family communication usually involves at least one access dimension and one target dimension. For example, a wife moves physically closer (space) to her husband in order to gain more affection (target) from him.

Using these six dimensions, Kantor and Lehr created a typology for viewing families, consisting of closed, open, and random types, acknowledging that actual families may consist of mixtures of types. The ways in which these three family types maintain their boundaries, or regulate distance through access and target dimensions, account for their differences in role enactment.

Closed families tend to regulate functions predictably with fixed boundaries. Such families interact less with the outside world. They require members to fulfill their needs and spend their time and energies within the family. Events in closed families tend to be tightly scheduled and predictable.

In the *open family,* boundaries tend to remain flexible when members are encouraged to seek experiences in the outside space and return to the family with ideas the family may use if group consensus develops. Open families seldom use censorship, force, or coercion because they believe family goals will vary, change, and be subject to negotiation. Members are more likely to concern themselves with the present, while energy is quite flexible.

Unpredictability and "do-your-own-thing" aptly describe the *random family.* The boundaries of space surrounding this family are dispersed. Family members and outsiders join in the living space based on interest or desire, or they voluntarily separate from one another without censure. Social appropriateness holds little importance for such members. Time is spent on an irregular basis. Energy in the random family fluctuates. The following example illustrates a random family.

I am next to last of 11 children, and by the time I came along, the family was in chaos. The younger kids lived with different relatives off and on until we were almost adolescents. When we did live at home, things were always unpredictable. Every morning my mother would put a big pot of cereal on the stove and people would eat when they wanted. You never knew exactly who was going to be sleeping where each night. When I was about 10, my parents got their own lives straightened out and enough older kids were gone so that we could live a more "normal" life, although I found it hard to suddenly have rules that were enforced and times when I had to be places.

Table 7.2 summarizes the characteristics that Kantor and Lehr delineated for each of these family types. You may identify more closely with one of the types, or you may find that your family incorporates two of the types. You may also realize your family has shifted in typology over the years. In Figure 7.3 we present a case study of three family types. Which one or combination describes your family?

A speculative comparison can be made between Fitzpatrick's and Kantor and Lehr's research. Olson's circumplex model of cohesion and adaptability can also be integrated into their thinking. The terminology each theorist uses can be clarified by remembering that Fitzpatrick's autonomy/interdependence is similar to Olson's cohesion dimension and Kantor and Lehr's affect dimension. Adaptability as used by Olson is similar to power (measured behaviorally) in Fitzpatrick and Kantor and Lehr. Fitzpatrick's ideology refers to meaning in Kantor and Lehr's

TABLE 7.2   Characteristics of Family Types

Type of Family	Use of Space	Use of Time	Use of Energy
Closed	Fixed	Regular	Steady
Open	Movable	Variable	Flexible
Random	Dispersed	Irregular	Fluctuating

thinking but does not appear in Olson's work. Communication is included in the behavioral data collected by Fitzpatrick. In Olson's research, communication appears as an enabling dimension, and as distance regulation in Kantor and Lehr's study. Whatever the family or couple type, adults use communication strategies in their various roles that maintain their type.

FIGURE 7.3   Examples of Closed, Open, and Random Families

The Closed Family: The Ward Family

Life in the seven-person Ward family is structured and predictable. Jack Ward and Lillian Ward have been married for three years. Jack was widowed for four years and brought 6-year-old twins to the stepfamily. Lillian was divorced at a young age and had three children aged 4, 7, and 9 at the time of the marriage. Her former husband has little involvement with the children. Jack and Lillian are the heads of the household and believe that family discipline is a training ground for achievement at school and financial success. Together Jack and Lillian have built a strong boundary around the marriage and family. Decisions are made at the parental level, usually announced by Jack. What the parents usually share about their private lives is revealed as a lesson to their children. Clearly, they are parents with a capital P.

In the Ward family, strong emotions are rarely expressed in public and affection is reserved for the appropriate time and place. Strong conflict is discouraged; polite disagreement is acceptable.

The Ward's family themes might be expressed as follows: "Be strong, self-sufficient, and stick together" and "The family comes first." Discipline is rigorously enforced throughout the family. Failure to carry out responsibilities at any level result in a loss of privileges. The strong boundaries keep friends at a distance.

Traditions are prized in this family. Holidays involve only family members who participate in predictable rituals designed to bond the members. These are times for storytelling, praying, and being together without interference.

The Open Family: The Parker Family

Events frequently take place at the last minute in the Parker household, which consists of four members—Doris Parker and her three children aged 8, 11, and 14. Doris's work pattern is one of taking it somewhat easy on a project and then launching a big, all-night push as her deadline nears. Her office work covers a desk at home, since she often works there to finish big projects. She is frequently behind schedule due to all her commitments. Somehow key tasks are eventually done before it is absolutely too late. Doris's tardiness is not due to laziness or lack of energy; rather, it comes about because she has so much to do. The children all have responsibilities but exceptions are made around school or religious group activities.

Friends and guests are frequently brought home by both mother and children. People may drop in or telephone at any time of the day or evening without feeling uncomfortable. Every once in a while a family member declares a need for "just us" together time, a request that is always honored. For the Parker family, there is no such thing as an absolute answer to the problems that arise. There are, however, certain points of view that members generally hold to be true, one being that safety and respect for family members are critical. Decisions are group projects. The Parker family members express their affection and their differences openly and often loudly. A key theme is: "The family must be free to fight and to love!"

Members enjoy being together for holidays and birthdays, but special circumstances are recognized. Other options may be negotiated but the centrality of the family must be respected.

The Random Family: The Connor Family

Life in the five-person Connor household is sparked by multiple projects, planned and spontaneous. "Go with the flow" is the byword in the household, which is formed by Mary and David, married for 19 years, and their two teenaged girls, Maggie and Michelle. Friends drop in at any time, often staying a few days or weeks, without much fuss or attention. In spite of their preference for spontaneity, the Connors are committed to huge holiday events, but rarely celebrate them in the same way from one year to another. Members are never sure who will be present or what the event will entail; there are few rituals, since repetition is not valued.

The Connor household is likely to be as cluttered with objects as it is with people. The hallway is typically strewn with clothes and the desks are piled up because the Connors are too preoccupied to take the time to tidy up routinely. The clutter is not of great significance. Clearly, it is more important that a developing school art project sits in the middle of the kitchen table than it is to impress visitors with order.

Each member complains that mealtimes do not provide a greater opportunity for emotional sharing and closeness. Yet, having a regular mealtime would interfere with each one's freedom. Therefore, the Connors often find themselves unable to ensure regular emotional connectedness. Closeness and intimacy do occur, but they occur spontaneously. When people see each other, great affection may be shared, or great conflicts may occur, if both parties are tuned in to each other. "Doing your own thing" and "Be yourself," within reasonable standards of ethics and safety, serve as the themes for this unpredictable family system.

Conclusion

This chapter took an interactive approach to roles, stressing the effect of family interaction on role performance. The distinction between position-oriented and person-oriented roles was developed and applied to communication. The five role functions were presented in a mobile model and explained with more emphasis placed on those roles that require more communication strategies. The development of roles takes part in a three-step process—role expectation, role enactment, and role negotiation—each of which have communication components.

Finally, the couple and family typologies, with their predictability, are viewed as sources for understanding the communication that helps to carry out role functions. A major consideration in examining roles or couple/family types is their dynamic nature, which is viewed in accordance with the personal developments and unpredictable circumstances faced by the people involved.

In Review

1. Discuss what you think will happen to roles in families by the year 2025. What directions do you see families taking in the future?

2. Compare and contrast the communication tasks required in carrying out the role functions involved in providing resources and nurturance for the family. Describe these functions in a family with which you are familiar.

3. Identify a real or fictional family that has changed over time. Note the role changes and give your reasons for these changes. What has been the effect on the system?

4. Give examples of partners you know that fit Fitzpatrick's couple types. Describe the sample communication strategies that they use.

5. Using one of the family typologies for roles (for example, Fitzpatrick's, Hochschild's, or Gottman's), analyze your family or another real or fictional family and explain how it fits or doesn't fit the type. Cite examples of communication patterns.

POWER, INFLUENCE, and DECISION MAKING

So children learn about power not just from what their parents try to teach them but also from observing their parents' interactions with them, with each other, and with other persons inside and outside the family. They learn, through trial and error and through example, which power strategies work, which ones are acceptable, and what they can get away with.

Hilary M. Lips, *Women, Men, and Power*

Who do you ask for permission to skip a family reunion? When trying to influence a sibling, do you offer to do a favor in return for another favor? When making a decision, does all your family sit down together and discuss the issue or does one member make the decision and the rest go along with it? How have these responses changed over the years? The answers to these questions tell you something about power, influence, and decision making in your family—concepts that we address in this chapter.

As you probably realize, the concepts of power, influence, and decision making are intertwined. A mother may use her parental authority as a type of power in trying to influence her teenage daughter to clean her room by saying, "You will do it because I told you to, and I'm your mother!" The Jamison family's decision to go to Disney World for their summer vacation may be the result of 10-year-old Ben's persistent attempts to influence his parents and sisters. TV dad Max Bickford (CBS's *The Education of Max Bickford*) used the fact that he had paid a $400 fee for his son's martial arts class as the reason behind his decision that the son couldn't quit the class.

However, despite how closely these concepts are tied together, they are unique enough that they deserve individual treatment. Family members use different types of power in a family, thus one family member's power does not always result in winning influence or having decisions made in the way that he or she wants. As you read this chapter, think of the ways in which power, influence, and decision making have played out in families that you have observed.

POWER

Each family member exercises a certain degree of power in order to have some control over his or her life. It is almost impossible to be a vital family member without becoming involved in power negotiations, positive or negative, overt or subtle. "Leave me alone," "It doesn't matter that much," "Why should I be the one to change?" and other such messages indicate how ingrained power issues are in family situations. The use of power produces changes that either improve or hinder family members' satisfaction. The feeling of having no power over family members is usually unbearable, but it is also undesirable to be too openly aggressive in making power plays (Green & Elffers, 1998).

Power operates transactionally in a family. It does not belong to an individual; rather, it is a property of a relationship between two or more persons. From a dialectical perspective, we define *power* by the way it is used to reduce or increase tensions when individual family members interact with each other over goals or attempts to change behaviors. This dynamic perspective emphasizes change and flux. The exercise of power becomes an important factor in regulating relational tensions between closeness and distance.

Every power maneuver has a systemwide effect. As one or more members exert power or respond to others' power moves, the whole system recalibrates itself. The system, through its adaptability mechanisms, reacts to all pressures and rebalances to respond to the power plays and players.

Power also affects perception and behavior. The way in which one family member perceives the power dynamics helps to determine and explain the reasons for that member's actions. The same power issue may be perceived differently by every other member. Montgomery (1992) notes how couples imitate other couples, and thus coordinate their relationship with a larger social order. Couples use their knowlege of how power operates within their culture to inform them about power in their own family. In the following example, a student explains how one family member attempts to seize power.

When my parents separated and Dad left the house, my domineering grand-mother became the ruling force. My mother would go along, out of respect for her age, even though she would disagree many times and secretly do what she wanted. Grandma would yell and scream if something wasn't done the way she wanted. We had no voice in her rulings. Each of us left home sooner than we might have in order to escape her domination.

The power dimension in a family system may vary greatly over time, depending on a host of factors, such as family structure, developmental stages, transitions, stresses, and the family's economic, cultural, or intellectual resources. Because the values, histories, and current socioeconomic factors of ethnic groups are different from the dominant white culture, family power processes may operate differently (Walker, 1993). One cannot assume that most African American, Hispanic, or Asian families exercise power in similar ways.

In order to begin to understand the complexity of power and its communication dynamics within family systems, you need to examine the aspects of power that impact family systems, the development of power in family systems, and how communication and power affect each other in family systems.

Aspects of Power in Family Systems

Power can be conceptualized as having various aspects. McDonald (1980) conceptualizes power to include three important aspects, all of which affect communication: (1) power bases, (2) power processes, and (3) power outcomes.

 Power Bases The bases of family power are resources used by family members to increase their chances of exerting control in a specific situation. Resources consist of whatever is perceived as rewarding to an individual or a relationship; it is anything that one partner makes available to the other to satisfy needs or attain goals.

McDonald's (1980) five resources serve as bases from which persons may derive power. They include normative, economic, affective, personal, and cognitive resources.

1. *Normative resources* refer to the family's values and to the cultural or societal definitions of where the authority lies. Normative definitions represent the culturally internalized expectations of what the family relationships should be—the perceived role ex-

power base - 1st us FOO.

pectations and obligations of members. For example, some families' norms require that the mother have the power in managing the children's day-to-day activities.

2. *Economic resources* refer to the monetary control exerted by the breadwinner and/or persons designated to make financial decisions. Economic power comes from wages earned and money saved or inherited. In some families, a breadwinning father may refer to the household income as "my money."

3. *Affective resources,* related to relational currencies, reflect who in the family nurtures others and how each member in the family meets his or her needs for feeling loved or belonging to the system. For instance, a mother may withhold her normal affection from a teenaged son who broke curfew.

4. *Personal resources* refer to each family member's personality, physical appearance, and role competence. They also include interpersonal factors that may cause the individual to be perceived as attractive or competent, and therefore accorded power or to develop a self-perception as such. For example, a grandson may have the ability to make his grandparents laugh by talking in a funny voice. He soon learns that using this voice allows him to say things that he otherwise would get in trouble for.

5. *Cognitive resources* refer to the insight family members have, or the sense of how their power influences their own actions and affects others. It deals with using intelligence to logically determine what power options are available. Some children learn at a young age what strategies to use when trying to get what they want from different family members.

No family member possesses all five of McDonald's (1980) power bases equally or uses all of them in a given situation or with a given person. Some may never be used, whereas others may be used in combination or only in certain situations or with certain other family members. It is possible for a husband to use normative and economic power resources extensively in his interactions, and simultaneously for his wife to use cognitive and affective resources in her interactions. You might exert power because of your education or assertiveness. Your sister's power may come from her strong personality, and your mother may have the authority to veto decisions. Children in the same family might use affective and personal power resources, especially when they are younger. This process is described by the following young respondent.

I can influence Fernando. I simply have to go about it the right way! He sets rules and expects the rest of us to follow. Then I join with my sisters and to-

gether we find ways to go around the rules. We tease him and keep bugging him until we wear him down.

Power bases are also related to factors such as income and culture. The more complex the family structure is in a culture, the less power wives possess and the more supervision they experience in extended families. In Turkish families, the higher a father's education is, the more decreased is his perceived power in relation to his wife and son (Schonpflug, 2001). The author of this study speculates that fathers with more education operate under a more egalitarian mode in the family.

 Power Processes Power processes are family communication practices that affect family discussions, arguments, decision making, and especially crisis situations. According to McDonald (1980), these power processes are attempts to control others through influence, persuasion (discussed later in this chapter), and assertiveness. Researchers have examined the number of times people talk, how long they talk, to whom they address their comments, and how long a talk session lasts (Johnson & Vinson, 1990). Their additional analysis of questioning, interrupting, and silence patterns led them to conclude that family members who talk most frequently and for the longest periods of time are dominant, but those who receive the most communication are the most powerful (Berger, 1980). As you know from your own experience, the longest or loudest talker may not hold the power. Effective communicators adapt their messages to different family members. One must distinguish between the power attempts a person makes and the final outcomes.

Certain power arrangements can increase marital satisfaction (Giblin, 1994). High levels of marital satisfaction occur most frequently among egalitarian (syncratic or autonomic) couples, followed by husband-dominated couples, and least among wife-dominated couples. Power balances are evidenced through language. Linguistic choices—such as using fewer first-person and more third-person narratives, and more descriptions—indicate tensions between deference and demeanor in power-imbalanced relationships (Buzzanell & Burrell, 1997).

All messages in a family are cocreated as a power process by the senders and receivers. Family members may send mixed messages, which are difficult to analyze accurately. When an individual says one thing but means and wants something else, confusion results. Contradiction often appears in the nonverbal aspects of a message. In analyzing power messages, both the content and relationship dimensions must be analyzed carefully to understand family communication. A family member who acts helpless can control the behavior in a relationship just as effectively as another who dominates, as this respondent reports.

My sister, I think, has a great deal of power in my family because she positions herself as dependent and helpless. Everyone is supposed to help Tamika because she can't cope. I think she is highly capable, deliberately or not, of manipulating everyone to meet her needs. She preferred to remain unemployed while she was single! And, now that she has a kid, she has a very good reason not to work and to need help in every way—money, child care, home, car. My mother falls for it all the time.

Messages created by ill or dysfunctional members can also influence family power. Families with alcoholic members have learned just how powerful that member can be. Everyone may learn to tiptoe around the drinker and develop strategies to minimize the alcoholic's verbal abuse. This places the alcoholic into a central and powerful position in the family, although he or she may be talked about as weak or helpless.

My sister and I would meet at the front door to our house after school to report to each other on our father's mood. He was either in a "good" mood (sober) or a "bad" mood (drinking) and Robin and I tailored our actions and plans to his mood. We learned to adapt to whatever mood and situation came our way.

Power Outcomes The final area, family power outcomes, focuses on who makes decisions and who wins. In this aspect, at least one family member gets his or her way or receives rights or privileges of leadership. McDonald (1980) equates power outcomes with control through decision making, implementation activities, and further defining the social-family context in which the power is carried out.

Power bases influence power outcomes. Family members who hold normative positions of authority may have the greatest power. Often, the balance of power rests with the partner who contributes the greatest economic resources. Sources of power may be tied to rewards. In a study of control in marriages, Ross (1991) equates control to various power dimensions. She concludes that marriage represents a trade-off for women. In general, marriage increases women's income resources, which increases their sense of control, but decreases their autonomy, especially their sense of independence.

Hierarchies in the family system establish guidelines for power processes that avoid conflicts yet affect power outcomes. Family members have orchestration power and/or implementation power. *Orchestration power* means that certain family members are allowed to make noncritical decisions. They usually make decisions that do not infringe on their time but determine the family lifestyle and major aspects of the system. The one with orchestration power can delegate unimportant and time-consuming decisions to the spouse or older child who derives *implementation power* by carrying out these decisions.

It is important to remember that each family uses a variety of power sources relevant to its needs and the personalities involved. Negotiation can result in mutually acceptable compromises on power issues. In some families, traditional roles, including the biosocial issue of male dominance, are clearly defined, and since no one challenges them, the family operates as if that were the only way to function.

Power Development

Due to the systemic nature of a family relationship, power develops through a transactional process. An alcoholic cannot control a spouse unless the nonalcoholic spouse permits it. A mother relinquishes her own personal control when she gives an "acting-out" child power over her. Only the small child who has limited means of resisting power moves must accept certain power outcomes; for example, an abused child has few means of resisting punishment. In some families, gender traditions limit power positions of women.

Spouses and Power Spousal authority may be examined by the number and type of areas over which each spouse exercises authority. In his review of power in families, Berger (1980) suggests that "the absolute number of resources a person brings to the marriage does not determine his or her power, but rather the relative contribution of resources to the relationship" (p. 210). He maintains that most of the studies he reviewed provide support for the resource theory but found notable exceptions, particularly in studies of other cultures. One exception seems to be in Taiwanese marriages, where the wife's resources gained from education and employment help to determine the balance of marital power (Xu & Lai, 2002).

Marital power reflects the extent to which one spouse loves and needs the other. The spouse with the strongest feelings may put himself or herself in a less powerful position because the person with less interest can more easily control the one more involved. The existence of an alternative relationship can provide power to one or another family member. However, options for couples are complicated: "The mere existence of alternatives does not ensure increased power for the spouse who has them; in addition, the other spouse must have some degree of commitment to the relationship so that the alternatives of the other spouse represent a threat" (Berger, 1980, p. 215). If there is little marital commitment, one spouse's affair may be viewed as a distancing act rather than a destructive one.

Couples may enter a relationship with unequal power, but the relationship can achieve balance over time. The following example illustrates how power changes over time in a relationship.

In the beginning of our relationship, Jack, who is older, tended to dominate. He had had a lover for several years and when that commitment ended, he had made up his mind to be more autonomous in any future relationship. I resented his treating me as if I were his former partner and assuming that we would conflict in similar situations in the same way. Now that we have been together a few years, he realizes that the past is not the present. We can make joint decisions, and both of us are much happier.

The spouse with the greater range of authority area has the higher relative authority. Four authority types describe the way in which married couples divide authority. Two are based on only one spouse having authority, and two describe couples with more equally divided power.

- *Wife-Dominant or Husband-Dominant*. In husband-dominated or wife-dominated families, major areas of activity are influenced and controlled by the dominant spouse. Dominance by one spouse permeates all areas of family power: the use of resources or bases, power processes, and power outcomes. One spouse demonstrates control of power in the system, while the other accepts such control. Thus, one spouse often orchestrates and the other implements the power.

- *Syncratic*. A syncratic relationship, characterized by much shared authority and joint decision making, implies that each spouse has a strong say in all important areas. This example reveals a couple that realized the value of their syncratic relationships.

When Kurt and I married, we agreed never to make big decisions alone, and we've been able to live with that. This way we share the risks and the joys of whatever happens. It just works out best between us if we wait on deciding all important matters until we sound out the other's opinions. It's when we decide over the little things that I know that each of us respects the rights and opinions of the other.

- *Autonomic.* In the autonomic power structure, the couple divides authority; that is, the husband and wife have relatively equal authority but in different areas. Each spouse is completely responsible for specific matters. The wife might have more power over the budget, vacation plans, and choice of new home, and the husband has more power over the selection of schools, buying anything with a motor in it, and whether the family moves to another state. Increasingly, couples indicate they achieve an equal balance of power. Peplau, Veniegas, and Campbell (1996) found that 48 percent of heterosexual women and 40 percent of heterosexual men stated their power was equal with their partner, and 59 percent of lesbians and 38 percent of gay men stated they had equal power in their partnerships.

Support groups for families with addicted members recognize how power transactionally affects all members. In these groups, such as Al-Anon, family members learn how to cope with some of the power maneuvers used by the alcoholic member. This includes learning how to ignore power moves that hook family members into nonproductive behaviors. Highly skewed relationships, such as extreme husband- or wife-dominance, have greater violence. According to Sabourin (1994), abusive partners aggravate one another through domineering behaviors. If both attempt control and neither submits, conflict escalates.

The degree of violence or abuse a parent experienced in his or her family-of-origin relates directly to the use of coercive power in families. The frequent observation of abuse in the family-of-origin consistently indicates a risk for wife abuse (Marshall & Rose, 1988). Negative emotions in family relationships can become more intense and irrational than those in other close relationships because families are together longer in an environment with closer and more frequent contact. Because family members assume their relationships have a long future, individual members may see this as a license to violate conversational and relational norms that they would not otherwise violate (Vangelisti, 1993).

Children and Power Children need to be included in any study of power because they impact family interaction. Traditionally, parents are expected to control and be responsible for their children's behavior. The law also places power in the parents' hands. In no other relationship within a family system does a person have such complete power over an-

⋆ Healthy Families negotiate power.

other as parents do over young children. Children may struggle to establish their position in the family, to gain certain resources, or to establish an identity. With the large increase in working mothers, both children and adolescents assume more personal and domestic responsibilities. This affects not only children's power but enhances their maturity and sense of self-reliance (Demo, 1992).

Often, children influence the interaction and outcomes of power struggles in families by using power plays such as interruptions or screaming. Children also may keep secret powerful information about abuse or neglect from the other family members or outsiders to maintain the family system. In many families, one spouse consciously or unconsciously co-opts a child into an ally position in order to increase the strength of his or her position. Similarly, children become adept at playing one parent against the other. "Daddy said I could do it" or "If Mom was here, she'd let me" has echoed through most homes as new alliances form. Children also gain power by forming alliances with one parent. Children may feel they have insufficient power to change other family members' behaviors (Vangelisti, 1994a).

Children engage in power struggles at very young ages.

Blended families often contend with children playing one side of the family against the other. "She can't tell me what to do; she's not my real mother" is the kind of communication that may cause years of pain while new roles and power are negotiated. Single-parent families display unique power alliances, due to the presence of one adult. A potential advantage for a child in a single-parent family is that the child may negotiate directly with only one parent for immediate answers and have direct personal power. However, the same child cannot form a parent-child alliance to try to change a decision the way a child can in a two-parent family, unless the parent or the child creates an alliance with a grandparent.

Some alliances continue in families over a period of time; others exist only for reaching a specific decision. The results of past alliances can obligate family members to feel that they must support another on an issue to repay a debt. For example, "Leonitas helped me convince Dad to let me buy a new 10-speed bike. Now I ought to help him argue with Dad to get his own car."

There are also cultural differences that affect power interactions in families. These remarks describe how the family-of-origin and cultural background influence power outcomes.

Within our Thai culture, children are taught early to defer and show respect to their elders. Given names are rarely used in conversation, except for older family members talking to younger ones. Respect for relationships are formalized verbally by the use of the term phi *for elder siblings and* nong *for younger siblings. The boy child is very important to Thai families and outranks any girl children.*

Although young children exercise power, they develop more independent power as they grow older when they demand and can handle more power within the family structure. A 6-year-old may fight for a new toy, whereas a 16-year-old fights for later curfews. Most of you have witnessed a small child explain computers, metrics, or a video game to a confused adult.

As families change in their life cycle, the original power relationship of a couple undergoes enormous modification as the family network increases, fragments, or solidifies. In addition to developmental issues, other forces affect changes in power, from inflation and environmental factors to changing cultural norms. Parents' competency in relating their needs and desires, first to one another and then to their children, affects power. Ishii-Kuntz (1994) notes in his research that children with highly involved fathers have higher cognitive competence, increased empathy, less gender-stereotyped beliefs, and more self-control. If a spouse falls ill, dies, or leaves, the remaining parent may return to the family-of-origin, seeking everything from shelter to advice, or may establish new ties with a child that involve sharing power differently.

Communication and Power

Certain family communicative acts can be identified that address power issues. Because of the nature of transactional communication, these communicative acts address power only when met with a response that engages them.

Confirming, Disconfirming, and Rejecting   These behaviors are strategies that affect power, and they can become a part of power messages when family members attempt to separate and connect in one-up, one-down subsystems. In a *one-up* position, one family member attempts to exercise more power control over one or more other members. The *one-down* member accepts from the one-up member the control implied in the messages (Escudero, Rogers, & Gutierrez, 1997).

Confirming implies acknowledgment and may be used to gain power when one tries to get another to identify with him or her, or when one tries to give rewards in order to gain power. The careful, nonjudgmental listener may wittingly or unwittingly gain power. The "silent treatment" represents a frequently used *disconfirming* behavior. One family member can put another in a one-down power position with the punishment strategy of disconfirmation. "I'll ignore him; he'll come around" represents such an effort. On the other hand, disconfirming a power message may serve as an effective method of rejecting power. The child who pretends not to hear "clean up your room" messages effectively deflects the parental power, at least for a while.

Rejecting messages tie directly to punishment messages and are often used as control in family power plays. "I hate you" or "I don't care what you say" may effectively halt control attempts. Hample and Dallinger (1995) state that individuals who sense they are being berated and stressed will avoid argumentative situations. The negative conflict behaviors of displacement, denial, disqualification, distancing, and sexual withholding can also be used as rejecting power moves.

Self-Disclosure   Self-disclosure serves as a major means of gaining intimacy within a relationship, but it can also be used as a power strategy when one attempts to control the other through the "information power" gained by self-disclosure. For example, when a self-disclosure (such as, "Well, you had an affair, so how can you talk?") is thrown back at a spouse during a fight, that person loses power.

Self-disclosure is often difficult for parents, but the mother cited in the following example gained greater closeness with her daughter.

One of the most meaningful times in my life occurred when my teenaged daughter and I had an all-night session about love, sex, and growing-up problems. It was the first time I honestly told her about what I went through growing up and how we faced some of the same things. I had always kept those things to myself, but I suddenly realized that she shouldn't feel like she was different or bad because of her feelings. It's scary to tell your daughter your faults or fears, but it certainly resulted in a closer relationship between us.

Men differ somewhat from women in using some kinds of self-disclosure in power processes. Wives disclose more descriptive information and share more intimate feelings with husbands than vice versa. Regardless of sex, the disclosure of highly intimate feelings requires reciprocity between partners (Dindia, Fitzpatrick, & Kenny, 1997). Applied to power, this would mean that the more equal and reciprocal the communication exchanges between family members, the higher the amount of honest self-disclosure that will occur. Especially with intimate self-disclosures, individuals adjusted their rates of disclosure to their partners' rates.

Dominance   According to a transactional view of relationships, power must be negotiated between and among family members. This transactional quality appeared in the research of Rogers-Millar and Millar (1979), who distinguish between dominance and domineering behavior. They define *domineering* as the sending of "one-up messages," or verbal statements claiming the right to dominate. For example, one spouse might say, "Be sure to have my supper ready at 6:00 P.M." A one-down statement from the spouse would be one that accepts the other family member's power. As a response to the one-up message about having supper ready, a one-down message would be, "I will."

This example shows the difference between domineeringness and dominance. *Domineeringness* comes from an individual's behavior, whereas *dominance* relates to dyadic relational behavior (Courtright, Millar, & Rogers-Millar, 1979). The first, one-up statement was domineeringness, but it took the one-down response to call this dyadic behavior dominance. Pure dominance means all one-up remarks made by an individual are followed by a one-down response from the other.

INFLUENCE

Influence occurs when family members use their power to try to change or modify each other's behavior or beliefs. Using McDonald's (1980) conceptualization, influence is a power process, and the terms *persuasion* and *control* are also used to describe this process. Influence in family communication is ever-present. Think about your last interaction with a family member and how influence was involved. Were you trying to influence a sibling to loan you some money? Did one of your parents try to persuade you to join the family for a family reunion over a holiday weekend? Were you involved in a debate over an issue, trying to influence a family member to change his or her opinion? Any parent will tell you of countless attempts to influence a child, whether it be trying to get a teenaged son to clean his room or to convince a 3-year-old daughter to eat her dinner.

Influence is a fundamental part of everyday interactions with family members. In fact, some researchers have suggested that all communicative events can be examined for persuasive qualities (Gass & Seiter, 1999). We will now look at the types of influence strategies family members use, who uses which strategies, and which strategies seem to be effective in producing desired change.

Types of Influence Strategies

To understand influence in families, we first need to identify the strategies that family members use in their persuasive attempts. A classic piece of research by Marwell and Schmitt (1967) delineated 16 influence strategies that people use in their daily interactions, including promise, threat, liking, debt, altruism, and punishment. These influence strategies seem to also be widely used in families. In one study, threat was the only strategy that was more likely to be used with a stranger than with a spouse (Sillars, 1980). Strategies can be thought of as being direct or indirect and as unilateral or bilateral (Falbo & Peplau, 1980). *Direct* influence strategies include bargaining, reasoning, and asking; *indirect* influence strategies include hinting and withdrawal (Falbo & Peplau, 1980). One study found that dual-career couples were more likely to use direct than indirect strategies at both home and work (Steil & Weltman, 1992). Bargaining and hinting are examples of bilateral strategies, and telling and withdrawal are examples of unilateral strategies.

Certain influence strategies are more likely to be used in specific situations. For instance, when making joint purchase decisions, marital and cohabiting couples more frequently use some influence strategies, such as bargaining and reasoning, than other strategies, such as acting helpless and displaying negative emotions (Kirchler, 1993). Adolescents also use a variety of influence strategies when trying to persuade a parent in a purchasing decision. From interviews with adolescents and their parents, Palan and Wilkes (1997) developed a list of influence strategies that adolescents use in purchasing situations. The four major categories of these follow, with examples:

- *Bargaining*. Offering to pay for some of the item, offering to do something to get the item, reasoning with arguments, or making negotiations
- *Persuasion*. Giving opinion, asking repetitively, begging, or whining
- *Emotional*. Showing anger, pouting, "sweet talking," or making parents feel guilty
- *Request*. Directly asking, expressing a need or a want, demanding

Parents have many opportunities to try to influence their young children. During play situations with preschool children, parents frequently use directive statements when trying to get their children to comply. Statements such as "Bring daddy the ball" or "Put the doll in her bed" are more likely to be used than prohibitory statements such as "Don't throw the blocks" (McLaughlin, 1983). Parents also try to influence their adolescent children, using a variety of strategies (deTurck & Miller, 1983).

Family members may also use influence strategies to try to persuade each other to modify health behaviors. In situations where spouses are trying to influence the health behaviors of each other, Tucker and Mueller (2000) found that the most frequently used influence strategies included the following:

- *Engaging in Health Behavior Together*. A wife who thinks her husband needs more exercise might ask him to join her on her nightly walk.
- *Engaging in Facilitative Behavior*. A husband may put a multivitamin on his wife's dinner plate or set aside money each month for her to spend on exercise classes.
- *Discussing the Health Issue*. A spouse might give a newspaper or magazine article to the other spouse about a health concern or issue and then request they discuss it.
- *Requesting That the Partner Engage in the Health Behavior*. One spouse might simply ask the other spouse to quit smoking.

If I didn't cook the broccoli or cut up the cantaloupe for dinner and put it on the table, my husband would certainly revert to his bachelor diet of frozen pizza, macaroni and cheese, and fast food. I also encourage him to make doctor and dentist appointments. Sometimes I remind him that married men live longer because they have their wives to help them take care of themselves. Although I say it in a lighthearted manner, I really believe that he is healthier since marrying me.

Factors Affecting Influence Strategy Use

Look back at the influence strategies explained in the last section. Which ones are you more likely to use with your family members? Most would probably answer, "It depends!" It depends on what outcome you are trying to attain from the influence strategy. It depends on the closeness and relational history with a particular family member. It depends on the power bases that you have in relation to that family member.

One basic question that many researchers have asked is if husbands and wives use influence strategies differently when trying to persuade a spouse. Traditional stereotypes of a wife nagging her husband come to mind for many people (Soule, 2001). However, in most marriages, the persuasion goes both ways as spouses try to influence each other. In fact, the more frequently a wife uses persuasive strategies, the more frequently her husband also does (Sexton & Perlman, 1989). When it comes to persuasion about health issues, wives and husband are equally likely to use influence strategies on their spouses (Tucker & Anders, 2001). Similarly, the sex of the parent and of the child does not affect the number of influence strategies used in play situations with preschool children, and parents make more attempts at influencing younger children in play situations than they do with older children (McLaughlin, 1983).

Men and women seem to be quite similar in the types of influence strategies that they use (Baxter & Bylund, in press). One exception is during purchasing decisions. Kirchler's (1993) research shows that women are more likely to report using strategies that are more partner-oriented, such as offering trade-offs, whereas men are more likely to make autonomous decisions and be less cooperative. As you might expect, children's influence strategy use in purchasing decisions changes over the years. Younger children (ages 3 to 11) are more likely to ask for products (Isler, Popper, & Ward, 1987), but adolescents use a range of influence strategies (Palan & Wilkes, 1997).

Although husbands' and wives' use of persuasive strategies don't differ much simply by gender, other personality factors may contribute to why a spouse chooses a certain type of influence strategy. Dual-career spouses who are less confident tend to be more likely to use indirect-unilateral influence strategies, such as withdrawing and doing their own thing, at home and work. Dual-career wives who rate high on nurturing are more likely to use indirect-bilateral strategies, such as smiling or suggesting, at home and work (Steil & Weltman, 1992). In purchasing decisions, type of conflict, marital satisfaction, power patterns, and relationship duration all affect the choice of persuasive strategy (Kirchler, 1993). Traditional couples are more likely to use influence strategies that focus on the positive or negative outcomes of the decisions, whereas separate couples use constraining messages. Independents are more likely to use a variety of strategy types, as they rely on more power bases than tradi-

*Parent credibility
increases when
parents model
good health
choices.*

tional or separate couples (Witteman & Fitzpatrick, 1986). Couples who
are more satisfied in their marital relationships are less like to use indirect
strategies in their influence attempts than are couples who are less satisfied in their marital relationships (Zvonkovic et al., 1994).

Remember that influence strategies aren't necessarily communicated
just once. Some researchers have examined the process of sequential
spousal influence attempts often called nagging. *Nagging* is "a form of
persistent persuasion that involves a persuader repeating him or herself
rather than escalating to a more aggressive persuasive strategy" (Soule,
2002, p. 217). For most married couples, nagging happens after a spouse
does not do what the other spouse asked. Further, spouses often report
concern about the other's well being as a reason for nagging, such as
about health issues.

The sex of the parent and child, and the child's age have been shown
to make a difference in the types of strategies parents use in trying to influence their adolescent children. In one study, adolescents were asked to
think of a situation in which their parents were trying to get them to help
with spring cleaning. Older adolescent boys reported their fathers to be
more likely to use specific influence strategies, such as pre-giving (such
as first giving the child permission to stay out late and then asking him to
do an extra chore the next day), whereas younger adolescent males said
their mothers would be more likely to use pre-giving (deTurck & Miller,
1983). The culture of the family also seems to play a part in determining
influence strategy use. In one cross-cultural study, researchers found

American mothers to be more likely to use directive statements, such as "Bring me the toy," than did Japanese mothers (Abe & Izard, 1999).

Influence Strategy Outcomes

Earlier, we asked you to think about which type of influence strategies you use with family members. If asked why, you'd probably reply, "Because it works!" When choosing an influence strategy, family members have a goal in mind of being successful in influencing the family member. Family researchers have also been interested in which influence strategies tend to result in compliance.

In spousal persuasion, spouses who are successful in gaining compliance generally rely more on messages that focus on the activity that is being requested rather than on messages about the power or control in the relationship. They also rely on questions and direct statements and request (Witteman & Fitzpatrick, 1986). Strategies such as agreement, explanation, and problem solving have also been shown to be effective influence strategies (Newton & Burgoon, 1990). In the specific realm of health behavior, effective strategies for both husbands and wives include engaging in the health behavior together, engaging in facilitative behavior, and providing emotional support (Tucker & Mueller, 2000).

With young children in play situations, influence strategy effectiveness doesn't depend on the gender of the parent or the gender of the child, but does depend on the child's age. For example, suggestions and questions don't work well for 18-month-old children, but they do for $3\frac{1}{2}$-year-old children (McLaughlin, 1983). Influence strategies that are strategically timed to the involvement the child currently has with a toy also result in higher compliance in play situations (Schaeffer & Crook, 1980).

During parents' interactions with their adolescents, effective influence strategies for parents differ by parent gender. Mothers are successful with frequent praise and moderate levels of attempted control, and fathers are successful with moderate to high levels of attempted control (Smith, 1983). When adolescents are trying to influence their parents to purchase something, reasoning is consistently reported as one of the two most effective strategies by adolescents, their mothers, and their fathers (Palan & Wilkes, 1997). The following comment from a 15-year-old female shows how well thought out these reasoning strategies can be.

First of all, I tell my mom or dad what they haven't *bought me lately. It gives them a guilt trip. It puts them in the right mindset, and then I go in for the kill. I say, "I need this because. . . ." And then I give three distinct reasons. I say the one that I think they'll go for first. But they have to be three distinct reasons. That way if one falls through, I can always depend on the other two.*

DECISION MAKING

Questions such as, "What should we do for Grandma's birthday?" and "Where should we enroll the twins in preschool?" represent concerns that involve family decision making. *Decision making* is the process by which family members make choices, reach judgments, or arrive at solutions that end uncertainty. Decision making means getting things done in a family when one or more family members need to agree with others to accomplish something (Scanzoni & Polonko, 1980).

You can see how power, influence, and decision making are closely tied together. Decision making allows differences between individual family members to be addressed. In addition, the decision-making process reflects individual differences. Family members can use power resources such as trade-offs, silence, or helpfulness as well as power processes such as influence or assertiveness processes. The decisions made in response to these efforts determine what occurs in the family system.

Decision-making processes help to regulate the closeness or distance of family members. The kind and quality of decisions determine how family roles, rules, or themes are enacted. It is through decision making that family members negotiate dialectical concerns of autonomy and connection. Couples develop a repertoire of strategies they use in the negotiation process to deal with the shifting needs for closeness and distance (Montgomery, 1992). Today's families struggle to find time to make careful decisions. The pressure on single parents and employed couples to set aside time to do intelligent decision making requires prioritizing among competing demands. For example, making decisions requires a couple to take the time to debrief and shift focus from outside jobs. The more complex the family system, the more important the decision patterns, as indicated here.

Both Mom and Dad work overtime. The oldest one home is in charge of decisions that involve those in the house. For example, when my older brother is home, he makes decisions on who can go somewhere or what friend can come over. If he's at work, I take over. My next younger sister does the same when I have something after school.

Decision making, like power, is a process that belongs to the family system, not to an individual. Therefore, decision making varies greatly among families because each family negotiates about values or resources differently.

Unlike a small group that comes together to accomplish a particular task, a family has a history of continuous interaction and consists of a combination of interdependent individuals. Even if the decision-making process results in turmoil, a family remains a unit, although sometimes a factional and unhappy one. This is not true of outside groups that often disband. Families tend to remain together even if members disagree. This creates what to outsiders may appear as irrational decisions or negative communication. Because family relationships are both involuntary and lengthy, members may use negative messages that ironically function to maintain the family system and the separate identities of a husband or daughter (Vangelisti, 1993). A study of parent-adolescent problem solving reveals that adolescents may vent great anger over the decisions on a particular issue, but not be dissatisfied with the overall family relationship (Niedzwiecki, 1997).

Family decisions can be either instrumental or affective. *Instrumental decisions* require solving rather functional issues, such as getting a job to pay the family bills or providing transportation. *Affective decisions* relate to emotions or feelings. Instrumental decisions tend to be more basic, since "families whose functioning is disrupted by instrumental problems rarely, if ever, deal effectively with affective problems. However, families

Joint decision making reflects shared family power.

whose functioning is disrupted by affective problems may deal adequately with instrumental problems" (Epstein, Bishop, & Baldwin, 1982, p. 119).

The location of a family along the cohesion and adaptability continuum affects their decision-making behavior. Highly enmeshed, rigid families may pressure members to reach predictable and low-risk decisions, whereas disengaged families may have trouble sharing enough information to make reasonable decisions. The length of time together also influences decision making. Early in their relationship, a couple may engage in arguments like others they have known well. Later on, they develop their own pattern. Understanding family decision making involves examining (1) types of decision-making processes, (2) styles of decision making, (3) phases in decision making, and (4) factors that influence decision making.

Types of Decision-Making Processes

Each family has its own way of reaching decisions on issues. Decisions can be reached through use of the following levels of agreement: (1) consensus, (2) accommodation, and (3) *de facto* decisions, each of which involve different degrees of acceptance and commitment (Turner, 1970).

Consensus   Consensus, the most democratic process, involves discussion that continues until agreement is reached. This may require compromise and flexibility, but the desired goal is a solution acceptable to all involved. Because each family member has a part in the decision and a chance for influence, they more likely will share the responsibility for carrying it out. Major purchases, money issues, and vacations are common topics for consensus discussions. The complexity of such decision making is described in the following example.

Every Tuesday night is family night, and everyone must be present from 7:00 until 8:00. This is the time when we make certain family decisions that affect all of us. We may make a joint decision about vacations and try to find a plan that will please everyone. All six of us have to agree to go ahead with the decision.

Accommodation   Accommodation occurs when some family members consent to a decision not because they totally agree but because they believe that further discussion will be unproductive. Consent may be given with a smile or with regret. The accommodation decision requires a great deal of trading, because no one really achieves what he or she desires. For example, you may want to go to a church picnic while someone else wants to play in three ballgames that weekend. This type of decision making occurs when families pressure for high cohesiveness and individual members feel they must "go along," as in this somewhat manipulative example.

It's just easier to agree with Dad and let him think his ideas are what we all want than to argue with him. He's bound to win anyway, since he controls the money. Sometimes when we humor his wishes, Mom, my sister, and I can then get our way on what we want to do—sort of a trade-off!

Sometimes family members line up on one side of an issue and vote. The minority views held by losing family members might have genuine merit, but the losers accept majority rule rather than cause trouble. In accommodation, decisions may favor a dominant member, and less aggressive family members may develop a pattern of submitting to their wishes. Accommodative decision making encourages distance and can also enforce negative family themes and images while implementing stereotyped thinking on biosocial issues, especially in cases of male dominance.

 De Facto *Decisions*   What happens when the discussion reaches an impasse? Usually, one member will go ahead and act in the absence of a clear-cut decision. This is a *de facto* decision—one made without direct family approval but nevertheless made to keep the family functioning. A fight over which model of VCR to buy while on sale may be continued until the sale nears an end and Mom buys one.

De facto decisions encourage family members to complain about the result, because they played either no part, or a passive part, in the decision. The family "decided" not to make a decision, and the family member who acts in the vacuum of that decision may have to endure complaints or lack of enthusiasm of those who have to accept the decision. Although many families, particularly rigid ones, seem to use only one type of decision making, more flexible families vary their styles according to the issues. Critical issues may require consensus, whereas less important concerns can be resolved by a vote or a *de facto* decision.

Styles of Decision Making

Families have distinctive styles for decision making. There is a uniqueness in each family's problem solving because the underlying reasoning differs from family to family. Vuchinich and DeBaryske (1997) suggest a family's decision making can be based on behavioral learning via role expectations, a shared worldview, or intrafamily structural alliances.

 "I Win; You Lose" (Zero-Sum)   Applied to decision making in conflict situations, the first and most primitive way to reach a decision is simply to insist on your own way. This means that in an argument, one person wins and one loses. This approach can lead to threats, yelling, browbeating, and slanting of the truth. The maintenance of an "I win; you lose" relationship requires coercive power, especially the use of fear and threat. Information is of little use, because too much evidence might weaken the position of the selfish family member who insists on his or her views. Some parents demand acceptance of their decisions, as in this example.

In our farmhouse you went along with parental decisions or you were punished—it was as simple as that. My oldest brother frequently rebelled, and my father would beat him. My mother usually went along with whatever my father said because I think she was scared of him, too.

There are only two circumstances in which families could survive using zero-sum confrontations (Broderick, 1975). One example would be if the wife and husband are closely matched, with each getting an equal number of wins and losses, the relationship could continue. Also, if the consistently losing partner feels there are no alternatives and lacks the emotional or financial resources to leave, he or she may remain in the relationship in spite of the heavy psychological cost of lower self-esteem. Children can be victims in this kind of household because they have no way to escape.

To be a constant winner requires defensive behaviors and putting up with the loser's submissive behaviors. To lose constantly requires a person to live with low self-esteem or to try to subvert the more powerful person. In many families, victories are hollow because they curb or destroy ideas and limit input from others that might lead to better solutions.

 Decisions via Rules   A second style of decision making involves the creation and enforcement of rules. Rules that evolve through repeated interactions affect decision making because, over a period of time, they become accepted ways to operate when problems arise. Rules in decision making certainly become a part of relational maintenance strategies affecting equity in marriages (Canary & Stafford, 1992). These strategies maintain a relational definition and safeguard the status quo, reduce or heighten the dialectical tensions, and increase or decrease affection between family members. Three types of rules can be distinguished in family decision making: (1) rules for dividing resources, (2) rules for assigning responsibility, and (3) rules for negotiation.

Rules for Dividing Resources   Dividing family resources among members requires decision making. This may include the dividing of family income into the amounts available for food, housing, tuition, and entertainment, or dividing living space, including which child gets which room, which children have to share a bedroom, and which shelves belong to which child or parent. Rules function to avoid confrontations and reduce power plays through resolving conflicts before they become problems. Rules require that family members carry around in their heads a whole series of predetermined decisions about matters of family living.

Rules of Designated Authority   Designated authority rules indicate who has the authority over certain areas. For example, Mother pays the bills and does the budgeting. Dad does the painting and refinishing and thus decides on the materials to use. Kohna plays in the band and therefore does not need to help with housework on weekends when the band travels. This type of rule, assigning responsibility, often relates closely to roles in the family. Whoever controls the kitchen and all of the activities that take place there has the authority to make the decisions in that area. Culture may play a significant role in designating authority. The following example illustrates cultural differences.

As an immigrant Assyrian family living in the United States, my family is quite different. I would describe our family as "closed" because we have learned that this works better if we are to keep our culture, language, religion, and traditions. My father makes all important decisions, so we don't make decisions like other families in our neighborhood.

Rules for Negotiation   Much rule-based decision making is based on negotiation and compromise. Over time, families can establish rules governing the acceptable process that decision making will follow when conflict occurs. Certain tactics, such as yelling or interrupting, can be outlawed. This approach implies that the decision reached may require compromise or self-control on one or more family members' part. Many current marital or family enrichment programs stress how to negotiate differences according to rules that allow all members of the system some input (Renick, Blumberg, & Markman, 1992).

In some families, each person has a right to decide what is negotiable and what is nonnegotiable for himself or herself. Others intimately involved have a right to know what is nonnegotiable and can question or evaluate it, but the final decision is up to the individual and is respected. For example, in some interfaith marriages, couples agree that each has the right to continue his or her religion. Thus, a choice to attend religious services is nonnegotiable.

Ever since the children have grown older, I have declared Saturday as my day to do whatever I desire. It is sacred to me and I do only what I want on that day, even if somebody else will be disappointed. I am wife or mother to four people during six days of the week, and I really need some scheduled time to myself and Saturday's it!

Decisions via Principle   The final style involves decisions by principle or contract. Few families actively operate at this high level, and those that do usually include older children and adults. It is based on a belief in the basic human needs of each family member and a desire to put the family's welfare above individual concerns. Family members operate on principles of fairness and care. For example, if either Dad or Mom works late, he or she calls the other and explains. The operating principle is that neither partner unnecessarily inconveniences the other. This type of decision making works in families with children if the parents have taught them how to use good judgment and value the rights, strengths, and limitations of one another. It requires empathy and cooperation. Disharmony can be handled as a temporary condition that will be resolved by fair decisions that restore balance to a family system. Principles are sometimes stated overtly, such as in family themes or rules. Other times, they are conveyed through key family stories.

Phases in Decision Making

Most family decision making goes through a series of phases to reach satisfactory or unsatisfactory decisions. A valuable way to consider phases is to use the family problem-solving loop developed by Kieren, Maguire, and Hurlbut (1996) (see Figure 8.1). The loop illustrates the phases of decision developed in the somewhat circular path families take when they make decisions. It also provides for shortened loops when decision mak-

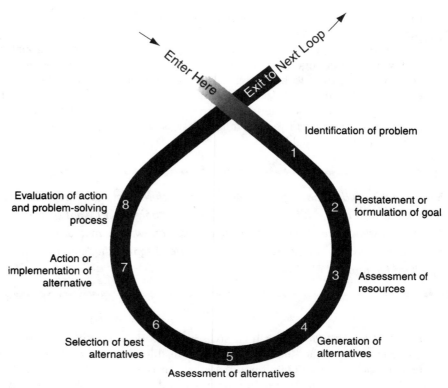

FIGURE 8.1   The Family Problem-Solving Loop

ing falters. It breaks the process down into eight steps that decisions proceed through in solving problems. Remember that we are presenting this as a general model of decision making. You can certainly see how families making decisions in their everyday lives may not follow this model precisely in this order or follow all of the steps each time.

Each of the eight steps of this model marks or identifies the beginnings and endings of different patterns of interaction in problem solving. Note each of the eight steps that happen in developing the loop. These eight steps can be condensed into four phases based on the similarity of activity performed by family members. Phases 1, 2, 3 (identification of problem, formulating a goal, and assessing resources) is labeled identification/clarification. Phase 2, called alternatives, covers steps 4 and 5 (generation of alternatives and assessing their value). Phase 3, designated as consensus building, includes step 6 (selecting the best option). It includes the attempts individual family members make to gain support for a solution. Phase 4 relates to the decision, covering steps 7 and 8 (accepting a decision, putting it into effect, and evaluating it as an outcome).

Decisions are never as simple as they appear. In examining the four phases in decision making, it is important to realize that the process may be short-circuited at any point by a family member or subsystem alliance that does not agree with certain choices. A family may reach a decision by skipping some steps. It may be difficult to identify which phases are being used in problem solving because family members are doing other things simultaneously and discussing decision options intermittently. Some families tend not to be rational or to follow steps in problem solving. These researchers believe that once problem-solving patterns are learned, either good or bad, they are resistant to change. In their study of 40 families, Kieren, Maguire, and Hurlbut report more support for a rational rather than a random pattern of decision making.

Reflect on how this next family effectively followed decision making in terms of the loop model.

My siblings and I and our wives actually went through a formal decision-making process as we decided how to take care of our elderly mother after she was unable to live alone. We went through all kinds of hassles on terms such as nursing homes, residential facilities, and social security benefits. We had to set monetary criteria for any solution based on a percentage of our salaries and based on a location that everyone could reach. Mother had to agree to the solution also. We agreed we could not force our solution on her. Each couple investigated different options, specific senior citizen housing options, live-in nurses, nursing homes, and specialized group homes. We finally reached two options that we could live with—a particular senior citizen facility or a nursing home. We discussed these with our mother who rejected the nursing home instantly but who agreed to the senior citizen housing facility.

This planned approach to decision making does not just happen in families. Some families become bogged down and never get beyond the first or second phase. In order to understand the complexity of the process, we need to examine what affects family decision making.

Factors Affecting Decision Making

Over time each family evolves some patterned ways of solving problems. The decision-making process is affected by multiple factors. In this section, we will discuss how the following affect decision making: (1) children, (2) gender influences, (3) the role of individual involvement and resources, and (4) outside influences.

The Role of Children   Since family-of-origin experiences affect all areas of your life, your decision-making experiences as a child impact your approach to adult decision making. In addition, your own children may affect your family's current decision-making processes. In certain circumstances, children share the leadership in decision making, especially when a child feels support from other members. For instance, one study found that children ages 9 to 12 are influential in family decision making about choosing a restaurant (Labrecque & Ricard, 2001). However, results from a study of high school students from diverse socioeconomic and ethnic backgrounds reveal that granting adolescents autonomy in decision making too early leads to lower levels of effort and lower grades for youth of both sexes (Dornbusch, Ritter, Mont-Reynaud, & Chen, 1990).

Moods of either parents or adolescents affect decision making. Niedzwiecki (1997) reports that problem solving should be postponed until moods are more positive or neutral. Children often respond best to positive emotional patterns of communication and perform less well when parents express negative emotions. Although negative feelings need to come out in decision making, the way in which they are treated will affect the outcomes. The "Let it all hang out" philosophy hinders family problem solving. When too many negative feelings surface during decision making, the focus shifts from problem solving to personalities. For daughters, the more adaptability, the more positive the outcomes on behavioral, psychological, and relationship measures. Such is not true for other family members (Farrell & Barnes, 1993). The results for boys show that more adaptability affects communication with parents and causes depression, but not cohesion or other behavioral and psychological outcomes.

As parents and children age, decision-making processes can take on a different meaning. Elderly parents may require caregiving decisions to be made by their adult children, which can be a difficult situation for families. Talks about preferences for caregiving may be useful to have earlier rather than later in the aging process. For mothers and adult daughters with close relationships, there may be little need to discuss the issues of future caregiving, because the mothers believe the daughters already know their preferences or because there is denial about the aging process (Pecchioni & Nussbaum, 2001).

Gender Influences   A family's role ideology and biosocial beliefs determine who carries out certain decisions and tasks. Thus, in male-dominant households, the husband may take over the financial decisions, the yard, and the basement, and the wife is in charge of the household operation, kin networking, and school contacts. Egalitarian couples will make more joint decisions. A study of differences between happily married and divorced couples reveals that happy partners practiced "more role specialization, with greater influence of the wife and less husband dominance in family finance handling, and greater joint and wife influence in decision making" (Schaninger & Buss, 1986, p. 129). Likewise, Wilkie, Ferree, and Ratcliff (1998) report that conventional gender roles only significantly affect marital quality indirectly through perceptions of fairness and understanding. These two qualities of fairness and understanding would certainly impact the emotional climate in decision making in a family. Fitzpatrick's couple typology research (1988) reveals that in casual conversations, both "independents" and "mixed-couples" types employed challenges and justifications to assert control over spouses, whereas "traditionals" used orders in decision making.

Outside factors impact decision-making styles. If men work in a participative work setting where the management encourages job autonomy, self-direction, and group problem-solving skills, they are more democratic fathers in child-parent relations, including more use of family decision making and consensus (Grimm-Thomas & Perry-Jenkins, 1993).

Frequently, employed women acquire more power than their husbands in decisions about money matters. In decision making, a wife's income was found to be highly correlated with direct bargaining and reward strategies (Zvonkovic, Schmiege, & Hall, 1994). Rural women who do not work outside the home, but indeed do field work on family farms, have no more, and possibly less, influence on decision making (Rosenfeld, 1986).

Individual Investment and Resources How many times have you dropped out of or avoided a family decision-making session because you did not care about the result? If you do not sense how things affect you, you are not likely to get involved, even though, as a family member, you will probably be affected. Mom's desire and need for a new refrigerator may not be perceived as important to a teenager. If money, or any shared resource, is scarce, decision making can become a competitive process for the limited resources. If each family member can become involved in agenda setting and has the right to raise issues and objections, the decision making prospers. Agenda-setting power rather than decision-making power better indicates marital satisfaction (Wilkie, Ferree, & Ratcliff, 1998). Discussion may be unimportant to some family members and critical to others.

Personal investment in decisions varies over time with the degree of separateness or connectedness within the family system. In close relationships in which each partner has multiple role functions, "individuals tacitly negotiate agreements to reciprocate support for critical components for each other's views of self or other role identities" (Stephen, 1994, p. 217).

Couples in distressed marriages will differ from those in a happier, nondistressed marriage in how they approach decision making. Each type of couple will manifest different degrees of motivation and use problem solving to further their agenda of wanting more or less cohesiveness. Couples in distressed marriages express more negative intentions toward mates than couples in the nondistressed group, probably because each feels discounted (Denton, Burleson, & Sprenkle, 1994). If couples express satisfaction with the decision-making process, conflict occurs less often. Dissatisfaction with process becomes a predictor of likely conflicts (Ballard-Reisch, Elton, & Weigel, 1993). Making plans involves the process of decision making. Investment in an issue impacts directly on decision making, as shown here.

I have learned that the best way to reach my partner with my needs is through persuasion. I suggest Carl consider the situation and see if he can think of some plan that will accomplish his goals with as little impact on me as possible. With a little charm thrown in, I might even venture an idea. I reveal my feelings, explain the situation as I see it, and listen to what he has to say. Then I ask for time to think about what we've said. Later, either can bring up the subject again and we'll both be better able to discuss it. Other decisions about our relationship, where there is not so much friction, are made by whoever really cares about the issue.

Outside Influences   All sorts of outside factors affect how a family makes decisions. Mom's salary, BJ's friends, and Mary Frances's teacher may all affect how a decision is resolved. Decisions within a family system often represent compromises or adaptations to other societal systems. School, corporate, and government systems impinge on families and influence decisions. For example, think of how a corporation affects family decision making. If the mother must travel, work overtime, or take customers out in the evening, the family makes decisions differently than if this were not necessary. The school-home interface requires other adjustments in decision making. "Latchkey kids," filling time between the end of the school day and the time a parent arrives home, make different decisions than children greeted by a parent at the door.

Decisions forced on a family by outside agencies restrict individual members' choices. Divorce, desertion, or death can greatly alter the decision-making processes in a family. If separating partners cannot reach decisions about money and property, attorneys and judges intervene. If there are children, decisions must be made regarding custody, visitation rights, and financial arrangements, and property or inheritance rights. Even in cases where spouses stay married, these decisions can be painful.

In this age of "experts," our family was almost ripped apart as my parents tried to make decisions about how to raise my younger brother, who has a serious attention deficit disorder. My mother was always wanting to follow the advice of a doctor or a teacher, my father wanted his family to make the decisions about Mario's care. My parents were constantly disagreeing with each other and the medical and educational experts.

Communication Skills in Decision Making

Family decision making can be enhanced by certain communication skills. Vuchinich and DeBaryske (1997) cite four initial items that, paraphrased in communication terms, form the basis for responsible family problem solving. They are (1) being open to allowing different family members to speak out; (2) avoiding negative messages, either verbal or nonverbal that convey hostility; (3) seeking more than one option as a solution; and (4) communicating in clear, positive remarks focused on the problem discussed. These four relate to the phases of problem solving and styles of decision making discussed.

Many families in solving problems have difficulty with disagreements, especially in the manner in which hostile messages are sent and received. Krueger (1983) reports that disagreements serve as a functional part of the decision-making process, particularly when both partners use positive communication strategies to express their differences. They may acknowledge the validity of another's ideas, indicate a willingness to incorporate part of another's solution, or praise the other's past contributions. She suggests this is true except when a sequence begins with a disagreement followed too rapidly by another disagreement, which signals the beginning of conflict escalation. Partners change subjects sometimes as a transition and at other times to avoid conflict. These changes indicate that couples do not focus for long periods of time on a single issue, thus demonstrating a cyclical and phasing model of decision making, with the couple taking up a topic and leaving it, returning later to reach a decision. In the "give and take" of exchanges over a decision, family members establish trust and a sense of fairness and equality. Disagreeing allows for minority alliances in a family to have an input and function as a source for ideas to include in a compromise decision.

You can conclude that communication plays a key role in determining the outcomes of family decision making. The way in which family members use verbal and nonverbal communication determines decision-making outcomes. The sending of mixed messages by one or more members affects decisions and may alter the cohesion and balance of the family system. Relationship satisfaction is highly related to skill in problem solving in married couples (Renick, Blumberg, & Markman, 1992) and cohabiting gay and lesbian couples (Kurdek, 1991). In the Kurdek study, the use of problem-solving strategies of negotiation and compromise led to constructive decision making; negative strategies such as coercion, withdrawal, and avoidance produced poor decisions and relational satisfaction. In comparing a sample of dating African American couples to white couples, Sanderson and Kurdek (1993) did not find significant differences in problem solving and happiness in relationships. What they did find was that couples, regardless of race, reported higher relationship satisfaction when there was frequent positive problem solving.

How well couples know one another's emotional responses to issues also affects decision making. Couples that were better at predicting the impact their messages had on their mates had higher positive feelings for one another (Burleson & Denton, 1997). They also found that distressed couples did not have poorer communication skills than nondistressed couples; rather, stressed partners expressed many more negative intentions toward one another. Unhappy couples communicated more ill will than poor skill.

The following principles could help guide family members in their decision making: (1) create a sense of justice by treating family members equally, regardless of sex or power resources; (2) create a sense of autonomy by respecting each family member's rights to free choices in order to carry out actions that enhance his or her life; (3) create a sense of caring by helping other family members achieve their goals; (4) create an awareness of which decisions lead to actions and behaviors that harm family members or place them at risk; and (5) create a sense of loyalty via keeping promises and carrying out decisions mutually agreed upon. These principles should enhance the self-concepts of each family member. This complex process of decision making can be helped by experiences of a life of shared communication, as described here.

For 52 years, Lambert and I made decisions together. We tried to spend our money as we both saw fit and discuss what was important to us. We usually shopped together for groceries, machinery, cars, and so on. Even on buying our tombstone, we looked them over and decided on one we both liked. Now he rests in front of it. We had our differences, but we always tried to see things from the other's point of view and eventually we'd resolve that problem. I miss him. We had a great life together!

Conclusion

This chapter presented an overview of power, influence, and decision making in the family. We discussed power bases, power processes, and power outcomes as described by McDonald's model and indicated how they affect cohesion and adaptability in family systems. Power in the system changes as the family system grows and develops. Spouses create power patterns, such as wife dominant, husband dominant, syncratic, and autonomic. Children wield power, often through power plays that gain attention. Families often involve member alliances that make certain issues predictable. Each family serves as a context for certain predictable communication strategies that fail or succeed only when they function within the transactional context. There are many types of influence strategies used by family members. Use of these strategies is predicted by context, age, gender, and personality traits. Effective strategies with spouses are often direct.

Through communication interactions, power and influence are employed in decision making, often using consensus, accommodation, or de facto decisions. These decisions may occur in families that govern their systems by styles such as "I win; you lose" confrontations, by the creation and maintenance of various types of rules, or by guiding principles of fairness based on conscience. There are eight parts in four phases in the decision-making steps that families use to communicate differences, yet solve their problems. Although compromise may be required, this problem-solving process has the potential to strengthen cohesion in the family.

In Review

1. How might power affect a family's cohesion and adaptability?
2. Analyze the power resources used regularly by members of a real or fictional family. Indicate how members use communication to convey their use of these resources.
3. Analyze the types of influence strategies used by a real or fictional family. Do you see any patterns of strategy usage? Which influence strategies seem to be most effective?
4. Give specific examples of how factors such as gender, age, individual interests, or resources affected a family's decision-making process.
5. To what extent should children be part of the family's decision-making process? How can they be guided to develop the communication skills necessary to participate effectively in such discussions?
6. Using the four phases of the loop model of problem solving, analyze how a family makes a decision on an important issue. Choose your family-of-origin if you like, but feel free to select another family you know well or a family in a movie, TV show, or novel.

COMMUNICATION *and* FAMILY CONFLICT

To find life again after the struggle, to see that some family fights have to be fought for family growth to take place is a key family characteristic of healthy families. Healthy families draw energy from their conflicts, reviving themselves through their awareness that most family feuds are natural steps in human development, and not signs that the family is failing.

Paul Pearsall, *The Power of the Family*

I f a family member views conflict as war, he or she will approach the whole process differently from a member who feels powerless when conflicts happen. Much of this indicates the negative connotations of conflict. Conflicts occur in all families. At times it feels like a home war is going on and part of the family soldiers have joined opposing troops. Gottman and DeClaire (1997) discovered that couples conflict over the same issues 69 percent of the time. Because the authors found many problems were insoluble, they advise, "We need to teach couples that they'll never solve most of their problems" and that they need to "establish a dialogue" with the problems (p. 20). Ongoing battles are debilitating.

Another way to view conflict is as a rational process, presenting conflict as an opportunity to resolve problems, as a better way to reach family goals (Buzzanell & Burrell, 1997). The increased societal concern with interpersonal violence publicizes the reign of terror in some families. Managing conflict outcomes needs to be a primary task for families in maintaining a fair relationship with a partner or children.

The mere absence of conflict does not make a family function well. Both functional and dysfunctional families conflict, but the functional family processes conflict more positively (Gottman, 1994a). In other words, functional family members engage in conflict when they struggle to make their differences more tolerable. The ways in which a family agrees are important, and the more agreement between members, the less likelihood of disastrous conflict. The ways in which a family disagrees are equally important. Some battle openly, whereas others covertly do one another harm. What is accepted as rational in one family may be perceived as irrational in another (Vangelisti, 1993). All family members help in either negative or positive ways to regulate the dialectical tensions that conflicts create within family systems.

One strong parent or sibling can suppress or avoid conflicts and provide necessary stability for other members to take coordinated actions that make the family system appear to be balanced. Over time, however, such suppression can have negative effects. Dysfunctional families may get stuck in a powerful conflict cycle and devastate one or more family members.

Conflict affects all areas of family life. Often, members escalate or avoid conflict. Conflict may create boundaries, yet boundaries may serve to reduce other potential conflicts. A family's themes or images will influence the amount and the type of conflict that develops. Conflicts can cause negative outcomes: injury, marital distress, divorce, confused children, depressed family members, or loss of property and money (Renick, Blumberg, & Markman, 1992). A family theme of "no conflict" can lead to future problems, as the daughters experienced in the following example.

In our family we were not allowed to fight. My mother wouldn't tolerate it! She would say, "God only gave me two little girls and they are not going to kill one another." Arguments were cut off or we were sent to our rooms. After she died we fought most of the next 10 years! We each had so many old resentments to settle. For over 2 years we didn't speak! Fortunately, we relearned how to relate to one another and now conflict only when necessary.

This chapter will examine the conflict process, a model of conflict styles, factors related to the conflict process, constructive and destructive conflicts, including violence, and communication strategies for managing inevitable and often necessary family conflicts.

THE CONFLICTUAL PROCESS

Family members who confront their differences can improve their relationships and accomplish more joint benefits that increase love and caring. Conflict can provide opportunities for valuable feedback that leads to innovations that enhance adaptability and cohesiveness. Think of conflict and communication as interdependent. Each affects the other. Communication either helps or hinders conflict and serves as a way to resolve conflicts or continue them (Hocker & Wilmot, 1998). The intensity of the conflict determines the kinds of messages produced, the patterns the confrontations follow and the interpretations placed on the communication cues (Roloff, 1996).

In thinking about conflict in families, it is important to remember that families act as systems, as discussed in Chapter 3. Because of family members' interdependence, a conflict between two members of the family will affect other members. A review of 39 studies found that parents' conflicts influence their parenting behaviors, consequently affecting their children (Krishnakumar & Buehler, 2000). These researchers commented that "the emotions and tensions aroused during negative marital interactions are carried over into parent-child interactions" (p. 30). For instance, parents who have high hostility within their marriage also use more harsh discipline with their children and show less sensitivity, support, and love to their children. Other research has found that when spouses have conflict one day, they are more likely to have tense interactions with their children the next day (Almeida, Wethington, & Chandler, 1999).

Families can have conflict over many issues. If you have siblings, or have been around sibling groups, you probably realize that siblings can quarrel over many issues—who gets the front seat in the car, how much time can be spent in the bathroom before school, and who gets to choose the Friday night video. More serious issues in families such as a teenager skipping school, a spouse's infidelity, or a parent's addiction might also lead to conflict.

In a study describing the different types of conflict that emerge in stepfamilies, researchers found that conflict that results in discussion and compromise can often lead to positive change (Coleman, Fine, Ganong, Downs, & Pauk, 2001). Although stepfamilies do encounter these various kinds of conflicts, there are also types of conflict that may be more specific to this family type (Coleman et al., 2001). Conflicts over resources, space, privacy, and finances may emerge as stepfamilies try to develop a family identity. One mother explained some of the conflict that emerged with her new husband over the financial support of her son: "I think he resented it if we went on a vacation to have to pay for [my son's] plane ticket or things like that. I think he did not want to have the responsibility of [my son's] college" (p. 65).

Conflict Defined

Conflict involves a process in which two or more members of a family believe that their desires are incompatible with those of the others. It may, but doesn't have to, include "displaying overt mutual exchanges of intentionally hurtful behaviors" (Weiss & Dehle, 1994). It may be the result of a perception, as when Malik believes that the degree of intimacy expected of him is too threatening or requires more of him than he is willing to deliver. Conflict may also develop over a difference in attitudes or values. Latricia, a full-time working mother, does not enjoy cooking and would prefer that the family went out to eat pizza rather than expect her to fix dinner. Conflict may also arise when one person's self-esteem is threatened by another. Conflict occurs when one person's behavior or desire blocks the goals of another, resulting in a "showdown" over values and resources as each family member seeks to satisfy his or her needs usually at some expense to the other. From a communication perspective, *conflict* may be viewed as "an expressed struggle between at least two interdependent parties, who perceive incompatible goals, scarce resources, and interference from the other party in achieving their goals" (Hocker & Wilmot, 1998, p. 12).

The conflictual process is very complex. Conflict has an individual dimension. The conflicts going on within an individual family member often can cause trouble with others in the family, such as when a father or daughter senses an incompatibility or inconsistency within their own cognitive elements (Roloff, 1987). A frustrated family member who is unhappy at work may act out the tension at home and create family struggles. In addition, family members may use conflicts in a dialectical sense to gain autonomy when they feel trapped and need to reduce connectedness. It is important to understand that not all dialectical contradictions involve conflict; those that do are referred to as *antagonistic* contradictions. Other contradictions that regulate tension are *nonantagonistic* when they do not lead to conflict. Usually these are intrapersonal in nature; "the individual experiences internally the dialectical pull between contradictory oppositions" (Werner & Baxter, 1994, p. 353). Antagonistic contradictions become external and result from an explicit mismatching of interests and goals of individual family members.

Conflicts in families stem from many issues and are handled in many different ways. Writing about conflict between intimate partners, Klein and Johnson (1997) state, "To achieve their goals, partners engage in a variety of conflict strategies, ranging from problem-solving and compromise, to unilateral accommodation and the use of insults, threats and physical force" (p. 486).

Change may trigger uneasiness and conflict. A new family member, the acquiring of a new job, the trauma of a divorce, or the loss of income all have an impact within the family system. Disturbances in equilibrium lead to conditions in which groups or individuals no longer do willingly what they are expected to do. Family systems experience a constant level of friction, since they continually change to survive and cope with conflict, either realistically or unrealistically.

Families who own and run businesses together may have additional opportunities for conflict (Klein, 2002). The following student's comment reflects some of the challenges family businesses can create.

My grandfather used some money he had earned selling a patent to open his own business. A very controlling and intelligent man, he spent a lot of time putting his business together and thus did not spend a great deal of time nurturing his relationship with my grandmother. I think that the conflict that exists between the two of them affects how they relate to their children. The overwhelming control that my grandfather had over his family created an immense amount of conflict even though my grandfather, my uncle, my aunt, and my father all work at the family business. My uncle and my father have a great deal of conflict with my aunt because they think she does not work as hard as they do and that she (and her family) get a lot of special favors from my grandparents.

Additionally, couples who cohabit may have different conflicts than couples who are married. For example, cohabiting women view money as a way to achieve equality, and thus they seek independence and want to avoid economic dependence. Cohabiting men expect economic equality more than married men. The cohabiting partner with the greater income determines more of the couple's recreational activities, including vacations. Cohabiting couples usually maintain separate checking accounts and when they do, they fight less about finances than do married couples.

Gottman and Krokoff (1990) found that some forms of confrontation during marital conflict precede increases in marital satisfaction. They concluded that conflict avoidance had negative long-term consequences. By exploring the process of conflict and how it can develop realistically or nonrealistically, and by becoming aware of better communication practices to use during conflict, one can better understand the development and management of family conflict situations. In some families, mismanaged conflicts can escalate into violence—defined as physical attacks, sexual abuse, and verbal aggression (Cahn, 1992).

Studies have concluded that conflicts are present in many successfully functioning marriages as well as in dysfunctional marriages (Gottman,

1994a). Even though all relationships have problems, successful ones involve partners who learn how to negotiate conflicts. In certain stages of courtship for some couples, there is little conflict, but conflicts develop as the relationship progresses.

Attitudes toward conflict emerge partially from cultural background. In some cultures, open struggle is commonplace and comfortable; in other cultures, verbal expression of differences are avoided at all costs. In many Asian families "saving face" takes priority; preserving harmony as a social group ranks over an individual family member's need to express strong feelings and inner thoughts (Kim, Shin, & Cai, 1998). By contrast, Mexican couples may fight more openly. In a study of conflict in low-income Mexican families, the more supportive the mother, the closer children felt to their mothers, the less depression they experienced as a result of the frequent parental conflicts (Dumka, Roosa, & Jackson, 1997).

Model of Conflict Styles

Every family dyad or triad disagrees differently. For example, your mother and brother exhibit a conflict style different from the one you and your mother exhibit. As you grew up, you learned how to manage or survive conflicts; this learning influenced the style of the conflict strategies you tend to use.

Kilmann and Thomas (1975) developed a model (Figure 9.1) to demonstrate that conflict style consists of two partially competing goals: concern for others (or cooperativeness) and concern for self (or assertiveness). Conflicts contain elements of both cooperation and assertiveness.

Competition and collaboration are at the top of the model. *Competitiveness* requires high assertiveness and going after what you want. Your concern for self is high; thus, you see conflict as a way to get what you

FIGURE 9.1   Conflict Styles

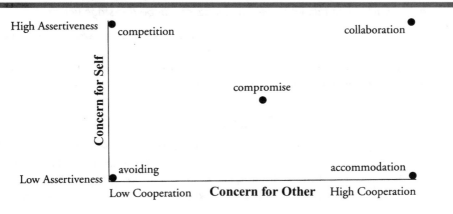

need, regardless of the concerns of others. Competition can be quite self-ish if it is your only style of conflict. It can mean "I win; you lose" too often and destroy cohesion within a family. The challenge is to compete to achieve personal goals without taking unfair advantage of other family members. Wilmot and Wilmot (1981) changed the term in Kilmann and Thomas's model from *high assertiveness* to a *highly competitive condition*.

Collaboration occurs when you show concern for those other family members as well as high concern for self. It often means finding an alternative or a creative solution that pleases all parties. It requires high trust and self-disclosure on the part of all members. Collaboration requires that conflicting members seek a solution that enables all parties to feel they have won without compromising issues vital to their needs.

A *compromise* represents a solution that partially meets the needs of each member in the conflict. In some families, the motto is "Be wise and compromise." Such a family theme tends to support giving in or giving up some of one's needs. At the lower right of the model is *accommodation*. This style of conflict happens when you are nonassertive but cooperative. It is the opposite of competition, because you meet the demands or needs of the other person but deny your own. Finally, *avoiding* implies an unassertive and uncooperative style in which conflict is not addressed. Sometimes it is wise to use a "pick your battles" approach; other times it is a powerful passive response.

This model of conflict styles provides a way of sensing how one family member's fights affect another's counterarguments through feedback. Where do you think the following example would fall on the model?

My father left my mother last year to live with someone else. I have become my mother's main support. She calls me at college almost every day and demands I come home for all kinds of silly reasons. Right now I can't seem to tell her to back off so I do whatever she wants and hope this stage will pass.

The conflict style model based on Kilmann and Thomas provides one view of how families use conflict; other strategies will be discussed later.

Stages of the Conflictual Process

Understanding how conflict develops permits you to unravel some of the complexity and places a point of anger or blowup into a larger context. We developed the following six stages as a model for analyzing the conflict process: prior conditions stage; frustration awareness stage; active conflict stage; solution or nonsolution stage; follow-up stage; resolved stage. These are represented in Figure 9.2.

As these stages are explained, think about a recent conflict in your family. Did each of these stages emerge as a distinct entity or was it difficult to know when one ended and the next began?

Prior Conditions Stage   Ongoing conflict does not occur without a prior reason or without a connection of the present event to the past experiences in the family. It does not emerge out of a vacuum but has roots in the history of the relationship. The family system establishes a framework out of which conflicts arise.

Prior conditions are present in the absence of conflict but, under pressure, come into play. Prior conditions that may affect a new conflict situation include ambiguous limits on each family member's responsibilities and role expectations, competition over scarce resources such as money or affection, unhealthy dependency of one person on another, and negative decision-making experiences shared by those involved in the conflict. Holiday times, income tax time, or the arrival of in-laws often are cited as prior conditions. Past experiences set the groundwork for new tensions.

Frustration Awareness Stage   The second conflict stage involves one or more family members becoming frustrated because a person or subgroup alliance is blocking them from satisfying a need or concern. This leads to an awareness of being attacked or threatened by something they have

FIGURE 9.2   Stages of Ongoing Family Conflict

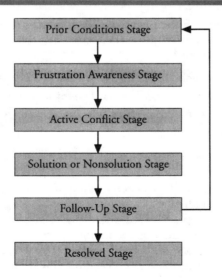

seen. One or more parties become aware of snappy answers, nonverbal messages in the form of slammed doors, or avoidance of eye contact. If you closely monitor any developing conflict, usually nonverbal cues of conflict appear before verbal ones. As you nonverbally become aware of the conflict, you might think, "He's really getting upset" or "I can feel myself getting tense." It is in this frustration awareness stage that one family member becomes increasingly aware that he or she is not communicating. This mismatching may be due to misperceptions.

Inaccurate perceptions can create conflict where none exists. Perceptions affect the degree to which the participants feel they will be threatened or lose if the conflict continues. Conflict may end at this stage if one party perceives that the negative consequences outweigh the possible advantages. "Backing off" from the issue ends the conflict but does not remove the causes or satisfy the needs that provoked it. This kind of unrealistic conflict may be avoided through self-disclosure: "I'm really just upset about the test tomorrow and I'm taking it out on you," or "You're right—I was selfish and I'm sorry."

It is during this stage, labeled "agenda building" by Gottman (1993), that cross-complaining may begin via a series of negative messages that the involved family members are unwilling to stop. *Cross-complaining* involves meeting another's complaint or criticism with one of your own while ignoring the other's point.

Active Conflict Stage In this stage, the conflict manifests itself in a series of overt verbal and nonverbal messages. This symbolic interchange can either be like a battleground or be relatively calm, depending on the family's rules and style of fighting. In some families, yelling and screaming signals the fight of the decade, whereas others exercise their lungs weekly over minor issues.

Unfortunately, my husband is the type who would rather yell. He is not always a fair fighter. When I want to talk and explain my feelings, and then give him a chance to explain his, he either goes into moody silence or explodes. I find both approaches useless.

Typically, conflict escalates from initial statements and queries to bargaining or an ultimatum. In the active conflict stage, there is a discernible strategy, or game plan, when one or more family members try to maneuver and convince others of the merits of an issue. The longer the conflict continues, the more the participants' behavior may create new frustrations, reasons for disliking, and continued resistance. Problematic couples usually escalate by cross-complaining. Functional couples tend to match positive remarks or coordinate negative with positive remarks.

Wives tend to have more other-directed and relationship-sensitive thoughts during active conflict; husbands are more likely to be concerned with the content of the message, their conversational role, and themselves (Sillars, Roberts, Leonard, & Dun, 2000). Thinking about the conflictual interaction in terms of a dyad (e.g., "We're getting more and more irritated," p. 490) is not frequent for husbands or wives. Wives and husbands also view their own communication during the conflict interaction as more favorable than the communication of their partner.

Solution or Nonsolution Stage   The active conflict stage evolves into either a solution or nonsolution stage. The solution may be creative, constructive, and satisfactory to all involved, or it may be destructive, nonproductive, and disappointing. The solution may represent a compromise or adjustment of previously held positions. In an interview, Gottman suggests that the task is to acknowledge other family members' shortcomings, to push for improvements but simultaneously communicate acceptance (Marano, 1997b). In this stage, how the conflict is managed or solved determines the outcome and whether positive or negative results follow.

Some conflicts move into a nonsolution. The conflict stops, but abruptly. Family members may not have the resources or talents to solve the problem, or, after going this far into the conflict process, they may recognize that they do not want the responsibility of carrying out what they demanded. Perhaps they decide they do not want to pay the trade-off costs of accepting a change they earlier demanded. Sometimes schedule demands result in one party leaving the interaction. Nonsolution brings the conflict to an impasse. Obviously, communication problems can develop if too many conflicts end with nonsolutions. However, every family lives with some unresolved conflicts, because the costs of an acceptable solution outweigh the disadvantage to one or more family members. Sometimes, when children mature, they make sense of conflict differently, as described here.

My sister and I are 13 months apart. We fought like cats through our teens. Jamie would always keep at me until I would reach the breaking point and I would say I was angry. Naturally, that was the red flag, and we would end up with my crying and her goading me on. It's ridiculous now when I think about how she manipulated me into crying. Then she would say she was leaving and disappeared. What manipulation!

Follow-Up Stage The follow-up stage could also be called the aftermath, because it includes the reactions that follow the conflict and affects future interactions, such as repeats of the same conflict, avoidance, or conciliation without acceptance. Grudges, hurt feelings, or physical scars may fester until they lead to the beginning stage of another conflict. The house may be filled with long silences, avoidance, or formal politeness. The outcomes may be positive, such as increased intimacy and self-esteem or honest explorations of family values or concerns. The members may exchange apologies or more to communicate about the fight. This aftermath stage is linked by a feedback chain to the initial stage, because each conflict in a family is stored in the prior conditions "bank" of the family and comes into operation in determining the pattern of future conflicts.

Resolved Stage This stage occurs when conflicts move out of the family system; they simply no longer affect its balance. For example, a husband and wife may conflict over priorities on bills to be paid. They negotiate and compromise on demands, then stick to their agreement. Time and developmental stages of each family member affect solutions to conflicts. For example, parental conflicts over who will take Chang to school decrease or disappear after he becomes old enough to walk there by himself; the same will be true of parental conflicts over dating rules and curfews when he becomes a young adult. Conflicts over space and territory among six children competing for three bedrooms no longer require solutions when all have left home and the "empty nest" remains.

It is important to remember that in the model (Figure 9.2) participants may "exit" at any stage. A drop-in visitor may interrupt during the frustration awareness stage and actually defuse the tension. One or the other party may disengage from the issue, give in, or shift the focus. Gottman (1982) found in analyzing the sequential nature of conflicts that an essential difference between distressed and adjusted couples was the ability of happy couples to de-escalate verbally potential negative effects. In a study of conflicts at the family dinner table, 61 percent ended in standoffs that were used as the easiest way to get out of conflicts (Vuchinich, 1987). The different family members involved most frequently used submission and compromise to close off conflicts. Renick, Blumberg, and Markman (1992) note that nondistressed couples exit out of the beginning stages of negative interaction cycles, whereas distressed couples engage in negative escalations.

FACTORS IN FAMILY CONFLICT

Family members fight with each other in different ways. Over time, most families develop their rules for conflictual situations, and each member stays within the calibrated levels, except for unique situations when he or she may go beyond acceptable fighting levels or reconciling behaviors. A tearful embrace may jolt the family pattern far more than a flying frying pan. Dialectical tension generated in conflicts is not a negative force but rather a part of the ongoing dynamic interaction between opposite views and needs of family members. It can be a positive force because the "interplay of opposing tendencies serves as the driving force or catalyst of ongoing change in relationships" (Werner & Baxter, 1994, p. 351).

Patterns of Family Conflict

In their major early study of conflict in early marriage, Raush, Barry, Hertel, and Swain (1974) found that "whatever the contributions of the specific partners, the marital relationship forms a unit, and the couple can be thought of as a system." Their analysis revealed that the marital unit was the "most powerful source in determining interactive events" (p. 201). Couples developed their own styles of conflict, which were unique to them. Soon after marriage, the system develops its own fight style.

Who starts conflicts? Do family members in their roles as father, mother, son, or daughter initiate more fights? According to Vuchinich (1987), parents start 47.6 percent of the conflicts and children begin 52.4 percent of them. More importantly, fathers have less conflict initiated against them, whereas mothers, sons, and daughters share about the same number of conflict attacks. Children start conflicts twice as often with mothers; sons initiate conflicts three times more frequently with mothers. Fathers start disagreements with their daughters three times more frequently than with their sons; whereas mothers counter this with starting conflicts twice as often with their sons.

Another pattern appears in conflict termination, with mothers most frequently involved in working out compromises, or standoffs, in which the family members agree to disagree and no one really wins. Daughters, more readily than sons or fathers, participate in the above ways of closing conflicts. In solving conflicts via submission, children acquiesce three times more frequently than parents. After standoffs occur, females initiate nonconflict activities twice as often. In families in which interactions are ignored or overt conflicts never occur because of child neglect or emotional maltreatment, problems just cause tensions with no relief (Wilson & Whipple, 1995).

In a classic study, Feldman (1979) views a couple's conflictual behavior as part of an intimacy-conflict cycle. Couples move from a state of intimacy as one member becomes anxious or fearful, which leads to conflict and separation. Eventually, one partner makes an attempt to patch up the differences. The desire for intimacy draws them back together. The need to be touched, reaffirmed, comforted, and nourished is a powerful conciliatory force in conflicts. At first, one partner might reject attempts to resume more positive communication, but the need for intimacy provides the motivation for repeated efforts to achieve it.

The couple's reconnection does not mean the problem between them has been resolved. Quite often, the issue has not been satisfactorily discussed or even fairly treated in the best interests of one or the other. Intimacy issues will again emerge into conflict when one partner feels threatened by the issue or aggressive enough to challenge. Have you heard people fighting and had the feeling you were hearing a rerun or rehearsed battle? The degree and limits of acceptable intimacy and acceptable conflict are important dimensions of a marital system's calibration. When these limits are violated, the intimacy-conflict cycle starts again.

Parts of Feldman's intimacy-conflict theory can be related to Baxter's views that individuals respond to contradictory demands by seeking to fulfill each demand separately. They do this through either cyclic alternation or segmentation responses. In *cyclic alternation,* first one partner complains or yells and the other responds. In conflict, husband and wife can "cycle or spiral between the two poles of contradiction, separating them temporally with each contradictory demand gaining fulfillment during its temporal cycle" (Werner & Baxter, 1994, p. 363). In *segmentation* the family members try to verbally group their complaints around a conflicting point. Segmentation involves separate arenas for dealing with opposites. A couple may fight about their household finances, but when it comes to making financial decisions for the family business, the husband has complete control. These authors report that cyclic alternation and segmentation are the most frequently used responses couples enact to manage the dialectical aspects of their relationship.

One common pattern of conflict that couples engage in is called the *demand/withdraw pattern* (Caughlin, 2002). In this pattern, one spouse uses a complaint or nagging behavior, while the other spouse withdraws, trying to avoid conflict. One spouse might nag the other about a chore that needs to be done. The more the spouse nags, the more the other withdraws, by ignoring or not answering the other. More frequently, the wife is the spouse complaining or nagging, while the husband is the one withdrawing. Marital dissatisfaction is linked with the presence of this type of conflict pattern.

Rules for Family Conflict

Members of family systems develop implicit and explicit rules governing the communication of conflictual messages. Jones and Gallois (1989) report that couples generate or employ four kinds of rules in resolving their differences: (1) rules governing consideration (e.g., don't belittle me; don't blame the other unfairly; don't make me feel guilty); (2) rules governing rationality (e.g., don't raise your voice; don't get me angry; don't be so aggressive); (3) rules governing specific self-expression (e.g., let's keep to the point; let's be honest; don't exaggerate); and (4) rules governing conflict resolution (e.g., explore alternatives; make joint decisions; give reasons for your views). Rules governing conflicts differ when couples are in public or in private. The rationality rules are used more in public settings; they are also more important to husbands than to wives. However, both agree that rationality rules are the least important. These rules can become a part of coping strategies both in private and public settings on how to vent negative feelings, how to avoid conflicts, and how to find support in others (Sillars, 1995; Noller, 1995).

Rules for conflicts in families with children have great variation. In some families, children cannot "talk back." In other families, children are encouraged to speak up about their feelings. In disciplining children for conflicts, the rules again vary. Some parents have rules that prohibit any hitting or verbal abuse; others believe spanking or screaming are appropriate. Couple roles frequently influence the conflict behaviors of their children, as in this story.

As a child I remember my parents referring to their rules for fighting, such as "Never go to bed mad" or "Never call the other person names." It seemed a bit silly at the time but, after the kinds of fighting I experienced in my first marriage, I made sure that my fiancé and I discussed fighting and set some rules for disagreeing before I would consider a second marriage.

Costs, Rewards, and Reciprocity

Part of a family's systemic function relates to how costs and rewards are negotiated. Conflict may result if a teenager believes the costs of living in a family (rules, obligations, and pressures) outweigh the rewards (emotional and/or economic). Partners stay together as long as the rewards for remaining in a system outweigh the pain or costs of leaving it. Caring for children may be part of a reward and responsibility component in a marriage and hold a family together for a time, but eventually, if serious conflicts continue, one of the partners will leave. To avoid constant conflicts, there must be sufficient rewards in the family system to justify remaining together.

When one family member does something special for another, a debt is owed. If the other fails to reciprocate, especially after several requests, conflict will start. Reciprocity becomes, or is a part of, the exchange of costs and rewards in the family. For the family to operate emotionally as a system, this reciprocity does not need to be equal either in amount or kind. Most family members do not keep an inventory up to date, but they know generally who owes them favors. Gottman (1994c) points out that the positive forms of reciprocity must outweigh the negative ones. Negative reciprocity definitely becomes a part of verbal abuse between partners when they match nasty replies in strongly responding to one another (Sabourin, 1996). Neither accepts the other's attempts to control. These negative exchanges escalate conflicts into "war" and power duels.

The amount of equity in different relationships impacts conflict. Equity in relationships occur when each family member receives rewards proportional to his or her costs or "If you each work equally hard, then equity demands that you each get approximately equal rewards" (DeVito, 1993, p. 285). A partner or sibling who feels unequal in a variety of ways will respond differently from one who feels equal. Canary and Stafford (1992) report that in equitable relationships, more maintenance strategies are used, such as positivity, openness, assurances, sharing tasks, and doing networking with family and friends. The implementation of these maintenance strategies within a family system would certainly modify conflict behaviors.

Couple and Family Types and Conflict

Couple and family types, as discussed in Chapter 7, can also affect conflict patterns. As a family evolves, the system develops conflictual behaviors that characterize the group if not the individuals.

The Fitzpatrick (1988) couple types demonstrate distinctive conflict behaviors. Her continued research with colleagues has strengthened her conclusions about types and conflict (Noller & Fitzpatrick, 1993; Fitzpatrick & Badzinski, 1994; Fitzpatrick & Ritchie, 1994). Traditional couples seek stability and resist change by confronting rather than avoiding conflict. However, they may avoid conflicts more than they realize. Traditionals more often collude with one another to avoid conflicts. Independents more readily accept uncertainty and change by confronting societal views on marriage in a much more direct communication style than traditionals. Independents do not run from conflicts. They resent a spouse who withdraws.

Vangelisti and Crumley (1998) believe that Fitzpatrick's independent couples and Gottman's volatile couples, plus some parent-child relationships, endure hurtful messages better than other types. Separates stress autonomy, especially by keeping their own space and distance as a strategy to avoid conflict. They hope to keep conflicts neutral and to a minimum. Separates appear angry toward a spouse who pushes conflict but withdraws when confronted. In conflict situations, independents receive satisfaction from self-disclosure, description, and questioning to receive further disclosure (Sillars, 1995). All this evidence lends further credence to our contention that conflict outcomes depend on the type of family and how individuals within the family or partners jointly in their interactions react or adapt to potential conflict stimuli. The conflicts are in their interactions and thus are unique to each family system.

Kantor and Lehr's typologies (1976) can predict how open, closed, or random families will behave in crises or conflict situations. These researchers hypothesize that closed families in conflicts frequently suppress the individual. This type of family operates successfully in conflict if members agree on solutions or accept those handed down to them. However, rebellion results when a member differs, and a permanent schism develops if one or more members refuse to comply with a major decision. Conflict in open families is usually resolved via group consensus in a meeting in which decisions are reviewed and modified. Conflicts are expected and welcomed if they make family living more meaningful. In decision making, every family member can reveal his or her feelings about an issue. This openness means that promises made in family conferences are kept. The random family demonstrates no set way to solve conflicts. No one person's views dominate, and ambiguity characterizes the negotiations. Emotional impasses occur when no solutions can be agreed upon. Solutions come spontaneously. Crises are not taken as seriously as in the open closed family types and are viewed more as an interruption of day-to-day events.

Conformity versus Conversation Orientation

Understanding the research results about conflict depends on how much family members use two types of communication labeled *conformity orientation* and *conversation orientation* (Koerner & Fitzpatrick, 2002).

In which kind of family did you grow up? Did your family use a conformity or conversation orientation in its conflicts? For example, if your family type was pluralistic, then children's views were heard in family disputes. There was a conversational quality about your disagreements. You could argue with Dad or your obnoxious sister. All siblings could develop verbal competence. Your parents would listen and not avoid conflicts, like a conformity-oriented family would. The interplay of these two orientations affects how family members engage in conflicts. Remember in Chapter 7 we referred to four types of families that are created with these two orientations (see Figure 7.2).

Pluralistic families report the least conflict avoidance but protective and laissez-faire families use it the most. Another valuable finding is "the more conformity family members experience in their families, the more likely they are to avoid conflicts . . . the stronger the conversation orientation . . . the less likely they were to avoid engaging in conflicts" (Fitzpatrick & Ritchie, 1994, p. 275). More than other family types, consensual families frequently vented negative feelings and sought outside support from friends and relatives to deal with conflicts, enabling them to better cope with negativity. Protective families conversely avoid outside social support but regularly vent negative feelings expressed in emotional outbursts (Koerner & Fitzpatrick, 1997). The importance of this study is that the results demonstrate how complex conflict dimensions are in families.

Understanding a person's family-of-origin family type may also help one understand that person's conflict behavior in romantic relationships (Koerner & Fitzpatrick, 2002). For the most part, young adults seem to approach conflict in their own romantic relationships in similar ways that their families-of-origin approached conflict. For example, persons from families with a high conformity orientation are more likely than persons from low conformity families to resist their romantic partners' aggressive moves and to engage in mutually negative behaviors with their romantic partners. Koerner and Fitzpatrick concluded that families-of-origin play an important role in socializing their children to conflict behavior.

Remember that in Chapter 7, we discussed Gottman's conflict types under couple-oriented types (1994a). Because his typology is based on how couples conflict, it is important to revisit it. As you may remember, Gottman found couples to fall into one of three types. *Validating couples* agree on many important areas. When they do disagree, they are respectful of each other and try to find compromise. *Volatile couples* are energized by conflict; they argue frequently. These couples are comfortable

Family pairs develop their own conflict styles.

with disagreement. *Conflict-avoiding couples* do whatever they can to refrain from conflict. They are more comfortable in a silent treatment situation than they are in a conflict. Also remember that Gottman has found that lasting marriages can exist in any of these couple types as long as the ratio of five positive interactions to one negative interaction has developed.

Family Developmental Stages

Conflict patterns change because the issues to be resolved in families vary greatly over the years. During the early years of marriage, a couple develops a fight style that may be modified as the family grows. In their analysis of couples who had a child within the first two years of marriage, Raush and colleagues (1974) identified three stages of development (newlywed, pregnancy, parenthood) characterized by varying conflict behaviors, including rejection. They compared these couples who became pregnant to couples who did not have a child during these same years. During the newlywed stage, the future-parent couples behaved more coercively than the nonparent couples, which may indicate greater stress due to impending parenting responsibilities.

Finally, during the parenthood stage, four months after the child's birth, both members of the couple appeared to handle conflict less emotionally and more cognitively than their matched counterparts. Yet, the reconciling behavior of the husbands returned to prepregnancy levels. The early stage of being a threesome may lead to difficulties, since roles need to be reworked when a new person begins to compete for affection, often causing one of the other adults to feel left out. Although a joyful time in most families, early parenthood provides great stress that can lead to significant conflicts (Stamp, 1994).

In the early childhood stage, parents often make decisions and solve conflicts by offering few options. As the child's ability to reason increases with age, the resolution of conflict relates closely to the type of family structure previously outlined. The adolescence period usually presents a greater number of family conflicts as young people search for independence and test rules and role expectancies. Intense peer pressure heightens conflict as family beliefs and practices are questioned. Teenagers make space and privacy demands, which may also cause conflict. Conflicts occur when adolescents question the patterns, images, and rules in their families. In families with delinquent adolescents, parents have difficulties in keeping established rules and expectations, praise their children less, and often give mixed messages and conflicting directives. Their family communication is characterized by "difficulty resolving conflicts, and unwillingness to compromise and a greater proportion of communication was misperceived" (Stith & Bischof, 1996, p. 113). When dating starts, mothers have more conflicts with children, especially daughters (Silverberg & Steinberg, 1987). Both adolescents and parents struggle when they face differences, as this student reports.

When I decided to go to New York for a "cattle call" for a possible movie part, it was the first time I actually argued with both my parents. During most of the argument, my father would not agree that we were in the midst of an argument. "We're just raising our voices," he insisted. This was his way of handling the conflict. He didn't want his little boy to grow up and leave. Finally, I stopped arguing about New York and argued about how he always denied we were fighting. Finally he admitted we were fighting. Two weeks later I went to New York City.

If families undergo separation and divorce, children witness a recalibration of the system, which usually involves a wider range of conflict behavior. If high parental conflict continues after the divorce, adolescents perform less well on both social and cognitive functions (Forehand, McCombs, Long, Brady, & Fauber, 1988). Excessive stepfamily family conflict is definitely detrimental. Cissna, Cox, and Bochner (1990) report that the main dialectical dilemma is to adjust to the voluntary marital relationship and the involuntary stepchild/parent relationship. Often there is great conflict between children and a stepmother or stepfather over accepting the new person with her or his different rules and expectations.

The *empty nest stage,* defined as the period when the youngest child leaves home, presents fewer problems in flexible families than in rigid types. Parents' loneliness, uncertainty, or worry over capabilities of young adult "children" to care for themselves largely disappear after two years. In fact, this stage has positive effects on the psychological well-being of some parents because their child has been successful in making it on his or her own. Conflicts develop when the youngest lingers and cannot make the transition into independent living.

Older married couples report significantly less conflict and greater happiness and life satisfaction than younger couples. Morale increases over time, and older couples evaluate their marriage in a positive manner and describe the quality of their marriages as improving (Steinberg & Silverberg, 1987). The return of adult children, often after divorce with children of their own, can reignite old conflicts and create new ones because parents are forced to help raise another family. They feel trapped into this second shift of parenting as grandparents.

Couples in later-life marriages (more than 40 years of marriage) look at conflict in a different way than they did in their earlier years (Dickson et al., 2002). Conflict is not as central to their day-to-day interactions as it was in their earlier years. Over time, these couples' beliefs about conflict and conflict behaviors have changed.

DESTRUCTIVE CONFLICT

Some conflicts have enormously destructive outcomes. We divide destructive conflict into two types—covert (hidden) and overt (open)—discussing how families use these types to cope with conflicts. Conflict styles may range from the very covert (the burned dinner, disappearance, or cutting joke) to the very overt (hostile words, pots or fists flying). Violence, whether in the form of verbal aggressiveness that abuses family members or physical attacks, fits under destructive conflict, representing the worst kind of conflict. Destructive conflict is illustrated in the following example.

One member of our family, my 20-year-old stepson, enters the house with a barrel full of hostilities and problems. He overwhelms my wife with yelling and screaming and a string of obscenities. My reaction is to tell him to shut up and not to have anything to do with him—certainly not to do anything for him. My wife seethes until she can no longer cope; then she explodes. After a litany of verbal attacks, she retreats behind a closed bedroom door—sealing herself off from the problem.

Covert Destructive Conflict

Covert conflict is sometimes called "guerrilla warfare" since feelings are hidden and messages are unclear. Sometimes family members cover up the hurt or express anger indirectly. They do this to preserve the balance in the system and keep the relationships together. To cope with verbal and physical attacks in conflicts, members often use covert strategies. Covert, or hidden, conflict usually relies on one of the following five communication strategies: denial, disqualification, displacement, disengagement, and pseudomutuality. One experiences the *denial* strategy most directly when one hears such words as "No problem; I'm not upset" or "That's OK, I'm fine" accompanied by contradictory nonverbal signals. Sometimes acquiescent strategies such as apologizing, pleading, crying, or conceding are ways that family members discount stronger feelings and deny their deeper meanings of hurt (Vangelisti & Crumley, 1998).

Disqualification occurs when a person expresses anger and then discounts, or disqualifies, the angry reaction: "I'm sorry, I was upset about the money and got carried away," or "I wouldn't have gotten so upset except that the baby kept me awake all night." Admittedly, some of these messages are valid in certain settings, but they become a disqualification when the person intends to cover the emotion rather than admit to it.

Displacement occurs when anger is directed to an inappropriate person. This is captured in the story about the man whose boss yelled at him, but he could not express his anger at the boss. When he arrived home, he yelled at his wife, who grounded the teenager, who hit the fourth-grader, who tripped the baby, who kicked the dog. When a person believes he or she cannot express anger directly, the person may find another route through which to vent the strong emotions. Displacement happens when a couple who cannot deal emotionally with their own differences turn a child into a scapegoat for their pent-up anger; they single out one person who becomes the "acting-out" child.

The *disengaged* family members live within the hollow shell of relationships that used to be. Disengaged members avoid each other and express their hostility through their lack of interaction. Instead of dealing with conflict, they keep it from surfacing. Some families go to extremes to avoid conflicts.

My wife and I should have separated 10 years before we did. I was able to arrange my work schedule so that I came home after 11 o'clock and slept until Carmen and the kids had left in the morning. That was the only way I could remain in the relationship. We agreed to stay together until Luis graduated from high school. Now I feel as if we both lost 10 years of life, and I'm not sure the kids were any better off just because we all ate and slept in the same house.

Pseudomutuality represents the other side of the coin. This style of anger characterizes family members who appear to be perfect and delighted with each other because no hint of discord is ever allowed to dispel the image of perfection. Only when one member of the perfect group develops ulcers, nervous disorders, or acts in a bizarre manner does the crack in the armor begin to show. Anger in this situation remains below the surface to the point that family members lose all ability to deal with it directly. Pretense remains the only possibility. Vangelisti and Crumley (1998) use the term *invulnerable responses* to describe family members who ignore messages, laugh, or remain silent. These responses may resemble pseudomutuality as a coping strategy in conflicts.

Very frequently, sexual behavior is tied to these covert strategies. For many couples, sex is a weapon in guerilla warfare. Demands for, or

Sometimes partners exaggerate nonverbally as part of their fight style.

avoidance of, sexual activity may be the most effective way of covertly expressing hostility. Sexual abuse, put-downs, excuses, and direct rejection wound others without the risk of exposing one's own strong anger. Such expressions of covert anger destroy rather than strengthen relationships.

Often, covert behavior is a rejection of family themes that discourage conflict or independence. Themes such as "We can depend only on each other" or "We never wash our dirty linen for others to see" encourages family members to hide conflicts. These covert strategies of conflict relate to the belief that conflict equals powerlessness (Buzzanell & Burrell, 1997). Family members view themselves as victims, powerless to change or influence others, thus they use less-threatening covert techniques to reduce conflicts.

Overt Destructive Conflict

Perhaps you could list overt forms of destructive conflict in families that you have observed in or lived through. These negative behaviors include hostile verbal aggression and physical aggression that can lead to violence. Domestic violence happens when one family member imposes his or her will on another through the use of verbal abuse and often force. This violence violates acceptable social norms, but may be tolerated within a particular culture. The violent member intends to inflict pain, injury, or suffering, either psychological or physical, on other family members (Cahn & Lloyd, 1996). Threats are violent messages that warn family members that they will be punished now or later if they do not comply with the wishes of the aggressive member (Roloff, 1996). The research on family violence indicates that partner and parent-child abuse become a part of role relationships. In physically combative families, such behaviors occur frequently enough for children, husbands, wives, or lovers to become accustomed to it. Some evidence suggests that when children are exposed to destructive conflict between adults, it affects their own conflict handling behavior (Davies, Myers, Cummings, & Heindel, 1999).

However, conflict does not always lead to violence. In some families, the outcomes of conflict are positive because the participants do not feel verbally threatened or that they are being coerced to accept predetermined conclusions. The nonverbal elements of loudness versus softness, calmness versus agitated, angry versus pleasant, when used reasonably, can lessen or increase conflicts. There is less likely to be verbal aggression in conflicts if the interactions are rational and paced at a rate that permits listening. As Jacobson and Gottman (1998) point out, every couple argues, but nonviolent couples are able to leave arguments before they turn violent. For a battered woman, it may be difficult to predict when a partner will become violent, and thus it is difficult to withdraw from the argument before the violence begins.

Think back to Chapter 8, where we discussed power, influence, and decision making. Our discussion of overt destructive conflict is tied to those issues. Lloyd and Emery (1994) write that if the purpose of conflict is to meet one's needs, and that if aggression adds to the chance of winning, the emotional and physical health of a partner becomes secondary. Some family members will win at any cost, as in war, or use aggression as power to attain the goal at the emotional expense of other family members. This power extends beyond physically abusive behaviors. Violent husbands seem to assume more of the power of decision making in their families than do nonviolent husbands (Frieze & McHugh, 1992). If the power dimensions are not equal between the sexes in the family, especially in the marital dyad, the conflicts that involve negative strategies could be attempts to more equitably balance the power domains. There are inconsistencies between men and women regarding reporting abuse. "Women often do not label their violent experiences as abusive" (Hamby, Poindexter, & Gray-Little, 1996, p. 137). Conflicts that include anger, physical abuse, and alcohol and drug use definitely do have long-term effects on women's health (Ratner, 1998). Thus, negative words and actions in conflicts can lessen family harmony. Sometimes power moves are expressed during talk about the most mundane activities, as in the next example, in which the mother asserts her expertise in shopping.

My mother always seemed to think that my father had some type of problem carrying out simple tasks. Every once in a while she would give him the shopping list to pick up a few things. When he would return home, my mother would find something that he did "wrong." For example, my dad did not get the exact meat that was on sale; he got four bags of grapefruit instead of three, or bought the wrong brand of napkins. Verbally aggressive comments such as "What is wrong with you? Are you stupid or something? Why can't you follow simple directions?" served as a spark to really set him off.

This conflict is likely about more than shopping. It is probably about their overall inability to communicate positively with one another. Often, what couples fight about is a cover-up for larger issues.

The terms *violence* and *aggression* are often used to generally define both physical attacks and verbal attacks. Physical violence such as hitting, screaming, kicking, teasing, grabbing, and throwing objects characterize some family conflicts. Men are more likely to bully, drive dangerously, hold and shake or roughly handle a child or partner than women and children, who more often endure these painful behaviors (Marshall, 1994). Women, because they are smaller in size and have less options for leaving relationships, are at greater risk for physical injuries (Whitchurch & Pace, 1993).

Verbal attacks also can characterize family conflicts and are significant. "Words hit as hard as a fist," according to Vissing and Baily (1996, p. 87). One particular type of verbal attack is called *gunnysacking*. A gunnysack is a burlap bag and is a metaphor for a deadly weapon that implies storing up grievances against someone and then dumping the whole sack of anger on that person when he or she piles on the "last straw." People who gunnysack store resentments and then dump out the gunnysack when a spouse, sibling, or parent does that "one more thing." The offender usually responds by attacking back, and the battle escalates. Families handle verbal attacks in special ways, such as described in the next example.

My husband is a workaholic. I resent that my husband does not share in the child raising. In fact, it really bothered me when he referred to his staff as his "family." It bothered me even more when his paralegal became more involved with him than we were. They went to play golf and to ballgames. I held my anger in for over a year and finally dumped all my resentments. We are at a standstill. Now he never talks about work; I resent him even more, and so the cycle goes.

In the following sections, we discuss violence and aggression in the contexts of intimate partner relationships and parent-child relationships.

Partner Destructive Conflict   Destructive conflict between romantic partners is widespread. Approximately three-fourths of all couples have admitted using threats of violence to one another (Cahn & Lloyd, 1996). According to the National Research Council's Panel on Research on Violence against Women, up to two million women are battered by an intimate partner each year (Crowell & Burgess, 1996). But violence may be even more prevalent in couples than these numbers indicate. *Common couple violence* is defined as "the dynamic in which conflict occasionally gets 'out of hand,' leading usually to 'minor' forms of violence, and more rarely escalating into serious, sometimes even life-threatening, forms of violence" (Johnson, 1995, p. 285). It is estimated that up to 50 percent of American couples experience common couple violence (Straus & Gelles, 1986). However, Olson (2002) advocates for a recognition of the diversity of common couple violence. Her research demonstrated that there are different types of violent couples: aggressive, violent, and abusive.

Conflict about certain topics is more likely than other topics to be accompanied by physical or verbal aggression between intimate partners (Olson & Golish, 2002). When asked to describe situations in which conflict resulted in aggression, participants in one study most frequently reported situations in which the behavior of the partner was problematic, such as drug/alcohol use, lack of motivation, or not coming home. Participants also reported life change events and the involvement of a third party (such as a past partner) to be accompanied by physical or verbal aggression. There also appears to be several different patterns in which the aggressive events occur over time. For example, some respondents reported that aggression became more severe during the course of the relationship. Others explained that aggression in their intimate relationship began as severe and declined over time. Stable patterns, cyclical patterns, and oscillating patterns (up-and-down) patterns also were reported.

In all conflicts, the language used by family members has a great impact on the outcome. Word choice reflects the degree of emotion and reveals the amount of respect the conflicting individuals have for one another. In Marshall's (1994) study of verbal attacks, he found that 77 percent of the males and 76 percent of the families had expressed threats of violence to their partners and received almost the same percentages of threats! Emotional hate terms ("You idiot!" "Geek," or "Liar") quickly escalate conflicts. In some families, swearing is an integral part of venting rage. In others, the rules do not permit swearing, but name-calling replaces it. Sabourin (1996) states that the damage from verbal aggression is underestimated because it "can lead to serious physical, psychological, and relational problems" (p. 199). Put-downs heighten conflicts and slow the solution process by selecting words that describe and intensify bad feelings. The use of one-up messages represent attempts to dominate or control others. These verbal stances used by dominant family members occur whenever they feel threatened. They overreact to neutral messages if challenged (Rogers, Castleton, & Lloyd, 1996). These attacks are usually accompanied by screaming or other negative nonverbal cues. Men more often blame their wives for using verbal attacks that get out of control, whereas wives more often make excuses for their spouses being violent (Sabourin, 1996).

Sabourin, Infante, and Rudd (1990) discovered that abusive couples exhibited significantly more reciprocity in verbally aggressive exchanges than did distressed, nonabusive control groups. For a majority of couples that used verbal aggression, the conflict did not lead to physical aggression, yet those who used the latter attributed verbal aggression as a catalyst for their physical acts (Roloff, 1996).

In their study of violence, Cahn and Lloyd (1996) cite evidence that physical violence occurs in one of six marriages. Other studies have explored abuse in same-sex couples. Like heterosexual couples, gay male and lesbian couples may use physically aggressive or occasionally violent tactics to resolve relationship conflicts (Kelly & Warshafsky, 1987). Although the patterns of conflict may be similar between heterosexual and same-sex couples, the stigmatization of such couples may affect their willingness to seek help and the responses of those called on to help (Renzetti, 1989). Thus, conflict and abuse plague same-sex as well as heterosexual couples.

Many studies have examined the relationship between a couple's abusive tendencies and the characteristics of their marriage. Indeed, Rogers, Castleton, and Lloyd (1996) found that couples who felt their marriages were satisfying reported using physical aggression about equally and repeatedly, according to their three-year follow-up.

In a study of abusive couples compared to nonabusive couples, the abusive couples showed more imbalanced patterns of cohesion and adaptability (Sabourin, 1992). This research found that abusive couples focused on relational issues but had no sense of intimacy between them. In their digressions in conflicts, abusive couples complained about each other or their children, argued over relational problems, and expressed their own feelings. Nonabusive couples were more focused on accomplishing tasks and expressed their beliefs that life is good and in the value of cooperation. By contrast, abusive couples had these themes: "It's the same old thing; we're in a rut," "If only we had more money," "If only he/she would change." More recent research has examined the differences of relationship quality between women in physically abusive relationships and women in nonphysically abusive relationships (Byers, Shue, & Marshall, 2001). Not surprisingly, women in physically abusive relationships report lower levels of relationship commitment and relationship quality as well as more verbal abuse than do women in nonphysically abusive relationships.

How a couple feels about their relationship also influences their complaint behavior (Langhinrichsen-Rohling, Smutzler, & Vivian, 1994). Couples who admit physical aggressiveness and rate their marital happiness as low or moderate use a higher frequency of nonsupport messages and more competitive symmetry because each partner tries to control the conflicts. Those who rate their happiness at higher levels do not do this. When physical attacks are related to marital unhappiness, there are definitely more adversive comments, greater reciprocity of negative behaviors, more angry responses and overt hostility, and both increased demand-withdraw strategies and poorer problem-solving skills used by both partners (Rogers, Castleton, & Lloyd, 1996). How families handle conflict resolution is central to understanding violence and abuse (Cardarelli, 1997). In a report that indirectly summarizes our remarks, except for those regarding extreme forms of overt violence, Buehler, Betz, Ryan, and Trotter (1992) found in a study of overt and covert conflict styles in families with adolescent members that parents' use of covert conflict style caused youth to internalize problems, but an overt style did not. Hostile interparental conflict styles that were overt were highly related to adolescent problems both inside the family and in the community.

Have you ever known two people who were in a relationship with an imbalance of power? The nature of this power imbalance may affect how partners express or deal with conflict. Cloven and Roloff (1993) found what they called a "chilling effect" when one partner had more punitive power and the other sensed less power in the relationship. The less powerful partner was hesitant to complain or express grievances. This chilling effect increased when the less aggressive partner felt that the more aggressive partner was less committed to the relationship, had more alternatives, or had less dependent needs regarding the love continuing. Undoubtedly, the chilling effect exists in many marriages and leads to destructive conflict.

Noller and Fitzpatrick (1993) report on an Australian study of 600 married and cohabiting couples stating there was more conflict in cohabiting couples, particularly violent conflict, saying, "Conflict seemed to come from the cohabiting lifestyle and to involve feelings of anxiety, guilt, and isolation from family and other sources of social support" (p. 229).

Parent-Child Destructive Conflict   In 1999, an estimated 1,070,000 children were victims of child abuse and neglect (Peddle & Wang, 2001). However, results of nationwide surveys of parents show that occurrences of child physical abuse is even higher than what is reported (Straus, Hamby, Finkelhor, Moore, & Runyan, 1998). Further, one study of sexual abuse of children and adolescents document that 9 out of 10 cases are never reported, and that 27 percent of women and 16 percent of men have been abused (Petronio, Reeder, Hecht, and Mon't Ros-Mendoza, 1996). Teenagers who observe their parents hitting one another are likely to hit their own spouses in later years. Cahn and Lloyd (1996) report that children who see their parents hit one another are also hit, that sons who have violent fathers become abusive to their wives, and that one in five who were sexually abused as kids repeat the abuse with their own children! Boys received more verbal aggression than girls, and both experienced more of it after age 6 (Vissing & Baily, 1996). Some children grow up accepting beatings as part of parents' rights in governing them. The following example illustrates what life is like for some of these children.

My father used to whip my brothers and me with a belt as punishment. As siblings, we had this plan. We were going to go to the police and tell them what he was doing to us. One time, my sister even took pictures of our backsides after a punishment. Once, my brother threatened my dad that he was going to call the police. That just made my dad angrier. My mother told my little sister that she could never tell about what dad did because then they would put him in jail, and my mother couldn't support all of the kids on her own.

According to Wilson and Whipple (1995), "Physical child abuse is a societal tragedy of immense proportion" (p. 317). They believe that abusive parents view their children as more difficult, and therefore need more power-assertive forms of punishment, such as threats, reprimands, whippings, and orders for complying instead of suggesting to children reasons for altering their behaviors. Abusive mothers ranked the values of punishment higher, more than abusive dads and nonabusive couples. Abusive parents send mixed messages by failing to enforce rules consistently and then hitting or kicking children for disobeying. The effects of physical conflict in families takes a severe toll on members' relationships, as indicated in the following example.

As I got older and more mischievous, I became more and more familiar with the sting of my father's belt and the resultant welts and bruises that were not only across my legs and backside, but around my wrists where my father held me so I couldn't get away. Finally, when I was about 11 and tired of being embarrassed to wear shorts in gym class, and of making up stories to explain my welts, I turned on my father as he brought down the belt, caught it and tried to yank it from his hand. I was never spanked again.

Because they have no alternatives, children learn to live with verbal abuse and hitting. Straus (1998) states that spanking is dangerous, that children are easier to discipline with time-outs and reasoning, and that hitting leads to other negative behaviors that create violence in adult life. Hitting children reduces the ability of parents to influence them, especially in adolescence when they grow too big to control by force. "A child should never, under any circumstances, be spanked," Straus declares (p. 648). He asked young adults to react to how they felt after physical punishment. Forty-two percent stated that they hated the parent who did it! He concluded that "corporal punishment does chip away at the bond between child and parent" (p. 644). The extreme result of hitting is the battered child syndrome—the ultimate form of handling conflict negatively. It can include sadistic beatings, sexual abuse, locking children in basements or in cages, burning flesh with cigarettes, and so on. When this kind of behavior happens or erupts within families, positive conflict solving does not occur.

Demos (1998) argues that child abuse is a "malignancy" in society that has increased parallel to increased killings of public figures and rising rates of street violence. The mixed message of love followed by hate and violence that some children receive in their families causes children to mentally seek ways to avoid getting hurt themselves. They adopt a "wait and see" attitude and hope the conflicts will not lead to additional violence. Obviously, there are influences from the outside world that affect the handling of conflicts within the inside world of the family. For example, one study indicated that fathers were less likely to use extreme measures of psychological control and guilt with their children when they had positive coworker relations and clarity from their bosses about their work role (Grimm-Thomas & Perry-Jenkins, 1993). Reduced work stress meant reduced home conflict.

Even during situations where there is no physical abuse happening, mothers who have more tendencies to be physically abusive interact with their children in negative ways. For instance, a mother's level of child abuse potential was found to be related to how much she used affirming or soliciting behavior in interacting with her child; women who had a higher child abuse potential were less likely to use such behaviors (Wilson, Morgan, Hayes, Bylund, & Herman, 2002).

Verbal abuse from a parent to a child also exists. In one study, mothers who tended to be more verbally aggressive in their behaviors were also more likely to vocalize negative thoughts about their children (Wilson, Bylund, Hayes, Morgan, & Herman, 2002).

Incest is the most extreme form of family violence. It is usually cloaked in family secrets with only the victim and the perpetrator knowing. Incest quite often is not revealed until adulthood, after the victim has left the family home. Petronio and colleagues (1996) in their study of sexual abuse in children and adolescents found victims bound by rules enforced by those who had violated them. The victims were vigilant about guarding the release of information about the abuse; they wanted to be in control of what would happen if they disclosed the truth. They concluded that "trust is so central in their decision to tell" (p. 196). Too many children fear they will be held accountable for any legal action, plus be beaten for their disclosure. The increasing evidence of this problem has led some researchers to warn that incest occurs in families that are not classified as pathological or perceived as dysfunctional. Incest is related to family stress, and poor management of conflict certainly heightens stress. It is important to note that extreme male dominance of the family, plus weakness in the mother caused by illness, disability, or sometimes death, correlates highly with rates of incest. Further, women who have been abused both in their families-of-origin and by their husbands are more likely to be forced to accept abuse, resulting in submissiveness. According to Ferguson (1996), "Perpetrators are most often fathers or father surrogates (stepfather, mother's boyfriend, uncle) and the victims are most often daughters" (p. 3).

Children are not always the victims, however. Sometimes parents are the recipients of physical or verbal abuse from their adolescent children. Parents in such situations often feel powerless to stop the abuse. They feel that they have lost the power to be a parent and that they can't turn to the legal system for help. A parent being abused by an adolescent may disengage from that child. Following a family systems perspective, it is not surprising that adolescent-parent abuse affects the parents' marital relationship as well as other family relationships (Eckstein, 2002).

CONSTRUCTIVE CONFLICT

Constructive conflict provides a learning experience for future conflicts. A couple's manner of dealing with conflict is probably established during the first year a couple is together and remains quite consistent. In fact, one study showed that couples in stable marriages lasting more than 20 years do not seem to change their conflict management styles significantly from when they were raising children (Mackey, Diemer, & O'Brien, 2000). Therefore, partners may create a conflict style in the first 24 months of togetherness that will characterize the next 50 years.

Indeed, a couple's ability to handle conflict well can have benefits for their children. "Children who see their parents successfully resolve conflicts and share affection might be expected to feel secure about the future of their family and about their own relationships" (Cox & Harter, 2002, p. 172). Children's witnessing of such resolved conflicts may also affect their responses to future conflicts that they encounter (Davies et al., 1999). Additionally, among engaged couples in which male partners had experience with parental violence, there was more negative communication and affect in interactions (Halford, Sanders, & Behrens, 2000) than in couples where the male partner had not experienced parental violence.

In successful conflict management, happy couples or children go through validation sequences (Gottman, 1979). They know they can either agree or disagree in arguments and bring out their ideas and feelings. If family members can listen to one another, they can better understand motives, opinions, and feelings. Because children are younger and have less vocabulary to use, they must have a climate in which they can ask if they understand what the message means. Children's responses to harsh messages vary greatly; some are so sensitive and will suffer; others do not show any harm for a long time (Vissing & Baily, 1996). Parents can effectively model conflict management, as illustrated by the following example.

One of the things that characterize both my parents is their willingness and ability to listen. They may not always agree with us or let us do the things we want, but no one feels like they don't care. At least we feel like they heard us, and usually they explain their responses pretty carefully if they don't agree with us. As a teenager, I was always testing my limits. I can remember arguing for hours to go on a coed camping trip. Mother really understood what I wanted and why I wanted to go, but she made it clear that she could not permit such a move at that time. Yet I really felt that she shared my disappointment, although she stuck to her guns.

In a study of couples and how they argue, it was found that, when disagreements were negatively responded to by both partners, they had an unhappy relationship. In this research, agreements and acknowledgments correlated positively with control mutuality and relational length (Canary, Weger, & Stafford, 1991). Another study found that romantic partners who had more displays and experiences of love also dealt with conflict more constructively than romantic partners without as many displays and experiences of love (Gonzaga, Keltner, Londahl, & Smith, 2001).

In a comparative study of the communication patterns of couples, Haefner, Notarius, and Pellegrini (1991) discovered that the husbands' preexisting level of marital satisfaction correlated closely with their positive judgments of their wives' problem-solving skills and how they were emotionally validated. Interestingly, wives' happiness related to the husbands' lower use of negative or inhibitory problem-solving behaviors.

Gottman (1994b) has concluded from his research with 2,000 couples that satisfied couples maintain a five to one ratio of positivity to negativity (1994). It was not the way couples handled their compatibilities that prevented divorces, but how they communicated about their incompatibilities. The single factor, five to one positive over negative encounters, determined longevity, despite fighting styles that ranged from openly combative to passive-aggressive. Additionally, couples who use a collaborative conflict management style (Figure 9.1) have been shown to have higher marital satisfaction than couples who do not use a collaborative style (Greeff & de Bruyne, 2000).

Other studies reveal that satisfied family members often overlook conflicts or choose communication behaviors that decrease the chance of escalation (Roloff, 1987), and families that control negative emotional behaviors have an easier time of solving problems (Forgatch, 1989). In conflict the use of direct strategies related positively to marital satisfaction. The use of indirect coercive strategies—such as complaining, criticizing, put-downs, and ignoring—led to unproductive negative conflict outcomes (Aida & Falbo, 1991).

Families seem to be able to manage conflict creatively by recognizing that they have a twofold responsibility: to meet their individual needs and wants and to further the family system. This requires give-and-take, resulting in compromise. The attitude behind this view enhances flexibility and helps to avoid conflicts that result from being too rigid and assuming that one family member's views must be followed. In a comparison of abusive and nonabusive mothers, Wilson and Whipple (1995) report that nonabusive mothers introduce more topics into discussions, give more verbal and nonverbal instructions, and utilize more signs of verbal and nonverbal affection. The nonabusive parents use more inductive or indirect strategies—such as time-outs, withdrawing privileges, explaining consequences, and so on—to discipline their children. If the system is flexible and differentiated, family members can more readily accommodate one another, learn new ideas from other members and themselves, and change. In a study of gay and lesbian couples and heterosexual couples, Kurdek (1994) found relationship satisfaction depended on the degree of investment in the partnership and the use of positive strategies to problem solve and resolve conflicts. Thus, a climate of validation or confirmation establishes the tone for constructive interaction.

Strategies for Constructive Conflict

Although Chapter 13 describes specific methods of improving family communication, three constructive conflict behaviors will be briefly discussed here: listening, fair fighting, and managing the physical environment.

Listening   A cornerstone to constructive conflict may be found in good listening behavior. Listening is an important communication skill to use to defuse conflict and help clarify and focus on the issues being debated. Empathic listening requires that one listens without judging and tries to hear the feelings behind the remarks. A remark like "You're really angry" or "That had to bring up all the sadness again" indicates to a family member that one has listened yet not become trapped within one's own emotions or thinking about "How can I best turn off this complaint?" Restating what one has heard a person say can be most helpful in slowing or stopping the escalation of conflict. "Wardell, are you saying . . . ?" Asking Wardell to repeat his point is another helpful approach. Some partners will go so far as to switch roles in a conflict and repeat the scene to check out the accusations. It gives the one partner a chance to try out the other's feelings.

Fair Fighting   Many bitter conflicts in families result from the use of unfair tactics by various members; such behavior can be changed with commitment to fair fighting. In a fair fight, equal time must be provided for all participants, and name-calling or "below-the-belt" remarks are prohibited. In this system, family members agree on how they will disagree. The procedures are agreed on with time and topic limitations. They can be used only with the mutual consent of the parties involved and the assurance that each will listen to the other's messages. Distressed couples have great difficulty in fighting fairly. They readily exchange one-for-one negative remarks and cannot cycle out of negative feedback loops. They continue blaming and fail to build on remarks that would lead to change and solve the conflict (Weiss & Dehle, 1994). An unfair example of conflict and the use of name-calling to "hit below the belt" is demonstrated in the following example.

My mother always used a lot of verbal attacks to "handle" conflict. Put-downs definitely intensified bad feelings. My mother knew the exact names to call me that really hurt. She used to call me Chubby, Fatso, and other similar words. These words only made me angrier and never settled any argument. My mother rarely used swear words when she was yelling, but if she called me those names, I would usually start swearing at her. When she went into treatment for drug abuse, the whole family got involved and through counseling we learned to avoid the "red flag" words that would set each other off.

In fair fighting, family members try to stay in the here and now. They specify what it is that they feel caused the conflict. Each family member takes responsibility for his or her part in the fight and does not blame the others. Jim tells his wife, "I really felt angry this evening when you told Marissa she didn't have to go to the program with us. You let her run wild." In this approach, Jim continues to release his anger during the time granted to him by his wife. According to the rules of fair fighting, he can express his anger only verbally—no hitting or throwing things. Michelle can deny the charges Jim makes, which can lead to a careful recounting of what was said and with what intended meanings. This often helps clear the air. She can also ask for a break until later if she becomes angry and cannot listen.

Sometimes flexibility and compromise will not solve conflicts. In these cases, the consequences outweigh the advantages. An individual's self-worth may be more important than family expectations. Some families permit members to decide what is negotiable and nonnegotiable for them. Stating "This is not negotiable for me at this time" enables one to own his or her position and part of the problem. Being tentative and including the phrase *at this time* leaves the door open for future discussion. Other items may legitimately be nonnegotiable for you on a permanent basis.

If I feel like Italian food and Roger, my husband, has his heart set on Chinese food, Chinese it is. I have never thrived on conflict, and will avoid it by settling for less, especially on "little things."

In the case of a more serious conflict, I try to problem-solve. I believe that two people in conflict should never go to bed mad at each other. If the problem is big enough to cause conflict, it is worth the time and effort to solve it, for the sake of the relationship.

It goes without saying that cross-complaining defeats the purposes of fair fighting. In cross-complaining, one partner ignores the complaint of the other and counters with his or her own complaint. Both parents and children can get caught up in an endless cycle of "You did this!" followed by "But you did the same yesterday!"

Whatever rules or methods couples use in their fighting, the nonverbal aspects of conflict need special attention. Careful monitoring of nonverbal cues often reveals the true nature of conflict (Gottman, 1994c). Gestures of threat, harsh glares, and refusals to be touched or to look at others indicate the intensity of the conflict. Gottman observed that "nonverbal behavior discriminates distressed from nondistressed couples better than verbal behavior" (p. 469).

Sometimes nonverbal cues contradict verbal statements. A receiver of such mixed messages must decide "Do I believe what I hear or what I see?" On the other hand, supportive nonverbal cues can drastically reduce conflict. For example, a soothing touch or reassuring glance has great healing powers.

Managing the Physical Environment   Choice of space may dampen certain conflicts. Reducing the distance between adversaries may help to reduce the noise level. Sitting directly across from someone makes for easy eye contact and less chance for missing important verbal or nonverbal messages. Conflicting family members need to be aware of all the factors that can escalate a fight. Choosing a quiet and appropriate space lessens distractions or related problems.

One thing I have learned about fighting with my teenaged son is never to raise an argumentative issue when he is in his bedroom. Whenever we used to fight, I would go up to talk to him about school or about his jobs in the house, and five minutes after we started arguing, I would suddenly get so upset about his messy room that we would fight about that also. By now I've learned to ask him to come out or to wait until he is in another part of the house to voice a complaint.

The rewards of better-managed family conflicts are numerous. Better use of positive communication practices stops the cumulative aspect of conflict. A series of minor conflicts left unsolved can escalate into separation, divorce, or emotionless relationships. Successful resolution of conflict that goes through the stages of our conflict model (Figure 9.2) leads to emotional reconciliation and affirmation of the participants. Knowing how to manage conflicts leads to a greater appreciation for the talents of family members and enjoyment of each of them in the here and now of living together. Gottman and Krokoff (1989) state that for long-term marital satisfaction, wives need husbands to confront areas of disagreement and to vent disagreement and anger openly. They also note these differences: Men in satisfied marriages de-escalate negative affect in low-conflict interactions; women in satisfied marriages de-escalate negative affect in high-conflict interactions. However, in unsatisfactory marriages, both partners abandon the de-escalation role.

In other forms of families, gay and lesbian, cohabiting, single-parent, and stepfamilies, the conflictual process can vary from married couples and their children. Conflicts differ for gay and lesbian couples in several distinct ways. They have no marriage license to slow down exit threats. In some sense they are voluntary relationships. They report less security in their future together and restrain conflict to survive as couples (Patterson & Schwartz, 1994). Homosexual couples in serious conflicts or in abusive relationships have less access to social support from others. Being a minority and also "in the closet" in so many cases limits their chances of getting help from family members and others who do not approve or understand their lifestyle. To disclose conflict problems may lead to rejection and ridicule. Another type of conflict often arises in gay and lesbian families when they have children from previous marriages, especially in the early years after divorce. This stepfamily form does not have universal acceptance and causes conflicts at holiday times, vacations, and visits from the children or arguments over who should have custody.

Conflicting cohabiting couples are more likely to be abusive than in dating couples of the same age. They conflict more on a larger range of topics and are twice as abusive, particularly in longer-term relationships (Magdol, Moffitt, Capsi, & de Silva, 1998). All of this information has an impact on conflicting constructively.

Children in single-parent families and stepfamilies may be exposed to intrahousehold fighting within their homes and to interhousehold conflicts with the biological parent living in another home. Children become tale bearers with stories from one home to their second home, which can cause conflicts.

The following summary of strategies for constructive conflict reflects integration of many pieces of prescriptive advice. As you will note, certain strategies are valued, but across different cultures, other strategies may be seen as more critical.

Elements of Constructive Conflict

The following characterize successful conflict management:

1. A sequential communication exchange takes place in which each participant has equal time to express his or her point of view.
2. Feelings are brought out appropriately, not suppressed.

3. People listen to one another with empathy and without constant interruption.

4. The conflict remains focused on the issue and does not get side-tracked into other previously unsolved conflict.

5. Family members respect differences in one another's opinions, values, and wishes.

6. Members believe that solutions are possible and that growth and development will take place.

7. Some semblance of rules has evolved from past conflicts.

8. Members have experience with problem solving as a process to settle differences.

9. Little power or control is exercised by one or more family members over the action of others.

Families that are inconsistent in going through the phases of problem solving do not see a new conflict as a challenge to think creatively; rather, they try to use old solutions. More consistent families have all members involved as they try to find new ways to creatively handle problems (Kieren, Maguire, & Hurlbut, 1996).

These goals are not achieved in families in which young people fail to learn these communication and problem-solving skills, because their parents either shield them from conflict or typically make the decisions. Remember, guidelines must be culture-sensitive to be effective. Encouraging a battered spouse or child to become more argumentative in an abusive family could make matters worse. Whitchurch and Pace (1993) caution that being confrontive "could backfire because with relational issues such as anger and control unaddressed," the conflict could escalate (p. 98).

UNRESOLVED CONFLICT

Unresolved conflict is associated with low relationship satisfaction (Cramer, 2002). What happens in the family if conflict cannot be solved? Usually, a loss occurs, which affects all members as psychological and/or physical estrangement creates and fosters separation. Young family members may remain in the home but withdraw from family activities until they go to school or establish a way to support themselves. If circumstances force a continued joint living arrangement, a wall of silence may become part of the family's lifestyle. Some members may be cut off from all contact with the family and may be treated as nonexistent, as in the following example.

When I married my husband, I was essentially making a choice between my parents and Joe. Joe is African American, and my parents said they would never speak to me again if we married. Although I knew they were angry, I thought that they would come around when we had a baby. Melissa is 2 years old now and my parents have never seen her. My brother and sister have been to see me, but I am "dead" as far as my parents are concerned.

In other couples, unresolved conflict may lead to violence (Olson, 2002). Many unresolved marital conflicts result in divorce, or dissolution of the relationship in cohabiting or homosexual couples. One or both members withdraw, seeing the ending of their formal relationships as the only logical solution. Yet, when children are involved, spouses are divorced from each other, not from the children, and the children not from one another. The system alters itself rather than ends. The original family system evolves into new forms, which may include new spouses and children. Legal action does not stop interaction of family members.

Some couples stop their conflicts short of separation because the cost of the final step may be too great; yet, the rewards of living together are too few. For these people, destructive conflict characterizes much of their continued shared existence. Such unresolved conflict may add great tension to the entire family system, but not always. When an issue is unresolvable, it may be more functional for the family to avoid the issue and direct its communication to areas that bring cohesion (Fitzpatrick, Fallis, & Vance, 1982). Gottman would modify this advice if the anger could be directed at a particular issue, and be expressed without contempt and general criticism. Gottman found in his research that "blunt, straightforward anger seems to immunize marriages against deterioration" (1994c, p. 46). Yet, over time, family members may learn to live with topics that are avoided because the pain of addressing them is too great.

Conclusion

Given the many stresses families face in today's world, conflict management becomes an important critical skill. Giblin (1994) summarized several studies and stated "Whatever the stress, the more partners are able to support each other, to understand and respond empathically, the greater their marital satisfaction" (p. 49). In this chapter, we have presented a variety of ideas about conflict. We view conflicts as inevitable, potentially rewarding, and leading to the resolution of differences with families. From a dialectic perspective, the potential for conflict is always present in families, the tension residing in the relationships and not individuals. Conflict is a dialectical force of opposites continually present in a state of fluctuation, adjustment, and change.

Some families develop effective conflict styles through discussion and negotiation. The following family realistically faced their problem when they sought outside help—a step that can reward a troubled family system.

When I asked my wife what she wanted for our twenty-fifth anniversary, she said, "Marriage counseling. The next 25 years have to be better than the first." I knew we had many fights, but I never knew she was that unhappy. I agreed to the counseling, and we really worked on our differences and ways of resolving them. After a few months, we were able to talk rationally about things we always fought over—money, my schedule, our youngest son. Next month we will celebrate our twenty-eighth anniversary, and I can say that the last 3 years were a lot better than the first 25.

In Review

1. Take a position and discuss whether conflict is inevitable and necessary for the development of family relationships.
2. Using the stages of family conflict, describe a recurring conflict in a real or fictional family.
3. Interview three persons about their attitudes toward conflict they learned in their family-of-origin and how they perceive they have learned to manage conflict today.
4. Relate examples from your own experiences with families that might agree with Gottman's conclusion that couples can conflict, but the ratio needs to be five positive experiences to one negative over time if a relationship is to last.

COMMUNICATION *and* FAMILY STRESS: DEVELOPMENTAL ISSUES

10

Families comprise people who have a shared history and a shared future. They encompass the entire emotional system of at least three, and frequently now four or even five, generations held together by blood, legal, and/or historical ties. Relationships with parents, siblings, and other family members go through transitions as they move along the life cycle.

Betty Carter and Monica McGoldrick, *The Expanded Family Life Cycle*

Families constantly change as time and events alter their lives; some events are developmental and predictable as years and physical growth lead to maturation. Other events occur that are unpredictable; out of sync with usual expectations, such as family disruptions caused by poverty, illness, unemployment, or abrupt endings of relationships that once met family needs. "Depending upon the resources they possess and their interpretations of the events, family members respond to these events with varying degrees of stress" (Aldous, 1990, p. 572). Major events impact developmental patterns. Some families experience an entirely different life from the majority of families in a community since "ecological and life course perspectives, as well as historical accounts of the lives of ethnic/minority families suggest that, in fact, the developmental pathways of African Americans, Hispanics, Native Americans and recent Asian American immigrants may be quite different from those of mainstream individuals" (Dilworth-Anderson & Burton, 1996, p. 326). Indeed, not all majority families follow the dominant pattern because they too are affected by poverty, homelessness, and unemployment, issues that impact some minority families, interrupting "normal" expectations in the life development. Any time there is either a natural change in the life of a family member or a catastrophic change, communication plays an important part in negotiating the transitions involved. One family's development evolves into another, like a great chain with connections from previous generations to the present. Family patterns affect three or more generations (McGoldrick & Gerson, 1985).

Like a mobile that cannot stop gyrating, families experience extremes when a variety of stresses pile up. It is unrealistic to take a rigid system's view and assume that strain can be reduced or completely eliminated by rationally realigning priorities and renegotiating responsibilities. We cannot assume that all family members have the resources to go through the years easily. For example, the pressures that adolescents can place on a family system are illustrated in the following example.

"Jesus, Mary, and Joseph, save my soul!" can be heard from the lips of my mother at least once a day. Mom thought three in diapers was bad but since has decided three teens are worse. Presently, we have three teens in Driver's Ed, three teens tying up the phone, three teens falling in and out of love. Mom threatens to run away once a day. Dad says we drive him crazy and should be locked up until we go away to college. We must be driving our parents nuts.

[handwritten margin note: Highest stress @ transition point]

Think about your own family. What has marked family changes? Some families emphasize *marker events,* or the transition points in human development, more than others do. A child's first steps, a confirmation or bar mitzvah, a teenager's driver's license, or a wedding may serve to mark major changes. Other families emphasize unpredictable crises as significant symbols of change—winning the lottery, a parent's cancer surgery, or the accidental death of a sibling may symbolize the greatest moment of change.

Family worldviews affect their perceptions of stresses that enter their systems. If one family perceives the world as chaotic, disorganized, and frequently dangerous, any change may be upsetting. If another sees the world as predictable, ordered, and controllable, change may be perceived as manageable. How a family responds to stress depends on its organizational structure prior to the stress and the values it upholds. The family's first response to stress may be to maintain balance in the system, but this may fail if the shock to the system is significant.

This chapter and the following one address family communication patterns related to developments and life-course changes that are somewhat predictable as well as the range of unpredictable stresses. Moving through stages of family development creates stress as family members separate from their families-of-origin, form their own familial units, and live together over a period of time. The next chapter focuses on unpredictable stresses and family interaction. Communication plays an important part in negotiating the transitions and coping processes. We also recognize that stress can be related to gender issues and that frequently men differ from women in how they handle stress.

OVERVIEW OF FAMILY CHANGE

Developmental Stage and Life-Course Issues

As you read the next two chapters, you will encounter the terms *developmental stage* and *life course*. Both are central to an understanding of change and communication in family life. First, we will discuss the developmental approach, sometimes referred to as *developmental stages*. Most early researchers accepted the position that individuals experience critical periods of change, or life stages, until death (Erickson, 1968; Levinson, 1978; Gilligan, 1982; Rogers & White, 1993). Sometimes these stages are referred to as *seasons* of one's life. Some authors use the term *life cycle* but others discount it because it implies a repeated circular sequence although families never go backward, or circle through the same experience (Aldous, 1996).

Communication between people not only reflects their environment but depends on their experiences and which stage they are at in the life cycle (Kohlberg, 1969). Hayes (1994) applies Kohlberg's ideas to what he calls a developmental constructivist perspective in which an individual moves through stages. Each stage enables the person to make more sense of a greater variety of experiences in more adequate ways. Stress occurs when the individual's levels of functioning and problems in his or her social environment do not agree. The original work on development related only to individuals; eventually, family theorists developed life stages or developmental models of families. Early thinking about family life reflected the position that "normal" couples remained intact from youthful marriage through child rearing to death in later years. It was assumed that the communication components of these developmental stages would also be predictable.

Originally, models of family stages applied to middle-class intact white American family developmental stages. Historically, events such as untimely death or divorce interrupted families from experiencing "on time" life cycle developments. Today, family theorists consider divorce or single parenting as a stage, suggesting a "Y" or "fork in the road" model of development (Ahrons & Rodgers, 1987). Carter and McGoldrick (1999)

Like individuals, whole family systems also pass through various "seasons" of their lives.

conceptualize divorce as an interruption or dislocation that restructures but does not end the family.

A *life-course approach* provides another valuable way to understand change and the stresses that accompany it. The focus shifts to under-standing "how varying events and their timing in the lives of individuals affected families in a particular historical context" (Aldous, 1990, p. 573). It includes changes in individuals, families, and social organizations over historical time (Price, McKenry, & Murphy, 2000). This perspective, for example, recognizes that individuals and families living in the new millennium are dealing with stresses unique to this historical period, such as environmental concerns, economic uncertainties, international adop-tion, cloning debates, homelessness, concerns about adequate medical care, globalization, new reproductive technologies, and terrorism.

Technology provides a means to see how current life course issues impact the family. Stress can be induced instantaneously via cell phones, laptops, home computers wired to offices, and beepers. All of these devices of the Information Age force attention to concerns as they occur (Goozner, 1998). These mechanical devices contribute to stress if they force people to be "on call" 24 hours a day. Laptops extend the workday; cell phones link parents and teens continuously. Family life has been altered by these technological devices.

The life-course approach operates at a different level of analysis because it is focused primarily on "how individual family members in connection with their participation in other groups orchestrate family event sequences" (Aldous, 1990, p. 574). Three types of time are considered in a life-course perspective: individual time, generational time, and historical time. *Individual time* refers to chronological age, *generational time* refers to "family time" or the positions and roles individuals hold in families (grandmother, breadwinner), and *historical time* refers to events that occur during the era in which one lives (e.g., Civil Rights Movement, September 11th).

Events in the life-course perspective often get labeled as "on time" or "off time." Individuals now marry later; have babies later, even into their early forties; start or are forced into entirely new careers, often at midlife; return to college to complete degrees—all "off time" with a strict time sequencing family process.

One way to recognize the connection between a life-course and developmental stage approach is by adding a greater number and variety of family stages. For example, establish a contextual frame for 18- to 29-year-olds who have not left home because of poorly paying jobs or need for job retraining or have returned because of failed marriages. Taking a life-course perspective suggests that when crises occur, an individual family member's education, income, occupation, values, and satisfaction or dissatisfaction with life may be more significant than timing in family stages.

Future families will be represented increasingly by elongated generational structures. Bengston (2001) reports that due to increases in longevity and decreases in fertility, the population age structure in most industrialized nations has changed from a pyramid to a rectangle, creating "a family structure in which the shape is long and thin, with more family generations alive but with fewer members in the generation" (p. 5). This will create shifts in relational interaction as elder generations compete for connection to limited grandchildren and great-grandchildren. Bengston makes the case for the increasing importance of multigenerational bonds because these changes will result in longer years of shared lives.

No single model can reflect all family growth complexities. The life course approach allows for more variation in understanding stress and sees differentiation as normal rather than as deviation. Some societal forces cause more differentiation in families, especially in low-income or high-income families (Hiedemann, Suhomlinova, & O'Rand, 1998). Following are some perspectives on family development with recognition of life-course issues, drawing implications for family communication.

Sources of Family Stress: A Model

In their work on change in the family life cycle, Carter and McGoldrick (1999) present a model depicting stressors that reflect family anxiety and affect the family system (Figure 10.1). Within the same family, individual members experience and react to these stresses differently. Stress

FIGURE 10.1 Flow of Stress through the Family

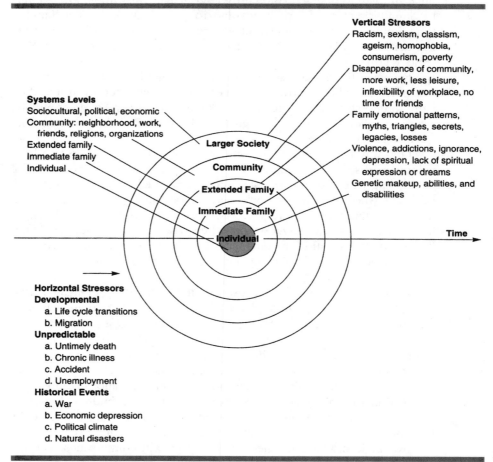

Source: From Carter, B., & McGoldrick, M. *The Expanded Family Life Cycle,* 3/e, © 1999. Published by Allyn and Bacon, Boston, MA. Copyright © 1999 by Pearson Education. Reprinted by permission of the publisher.

varies with the age of each family member and their position in their life cycle.

The vertical stressors include unique family patterns of relating and functioning that are transmitted across generations, including family attitudes, values, expectations, secrets, rules, societal pressures, and individual makeup. In other words, "These aspects of our lives are like the hand we are dealt" (p. 5). Many of these communication-related stressors were discussed as the images, themes, myths, rules, boundaries, and expectations that come from the family-of-origin.

The horizontal flow in the system includes the anxiety produced by the stresses on the family as it moves across time—both the predictable, or developmental stresses, the unpredictable events that disrupt the life cycle, and major historical events. Pressures from these current life events interact with one another and with the vertical stressors to cause disruption in the family system. The greater the anxiety generated in the family at any transition point, the more difficult the transition.

The past and present family stresses are affected further by all levels of the larger systems in which the family operates. These are the life course concerns—social, cultural, economic, and political contextual factors. One's community, extended and biological family, and personal resources also contribute to the process of moving through life. This model is too complex for us to develop in two chapters, yet it gives you a sense of the enormous number of life variations experienced in the everyday world.

The developmental approach goes through stages that suggest a linear progression of families moving through the life cycle, but some families follow a nonlinear sequence reflecting the life-course approach that has been affected by social and structural issues such as racism, unemployment, and poverty. As one moves through phases of one's individual and family existence, these forces will positively or negatively influence the process. Thus, these three major factors—vertical stressors, horizontal stressors, and system levels—taken together put a family's life cycle and its life-course position into perspective.

FAMILY STAGES AND LIFE COURSE

We will examine the life cycle or stages approach and then intersperse comments about how the life-course approach broadens and recognizes differences that affect family communication. Family researchers have attempted to apply the stage concept to whole families so that the entire system may be thought of as moving through particular stages. Experts (Carter & McGoldrick, 1999; Duvall, 1988; Hill, 1986; Glick, 1989) describe the process in anywhere from 6 to 12 stages. Such analysis has difficulties, because families consist of several individuals in different life stages, but it becomes more manageable than trying to account for each person. Such schemes provide simplicity but do not account effectively for families with numerous children or widely spaced ages of children as they go through the middle stages of development. Nor do they focus on adult developmental stages or tasks unrelated to childrearing. No matter which framework is adopted, communication emerges as a critical issue at each stage. The following stages are most appropriately applied to the two-parent middle-class American family life cycle. These stages, detailed by Carter and McGoldrick (1999), will be used for discussion. Table 10.1 describes the stages of the family life cycle.

Leaving Home

Although this first stage, leaving home, is not found in other life cycle lists, Carter and McGoldrick include it as an essential stage that recognizes the young adult coming to terms with his or her family-of-origin and separating or leaving home to enter a new cycle. The unattached young adult faces developmental tasks in areas of work and relationships. These will play out differently, depending on social class and ethnicity.

Unless this task is successfully handled, communication problems can develop in the stages that follow. Young people need sufficient autonomy to separate and achieve their goals independently. If they remain enmeshed and overly dependent, this will affect their choices or options throughout their lives. The goal is healthy interdependence, with the parents letting go and the young adults establishing careers, completing school, finding close friends, and establishing peer networks, defining the "self" as separate yet a part of the family-of-origin. Cain (1990) indicates that young adults faced with their parents' divorce may experience severe life disruption. The ideal would be for the young adult to feel free to achieve his or her own goals and command the respect and encouragement of the parents, even if they might have hoped for other outcomes. Successful resolution of the single young-adult stage requires "(1) an ability to tolerate separation and independence while remaining connected; (2) a tolerance for differentness and ambiguity in career identity of adult children; and (3) the acceptance of a range of intense emotional attachments and life styles outside the immediate family" (Aylmer, 1988, p. 195). Young people and their parents need to find less hierarchical, or vertical, ways of communicating and to adopt more horizontal, or adult-to-adult, communication patterns. This is not always easy, as seen in following example.

Ending college has been a period of great stress for me. My family always refers to me as the "gazelle"—frightened by conflict. Yet I'm now battling with (handwritten top margin) marriage → changing of two entire systems & an overlaping to develop a new system

TABLE 10.1   The Stages of the Family Life Cycle

Family Life Cycle Stage	Emotional Process of Transition: Key Principles	Second-Order Changes in the Family Status Required to Proceed Developmentally
Leaving home: single young adults	Accepting emotional and financial responsibility for self	a. Differentiation of self in relation to family of origin b. Development of intimate peer relationships c. Establishment of self in respect to work and financial independence
The joining of families through marriage: the new couple	Commitment to new system	a. Formation of marital system b. Realignment of relationships with extended families and friends to include spouse
Families with young children	Accepting new members into the system	a. Adjusting marital system to make space for children b. Joining in child rearing, financial and household tasks c. Realignment of relationships with extended family to include parenting and grandparenting roles
Families with adolescents	Increasing flexibility of family boundaries to permit children's independence and grandparents' frailties	a. Shifting of parent/child relationships to permit adolescents to move into and out of system b. Refocus on midlife marital and career issues c. Beginning shift toward caring for older generation
Launching children and moving on	Accepting a multitude of exits from and entries into the family system	a. Renegotiation of marital system as a dyad b. Development of adult-to-adult relationships between grown children and their parents c. Realignment of relationships to include in-laws and grandchildren d. Dealing with disabilities and death of parents (grandparents)
Families in later life	Accepting the shifting generational roles	a. Maintaining own and/or couple functioning and interests in face of physiological decline: exploration of new familial and social role options b. Support for more central role of middle generation c. Making room in the system for the wisdom and experience of the elderly, supporting the older generation without overfunctioning for them d. Dealing with loss of spouse, siblings, and other peers and preparation for death

(handwritten margin notes)
- Problem if parent or child doesn't recognize need to change.
- most complex stage — boundries are critical
- hardest part for satisfaction for couple
- most couples in therapy have young children
- form new boundries
- Sandwich gen.
- boomerang gen.
- empty nest synd.
- relinquish power

Source: From Carter, B., & McGoldrick, M. *The Expanded Family Life Cycle,* 3/e, © 1999. Published by Allyn and Bacon, Boston, MA. Copyright © 1999 by Pearson Education. Reprinted by permission of the publisher.

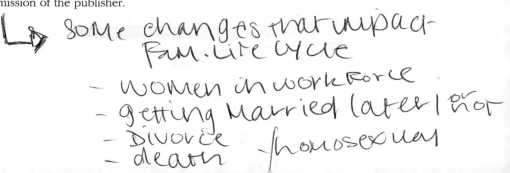

(handwritten notes)
└→ some changes that impact fam. life cycle
- women in workforce
- getting married later / or not
- divorce   / homosexual
- death

my parents to support my desire to go on a year-long mission for my church.
They see this as inconceivable. I am struggling with my need for indepen-
dence and the chance to move on my own.

There is a definite connection between what happens to single young adults in their leaving home and their transition into the next stages of family development. Fiese, Hooker, Kotary, and Schwagen (1993) go so far as to state that "the marital dissatisfaction reported during the early stages of parenting is best predicted by premarital relationship satisfaction" (p. 634). Yet, many young adults continue to live at home because they are single parents, it is not culturally appropriate to live apart from the family at their age, or they are helping support the family. For example, Latinos leave home typically to form a family of their own; moving out tends to be a prolonged process due to intense family ties (Falicov, 1999).

Part of young adulthood involves investing in intimate peer relationships, some of which may be romantic, and beginning the process of exploring deep interpersonal connections. Thus, young single adults must experience an individual orientation, or autonomy, in order to move toward future interdependence and attachment. Individuals use stories to recall how their relationship developed in the courtship period (Orbuch, Veroff, & Holmberg, 1993). Although "coming out" occurs over time, young adulthood is the time when lesbians and gay men usually begin the process (Fulmer, 1999). Many experience major family stress or they attempt to negotiate their identity and presence within the immediate and extended family network. If they do not declare their sexual preference openly, a whole series of family secrets can develop, with some siblings and friends knowing and others not. Then communication becomes even more complicated.

The Couple

Marriage affects all family members and generations and requires that the couple negotiate new relationships as a twosome with many other subsystems: parents, siblings, grandparents, nieces and nephews, and friends. Unresolved family issues move into the marriage (McGoldrick, 1995). Marriage, however, is no longer the defining marker of entering adulthood nor is it the highly predictable event it once was.

Courtship may be viewed as a decision-making time because "the decision to marry is a prediction about how one person's life with another person will evolve in the future based on how it has evolved in the past" (Yerby, Buerkel-Rothfuss, & Bochner, 1990, p. 98). Today, many do not want to make such a decision.

Couples entering a relationship must resolve three developmental challenges in order to achieve satisfaction in later stages: commitment, power, and closeness. *Commitment* requires each to make the other his or her primary partner and lessen their ties to parents, siblings, and friends. *Power* reflects the dialectical tension between self-determination and yielding power to the partner for the enhancement of the relationship. *Closeness* relates to establishing a balance between separateness and attachment that is mutually satisfying for the couple. In this early stage, a couple develops rules for distance regulation and negotiates a mutually satisfactory degree of separateness and connectedness. Partners use verbal and nonverbal cues to negotiate what is an acceptable and nonacceptable distance, as the following example illustrates.

Sometimes I feel like a piece of Swiss cheese—full of holes. I grew up in a non-touching, often violent family. I realize I hunger for touch and affection. I can cuddle and hold my partner for long periods of time, but he gets uneasy after a while. We have to reach a point where both of us are comfortable.

Courtship and engagement involve a couple's attempt to move to deeper levels of communication. Partners establish through verbal and nonverbal permissions their relational boundaries. Certain topics, feelings, or actions may frighten or offend the other. They create rules that govern their communication when they encounter these issues.

Quite often, verbal and nonverbal signals from the couple indicate a deepening relationship. Significant jewelry may be exchanged, such as an engagement ring; invitations to attend special family events such as weddings or holiday dinners are extended; and so forth. This may not occur in same-sex relationships in which the deepening of the relationship may be hidden from relatives or co-workers. As you read the following example, think of the way it would happen in your family.

In my family, we always knew when relationships were serious when the annual family reunion time arrived. If you brought someone, you were expected to introduce this person to each member of the clan. However, you didn't go through this, and take all the teasing that followed, unless an engagement was to follow. Bringing a partner to the reunion signaled an impending marriage.

The act of bonding, or institutionalizing, the relationship may change the nature of many relationships. Some parents may not be prepared for the separation issues involved. Each family faces the questions of re-alignment, such as, "How willing are we to accept a new member as an in-law?"

The premarital period provides the time for self-disclosure and ne-gotiation. The following issues may need discussion: time with friends, desires for children, sexual needs, career and educational planning, reli-gious participation, money management, housing, in-laws, and accepta-ble conflict behaviors. The trend today is for shorter engagements, with many couples living together before this period. Based on their review of premarital relationship stability, Cate, Levin, and Richmond (2002) devel-oped a commitment model that includes intimacy-oriented relationship behaviors of self-disclosure, frequency of interaction, diversity of interac-tion, impact of interaction, and sexual intimacy.

Each person has to deal with the move from autonomy to attachment. The actual ritualized event and wedding ceremony is a communication event—a sign to the outside world that the ultimate formal bonding has occurred. In U.S. society, "Marriage is the only sexual relationship where partners can expect to receive public approval, through formalized rituals such as weddings and baby showers as well as a host of informal oppor-tunities to 'do marriage'" (Patterson & Schwartz, 1994, p. 4). For some couples, the wedding ceremony serves as a symbol of negotiating inter-cultural differences (Leeds-Hurwitz, 2002).

Marriages between young adults involve certain predictable tasks for most couples (Aldous, 1990). It is a time of (1) separating further from the families-of-origin; (2) negotiating roles, rules, and relationships; and (3) investing in a new relationship. Marriage at this time may continue unre-solved conflicts with the parents. This is a period of unconscious negotia-tion between the couple and their families-of-origin regarding how the old and new systems will relate to each other (Fiese et al., 1993). Some first marriages occur when partners are in their late twenties or thirties and have resolved some of these family-of-origin issues. Sometimes mar-riage holds surprises even when couples have known each other a long time, as noted in the following example.

I had known my husband since childhood, and we dated since our junior year. Our parents knew each other and we attended the same church, yet we had some real difficulties in the first years of our marriage. I had difficulty in the following areas: First, learning to live with my husband's habits. Second, trying to be a full-time employee and a housewife. Third, deciding at which family's

house to celebrate holidays. Fourth, telling my husband when I was angry,
and fifth, dealing with the biggest problem—my husband's mother.

The initial stage of marriage is characterized by close monitoring of the relationship and more frequent and intense communication about the relationship than at any other stage (Sillars & Wilmot, 1989). As spouses move through this period, many report that romance moves into reality. Most couples experience a shift in their social networks. Early marriage is accompanied usually by a decline in contact with each partner's old friends.

In recalling stories about how they met and became a couple, there definitely were cultural differences between African American and white couples. African Americans reported more conflict in the early stages of their relationship than whites (Orbuch, Veroff, & Holmberg, 1993). Further results from this study indicated that men initiated more relationship maneuvers than women, women had more vivid memories of relational events than men, and that couples who remembered a positive relational development were happier in the third year of their marriages than those who told negative stories.

As you may imagine, the images, themes, boundaries, and biosocial beliefs experienced by each partner in the family-of-origin affect the new system's development. A woman whose image of a husband is one that is strong, unemotional, and powerful puts great pressure on her new husband to deal with such expectations. If one partner has experienced themes of open sharing and flexible boundaries, and the other partner has experienced the opposite, much negotiation will be required.

Couple conflict patterns tend to establish themselves within the first two years of marriage and demonstrate great stability; a greater proportion of communication is devoted to marital conflicts that gradually surface (Sillars & Wilmot, 1989). Usually, the balance of power between a couple is established early in the marriage and is based on decision-making behaviors and role performance.

A couple's ability to invest in their new relationship relates directly to the quality of their communication. This is a time of investing in the system, risking self-disclosure, and building a pattern of sexual communication. Time, energy, and risk taking nourish the relationship and establish a range of acceptable intimacy for the system. In courtship and marriage, couples go through these tasks "on time" in a linear life cycle.

But what about couples who do not marry? Taking a life course or nonlinear approach recognizes that marriage may be delayed, follow the birth of one or more children, or never occur. Because of racism, unemployment, welfare rules, and poverty, many couples follow a nonlinear path of relationship development. Such families construct "developmental pathways in which the timing and ordering of life course transitions such as marriage and childbearing are not comparable to mainstream patterns" (Dilworth-Anderson & Burton, 1996, p. 328). In gay and lesbian couples, few have a public commitment ceremony to mark the stage of their relationship and must invent some "marital rules" and borrow or avoid others (Patterson & Schwartz, 1994, p. 4).

Recent research indicates marriage is good for one's health, especially male health. Waite and Gallagher (2000) summarize the research on the "marriage advantage," reporting, "Both men and women live longer if they are married than if they are not" (p. 51) although men gain larger health benefits. Among the possible communication-related reasons for such findings are that wives "nag" them about their health by discouraging drinking, smoking, and speeding, and by encouraging good eating and sleeping habits and by managing doctor contacts. In addition, partners have someone to talk to about personal topics.

For some couples, this two-person system will be their permanent form. Partners may choose not to add children to their lives or may find it difficult to bear or adopt children. Yet, for most couples, the two-person system eventually becomes a three-person system, with pregnancy heralding the transition to a new stage.

The period before the children began to arrive was a critical point. If we had not established a really strong, trusting relationship in those first 2 years, we would have drifted totally apart in the next 23 years of child rearing. We lost most of our time together. If I had it to do over, I would have waited 5 years before having children, to share who we really were before we tried to deal with who the four new people in our lives were.

Families with Children

As parents, adults move up a generation, becoming caregivers to the younger generation. One of the most important choices a couple makes concerns childbearing. Such a decision should, but frequently does not, involve intense communication—self-disclosure regarding the needs and desires of each partner—and how a child could fit into their lives. Input from all sources affects such a decision. The media, parents, friends, and other relatives often pressure the couple to fulfill parental roles and subtly suggest that they are being selfish if they do not. Men may perceive children as a way to prove themselves as mature and responsible. Young adults with divorced parents may be ambivalent toward parenting. However, producing a child is partially ego fulfilling, and partners may desire to be the idealized parents they never had.

There is so much that could be discussed in examining parent-child interaction. The following sections can only highlight certain communication issues. A key thread running through parent-child interaction is the bi-directional nature of this relationship, meaning that parents are not the sole influence in this relationship. Children also influence parent behaviors (Saphir & Chaffee, 2002). In examining the periods of child growth and outward movement, three phases will be discussed. Remember that each family will experience each phase differently, depending on its size and the ages of its members. The three phases are:

- Family with first child
- Family with preschool children (3 to 6 years, possibly with younger siblings)
- Family with school-aged children (oldest child 6 to 12 years, possibly with younger siblings)

Although the life course varies for single unwed parents, gays or lesbians with children, and unmarried cohabitors, they will go through variations of these same phases. In unmarried situations, relatives or hired child-care resources are used so parents can work. Single white women end pregnancies at a higher rate than minority women who tend to add children to the existing family system. Increasing numbers of gay male couples are adopting and lesbians are bearing children.

Family with First Child Parenthood is now coming later in life for most couples because the age at first marriage has steadily increased. On the other hand, approximately 33 percent of children are born to unwed mothers, frequently teenagers. This means these youths go from adolescence right into adult status as parents—a shortened stage or life course event. Parenthood speeds up their whole life-course trajectory. Pregnant teens can make their mothers into grandmothers at age 30 or 32, telescoping all life stage changes into shorter time frames. How different the communication within the family becomes! Normal adolescent communication issues of dating and choosing the right high school or college courses are replaced with talk about breast-feeding, dropping out of school, and supporting the baby.

For young married couples, pregnancy occurs relatively close to the marriage. Because about one-fifth of all children born to married couples in the United States were conceived before marriage and many others are conceived during the first two years, many couples do not experience a lengthy period of intimacy before the child arrives.

Parents play a major role in developing a child's communication competence.

No matter when it occurs, the first pregnancy signals significant change in the couple's relationship. The intensity of the desire for a child by one or both spouses influences the communication about the parenthood stage from the very beginning. When a couple desires a child and the pregnancy is uncomplicated, this can be a time with much intimate communication. Yet, subtle communication changes occur as well as changes in conflict patterns.

Today, more never-married women as well as members of gay and lesbian partnerships are choosing parenthood. With the growth of new reproductive technologies (NRTs), parenting options are extended to many who previously would not have been able to produce biological children. Assisted reproductive technology has contributed to the birth of over 300,000 babies since 1977 (Parke, 2002). The NRT option creates communication challenges, both in terms of decision making, privacy, and explanation to others in the family network.

Three factors that influence couples during the transition to parenthood are their views on parental responsibilities and restrictions, the gratification child rearing holds for them as a couple, and their own marital intimacy and stability. Middle-class mothers differed from lower-class mothers in their response to the stress of motherhood both during pregnancy and in the years following. Middle-class women feel fewer pressures than lower-class women, who must worry more about support and work roles (Reilly, Entwisle, & Doering, 1987). Stamp (1994) stresses the importance of the transition into parenthood, suggesting that new parents "need to renegotiate the reality of their marriage due to both the presence of the child and to their transformed presence with one another with the addition of a new role" (p. 109). Additional communication may center on the role of the father in the birth process, because men may feel left out or abandoned at this crucial moment. Being present when the child is born has a great impact upon a couple, as reflected here.

I have never felt closer to my wife than at the moment of Brian's birth. I helped her breathe, wiped her forehead, and rubbed her back between contractions. I actually felt a part of the birth process. When Brian was finally delivered, Wilma and I cried and laughed and cried again because of the power of the drama we had created. It's indescribable—to share in the birth of your own child.

If you have ever lived with a newborn baby, you are well aware how one extremely small person can change an entire household. Sillars and Wilmot (1989) compare the adjustment following childbirth to the adjustment following marriage, saying, "There is a gradual decline from the emotional high experienced initially to a state more tempered by negative as well as positive feelings" (p. 233). The initial question is: To what extent is there space in the environment for a child? According to Bradt (1988), children can be born into an environment that has space for them, has no space for them, or has a vacuum the child is expected to fill. "Whether they are living with one parent or two, and whether living with biological parents or stepparents, family processes are critical to children's development and well-being" (Demo, 1992, p. 110). It is different with adopted children because usually the child has been wanted for a longer period of time and fills a void. At the point when the dyad becomes a triad, alliances or subsystems emerge. All family members cannot receive undivided attention at the same time. Such triangling has the potential to evolve into powerful alliances.

New parents must deal with the following communication-related issues: (1) renegotiating roles, (2) transmitting culture and establishing a community of experiences, and (3) developing the child's communication competence. Moderately flexible families are likely to weather this period more easily than are relatively rigid systems.

Spouses may lose sight of each other for a period of time. Due to parenting roles, new parents may feel inept at caring for their child. Because mothers traditionally have taken the major responsibility for child care, until recently few fathers have been exposed to much modeling regarding how to share the care-giving role. Women become depressed when they feel overwhelmed with work and child care. They feel "anger, resentment and hostility toward their husbands or partners for failing to share in childcare responsibilities" (Weldon, 1997b, p. 3). Currently, family life education is increasingly supporting equal roles for male and female, and young men are presented with a wider range of models of male family life (Hey & Neubeck, 1990).

Increasingly, couples with careers are delaying having children. In a study of "on time" (becoming a father by age 23) or "off time" (becoming a father after age 40), the results indicate that late-timing fathers are more involved with their children and form more affective ties with them. Based on the life-course perspective, the results suggest that "late fathers are more able than early fathers to be active parents and to feel positive about the experience because of reduced role demands they face in other social spheres" (Cooney, Pedersen, Indelicato, & Palkovitz, 1993, p. 213).

Intimacy between the couple certainly changes with the birth of a child. Privacy is almost impossible when the baby screams for attention. Although research points to increasingly positive involvement of the father in parenthood, the birth of a first child tends to have a "traditionalizing influence in marriage, prompting greater role specialization, male-dominated decision making and a shift toward traditional ideology" (Sillars & Wilmot, 1989, p. 253).

The first child represents a link to posterity and continuation of the family name and heritage—a potentially heavy burden. Naming the child becomes a communication event. Names may serve to link family generations or reflect dreams of a parent. Couples that become involved in talking to one another, talking to friends and kin who have children, or take parenting classes reported less stress in the first year of parenthood (Gage & Christensen, 1991). When you think about your own children or your future children, what parts of your background do you want to pass on to them? Do you wish they could experience the same type of Passover Seders you did as a child? Do you want them to have a strong Yoruba, Italian, Chinese, or Russian identity? Such are the issues of transmission of culture, as indicated in the following example.

The birth of our first child revived many issues that we had fought about in our courtship period and that we finally agreed to disagree about. Sean and I were from very different backgrounds, religiously, culturally, and even economically. As a couple, we were able to ignore many of the differences, but once Wendy was born, we each seemed to want certain things for her that we had experienced growing up. And our families got into the act also. We've dealt with almost everything except religion, and we are due for a showdown, because Wendy is now 5 and should begin some religious training soon.

For many people, a child represents a link to the past and the future, a sense of life's flow and a sense of immortality. Hence, children often serve as receptacles for what parents consider to be their best parts, strengths, and expectations for the family. Once a couple becomes a triad, certain dormant issues may arise—particularly unresolved ones. A father's unfulfilled dreams may be transferred to his son. Spousal conflicts may arise over what is to be "passed down." The transmission of both the cultural heritage and the family's own heritage is a demanding, frightening, and exciting task that depends on communication. As additional children arrive, the process will be repeated and extended, as this observer reports.

It was amazing for me to watch my sister and her husband with their first child. After almost 25 years, my sister could remember so many of the songs that our mother sang to us as little ones. She and Lee took great pleasure in creating new words and expressions from things that Jonathan did. They set certain patterns for birthday parties, established Friday nights as "family night," and began to take Jonathan to museums, children's theater, and library storybook programs together. They created their own world, which now incorporated a little boy.

Through communication, new patterns of life are formed and maintained in response to the arrival of a child. Young parents who have not had extensive contact with their own parents may suddenly feel a need to connect their child to grandparents and other relatives. Contact with the extended family tends to increase. Appropriate family and friend boundaries usually require careful consideration and negotiation.

Unmarried mothers often depend on grandparents for housing and sharing child care. These unmarried mothers and their parents follow different life-course trajectories than a traditional couple with occasional help from grandparents. Communication reflects the stress. Grandparents have to repeat parts of a life stage they have already lived through. Some grandparents welcome this; others feel guilty that their own children cannot take care of themselves or "their kids." Often, the unmarried mother at ages 14 to 16 has a working mother somewhere between ages of 30 and 35 and the great-grandparents have to shoulder the child-care responsibilities.

Finally, parents are deeply involved in providing their children with a means to deal with interpersonal relationships. Their relationships serve as the child's first models. The moment of birth exposes the child to the world of interpersonal contacts, when a powerful parent-child bonding process begins through physical contact, facial/eye contact, and reciprocal vocal stimulation. Parental warmth, support, sensitive responses, and children's temperament and signaling interrelate to create parent-child connections (Peterson, Madden-Derdich, & Leonard, 2000).

The child makes its first contact with the world through touch, and this becomes an essential source of comfort, security, and warmth. The first few months mark the critical beginning of a child's interpersonal learning. A child's personality is being formed in the earliest interchanges with nurturing parents. Children begin to respond to words at age 6 or 7 months; by 9 or 10 months, they can understand a few words and will begin to use language soon thereafter. Parents set the stage for positive interpersonal development by verbally and nonverbally communicating to a child the feeling of being recognized and loved. Stamp (1994) summarizes much of what we believe when he states, "Couples do not become parents just by virtue of having a child: parenthood is constituted and maintained through conversation" (p. 109). Such conversations occur between partners and between parent and child. Eventually, conversations include stories: birth narratives for biological children and entrance narratives for adopted children (Krusiewicz & Wood, 2001) that reveal a child's identity and family events surrounding his or her arrival.

Many couples experience a decline in marital satisfaction with the birth of the first child. An infant causes the couple to feel fatigued, frustrated, and tied down, with little time for self or spouse (Belsky, Youngblade, Rovine, & Volling, 1991). The baby's fussy behavior is stressful to both parents, but less to the father, since some men distance themselves until the wife adapts to the mother role. Sometimes this period has been described as the "baby honeymoon is over!"

In a comparative study of couples who became parents in either the first or second year after they married with couples who remained child free, the parents' group became more task oriented and child focused and experienced more traditional division of tasks. Women's expectations and adjustments to parenthood after one year were significantly less than they indicated they hoped for when interviewed during pregnancy. Adjustments were more difficult when expectations of more help from the husband and extended family diminished, or when mothers felt less competent and satisfied with mothering (Kalmuss, Davidson, & Cushman, 1992). Carter (1999) summarizes the gender issues of today's parenting, saying, "In spite of all the actual changes in our lives and in our beliefs, the two sacred cows—a 'real man's' career and a 'real woman's' mothering—maintain a stubborn hold on our emotions" (p. 255).

In summarizing 20 years of research, Cowan and colleagues (1985) concluded that first-time parents are at risk for personal and marital distress that often continues until after a child is 2 years old. As more children arrive, variations of this process occur. Nevertheless, later births do not cause as many major changes as the first one (Terkelsen, 1980). Increasingly, with the current birthrate, many parents raise only two children.

Family with Preschool Children   The preschool family (child 3 to 6 years) experiences less pressure than in the previous period. Parents have learned to cope with a growing child. Barring physical or psychological complications, the former baby now walks, talks, feeds, and entertains himself or herself for longer periods of time.

Watching 3- or 4-year-olds, one will be amazed at language skills. A 4-year-old may produce well over 2,000 different words and probably understands many more and can identify tasks and expectations according to gender. Children at this age begin to develop more sophisticated strategies for gaining such ends as later bedtimes or favorite foods. As children become more independent, parents may directly influence their language acquisition skills through enrichment activities such as reading, role playing, and storytelling. The parents' own communication behavior in this stage serves as an important model for the child. A study of African American fathers of preschoolers reveals the "fathers' ability to communicate effectively within the family was significantly associated with the fathers' involvement in child care and socialization" (Ahmeduzzaman & Roopnarine, 1992, p. 705). In a large national study of maternal competence and the effects on children 4 years and younger, it was found that "the characteristics of the mother, household, and child collectively influence the quality of the home environment and success of the child's developmental processes which mediates the influence of demographic and socioeconomic variables" (Garrett, Ferron, Ng'Andu, Bryant, & Harbin, 1994, p. 147).

Communication with children will differ depending on the extent to which the family is position oriented or person oriented. A child in a position-oriented family is required to rely on prescribed communication behaviors, but the child in a person-oriented family is more likely to use a range of communicative behaviors. The difference is essentially the degree to which the child is provided with verbalized reasons for performing or not performing certain functions at certain times with certain individuals. Persons growing up in a household where things are done "because I am the father and you are the child" do not gain experience in adapting to the unique individuals involved.

Parenting young children is stressful and joyful. In addition to relating to parents and other adults, children may have to incorporate new siblings into their world. During this period, many couples or single parents have more children, increasing the complexity of the family's relationship network. The arrival of second and third children moves the triad to a four- or five-person system and places greater stress on the parents. Additional children trigger a birth-order effect, which combines with sex roles to affect parent-child interaction. You may have heard characteristics attributed to various people because "She is the middle child" or "He is the baby of the family." There appear to be differences in parent-child communication based on sex and position (Sulloway, 1996). Each additional child limits the amount of time and contact each child has with the parents and the parents with each other.

Sibling competition is more prevalent when children are close in age and the same gender because they have to share parental attention. The sibling relationship is predictably the longest shared familial relationship. It is typically seen as moving from "closeness in early life, distance in middle life, and back to closeness in later life" (Nussbaum, Pecchioni, Baringer, & Kundrat, 2002, p. 379).

In a comparison of parenting and children's social, psychological, and academic success across varied family structures, it was reported that biological or adoptive parents in never-divorced families used more positive parenting and co-parenting practices than did single-parent or cohabiting couples. Children in intact families showed higher levels of adjustment (Bronstein, Clauson, Stoll, & Abrams, 1993).

The pressures of parenting are captured in the following example.

Angie was 3 years old when Gwen was born, and it was a very hard period for her and therefore for us. Angie changed from being a self-sufficient, happy child to a whining clinger who sucked her thumb and started to wet her pants again. Jimmy and I had to work very hard to spend "special" time with her, to praise her, and to let her "help" with the baby when she wanted to. Luckily, Gwen was an easy baby, so we could make the time to interact with Angie the way she needed us to.

The example illustrates why parents need direct communication with an older child or children before the next baby's birth or adoption and during the months that follow. Siblings 3 or more years older are more likely to treat the baby with affection and interest, because they are more oriented to children their own age and less threatened by the new arrival.

A sibling closer in age may engage in aggressive and selfish acts toward the baby.

In the 3- to 6-year-old stage, children begin to communicate on their own with the outside world. Some attend preschool. At 5 years old, most enter kindergarten. From their young peers, children learn about friendship and establish relationships outside the family. Children's interactions with one another vary in response to each other's gender and social characteristics such as dominance or shyness.

Quality of, and access to, day care or child care is related to income. Excellent day care, more available to higher income families, provides parents with peace of mind and helps develop children's skills. For poor children there are some funded day-care programs but for many middle-class parents they are not affordable. Such additional care could reduce stress and lead to improved parent-child and parent-spouse communication. A study of Mexican and African American working mothers reports the difficulty in finding day-care providers that do not racially insult their children or put them down for their cultural differences. Speaking Spanish was often not permitted (Uttal, 1998). This reality affected communication and required the mothers to reduce stress by explaining to their children "about race relations with white society and how to navigate them" (p. 605). African American parents have an additional task of preparing children to deal with racial derogation (Ferguson, 1999); these parents often rely on an imperative style to protect their children from racism (Daniel & Daniel, 1999).

We do not know directly how much stress economic issues place on the family, but they certainly affect communication. In a study comparing Latino, African American, and Caucasian children, Latino children are three times more likely to live at the poverty level than whites, and this rate increased faster in the past decade than for African American children.

Family with School-Aged Children The school-aged family experiences new strains on its communication as the children begin to link further with outside influences. The family system now overlaps on a regular and continuous basis with other systems—educational, religious, and community. Families with very strong boundaries are forced to deal with new influences. Schools provide an introduction to a wider world of ideas and values; new beliefs may be encountered, and old beliefs may be challenged.

School-aged children spend many hours away from the home environment and influence. In addition to the school experience, religious organizations provide educational and recreational events. Community organizations such as the Scouts, sports leagues, and 4-H clubs compete for family members' time. During this period of growth, the child comes under the influence of peer pressures, which may conflict with parents' views. Often, conflict develops, because the child feels compelled to please friends rather than parents. Mothers who take time to communicate with their children and listen empathically to them when disciplining or comforting have children who are less rejected by their peers and more frequently chosen as companions (Burleson, Delia, & Applegate, 1992).

As children continue their emotional and physical growth, their communication skills change. Negotiation and priority setting become important aspects of child-parent communication. Children's use of persuasive message strategies develop with advancing age in their life course. Kline and Clinton (1998) report that children ages 5 to 8 use one to two different arguments in beginning to make persuasive messages; children ages 9 to 12 create two to four arguments; and children aged 13 and older used three or more arguments. Summarizing studies of children's speech, they report 5- to 6-year-olds used more pleading, sulking, threats, and requests. Between third grade and eleventh grade, children increasingly use more compromises, arguments that advance their views, more appeals to what they think society expects, and more deliberation about competing alternatives. Children develop more persuasion strategies. "Second and third graders use unilateral or coercive strategies such as threats, punishments or appealing to adult authority. Fourth and fifth graders are more likely to use reciprocal strategies such as interpersonal bribes, coordinated teamwork or attempts to convince the other that he/she is wrong" (Kline & Clinton, 1998, p. 121). From an early age, children develop ways to produce messages that adapt to listeners and learn to create counterarguments to manage stress. During this period, a child's communication competence increasingly impacts parental decision making.

Given that the number of children of immigrants has reached the highest level in U.S. history, many school-aged children have become "family translators," a role that creates a significant power shift. A 10-year-old might translate for his mother during parent conferences, siblings' medical appointments, or social service meetings. Such role reversals can be stressful for all involved.

During the school years, the identity of the family as a unit reaches its peak. The family can enjoy all kinds of activities, which bring a richness to the intimacy of the family relationship. Due to the intense activity level, some partners neglect their own relationship or use the children as an excuse to avoid dealing with marital problems. Involvement with children may lower parent self-esteem, a reflection of the stress of active parenting (Hawkins & Belsky, 1989).

Families with Adolescents

The family system is significantly transformed as members attempt to manage the adolescent stage, which is commonly thought to begin at puberty and often referred to as teenaged years. Some parents communicate to their children to "hurry up and grow up" and promote this agenda by allowing early dating, relaxed curfews, and dressing like adults. Other parents encourage the opposite, with an attitude "You're only young once; enjoy it." Adolescents experience physical, sexual, and emotional changes. Regarding physical maturation, families differ greatly biologically; some children begin puberty very early while others are "off time." Some adolescents become pregnant, drop out of school, or become involved in drugs, essentially shortening the adolescent development phase. A dropout at age 15 without a job or a 14-year-old with a baby face different stresses than those who move more slowly through this stage. Although a number of investigations suggest that the extent of adolescent and parental turmoil during this period has frequently been exaggerated, there is general agreement that adolescence, and particularly early adolescence, has traditionally been a challenging and sometimes trying time for both youth and their parents (Reuter & Conger, 1995).

Hormonal changes impact moods, aggression, and feelings of self-worth. In his review of adolescents' impact on parental development, Farrell (2000) asserts that adolescent development affects immediate states such as mood, distress level, or well-being as well as sense of identity and generativity. This bi-directional influence process is particularly obvious during adolescence.

Teenagers experience internal struggles in coping with changes and individuation particularly in areas of sexuality, identity, autonomy, and friendships (Blieszner, 1994). These struggles affect the entire family at a time when parents may be facing predictable midlife issues. For most adolescents, prior interest in same-sex friendships switches to a growing interest in the opposite sex: "All he does is chase after girls now instead of fly balls." "Keep out" signs appear on doors; phone calls become private. Teenagers establish strong topic avoidance in relation to parents (Guerrero & Afifi, 1995). The upsurge in sexual thoughts and feelings serve as an undercurrent to many interactions that may make parents uneasy because they are forced to consider their child as a sexual being. Young people begin to set their own physical and psychological boundaries, which may limit communication with some or all family members.

Adolescent self-esteem is related to family relationships. Through communication interactions, adolescents gain a sense of their own identity. Manning (1996) reports adolescents in their communication are most concerned about identity protection and management of the outcomes of their remarks. Teenagers care greatly about what peers, parents, and other adults think of them. They trust people who keep personal information private. Other adolescent concerns include appropriateness, disconfirmation, conflict, control, and insecurity. Teens see communication as inappropriate when others talk as if they know about things they don't understand, express little care for what they say, or act superior, especially when challenged.

In describing her experience in counseling teens, Preto (1999) concludes, "Girls are more likely to let parents know what they feel by yelling, while boys are more avoidant and tend to deal with situations by leaving the scene" (p. 280). Fink, Buerkel-Rothfuss, and Buerkel (1994) report that the father's negative behaviors of verbal aggression, high control, lack of involvement with their families, and personal dysfunction can damage father-son communication. Obviously, the relational dialectics of closeness and distance with parents affect stress. The need for privacy often accompanies the search for identity, as illustrated here.

I grew up in a home where doors were always open, and people knew each other's business. I remember going through a terrible period starting at the end of junior high when I hated sharing a room with my sister. I would spend hours alone sitting on my bed listening to music with the door shut, and if anyone came in, I would have a fit. I even locked my sister out a number of times.

A major task of adolescence is to loosen family bonds while establishing friendship bonds with peers. If the family atmosphere is warm and supportive, adolescents successfully negotiate differences with their parents (Reuter & Conger, 1995). If the atmosphere is hostile and coercive, adolescents rebel, conflicts escalate, and disagreements are unresolved. Reuter and Conger's study was repeated over a four-year span, and the behaviors that affected communication in the first year escalated by year 4. Negative strategies increased in negative families and positive strategies increased in positive families. Thus, stress was much higher and more frequent in families in which parents were overly dominant, demanding, and coercive. The quality of the relationships teens had with their parents prior to this period foreshadowed their behaviors in adolescence. This study reports that "families entering adolescence showing a straightforward communication, attentive listening, and warmth tended to remain at highest levels of warm interaction one year later" (p. 446).

The more time parents spent with adolescents, the more frequent but shorter the conflicts (Vuchinich, Teachman, & Crosby, 1991). Conflicts with adolescents occur most frequently over simple items, such as chores and dress, rather than over bigger issues, such as drugs and sex (Barber, 1994). If a child has a positive perception of parents communication, there is a greater likelihood of a positive relationship and positive self-image (Bollis-Pecci & Webb, 1997, p. 4).

Adolescents are engaged in a process of finding themselves, a process dependent on communication experiences with peers. Such companions serve as relatively noncritical confidants, supporters, and listeners

(Blieszner, 1994). Concurrently, a young person becomes more other-centered and begins to develop a true sense of empathy and the ability to take another's perspective. Parents can raise self-esteem in adolescents by being supportive, demonstrating physical affection, maintaining contact over these years, and offering companionship (Barber, Chadwick, & Oerter, 1992). These parental behaviors would certainly improve communication by reducing tensions within the family environment.

For African American adolescents, racial esteem is the primary predictor of self-esteem. Diggs (1994) reports, "Parental communication, particularly mothers' remarks about self and race, is of greater relative importance than peer's communication in shaping the self-worth of children at the young adolescent stage" (p. 2). Peer communication about race and self ranks second.

Personal decision making provides a sense of autonomy for teenagers. The changes between the ages of 13 and 19 coincide with the individuation that occurs when a young person becomes self-reliant and insists on making up his or her own mind. This leads to independence and confidence in decision making. By asserting his or her developing talents to speak out, work, or perform tasks without constant help and supervision, the adolescent signals to parents that past communication directives no longer fit the situation. Boys sometimes feel they are caught in a trap between their mothers and fathers. While still wanting their mother's care and protection, they sense their father's expectations that they not become "feminized" (Goldner, Penn, Sheinberg, & Walker, 1990).

The adolescent's struggles to work through developmental tasks of sexuality, identity, and autonomy send reverberations throughout the family system. The sexual awakening of their children has a powerful effect on many parents. Udry and Campbell (1994) summarized many research studies about adolescents and sex. They state the following about teen sexuality over the life course: African Americans start earlier than whites, with some males beginning before puberty; adolescents who frequently attend church start later; adolescents with educated parents start later; teens from mother-only households begin earlier; those who begin early have lower grades; those with sexually active friends often imitate their behavior; and friendship influence is greater for white females, but less for white males or black females. Opposite-sex parents and children may find a gulf between them as a response to the power of the incest taboo in society. Unfortunately, in many families this results in the end of nonverbal affection, as illustrated in this example.

I will never forget being hurt as a teenager when my father totally changed the way he acted toward me. We used to have a real "buddy" relationship. We would spend lots of time together; we would wrestle, fool around, and I adored him. Suddenly, he became really distant, and I could not understand whether I had done something. But I did not feel I could talk about it either. Now that I am older, I can see the same pattern happening with my two sisters. Obviously, within his head there is a rule that when your daughter starts to develop breasts, you have to back off; and for him, that means having almost no relationship at all. Now I can understand that it hurts him as much as it hurts us.

Parents and children of the same sex may face internal conflicts if they perceive a major contrast between their children's budding sexuality and their own sexual identity. Such conflicts are tied to the parents' stages of development and negative self-evaluations. Because facing this issue would be uncomfortable, such perceptions may result in conflict over more "acceptable" issues such as friends, money, independence, or responsibility. For gay and lesbian adolescents, this is the time they are likely to label and understand their sexual orientation and face questions and fears about the coming-out process. If they do disclose their sexual orientation, they are more likely to tell mothers, and there is more concern about fathers' reactions (Preto, 1999).

In spite of differences, data indicates that between two-thirds and three-fourths of adolescents feel close to their parents, accept them, and say they get along (Demo, 1992). These results differ for families that consistently used a negative style of communication that is hostile and coercive, which had to exhibit a negative "sequential path that spirals downward from growing family hostility into increasing problem-solving difficulties and heightened and persistent parent-adolescent conflict" (Reuter & Conger, 1995, pp. 445–446).

The extent to which parents "practice what they preach" affects communication on sensitive topics. A study on parent-child communication about teen tobacco and alcohol use confirms that parents generally express less directive communication and talk more about softer issues; more educated parents talk less about rules or consequences. Yet, parents who smoke tend to discuss rules more frequently than nonsmokers, and parents who drink talk less about rules than nondrinkers (Ennett, Bauman, Foshee, Pemberton, & Hicks, 2001). The authors speculate that there is greater negative sound opinion regarding youth smoking. They also found parent modeling was more important than communication on the topic.

Adolescents are more likely to accept parental guidelines when they have clear, open lines of communication and feel that their parents respect their values. Yet, "all adult children report a sharp adolescent slump in intimacy" (Rossi & Rossi, 1990, p. 279). Usually only after adolescents achieve adulthood and independence do they feel closer to parents. Knowing this characteristic of adolescent-parent communication can reduce stress on parents who sometimes feel that they have failed when their adolescents reject them and their ideas. Closeness to parents during childhood and through the years of growing up is "more telling for the well-being of adolescents than is father presence during childhood" (Wenk, Hardesty, Morgan, & Blair, 1994, p. 229).

The exploring adolescent often challenges family themes, boundaries, and biosocial beliefs (Barber, 1994). He or she is forever introducing the family system to people or modes of behavior that may threaten the family's identity. As the adolescent begins to separate from parents, stays out later, and evades questions about friends, some parents become suspicious. Parents have trouble detecting deceptions by their children, partly because children vary in their communication strategies that include lies. Sometimes it is a "no-win" experience, since "some parents perceive completeness of information as a sign of deception, while others see incomplete answers as an indication of lying" (Grady, 1997). A relatively flexible family may encounter less difficulty with an acting-out adolescent than a family with rigid rules. In Puerto Rican families when both parents work, the family becomes more open because young daughters are required to take over household responsibilities, including the care of siblings (Toro-Morn, 1998). When this happens, adolescence is shortened because these teens have to communicate as adults to control and protect siblings.

Adolescents are more likely to accept parental guidelines when they have clear, open lines of communication and feel that their parents respect their values. The more open the communication, the greater sense of equity that is expressed in mother-adolescent relationships (Vogl-Bauer & Kalbfleisch, 1997). In addition, the more parents are aware of their adolescents' moods and refrain from forcing discussions or decisions during a negative period, the more positive are the eventual outcomes (Niedzwiecki, 1997). Communication that supports gradual separation, rather than pushes persons away from one another or holds them rigidly close, eases the transition. Failure to negotiate the adolescent stage successfully, as reflected by an increase is suicides, has caused concern among family experts.

Launching Children and Moving On

The departure from home of the older children signals one more major stage and family reorganization. Most theories propose some variation of one of the following scenarios: (1) the "empty nest" model, which suggests that at least one of the parents is having difficulty letting the children go; and (2) some variation of the curvilinear model, which concentrates on the increased freedom and independence of the parents

(Vaillant & Vaillant, 1993). The transitional tasks related to this stage include (1) the transition of parent-child to adult-adult relationships, (2) changes in function of marriage, (3) family expansion to include in-laws and grandchildren, and (4) opportunities to resolve relationships with aging parents (McCullough & Rutenberg, 1988). Except for marital change, all of these transitional tasks affect all parental-child relationships.

This is the period when parents move from being responsible for children to a sense of mutual responsibility between caring adults. This may differ in highly communal role-bound cultures in which parents and children retain a more position-oriented relationship. When young people start living on their own, especially if they support themselves, they more readily take on the responsibilities of adulthood and begin the process of becoming emotionally comfortable living apart from their families-of-origin. It is a time of vacating the bedrooms, sending along the extra coffee pot, and letting go of the predictable daily interactions at breakfast or bedtime that tied parents and siblings into a close, interactive system.

If the separation takes place without significant struggle, communication usually remains open and flexible. Frequent contact with parents and siblings via phone calls, letters, e-mail, or visits maintains family links and strengthens the bonds. At this time, communication issues may involve handling money, negotiating living space, making career decisions, keeping regular hours, or staying in contact.

Since I've been in college, I call home about once a week and sometimes I sense that my mother is upset about something. If I ask about it, she will say something like, "Oh, don't you worry about it. It's not your problem; you don't live here anymore." That upsets me, because I still feel I am part of the family.

The high cost of living makes leaving home difficult. Today, many college students live at home or college graduates return home to live due to economic pressures. Married children are divorcing and returning home as single parents because of financial difficulties. A counter-trend involves young people leaving home to live independently prior to marriage, with increasing numbers entering cohabiting relationships. More women than men who move away from home marry later than those who stay with a parent (Waite, 1987).

In middle age, many families find themselves stressed trying to care for two or more generations and live their own lives. Approximately three-quarters of caregivers are women, many of whom work full time. Caregivers have been labeled the "sandwich generation" as they struggle to meet their children's needs, their own desires as an aging couple, and the needs of their parents (Brothers, 1998). As the elongated generational structure becomes the norm, grandparents and even great-grandparents may rely on the two younger generations for emotional and physical support.

Conflict may occur when young people remain home during their early twenties, because established family rules and regulations tend to be challenged. "You don't need to wait up for me—I'm not seventeen!" "Pay room and board? I can't afford it and make car payments," are typical comments. If young adults remain longer than expected, some families develop adverse effects. If parent-child conflicts created problems in earlier years, this pattern is likely to continue (Aquilino & Supple, 1991). Some parents want time alone as a couple, and if the children delay leaving, this may create frustrations and negative communication patterns.

Leave-taking varies greatly. Stress seems less for males, but females often use leaving home as a way to cope with problematic family issues. Other factors that cause increased parent-child conflict are adult children remaining financially dependent and unemployed. The returning home of divorced or separated children, especially with their children, increases parents' dissatisfaction with joint living arrangements.

Some parents force a leave-taking before their children may feel ready for the break, often resulting in hard feelings, conflict, and resentment. Many children resist being "on their own," and others cannot wait "to get out of the nest." In some communities or cultures, departure is expected; in others, daughters especially may remain home indefinitely. Parenting varies from culture to culture, but a large study of African American, Hispanic, Asian American, and Caucasian two-parent families revealed that there are more similarities than differences in parenting attitudes, parenting involvement, and parenting behaviors, including leave-taking (Julian, McKenry, & McKelvey, 1994).

Major changes occur in the husband-wife relationship after children leave, as opportunities for increased intimacy present themselves. Mothers in the launching stage, whose children are getting ready to leave home, are seldom enthusiastic. Fathers with fewer children report greater unhappiness over their leaving than do fathers with more children. Also, older fathers react more strongly than younger fathers. It is only after the children are gone that the second honeymoon occurs—if it is going to. Single parents may experience even more dramatic shifts; some may have put their adult relational lives "on hold" to raise children, while others may find the personal life versus parental responsibility struggles diminish significantly. The amount of stress in this phase relates closely to the parent-child relationship prior to the transition. Aquilino (1997) found that "earlier levels of closeness and conflict set the stage for intergenerational solidarity in adulthood" (p. 683). The patterns of communication learned in earlier interactions with their children predict how parents relate to their children upon leaving home.

In the following shortened Christmas letter, one couple expresses what it is like when the third and last child leaves home:

We ran out of luggage this fall.
Three college-bound family members moved out,
or in and out,
over more than 3 weeks,
taking with them all the shampoo, Coke, scissors and CD players,
leaving things eerily silent.

Two parents and two cats contemplate the stillness.
According to Charlie's metaphorical explanation,
"It's like we lived next to the El for 20 years and we've moved."
Train cars rumble by occasionally
dropping off young adults looking for clean laundry or food.
Kids roll out; bills roll in.
E-mail silently links us . . .

Letting go is never simple.
Letting go of children is excruciatingly complicated . . .
We are at the stage of swinging doors,
ins and outs,
noises on and noises off.
It is a bittersweet moment in time.

Communication and stress vary at this point on the life course. Most parents successfully launch their children, but a significant number have their plans interrupted by responsibilities for their children and their children's offspring. In offering shelter and care, they repeat an earlier part of their life trajectory by having to go back through parenting. Others experience "getting younger while getting older" as "age is no longer a predictor of life stage for a very large number of Americans" (Rubin, 2001, p. 62). Due to technological advances, women in their forties are having their first children, 50-year-olds are paying to look 10 years younger, and 60-year-olds are jogging daily. Therefore, describing the predictable midlife transition is no longer simple.

There have been fewer communication-related studies in later-life married men. Early research indicated that wives tended to become more assertive and men become more affiliative and expressive. In their study of storytelling of middle-aged couples, Dickson and Walker (2001) found that husbands revealed higher levels of emotional expression, politeness, and openness, compared to their wives.

Spouses who have allowed their children to become their main focus for so many years may find themselves somewhat unconnected. Partners may sense a distance between them and feel unable, or unwilling, to try to reconnect. For many couples, the readjustment to a viable, two-person system requires hard work. Divorces occur frequently in this midlife transition period. How difficult the transition can be for some women is reflected in the following example.

When the children left, I discovered myself living with essentially a mute man. We hadn't realized that for years we had talked little to one another—that most of our communication was with the children or about them. Since we both worked, always took vacations with the kids, and kept busy chasing after kids' activities, we never had time for ourselves. Now I've got time to talk, and I have to compete with TV—that's the "other woman" in my house.

By this point, parents and their adult children have negotiated, and may continue to negotiate, issues such as privacy rights and the management of intergenerational boundaries (Cooney, 1997). Such issues may be confounded if either party becomes financially or physically dependent.

The experience of being a grandparent or grandchild is becoming more and more common, given increased longevity. A child today has a 50 percent chance of having two living grandparents plus one or more great-grandparents. It is predicted that by 2020 the number of adults aged 65 and over will increase from 33.2 million to 53 million, with the 85 and up group expected to double by that date (U.S. Census, 1997). These facts indicate a large pool of grandparents and great-grandparents, and a significant change from previous decades. Children in blended families may experience up to eight grandparent figures. Given the reality of a mobile society, some grandparents and grandchildren experience limited and formal or distant contacts. In a comparative study of African American and white grandmothers, African American grandmothers had a greater number of exchanges and contacts with grandchildren than white grandmothers. In later years, moreover, aging African American grandmothers received more help from grandchildren than did white grandmothers (Kivett, 1993). Parents tend to give priority to adult children with greater needs, especially to divorced daughters with children and to unmarried daughters (Aldous & Klein, 1991). Grandparents are being called on to take a more participative role in modern families, particularly in situations of divorce and dual-career marriages.

Grandparents can range in age from age 28 to 90-plus, and grandchildren range in age from newborns to retirees. Styles of grandparenting vary. Neugarten and Weinstein (1964) in an early study classified five grandparent styles: (1) formal, (2) fun seeker, (3) second parent, (4) family sage, and (5) distant figure. Such roles may vary across ages. For example, one study reports that children ages 4 to 5 like indulgent grandparents, at ages 8 to 9 they preferred fun-loving ones, and at ages 11 to 12 they begin to distance themselves (Barranti-Ramirez, 1985). Grandchildren indicate the predominant style of communication for grandparents is that of fun seeker (Eckloff, 1994). She concludes that maternal grandparents have closer relationships and more communication with their grandchildren than with paternal grandparents.

Assuming the role of grandparents opens the door for unique communication experiences. Walsh (1999) points out that when adult children become parents, this can be an opportunity for reconnection and healing of old wounds; there is a new understanding of what parents do.

Grandparents and grandchildren who interact frequently express feelings of closeness; some grandparents experience continuity, and grandchildren develop added self-identity through storytelling and oral history. Grandparenthood provides an opportunity for new roles and meaningful interaction, because it usually does not entail the responsibilities, obligations, or conflicts of parenthood. Stress can result if grandparents are drawn into parental conflicts. Occasionally, grandparents act as a refuge for children in a strife-torn family. Geographically separated grandparents and grandchildren have greater opportunities to communicate regularly today because of e-mail; many seniors are encouraged to go online by relatives, and a prime motivation is to connect with their children and grandchildren, rather than with friends (Wired Seniors, 2001).

In certain ethnic groups, grandparents are expected to assume a major role in child rearing. However, in other cultures, if grandparents are coerced into child care, they are likely to resent it. In most African American families older family members play many roles—adviser, mediator, financial supporter, health resource, and transmitter of culture. "Grandparents often have relationships with their grandchildren that are as close as, if not closer than, the relationships they have with their own adult children" (Hines, 1999, p. 339). Increasingly, some grandparents are forced to raise their grandchildren due to the dysfunctional behaviors of their children. There has been a 40 percent increase in middle-aged and older adults caring full time for grandchildren. This has happened because parents became involved in drugs; babies were born to young mothers who essentially abandoned them; children are abused or neglected; or parents cannot hold jobs or contract illnesses, such as cancer or AIDS (Pinson-Millburn, Fabrian, Schlosberg, & Pyle, 1996). Such cross-generational contact provides opportunities for extended transmission of culture and for development of a sense of family history.

In addition to embarking on grandparenting, the middle-aged generation has to deal with changing relationships with their parents and their retirement, disability, dependency, or death. In spite of the decisions about major changes in midlife, this period can be a happy one for families. Financial worries lessen if money has been managed well over the years. Family income tends to be at its highest level. Children become less of an everyday concern and a couple or single parent may have the opportunity to focus on old or new relationships and experiences.

Families in Later Life

Family relationships continue to be significant throughout later life. According to the 2000 U.S. Census, 12 percent of the U.S. population is over age 65; 9 percent of American households belong to a householder 65 years old or older. Approximately one-third of men and over one-half of women live alone. Most of those with children report that a child could be there within minutes if needed and tend to maintain at least weekly contact. The myth of the isolated elderly is not reality for the majority of older Americans. Total isolation is very rare. As families grow older, the more frequently they interact with relatives, and the higher they rank their happiness (Ishii-Kuntz, 1994). Because people live longer today, some 34 percent of adults aged 65 to 69 now work because they wish to do so or fear that they will not have enough money for health care or other major expenses (Lewis, 1998). If they have to work in addition to care for their grandchildren, stress increases.

Older family members face issues of self-identity related to retirement, health concerns, interpersonal needs (especially if they lose a spouse), and facing their own death. Some couples experience "re-entry" problems when one or both return to the home and remain there 24 hours of most days. The increased contact may lead to a deepening of the relationship or result in friction from the forced closeness. Retired persons may undergo severe role adjustments to the loss of certain functions (e.g., providing) that served as self-definition. Today, many older Americans retire more than once, having started new careers or jobs after a traditional retirement. The loss of a large social communication network places increased pressure for intimacy on the couple. Yet, this may be a time of rejuvenation. The couple now has time to enjoy one another. However, many older people are not like the couples just discussed. They face a different communication challenge since, as noted earlier, many live alone. Sheehy (1998) reports the following: Men have a more difficult time transitioning from midlife to old age; women reach out from midlife and beyond using communication to extend and multiply friendships for nurturance, whereas men rarely make new friends; and

Later life conversations and communication contribute to an individual's well-being.

men are less introspective and become emotionally more dependent on their wives.

During old age, many family relationships are emotionally important even if there is limited direct contact, as these are sustained by memories of intense interaction (Bedford & Blieszner, 1997). Although historically, limited geographic mobility served as a major source of interpersonal loss, new technologies provide greater opportunities to bridge the distance gap. For example, although only one-quarter of seniors over age 65 use the Internet, 93 percent of users over age 65 send and read e-mail (Wired Seniors, 2001). This number will rise annually.

Another issue that affects communication involves family members' health and declining strength. Ill health creates a need for nurturing communication and taps a couple's physical, mental, and financial resources. Weiss (1997) catalogs a list of what happens to many aging adults: Vision declines and lenses thicken; ears lose the ability to detect higher-pitched tones and, later in life, low pitches; senses of smell and taste grow duller; skin grows thinner; muscles waste and fat accumulates around the waist; and so on. The list does not need to get any longer to convince one that physical changes connected with aging affect interpersonal relationships and can contribute to loss of self-esteem. In addition to these normal body changes, all disabilities add to stress levels as older adults try to communicate. Such health concerns compound the problem of maintaining relationships. Frustration and low self-esteem may make individuals reluctant to initiate contact, and listeners may become impatient with the older person's infirmities.

Interpersonal communication becomes increasingly important at this stage. Many older family members engage in the "elder function," or the sharing of the accumulated wisdom of their lives with younger people, usually family members. There is a need to feel useful to the coming generation, and, for many older persons, such feelings come from revealing information or spinning stories designed to guide the younger listener. The focus of reminiscence is usually the family. It can be used as a coping mechanism, to defend self-esteem, to feel loved, to gain self-awareness, or to see oneself in a larger historical context. This oral history can enrich a family, especially its members' sense of their family-of-origin (Wolff, 1993). It gives the elderly a chance to communicate to those they love, helped raise, or even harmed. Some need to "set the record straight" or to correct, and express sorrow for mistakes. More old people are writing their memoirs, not for publication but because they "want to leave a record of their lives for future generations" (Harker, 1997, p. 32). Many journaling and autobiography writing classes are being offered by senior centers. The importance of this storytelling is demonstrated in the following example.

I'm glad my Dad, Bill, lived past 75. Only then did we come to terms with one another. Long after he retired, he mellowed, had a stroke, and became approachable. He talked about the depression, the war years, and the struggle to pay for the farm. Then I sensed what had made him so tough and noncommunicative.

Two basic functions seem to be served by the elderly parent-adult child relationship: sharing affect and mutual aid. Positive affect provided to the elderly by their children significantly increases their feelings of well-being (Barnett, Kibria, Baruch, & Pleck, 1991). Although older Americans see their children with some regularity, many older persons are prevented from maintaining the interpersonal contacts they desire due to concerns of economics, safety, and health (Aldous & Klein, 1991). Rising costs of living restrict the travel and entertainment aspects of older persons' budgets, and many urban senior citizens do not feel safe attending evening meetings or social activities. Inflation has increased stress on older Americans as more fall below the poverty level. Poverty rates are higher for elderly women, African Americans, Hispanics, and single persons.

Older couples who reach their retirement together may turn inward toward each other and share their remaining years intensely. Loss becomes a part of aging, and this increases when close friends and relatives die. When needed, elder care is most often carried out by daughters; often the oldest who lives within five miles of the parents. This care-giving daughter is more likely to be divorced, widowed, or never married (Weldon, 1998).

The developmental stages of both middle and older years are important periods for reflection. Intrapersonal communication about the meaning of one's life allows an individual to put life in perspective. The intrapersonal communication has systemic effects, because how the aging individual comes to terms with his or her own sense of wholeness affects other members' sense of identity.

The loss of an elderly family member may be seen as "on-time" within the life course, but this does not diminish the grief. Functioning families find ways to acknowledge death as a normal and appropriate topic throughout life; therefore, an aging member's death can be openly addressed. Death decisions related to aging frequently forces end-of-life decision making (Hoppough & Ames, 2001). Although death remains a difficult or taboo topic in many families, others, particularly those with strong ethnic ties, are able to confront the issue more directly and realistically. For example, within Mexican American families, events surrounding death bring a family together to express emotions freely, reinforce family cohesiveness, and involve all ages in related ceremonies and support for each other (Martinez, 2001).

After the death of a spouse, cohabiting partner, or lover, the other must face the adjustment inherent in becoming a widow, widower, or single person without a lover. Working through the grief period, such a person may make great demands on friends or family members who are resentful of, or unprepared for, such pressures. The surviving member of a couple has to renegotiate roles and boundaries as he or she attempts to create or maintain interpersonal contacts. It is important that older family members have a say in their care and be a part of all communication that concerns them as long as possible.

Much to the surprise of their adult children, many widows or widowers begin to date. The importance of dating among older persons is growing, not necessarily as a prelude to marriage. Interpersonal motives for dating include meeting possible mates, meeting possible dates, exchanging intimacies, remaining socially active, interacting with the opposite sex, engaging in sex, and maintaining a stable identity. Often, relationships with siblings emerge as very significant during this period, as family and memories take an even greater importance.

Eventually, an elderly person must confront his or her own death. Many families resist addressing the issue directly with the elderly member, yet relationships that allow discussion of death and that provide direct emotional support are more helpful. Family members—particularly adult children—may face their own crises as they try to (1) deal with the loss of the generation that separates them from death, (2) make sense of the experience, (3) anticipate shifts in the family formation, and (4) deal with their own feelings. Often, these concerns get in the way of saying farewell in a direct and meaningful manner. More will be discussed about this kind of stress in the next chapter.

TRANSITIONS BETWEEN STAGES

It is important not to underestimate the effects of transitions between each of these developmental stages that are part of varying life courses. Dysfunctional families have members who fail to make these transitions at the appropriate times in their lives. These members cause imbalance in their family systems by remaining at one developmental stage and not moving on. They are "off course" in not proceeding through expected changes in the life cycle stages. In these troubled families, there is a piling-up effect, with one or more members stuck at the same stage. Some of these same family members experience external stresses (illness, separation, divorce) simultaneously with developmental changes and become unable to cope. However, functional families take these changes in stride and experience the transitions with temporary, but not permanent, stress.

Relational and marital satisfaction vary across time with consequent effects on family communication. In a variety of studies that followed couples from the childless stage through the years of childbearing, adolescence, and stages beyond, results indicated a steady decline in satisfaction that did not level off until the children began to individuate and separate from their parents. Then, satisfaction increased in the postparental period when the children left and established their own families (Giblin, 1994). Some more recent studies suggest greater variation. Not only does this show differences in perceptions by family members but differences between stages that affect communication. It is interesting to note that families cope with these stresses by using the communication strategy of reframing their difficulties in ways they could manage. This requires the communication skills of negotiation, problem solving, and decision making.

Functional families experience transitions as challenging and, at times, unpleasant events, but not as long-lasting negative influences. Transitions into marriage or birth of a child, for example, affect family functioning, but the family progresses through them as a normal maturation process. Transitions out of marriage—such as divorce, desertion, or death—have negative effects and cause higher stress over longer periods of time (Belsky et al., 1991).

Frequently, typical transitions are replaced by idiosyncratic transitions, such as gay or lesbian commitments, family formation through new reproductive technologies, foster placement, or the end of cohabiting partnerships; these moments need their own adapted rituals (Imber-Black, 1999). Importantly, Lavee and Olson (1991) report that the impact of transitions and the intrafamily strain on the family system are not determined by either the levels of cohesion or adaptability alone but by the interaction of the two dimensions. They suggest some families become more crisis prone and others more adaptive while moving through the life cycle stages. The authors discovered differences on cohesion and adaptability scales in the Circumplex Model of Family Systems related to a family's response to stress. Earlier research had indicated that families could be more accurately described on cohesion and adaptability scales as (1) flexible-separated (high on adaptability and low on cohesion), (2) flexible-connected (high on adaptability and cohesion), (3) structured-separated (low on both cohesion and adaptability), and (4) structured-connected (high on cohesion and low on adaptability) (Olson, Lavee, & McCubbin, 1988). Using this family system typology, Lavee and Olson (1991) report that marital adjustment to stress was an important predictor of adaptation, affecting perceived well-being directly or indirectly, for connected but not in separated families. Further, a direct effect of intrafamily strain on well-being was found in flexible but not in structured families. Other conclusions indicate that flexible-connected families are more affected by the pileup of stressful events but not by predictable transitions, whereas the structured-separated families have greater difficulty with transitional changes in the life cycle. The flexible-separated and structured-connected types experience difficulties with both transitions and stressful events.

Throughout this chapter we have cited evidence that indicates the great variations in how families cope with stress. Some families experience a roller-coaster effect with little relief, especially when multiple stressors accumulate (Burr, Klein, & Associates, 1994). As they struggle with change and transitions, most persons experience life in its moments, and often ignore the larger process. In short, the movement across the life span becomes lost in the moments.

Conclusion

This chapter provided an overview of the effects of developmental stresses on communication within families and how these affect the life course. Olson (1997) summarized well the impact of stress when he stated, "All stressors either begin or end up in the family" (p. 261). Some stresses may come from outside the family system;

some are created inside the family system, but all affect the family. After indicating how individuals move through a life cycle, the chapter focused on a stage model for intact U.S. families. The stages included are (1) single young adults, (2) the couple, (3) families with young children, (4) families with adolescents, (5) launching children and moving on, and (6) families in later life. As families move through the years, each generation faces predictable developmental issues as couples marry, beget children, and live through stages of child development superimposed on individual adult developmental changes. As children leave home to form new systems, the original couple faces the middle years and adjustment issues. The cohesion-adaptability axis overlays each family system's personal growth, while themes, images, and biosocial beliefs may be challenged as the years pass. Throughout the chapter, research has been included on how the individual's life course can be altered by the "on-time" or "off-time" sequencing of life cycle or developmental stages.

The entire family developmental process is extremely complex and challenging. Achieving the developmental tasks in each stage represents accomplishment and psychological growth for each family member in his or her life course. Stress gets expressed in the intrapersonal and interpersonal communication that follows as the family member struggles for balance in the dialectical tension between self needs and family system needs. Coping requires continual conversation.

In Review

1. Reflecting on your own family or one you know well, compare and contrast how the stages of development affected the life course. Cite examples of "on-time" and "off-time" events that altered the life course.

2. Discuss what impact different cultural backgrounds have on the communication in various stages of development on children and parents. Does being Asian American, Hispanic, African American, and so on affect developmental issues?

3. Using your own family or a family you know well, give examples of verbal or nonverbal communication patterns that seemed commonplace at different developmental stages in the family life cycle.

4. Referring to your own family or a family you have observed, describe how a couple has dealt with the communication tasks of incorporating a child into their system and dealing with the following communication-related issues: (a) renegotiating roles, (b) transmitting culture, (c) establishing a community of experiences, and (d) developing the child's communication competence.

5. What appears to characterize communication in families during the period when there are one or more adolescents living within the system?

6. How is communication affected by the moving out of young adults in the launching stage in two-parent systems or in single-parent systems?

7. Compare and contrast communication patterns you have observed in the interactions between middle-aged and older family members. To what extent were reminiscing, reflection, and sorting out important to members at these stages?

FAMILY COMMUNICATION *and* UNPREDICTABLE STRESS

11

The loss of a child is one abyss from which few families return. Some claw their way again toward the light, perhaps finding a narrow ledge where, in time, memory can shed its skin of pain. Others dwell in darkness forever.

Nicholas Evans, *The Loop*

"Never would I have predicted we'd have to deal with something like this." These words have been spoken by countless family members as they faced unforeseen challenges, such as the loss of loved ones on September 11, 2001. Every year brings major and minor challenges. On the West Coast, terrible storms wreak havoc on families with mudslides, torrential rains, and destroyed homes. Shootings within schools terrorize children, while on the streets some witness death up close. The continuing violence in our communities adds stress whether in the form of "road rage," domestic violence, anti-gay hate crimes, or knife attacks that maim or kill. Add to this figure the hundreds who die in robberies, drug wars, and drunken driving accidents, and the human costs involved in these tragedies becomes apparent. Every one of those killed or injured had people who loved them—fathers, mothers, brothers, sisters, friends, partners, or stepparents. These catastrophes represent only one kind of unpredictable stress that families fear. Families can also live in dread of losing a father suddenly because of an artery blockage, a mother relapsing into alcoholism, or a young son diagnosed with leukemia. What happens to a family system when events occur that the family has had no preparation to cope with? How does communication function in these circumstances?

The previous chapter focused on family developmental issues that are framed by the life-course issues, explaining changes that cause predictable stress in families from infancy to death. The stages a family passes through has an overall timetable or temporal quality with expectancies as to when transitions would occur. The absence of "on-time" movement through the stages creates stress. Critical role transitions become a part of developmental change, such as getting married, establishing careers, first parenthood, or having children leave home.

This chapter discusses those unpredictable events that cause great stress in families. "Unlike family development, unpredictable family stress is largely concerned with *unexpected* events in the lives of families" (Aldous, 1990). Depending on their resources and their interpretation of the events, family members respond with varying degrees of stress. The unpredictable stress in families caused by divorce, remarriage, and teen pregnancy leads to changes in the lives of family members, interrupting gradual family development processes. Later marriages, cohabitation, or stepfamily formation make it difficult to predict the points of stress family members experience going through developmental changes (Aldous, 1995). The later arrival of children, the greater number of years between children, and the decline in number of children all affect time in any life cycle stage. Unemployment and job shifts may affect timing of developmental cycles. Remember, in the family development approach, change is conceptualized as systematic shifts through a sequence of stages. A life-course perspective suggests that when crises occur, a family member's education, income, occupation, value structure, and satisfaction or dissatisfaction with life may cause more changes than timing in family stages. Issues of life cycle and life course simultaneously bear on how a family responds to unpredictable stress.

Unpredictable stresses are brought about by events or circumstances that disrupt life patterns but cannot be foreseen from either a developmental or life-course perspective. Such stresses may be positive, although more frequently they are perceived as negative. These are the "slings and arrows of outrageous fortune," or shocks to the system. Such stresses conjure up images of loss such as that involved in untimely death, divorce, economic reversal, or serious injury. Some positive events—such as a large inheritance, winning the lottery, a job promotion or transfer, or the rediscovery of long-lost relatives—are also stresses for the system. These unpredictable stresses can maximize the dialectical tensions between individual family members and others or between the family and its environment. For example, a sudden death, a long-term illness, or a severe injury of a parent or child can change a family from one that copes well with ordinary stresses to one that cannot cope with a critical major stress.

There may be certain overlaps between unpredictable stress and developmental and life-course issues. Becoming pregnant or having a child may be considered a developmental event, but an unwanted pregnancy or the birth of a child with a severe handicap may also be classified as an unpredictable stress. Whether the entire family or only certain members are initially affected by the event, the family system will eventually reflect the tension created by the loss in its interaction patterns.

Crises occur when a family lacks the resources to cope or when a "family demands significantly exceed their capabilities" (Patterson, 2002, p. 351). All families undergo some degree of strain or stress. *Strain* can be defined as that tension or difficulty sensed by family members, which indicates that change is needed in their relationships and their family environment. *Stressor events* discussed in this chapter are characterized by unexpectedness, their greater intensity and longer duration, and their undesirability and serious effects (Lavee, Sharlin, & Katz, 1996). Think about the stresses of a family dealing for over 20 years with what became a fatal illness for three members in this example.

There were nine children in our family, and three had muscular dystrophy. I remember how hard it was for Mom to accept their illness. She wouldn't talk about it within the family. Her rule was that it was better not discussed, yet I would find her alone in her room crying. We all learned from Marilyn, Dan, and Virginia. Communication reached a tense stage when Marilyn was the first to die. We sensed the fear and panic in Dan and Virginia. It took time to get them to talk about these fears and finally, near their own deaths, they would joke about who was going next. All of this was strictly among Dan and Virginia and myself. Mom, Dad, and the rest couldn't handle any humor on the subject. I feel they would like to have shared these feelings with all of us, but some of the living in our family put great distance between themselves and those who were dying.

The previous chapter contains a model of family stressors (Figure 10.1) and a description of the developmental stresses a family faces. This chapter concentrates on the second type of horizontal stressors—the external, unpredictable stressors. It examines (1) coping with unpredictable stress (including the stressors), a model for coping, and the stages of crisis; and (2) communication patterns for coping with stresses such as death, illness, disability, and divorce. It also links these stressors to the systems or the life-course frame of the model.

UNPREDICTABLE STRESS AND FAMILY COPING PATTERNS

Stress involves a physiological response to stressors—events or situations that are viewed as powerful negative or positive forces. Individuals or families under stress reflect this in physiological changes and anxiety as they attempt to cope.

Systems under stress tend to fall into predictable patterns, some functional, some dysfunctional, as the members try to handle the anxiety. As you might imagine, what is a major stressor to one family may be a minor concern to another. What one family does to reduce tension differs greatly from another family's strategies. In order to appreciate the process of coping, the family stressors, models of coping, and stages of crisis must be examined.

Stressors

Family researchers have examined stresses and crises for over 50 years. In his early classic work, Hill (1949) identified family disruptions that cause crises. These include (1) the coming apart of the family due to the death of a member; (2) the addition of new or returning family members; (3) the sense of disgrace, which may result from infidelity, alcoholism, or nonsupport; and (4) a combination of the above, which could include suicide, imprisonment, homicide, or mental illness. Stressors such as drug abuse, abortions, forms of violence, and teenage suicide are more prevalent today. Major stresses throw a family system out of its normal balance, and precipitate long-term change. Although there is knowledge that death is inevitable, that accidents happen daily, or that serious illnesses can happen to anyone, the actual occurrence of these events brings challenges that test the limits of endurance. These struggles affect all family members.

How well a family copes depends on several factors. In early work, Bain (1978) claimed a family's coping capacity was tied to four factors: (1) the number of previous stressors the members had faced in recent years, (2) the degree of role change involved in coping, (3) the social support available to members, and (4) the institutional support available to members. Past experiences with crises prepare family members to understand new crises when they occur; they may also retraumatize family members. The piling up of sad, unpredictable events affects coping, as does the amount of recovery time between jolts to the system. For example, the severe illness of a child is likely to be very difficult for a family who has recently dealt with major financial or marital problems. It may cause greater strain if a parent has to change roles, such as giving up a career, to tend the child. The rallying of support from friends and family members to assist or offer empathy lessens the stress. Yet, often a family has to ask for the support and not assume people will know what is needed or know how to respond. The following observation by a teacher attests to the importance of support at the time of crisis.

Unexpected death of a parent sends a family into shock and role confusion.

As a teacher, I watch a few students' families undergo divorce each year. The ones who seem to cope reasonably well with the pain are those that have some strengths or resources to bring to the process. Usually this is the family that has strong extended family or neighborhood friends and the family that tells the school or church what is going on. In short, this family lets people in on the pain—asks for some help.

Throughout the family stress literature, writers emphasize the possible productive outcomes of dealing with stress as well as the difficulties inherent in such a process (Burr, Klein, & Associates, 1994). Certainly some families fare better during stressful situations than do others. Researchers use the word *resilience* to refer to a family's ability to "do well in the face of adversity" (Patterson, 2002, p. 350). A family who suffers through the loss of a child and is able to build intimacy during the process of grieving, rather than become more distant, would be considered a resilient family. Patterson points out that living in poverty or in violent neighborhoods affects a family's ability to be resilient. Resilient low- to low-middle–income families are characterized by internal strengths complemented by community support services, religious programs, and a sense of belonging to the community.

Farm families have been especially prone to family stressors due to their dependence on weather patterns. Teens in these families who reported being able to have their families help them deal with stress were more satisfied with their families (Plunkett, Henry, & Knaub, 1999).

Family Stress Model

Each family exhibits unique coping behaviors. *Coping* implies "the central mechanism through which family stressors, demands, and strains are eliminated, managed, or adapted to" (McCubbin, Patterson, Cauble, Wilson, & Warwick, 1983, p. 359). The primary model currently used to understand family crises evolved from R. Hill's original model, which proposed that:

> A [the stressor event], interacting with B [the family's crisis-meeting resources], interacting with C [the family's definition of the event] produces X [the crisis]. (McCubbin & Patterson, 1983b, p. 6)

The stressor, *a*, represents a life event or transition that has the potential to change a family's social system—indeed, its life course. Such events as the loss of a job, untimely death, serious illness, or good luck in the lottery may fall into this category. The *b* factor represents the resources a family can use to keep an event or change from creating a crisis, such as money, friends, time and space, or problem-solving skills. This factor ties into a family's levels of cohesion and adaptability in terms of how it has learned to deal with various crises over time.

The *c* factor represents the importance a family attaches to the stressor *a*. For example, in one family, a diagnosis of a member's juvenile diabetes might overwhelm the entire system, whereas another family might cope well with that news, perceiving the diabetes as a manageable disease, one not likely to alter their lives drastically. The definitions of both the family and families-of-origin may come to bear on the perception of crises. For example, a three-generation family that has never experienced a divorce may define a young granddaughter's marital separation as a severe crisis. A multigenerational system with a history of divorce may not see the separation as a crisis. Together, *a, b,* and *c* contribute to the experience of stress that is unique to each family, depending on its background, resources, and interpretation of the event.

The *x* factor represents the amount of disruptiveness that occurs to the system. It is characterized by "the family's inability to restore stability and by the continuous pressure to make changes in the family structure and patterns of interaction" (McCubbin & Patterson, 1983b, p. 10). In short, it is the family's total experienced anxiety and demands that the family cannot assimilate.

McCubbin and Patterson (1983a) have developed a Double *ABCX* model based on Hill's original work that incorporates postcrisis variables (Figure 11.1), or the next stages of coping. Although Hill's *ABCX* model focused on precrisis areas, the Double *ABCX* model incorporates the family's efforts to recover over time. In this model, the *aA* factor includes not only the immediate stressor (e.g., death) but also the demands or changes that may emerge from individual system's members, the system as a whole, and the extended system. McCubbin and Patterson suggest that the *aA* factor includes (1) the initial stressor or developmental stage issues, (2) normative transitions, (3) prior strains, (4) the consequences of the system's coping attempts, and (5) ambiguity. Imagine, for example, the death of a man, age 36, in a family with a wife and three daughters, ages 6, 10, and 12. If a young father dies, the system must deal with the immediate loss as well as economic uncertainty and changes in the mother's role. In addition, the developmental stage of some children may soon require the family to cope with an adolescent's need for independence. This is compounded by any prior strains, such as in-law problems or mother-daughter conflicts. A consequence of the family's attempts to cope might be the mother's new job, which keeps her from meeting the children's needs for active parenting. Finally, ambiguity might be caused by the confusion of new roles now that the father has left the system. Boundaries shift as the life course changes later. Mother might consider remarriage. Changes become expected. Thus, *aA* is broader than the original conception of *a.*

The *bB* factor represents the family's ability to meet its needs. This factor includes family resources from an individual, system, and commu-

FIGURE 11.1   The Double ABCX Model

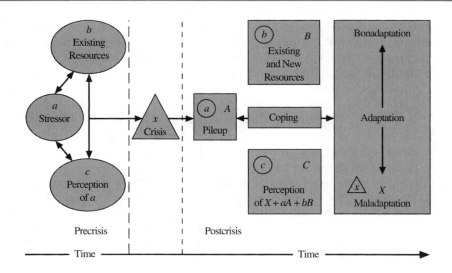

nity point of view. A family may use existing and expanded resources. Existing resources are part of a family's background. In the case of death, these may include the ways in which a family coped in the past when the father was gone on business. The expanded family resources emerge from the crisis itself. A widow may create such resources by studying accounting, which leads to a well-paying position, or by sharing in a widows' self-help group. The emerging social systems are a critical element in the *bB* factor.

The *cC* factor is the way in which a family interprets a crisis, including the meaning the family gives to the stressor event and to the added stressors caused by the original crisis, plus its perception of how to bring the family into balance. When a young father dies, a family must cope with that event and its meaning. If the widow comes to believe she has lost her only chance at happiness in life, her perceptions will strongly influence her attempts at recovery and the attitudes of her children. The members must also interpret the changes in finances, changes in the mother's role, and how the entire family is affected. Families who cope well can manage the situation through flexible changes in responsibilities and through support of one another. Families who have difficulty coping cannot see a sense of challenge and find themselves overwhelmed, with little sense of hope or opportunity for growth.

The *xX* factor is the effect of the family's adaptation on the individual system and community levels. Family adaptation is achieved "through reciprocal relationships where the demands of one of these units are met by the capabilities of another so as to achieve a 'balance' of interaction" (McCubbin & Patterson, 1983a, p. 19). If members' demands are too great for the family's capabilities, there will be an imbalance. There will also be imbalance if the family demands more than the community is capable of providing. For example, the family and work community may create an imbalance by demanding too much of one parent. The positive end of the continuum of outcomes of a crisis, called *bonadaptation,* is characterized by balance between (1) member and family and (2) family and community. The negative end, or *maladaptation,* reflects imbalance or severe losses for the family. In some families, drastic changes allow members to renegotiate their relationships in positive ways. Thus, disruptions may be resolved in positive or negative ways. The whole family system reacts to the crises, even down to its youngest member as shown in the following story.

In the summer of 1994 our son, Mitchell, came home to die. He had lived an independent life since his AIDS diagnosis four years earlier, but the shadow of the crisis was always there—waiting. My top priority was to help Mitchell. Our first grandchild, Hannah, was 2 years old when Mitchell came home. She had been coming to our house every Wednesday since she was an infant. Hannah had her own room that was fixed up just for her. Because of Mitchell's needs, the visits stopped. Weeks later she came over with her mommy only to find all of the toys had been replaced by hospital equipment. The expression on that little face was one of complete bewilderment. We said and did all of the right things but Hannah was angry with her Grandma for a long time.

Burr, Klein, and Associates (1994) challenged the assumptions that support the Double *ABCX* model and some inconsistencies in the assumptions used to explain how the model operates. The intent of the model is to identify causal relationships that specify recognizable patterns. What happens in *a, b,* and *c* factors determines *x,* or the degree of crises in a family. This approach does not provide adequately for the piling up of processes simultaneously and the fact that stress can come into a system at any time. To overcome this rigidity, Burr and associates have added to the model concepts of "rules of transformation," "boundary ambiguity," "stress piling," and "feedback loops" for alternative causes and effects, and different levels of "coping strategies" for individuals within families. Later in this chapter we will discuss these levels of coping. To improve these models of stress, Olson (1997) developed a multisystem assessment of stress and health (MASH), which focuses on four areas of life (individual, work, couple, and family) and extends into a biopsychological approach that measures the relationships between stress, coping, system variables, and adaptation in the four areas of life.

All unpredictable stresses affect cohesion and adaptability and may modify boundaries, themes, images, and biosocial issues. A family with a high capacity for adaptation and above-average cohesion is likely to weather stressor events more easily than families who are rigid and fragmented. More adaptable families have the capacity to find alternative ways of relating and can adjust their communication behavior to encompass an event, but this is not easy. Family caregivers for chronically ill members reported that 55 percent spent less time than other family members, and gave up hobbies, vacations, and personal activities. Another 15 percent suffered physical or mental problems and 7 percent experienced financial hardship (National Council on Family Relations, 1998).

During a crisis, family members often want to rely on each other for comfort and support, a behavior that cannot suddenly occur if the family has a history of separateness. Families with rigid boundaries may be unable to cope adequately when severe external stresses occur. *Boundary ambiguity* increases stress. This term refers to the degree of uncertainty in family members' perceptions of who "belongs," who is expected to function in various roles, and how much openness there should be in the system to permit various outside resources to be used to deal with stress. By greatly limiting communication with such institutions as hospitals, courts, and schools, members deprive themselves of necessary information and possible emotional support. Additionally, boundaries that prevent friends or extended family from knowing about the stressor reduce sources of comfort that might help "carry" a family through a critical period. In African American families, crises among older parents trigger higher expectations of filial responsibility. Such parents are "more likely to receive assistance from both descendants and formal service providers" (Lee, Peek, & Coward, 1998).

Seemingly positive events—even increased longevity—can create great stress. The facts clearly indicate that family members are living longer. In one sense, that is good news, but who in the family accepts the burden of caring for aging parents? Newspapers contain accounts of the pressure put on lottery winners by the expectations of family and friends and the loss of a settled way of life. A long-wished-for promotion may be accompanied by the loss of familiar coworkers, pressure to succeed at a new level of responsibility, and the possibility of a stressful family move to a new city or neighborhood. Family members may find it painful to cope with the departure for college of a much-loved child. Great joys may be accompanied by great losses.

The picture is not entirely negative, however. On occasion, communication improves when the family deals with major crises. In a large study of a series of unpredictable crises, including bankruptcy, infertility, and muscular dystrophy, Burr, Klein, and Associates (1994) note that 29 percent of the family members report a lasting and definite increase in positive communication techniques. In addition, 21 percent relate early increases in better communication with later variations, and do not return to the low levels of communication experienced before the crises. Better communication included less conflict, more positive statements, and special remarks that nurtured and supported family members. The conclusion of the researchers was that most families under stress realize that they need to communicate better and so they listen more effectively to one another.

Because communication affects and is affected by all these behaviors, it plays a central role in the experiencing and eventual resolution of such stresses and contributes specifically to the family's movement through stages of stress reaction. In some families, members use direct verbal messages to explore options, negotiate needs, express feelings, and reduce tension. In other families, the members' stress may be apparent through the nonverbal messages that indicate their anxiety and other feelings. Members constantly interpret others' verbal and nonverbal messages as part of the coping pattern.

Stages of Family Crisis

In any serious crisis situation, a family goes through a definite process in handling the grief or chaos that results. Depending on the event, the stages may last from a few days to several months or years. These stages may be more pronounced in the case of a death, divorce, or news of an incurable illness, but in any crisis, family members experience a progression of feelings from denial to acceptance. Yet, since no two families accept crisis in the same way, family systems are characterized by *equifinality,* which means each family will reach the final stages of the process in a variety of ways. The following stages approximate the general process of dealing with severe stress. Although the stages usually follow one another, they may overlap, and some may be repeated a number of times.

1. Shock resulting in numbness, disbelief, or denial
2. Recoil stage resulting in anger, confusion, blaming, guilt, and bargaining
3. Depression
4. Reorganization resulting in acceptance and recovery (Kubler-Ross, 1970; Feifel, 1977; Mederer & Hill, 1983)

The process of going through such stages after a serious life event usually results in transformation of the system. Persons may find themselves more separated from, or connected to, different members and may find a shift in adaptability patterns. Communication behavior reflects and aids progress through the stages. Understanding the process allows one to analyze others' progress through the stages or to be more understanding of one's own behavior and personal progress.

Shock   At the *shock stage,* family members tend to deny the event or its seriousness. Denial comments such as "It can't be true," "It's a mistake," or "He'll be back" are accompanied by nonverbal behavior, such as setting a dead person's place at the table, awkward attempts at smiles and encouragement with a terminally ill person, or spending money lavishly when the paycheck has been cut off.

Most persons move from this stage, exhibiting behaviors that indicate a recognition of reality. Family members acknowledge their grief and feel the pain of the loss. Withdrawal or quietness characterizes communication of those who find it hard to cry. The truth of the crisis news begins to take on fuller meanings, such as "Mom will never be the same" or "She has left and will never return." Denial is transformed into an intense desire to recapture what has been lost, especially in the case of a family death, desertion, or severe injury. This may lead to attempts to recapture memories, for example, "I keep expecting to see her in the kitchen."

Recoil   After the initial blow, the family may move into the *recoil stage* of blaming, anger, and bargaining. Blaming often takes place as the grieving family members seek reasons for what has happened. This may include blaming the self ("I was too trusting; I should have watched her more closely" or "I never should have left town") or blaming others ("It's his own fault" or "The doctors never told us the truth soon enough"). Such behavior may be interspersed with feelings of "It's not fair." Anger may be directed at the event or person most directly involved or may be displaced onto others, such as family members, friends, or coworkers. Attempts at real or imagined bargains may occur ("If I take a cut in pay, they could hire me back," "If you come back, I'll stop gambling forever"). Thoughts that the world is unfair, that God has been cruel to let this happen, or that a child's potential will never be realized fill the minds of family members and then are released to one another.

Depression   Anger slowly turns into depression; an ovewhelming sadness permeates the family members' thinking. Whereas anger is directed outward, depression is directed inward. Usually, family members need to talk about what has happened. In fact, they often retell the crisis story over and over. This is a normal and healthy response especially for families experiencing a long period of suffering because of death, incurable illness, permanent injuries, a long jail sentence, or mental breakdown. People outside the family often fail to understand the need to talk and may attempt to avoid the subject, not recognizing that support may be possible only from those not as directly affected. Often, family confusion and disorganization may be so great that outsiders tend to take over and guide decision making. This could easily have happened in the following example.

I have never felt so much sorrow and stress as when my wife left with the children and I was without the daily company of my kids. Among other things, life became totally unpredictable and I felt I lost my identity. For months I functioned in a total fog.

Reorganization   Grief-stricken people normally pass through this stage to what they describe as a "turning point." Graham (1997) studied the communication between divorced couples and identified eleven turning points in which the communication changed, usually from negative to more positive over time. A frequent pattern she labeled "gradual relational progress" meant the couples through "trial and error eventually fig-

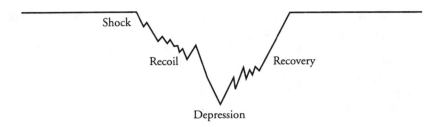

FIGURE 11.2   Linear Scale of Emotions during Crisis

ure out how to proceed in the new relationship." Usually, a decision marks the turning event. It may be a decision to take a trip, to sell a failing business, to get rid of mementos that serve as daily reminders, to register with a placement bureau, or to join Alcoholics Anonymous. This decision signals that the individual has moved into the fourth crisis stage—reorganization of events in his or her life to effect a recovery. This stage is characterized by family members' taking charge of their lives and making the necessary changes forced on them by the crisis. It may take 6 weeks for one family to recover from a job loss. It may take another family, suffering a death or divorce, anywhere from a year to 18 months to achieve a semblance of balance in the system.

If emotions in crises could be diagrammed, the line would descend to the lowest point with depression. The descent begins with the impact of the news and continues the downward spiral with some rises in the recoil stages to descend again as reality returns (Figure 11.2). Eventually, most people reach a level of recovery.

Throughout this process, communication links members in sharing their reactions and links one or more to outside sources of institutional or social support, which can provide acceptance of the emotions that need to be expressed. If family members are cut off from support or unable to communicate about the loss, the process may be incomplete—they may be stuck, unable to complete the process and reach acceptance. The next section will consider some common types of family crises and communication issues involved with each.

COMMUNICATION AND SPECIFIC CRISES

Communication patterns and networks shift dramatically when members face major life crises (Brubaker & Roberto, 1993). Interaction becomes unpredictable as individuals withdraw into silence, explode into anger, or move into constant talking as a way to handle the stress or grief. Although this section focuses on three major crises—death, illness, and divorce—remember that less dramatic events, such as moving or losing a job, also disrupts the family system. These events alter hopes and fantasies by introducing new tensions between family members and their environment. Any stress, particularly unpredictable, makes it difficult to maintain relationships. Crisis forces parents and their children to use different relationship maintenance strategies because frequently dialectical pressures shift and what previously worked no longer address the situation (Baxter & Dindia, 1990). The crisis event can force openness and expose a family to public scrutiny, as for example in the case of a suicide, teenage pregnancy, or drug arrest. The event may create closeness and connection as the family attempts some sort of a united front to cope or to support one another. Autonomy needs may be set aside in the early stages of dealing with a crisis. Variations in the predictability-novelty dialectical tension in individual family members' communication may be exacerbated when the crisis demands response from each family member.

Untimely Death

The finality of death closes off relationship options, making it an emotionally overwhelming crisis for most families. Although the death of any family member carries with it a sense of grief, the death of an elderly person who has lived a full life usually does not generate the anger aroused by untimely death, nor does it carry the potential for major role changes among young or middle-aged family members. However, untimely death of younger and middle-aged family members serves as a major unpredictable crisis for all families (DiGiulio, 1992). Surviving partners are not prepared to be called "widow" and "widower," and for cohabiting or same-sex partners, there is not a word that designates the loss of a partner. Untimely death throws a family into severe shock, allowing no chance for farewells or the resolution of relationship issues, and it often results in prolonged mourning across many years (McGoldrick & Walsh, 1999). Prolonged illness, on the other hand, often provides the family with the opportunity to mourn, say farewells, and resolve relationship issues.

Communication within families dealing with death ranges from the highly intense and emotional to the very superficial and denial oriented. Variables to consider are how family rules impact communication about death; myths that sustain or create blocks to open communication on the subject; ethnic or religious differences such as attitudes toward death and mourning rituals; and the family's experience with previous losses (Brommel, 1992). Persons who are dying and their family members often resort to verbal games to maintain a two-sided pretense that "everything is going to be all right." Family members in their own grief may go into a denial of the information of a terminal illness. They shield the dying from such knowledge and develop communication rules to support this fiction. Triangles may form when two people draw in a third to relieve tension, or subgroups may collude to avoid any discussion of the impending death. Frequently, the dying member knows and then has to play the game of "not knowing" to protect the rest of the family. Such rules block the dying family member from dealing with all the interpersonal feelings, as well as with their immediate fears and loneliness. Some family members resent the dishonesty involved, as explained here.

I will never forget my uncle complaining bitterly two days before he died about his family treating him like a helpless child and insisting he would recover whenever he started to talk about dying or his fear of never leaving the hospital. I was only 14 and did not fully understand what he was trying to tell me at the time, but I never forgot his pain or anger as he tried to explain the feeling of dying without emotional support.

The dying person has his or her own grieving to do since he or she is about to "lose everything which is important and everyone who is significant to him and whom he loves" (Dunlop, 1978, p. 2). In determining whether to tell a patient, one should consider the following: (1) the dying member's emotional and intellectual resources to handle the news, (2) what the dying member already knows or has guessed, (3) the personal meaning the disease has for the dying individual based on his or her knowledge of others who had the same terminal illness, and (4) the degree to which the dying member wants to know his or her fate. Deciding whether to tell the dying person requires considerable skill in assessing verbal and nonverbal communication from that person.

Kubler-Ross (1970) suggests that death should be regarded as an "intrinsic part of life" and discussed openly like other events in family life, especially since almost all terminally ill patients are aware of it. The question should change from "Do I tell?" to "How do I share the information?" If a family confronts the issue openly, members can go through preparatory grief together, which facilitates the later bereavement process.

Even those persons who choose their own death through suicide find that many of their preparatory messages are denied; their attempts to communicate suicide plans go unrecognized until after the event. Parents of young people are advised to watch for such behaviors as talking of suicide, giving away possessions, acting abnormally cheerful after depression, and losing appetite (Shreve & Kunkel, 1991). Those who deal with the elderly are advised to look for depression, withdrawal, isolation, changes in sleep patterns, lower self-image, and prolonged bereavement. However, many refuse to interpret these messages as they are intended. Kubler-Ross's classic five stages present one model for the process of dying: (1) denial, (2) anger, (3) bargaining, (4) depression, and (5) acceptance. The sequence of stages may vary, but eventually, the dying person will progress through all of them if he or she lives long enough and does not become stuck at a particular point, since the length of time one stays in a stage varies according to the individual. Persons may move back and forth through the stages, reworking certain issues.

Persons preparing for death need to express their denials—to articulate why such cannot be the case and to explore other remedies. They need to vent their anger at themselves, those they love, and possibly at God, science, medicine, or other institutions. Children in families where a member dies by homicide often feel anger toward the police officer or other person who delivered the news (Clements & Burgess, 2002). Bargains must be struck or attempted—silently and openly. Finally, the loneliness, fears, and practical concerns must be unloaded, ranging from "What is really on the other side?" to "How will they cope in school without me?" When a person facing death prepares a written advanced directive (a statement about his or her wishes for care), he or she may lessen the stress that family members feel at the time of death (Tilden, Tolle, Nelson, & Fields, 2001).

Dying persons need empathic listeners who do not insist they will be better if they think about something else. Although watching a person die can be devastating to the family members, terminal illness (unlike sudden death) does provide the family potential to resolve relationship issues and to say the "final good-byes" (Herz, 1980). One man's experience facing the death of his partner is exemplified by this example.

We had been together for several years as partners-in-life. We knew that each of us cared for the other but we had intimacy issues because we found it difficult as two men to talk about what we really felt about one another, our relationship, and our kids from previous marriages. His illness changed all that! We began to have long talks late into the night, pouring out all the things we had never said, and trying to say what needed to be said about a future I would face alone. He not only helped me to accept his leaving, but he reconnected with all his siblings and his mother, in deeper more meaningful ways. They all came for a weekend three weeks before he died and I made a two-hour video of each of them reminiscing about happy and sad times in their lives. Each told him what his life had meant to them and he did the same. He wanted this tape to be his gift of remembrance. Never was communication better or easier for him and those he loved than in his last few months!

After the death of a family member, the remaining members go through a continued bereavement process. An unexpected death, either by accident or illness, forces a family into an initial state of shock. Eventually, the shock wears off and the bereavement process begins. The event traumatizes the family, even in cases in which members know of an impending death. The survivors experience anger and depression. In the year after a death, widows and widowers had rates of depression ranging from 16 to 36 percent, compared to 8 percent for comparable married partners (Brown, 1990). There may be many regrets about unspoken issues: "If only I had told him how much I loved him," "If I had only taken time to listen to her." Survivors, too, need supportive listeners. Listening, being there, and acting as a communicative reflector are key communication strategies.

During the grieving process, family members will be upset and irrational and will communicate differently. If the death has been caused by a long terminal illness or injury, the bereaved may have been so occupied with caregiving that only the death frees them to get in touch with their feelings. Many bereaved persons report the sense of a continuing relationship with the deceased and a sense of being unfinished with the relationship because they wanted to do or say additional things.

Much also depends on the place that the deceased filled in the family system. The death of a parent of young children leaves many child rearing and family support responsibilities to the remaining parent. The surviving spouse must grieve and take on new role functions. Loneliness results from the desire for emotional intimacy. The survivor wants to interact with the partner who is not available and cannot return. If the household contains young children, the remaining person has to help them through the crisis without allowing his or her own emotions to create distance from the children. Parents who have lost a child to accident, suicide, or homicide report most frequently using private prayer and church attendance to help them grieve (Murphy, Johnson, Lohan, & Tapper, 2002).

The death of a child carries with it the loss of parental dreams of their child graduating, marrying, and having children, thus creating extreme family pain. Family disruption is a common aftereffect, with divorce or separation occurring in a large number of the cases (Herz-Brown, 1988). Siblings may experience great stress and pressure. Adolescents who lose their siblings in a sudden, violent death experience a painful and complex grieving process for up to two years (Lohan & Murphy, 2002).

The death of a child with a disability or chronic illness may also have negative financial effects on a family as social security benefits end (Corden, Sloper, & Sainsbury, 2002). Deaths of healthy or unhealthy children also require parents to pay for funeral costs. Some young parents are unprepared financially to pay for burial and funeral costs for their infant, and so accept help from both sets of grandparents to pay for these costs.

Other families may not have such resources. The extended family system also experiences stress when a child dies. This young mother was bothered by her older brothers' response after the death of her infant daughter.

When they came to visit at Christmas, they didn't even ask to see her grave. I wanted them to go and to be a part of it. I guess I don't know how I would be if it happened to someone else and I didn't experience it, but it just frustrated me a lot because it was like she never existed to them. I think it took them by surprise that we talked about her so openly. I think that scared them because they didn't know how to react.

Many family members experience a return of sadness or withdrawal on anniversaries of deaths. Such dates, as well as significant holidays, serve as markers of loss, forcing memories to surface with great force. Thus, the death of a family member alters the entire family system, requiring the other members to go through a grieving process with as open communication as possible.

Family-of-origin culture plays a significant role in how a family deals with death. In general, African American families, Irish families, and Italian families believe in a "good" send-off. White Anglo-Saxon Protestant families may limit their emotional expression. Puerto Rican families, especially the female members, suffer publicly. Jewish families, reflecting a tradition of shared suffering, tend to deal openly and directly with death. Chinese families believe a "good death" includes relatives surrounding the dying person. Cultures with rituals for dealing with death, a strong sense of community, and tolerance of verbal expressions provide members with greater support. In addition, religion or spirituality can offer meaning about death and provide comfort and support (McGoldrick & Walsh, 1999).

Illness or Disability

A family with a seriously ill or disabled member goes through an important coping process before coming to terms with the problem. In families where a member has suffered a stroke, the Double *ABCX* model has been shown to be a good model for the family's experience (Clark, 1999). Using the Double *ABCX* model in a research study, Bigbee (1992) discovered a strong relationship between family stress and family illnesses. Those families that demonstrated hardiness—a personality construct composed of control, challenge, and commitment—handled stress far better than those families that did not possess it. Coping with a child's birth defect or the effects of a debilitating disease or accident requires major adjustments involving physical and emotional energy. The immediate disruption of the family in no way equals the long-term drain on family resources and energies required to help the injured or sick family member deal with what may be a lifelong situation. Illnesses with multiple hospitalizations slowly wear down the energies of family members, making the sick members feel they are a burden.

The mourning process that parents of affected children undergo are similar to stages of coping with death. The stages include impact, denial, grief, focusing outward, and closure, each with a communication component.

At the *impact* stage, the family learns, immediately or gradually, of a child's serious illness. Anxiety and tension characterize this period. Usually, the family responds in a frantic and disorganized manner. At first, the family can absorb very little information and has very limited responses. Usually, the *denial* state follows, carrying with it a sense of disbelief and distorted expectations. Parents may reject the diagnosis, fictionally explain the child's failure to perform normally, and find themselves unable to hear what others are saying about the problem. It is a period of fear and isolation.

Anger and sadness characterize the *grief*. Parents question why this happened to them. Children question why their sibling has to suffer. They may blame each other for the difficulty, isolate themselves from interacting with usual friends or extended family, preventing open and supportive communication.

Eventually, parents move toward the *focusing outward* stage, beginning a process of seeking information, discussing options, asking for help, expressing feelings, or forming a support group. Signs of relief are evident at this point as the family moves toward dealing with the issues. The *closure* stage represents a reconciliation with reality and a sense of adaptation to the child's needs. The family pulls together and adjusts in ways that allow the member of the altered system to move forward and to communicate directly about its concerns. In a study of cancer patients, Gotcher (1993) found that the communication of emotional support was the most important predictor of effective adjustment. Parents do not dream of giving birth to a child with a disability. The family must grieve the loss of a limb or mental capacity before they can become fully attached to this child. In addition to the emotional stresses, the financial demands can send a family into economic turmoil.

A serious illness or disability affects the overall family. Many adults who become ill also have parents who are affected by the illness. These parents do not get the same help in coping with their child's illness as the child's spouse and children do, often being left to cope alone with their feelings (Gilbar & Refaeli, 2000). As might be predicted following the onset of a chronic disease, it is typical for a patient to assume a central position in the family. This shift in focus, if continued over a longer period of time, affects marital and other parent-child relationships. Parents who are forced to focus on a sick and demanding child have little time or energy to deal with each other. A study of the coping patterns of parents with a child with cystic fibrosis found that both parents contribute to the coping process, but the mother's coping behavior focuses more on the interpersonal dimensions of family life—family cohesiveness and expressiveness (McCubbin et al., 1983).

Parents of children with spina bifida who were older and who had older children reported higher levels of stress in one study (Macias, Clifford, Saylor, & Kreh, 2001). In many situations, families must spend a great deal of time with a child in the hospital or in doctors' offices. In a pediatric intensive care unit, parents express a desire for communication that would foster family normalcy, respect family rights, and strengthen the family as a whole (Tomlinson, Swiggum, & Harbaugh, 1999). At one hospital, some parents were given the expectations of their roles while their child was in the hospital. Parents who received these in spoken and written form, or just written form, better understood what their roles were (Adams & Parrott, 1994).

The disability puts stress on the marriage, usually in negative ways. In fact, research reveals a high divorce rate among people with disabilities (Braithwaite & Thompson, 2000). For some couples, one child's disability limits their choice to add another child. Couples with disabled children have reported their inability to go to certain places or do certain things together. They may confront greater dialectical tension between predictability and novelty than before. Neither partner feels free to go to places or begin new projects because duty compels each of them to be there for the other or their child. The stresses are heightened when single mothers have the main responsibility for their disabled child (Gottlieb, 1997). Siblings are significantly affected by a brother's or sister's illness or disability. Research on sibling response indicates that siblings may have a surprising lack of information about the disability. This lack of information may confuse siblings in the following ways:

1. They may feel responsible for a particular condition.
2. They may wonder whether it can be transmitted or "caught" and whether they are susceptible to the same disorder.
3. They are confused about how they should communicate to family and friends about the handicap.
4. They wonder what implications a brother's or sister's handicap has for their future.
5. They may feel perplexed and overwhelmed by such discomforting feelings as anger, hurt, and guilt. (Seligman, 1988, p. 168)

In a study of the siblings of children with Down syndrome, one researcher found that many of these siblings have a positive experience in living in such a family. These siblings had above-average self-concepts, were socially competent, and had low numbers of behavior problems. Siblings did better in families that had less demands, more resources, and better coping and problem-solving skills. The siblings in the study stated that they had learned patience, love, and courage from their siblings with Down syndrome (Van Riper, 2000). Parents attribute about twice as much of their stress to a child with a disability than they attribute to the youngest sibling in the family without a disability (Baxter, Cummins, & Yiolitis, 2000). Siblings must adjust to whole new interaction patterns, as shown here.

A year and a half ago, my brother, Steve, suffered a paralyzing head injury when he swerved his motorcycle to miss a dog. He dreams of driving his Chevy pickup again but he knows he might live the rest of his life in a nursing home. When asked when he expects to get out, his eyes go blank. "Never," he says. My father discourages such talk. "Now if you work real hard you might get your legs going again, right?" he says. Steve's eyes grow red. "OK," he replies and stares at the wall. It pains me to see him like this.

As in the Double *ABCX* model described earlier, the family organizes its current resources at the outset of the crisis and then attempts to develop new resources to carry them through the crisis. A study of people with a disability indicated that they wanted to be acknowledged as persons first, especially with outsiders, and then hoped to keep the focus on the relationship rather than the disability (Braithwaite, 1991). The frustrations involved are revealed in the following example.

I certainly knew I had multiple sclerosis! I knew that if I started using a wheelchair, I would lose more than I would gain, including a feeling of control over my life and my disease. I had difficulty with steps, and not all buildings had friendly ramps. I left for classes a half hour early. I pulled myself up the steps slowly, using the railing for support. Too often I would be stopped and would have to listen to remarks that internally sounded like "Oh, Marilyn, you poor thing." I resented the intrusions—it may have been a beautiful day and I was

*thinking about the novel I read for my English literature class, and these clods
had to remind me that I was a cripple!*

The ability of family members to communicate in a direct and supportive manner directly influences the coping process. The availability of support from the extended family varies greatly, especially when the family with a severely ill member lives miles or states away. In a study of intergenerational help within Mexican American families, Dietz (1995) reports strong support for taking care of the elderly when ill. Also affecting the coping process may be the social support the family perceives that it has. In a study of families with a child who is diagnosed with congenital heart disease, the more social support a parent perceived, the higher level of coping he or she reported (Tak & McCubbin, 2002).

A particularly difficult situation that many families encounter is when a family member is diagnosed with Alzheimer's disease. In recent years, public figures such as former President Ronald Reagan and actor Charlton Heston have been associated with Alzheimer's disease. Spouses of men and women who are in nursing homes and have Alzheimer's make sense of their marriage to the spouse in different ways. Some continue to strongly view their relationship with their spouse as a couple, while some spouses consider themselves to be "unmarried marrieds." Others fall in various places on the continuum between those two (Kaplan, 2001).

When a woman has breast cancer, she as well as her family have to adjust to changes. One study found that families dealing with breast cancer that were more flexible, that could balance family and illness needs, and that had prior ability to cope with stress had more positive outcomes (Radina & Armer, 2001). The roles of husbands of women with breast cancer are affected at home and work, especially when the wives are unable to do the tasks at home that they usually did and when the family has children (Hilton, Crawford, & Tarko, 2000).

Another form of illness that impacts the family is addiction to drugs or alcohol. If one or more members are addicted, the entire family has to do a constant verbal "dance" about the problem. Such families are characterized by the rules, "Don't talk, don't trust, don't feel." The questions arise—What do you tell? When do you openly seek help and end the secrecy? How do you communicate with a family member who is in an altered mental state while under the influence of alcohol or drugs? Having an alcoholic parent or a drug-addicted adolescent is like having a wounded bear sleeping in the middle of the living room; everyone has to tiptoe around and fears when the animal awakes and starts thrashing around. The stress is monumental. In a study of communication between alcoholic parents and their children, Menees (1996) reveals that the coping strategy of "venting" improved the children's self-esteem. If they can vent their feelings about their parents' drinking, they maintain better self-esteem because venting serves as a protective factor and reduces stress. The closed boundaries of most alcoholic families inhibits recovery and support.

Families from different cultural backgrounds may cope with alcohol or drug addiction differently. Close family members of someone with a drug or alcohol problem in both Mexico City and southwest England were interviewed about coping strategies. Family members in Mexico reported less coping by withdrawing than did those from England. Fathers of drug-addicted family members in Mexico City were likely to perform what the researchers called "low tolerant-inaction." These fathers didn't tolerate the behavior but didn't try to do anything about it (Orford, 2001).

Separation/Divorce

Divorce is a major disruption of the family life course and is characterized by loss, change, and complexity. The normal life cycle tasks are interrupted and altered by the divorce process, and continue with greater complexity (Peck & Manocherian, 1988). Unlike death, which forces a family to adjust to a smaller number of members, the family in a divorce must adapt to an altered state (Bay & Braver, 1990). Wives are more likely than husbands to plan longer for leaving and to leave the marriage. Divorce is not often the result of one negative occurrence in the marriage. Instead, it is usually the result of unhappiness and problems that have developed over time (Hetherington & Kelly, 2002).

When children are involved, a couple becomes divorced *to* each other rather than *from* each other. Family members remain linked around the children and must find ways to function as an ongoing altered system in which former partners function as co-parents. Whether divorced or not, when parents cannot control their negative and hostile messages or cooperate to solve problems, their children are at risk for academic and behavior problems (Cowan & Cowan, 1997). A father who pays child support, visits his children, and participates with his former wife in child-rearing decisions has a happier outcome than other divorced persons (Seltzer, 1991). However, all too many fathers disappear and do not pay (Meyer & Bartfeld, 1996). And when they do not pay, both stress and negative communication escalates. Hochschild and Machung (1998) report that over half of the children of divorced women had not received a visit or call from their father in the past year. Two-thirds of fathers divorced more than 10 years had not had contact with their children in the past year. Over time, many fathers disappear and abandon their children, leaving them with intense feelings of loss and unrealized opportunities for companionship and communication. Wallerstein and Blakeslee (1989) found that one in four children experiences a severe and lasting drop in their standard of living and observe a major discrepancy between their mother's and father's homes. The result was, "They grew up with their noses pressed against the glass, looking at a way of life that by all rights should have been theirs" (p. 298).

A systemic view of divorce acknowledges that both partners contribute to the dissolution of a marriage. When one thinks about the variety of issues in most divorces, it is often difficult to assign blame, since the immediate split may have been preceded by months or even years of dysfunctional communication. In fact, some research on characteristics of couples' communication goes so far as to predict their likelihood of divorce (Gottman, 1994a, 1994b; Buehler, Gottman, & Katz, 1992). Gottman's research via videotaped interviews revealed that negative attitudes toward their partner, especially contempt, destroyed relationships over time. The study by Buehler and colleagues predicted divorce accurately from whether a husband or wife viewed their relationship in terms of "we-ness," rather than distancing themselves from the marriage by using "I" and "you" references repeatedly. Honeycutt (1997) extended the previous research by using couples' oral histories to predict marital happiness and applying Fitzpatrick's couple typologies to ascertain differences between the types. He reports that husbands' happiness depends on their wives' positive responsiveness, on husbands' as well as wives' use of "we-ness," and on husbands' fondness for their wives. The wives' happiness relates more to their fondness for their husbands; and the wives' using "we-ness" terms (p. 19). Traditionals and independents display more fondness in their interactions than separates. They also indicate less excitement and less internal joy in recalling or imagining better scenarios. To examine future stress, Gottman, Coan, Carrere, and Swanson (1998) studied newlywed communication; interactions and divorce and stability were predicted accurately 83 percent of the time and satisfaction in the marriage with 80 percent accuracy. The stressful patterns of communication predictive of divorce are negative "start-ups" by the wife; husbands' refusal to accept influence from wives; wives' reciprocation of low intensity negativity in kind; and the absence of de-escalation of low intensity negativity by the husband. The researchers conclude, "The only variable that predicted both marital stability and marital happiness among stable couples was the amount of positive affect in conflict" (p. 17).

The separation and divorce processes essentially follow the mourning pattern described earlier. At some point, the spouses mourn the loss of the relationship, although one or the other may have emotionally divorced the other years before the divorce became a reality. Initially, spouses may deny that anything is really wrong and communicate to children or others that "Our problems aren't all that serious" or "Daddy will be back soon, so don't tell anyone he's gone." As the reality takes hold, anger, bargaining, and depression intermingle. There may be attempts at reconciliation: "We had a great thing going once; we can have it again." Reconciliation does work for 30 percent of couples in a first marriage. Two factors that correlated highly with successful reconciliations were both partners having a religious similarity and cohabitation before marriage. Failed attempts may be met with such messages as "How can you leave after all I've done for you?" and "What kind of a parent would move out on their children?" Painful accusations and negative conflict are often heightened by the adversarial positions required in legal divorce proceedings. Finally, depression reflects the sense of loss and/or rejection, often accompanied by great loneliness and a sense of failure (Hetherington & Kelly, 2002).

According to Knapp and Vangelisti (1992), a relationship that is coming apart reflects (1) a recognition of differences, (2) an experience of constricted communication, (3) a sense of stagnation, (4) a pattern of avoidance, and, finally, (5) the immediate or protracted experience of termination. Partners at these stages create messages that communicate an increasing physical and psychological distance and an increasing disassociation from the other person. A complicating factor is that most parents, while trying to come apart from each other, are still trying to maintain a relationship with their children (Graham & Edwards, 2002). "Many post marital couples struggle with the necessity of maintaining a relationship with a person whom they have chosen to no longer be married to. It seems that the desire and responsibility one might feel to stay connected to one's former spouse is fraught with contradiction" (p. 14).

Individuals leaving intimate relationships may rely on rituals to disengage from one another. The rituals serve as communication metaphors for their feelings (Bruess, 1994) and include letters, refused phone calls, listening to sad music, retrieving or returning gifts from their partner, and losing weight to look better and start over. Some ex-spouses may participate in a religious divorce ceremony to mourn the death of the marriage with family and friends. To reduce stress, departing partners enact ritualistic behaviors that empower themselves to overcome the struggle (Emmers & Hart, 1995, p. 18).

Divorce pressures are intensified by the predictable and problematic withdrawal of social support. In divorce, social support falls away (Arendell, 1998). Some friends are afraid to "take sides," or they act as if they believe divorce might be contagious. Fear of the loss of children haunts many fathers. In divorce, fathers receive custody of children 3 to 4 percent of the time (Hines, 1997). Although quite small in percentage terms, the number of "father-only families" and "father and stepmother with custody of his children" families are growing. Interestingly, there are more sons than daughters as well as older children in these father-led families.

Studies have shown adverse effects of divorce on children (Lorenz et al., 1997; Hines, 1997). Although divorce is often a badly needed fresh start for the parents, divorce is a much different experience for the children (Wallerstein, Lewis, & Blakeslee, 2000). Some have indicated problems in the predivorce, transition, and early postdivorce periods, with children acting out their frustrations and rage. Wallerstein (1997) reports after 30 years of research on how divorce affects children that it is worth remembering that typically in families with children only one person wants the divorce. Children fear that if one parent can leave, so can the other!

Children are often affected by parents' marital problems long before and long after the divorce. One longitudinal study found detrimental psychological and academic effects on children from about three years before to three years after the divorce (Sun & Li, 2002). Adolescents experience accelerated parent-child separation, which may promote earlier individuation, ego maturity, and courtship activity. Children from divorced homes are more likely to rate their parents, especially fathers, less favorably than children from intact families. Many children witness intense verbal and physical anger acted out by parents in the acute stage of divorce. Over time, the system recalibrates itself to deal with its altered course and its new communication dynamics. The presence of siblings makes the transition easier to manage because they may protect each other from parents' attempts to hook them into the struggle, share the "care" of a distraught parent, and support each other (Hines, 1997). Indeed, siblings often become closer after a divorce and their close relationships frequently carry over into adulthood (Wallerstein et al., 2000). Most children experience a sense of confusion and chaos when parents divorce. The following example illustrates what may happen if those fears are not addressed.

When my parents divorced, although it was a relief from the fighting and constant tension, I experienced a sense of loss and many new fears about their future as well as my own. As a child who experienced divorce, I was expected to "bounce back." I was just expected to adapt, but without being given time to express grief. As a result, I repressed these feelings and fears, and since they were never really addressed, they resurface now, years later, to haunt me.

Comparing adult children of divorce with adult children from intact families, Wallerstein and colleagues (2000) studied the long-term effects of divorce on children. By interviewing these adults, they found differences. First, children who grew up in divorced families didn't have happy memories of play as did those who grew up in intact families. "Instead of caring about who finds who in a game of hide-and-seek or who is at bat in the local softball game, children of divorce have other, more pressing concerns. Is Mom all right? Is Dad going to pick me up tonight? Can I bring my new friend over to the house to play if no one is home?" (p. 19). Another difference found was that those who grew up in intact families were much more likely to be able to tell the story of their parents' courtship than those from divorced families. Children from intact families also received more financial support through their college years. Wallerstein and colleagues conclude that growing up is harder in a divorced family than in an intact family. However, the researchers also write of adult children of divorce who, despite the odds against them, created good lives for themselves with happy marriages, children, and successful careers.

Although there is limited information on communication during the divorce process, current research indicates that most couples do not discuss this decision in lengthy detail with their children. Few divorcing parents have appropriate conversations with their children about the divorce for a variety of reasons. The parents often do not have correct information about how to have such a conversation, the parents may be angry, and the parents are often overwhelmed. "This means that the child, especially the preschool child, often learns about the divorce in the most traumatic way possible when she wakes up one morning to find that her father and his belongings have vanished into thin air" (Wallerstein et al., 2000, p. 47).

In many cases, children are informed about the divorce but not encouraged to discuss their concerns. In their study of the long-range effects of divorce, Wallerstein and Blakeslee (1989) suggest, "Nearly 50 percent of the families that we counsel waited until the day of the separation or afterward to tell their children that their familiar world is coming apart" (p. 302). Whereas loss through death involves a socially expected mourning period, there is no sanctioned mourning period for the loss of the "family that was." Just as there must be support systems available to the child at the time of divorce, there must also be resources available during the postcrises period. Divorce forces a division of parental assets, and messages about the availability of money suddenly become frequent. Children who have never been concerned about family resources are faced with new realities—a smaller home, sharing rooms, moving, fewer vacations, less clothing, and so on (Ono, 1998).

Numerous researchers have debated the effects of the single-parent family, especially the impact on children. They report that it is important to distinguish between life in conflict-laden, intact families and life in well-functioning, single-parent homes, concluding that the latter leads to better adjustment (Pinsof, 1997). In comparing adaptation in divorced and nondivorced families, Hetherington (1987) found that children fare poorest in dysfunctional families that remain together. Divorce and adjustment to life after divorce are often influenced by the emotional climate of the marriage (Hetherington & Kelly, 2002).

Usually, communication between former spouses becomes less conflictual in the years following a divorce. Lorenz and colleagues (1997) report that divorcing mothers experience a piling up of stressful events and depressive symptoms right after the divorce but they diminish over the next three years. In comparison to a married sample, however, divorced women reported a higher number of stressful events and depression symptoms at the end of the multiyear study.

Women find talk to be helpful in dealing with divorce during the first year following it. Men, however, are less likely to talk about it. Hetherington and Kelly (2002) suggest that this is because men have lost the person they disclosed the most to previously—their wives. Because of stress from the divorce, men and women experience more health problems in the early years after divorce, including depression, alcoholism, sleep disorders, and pneumonia. However, women who were previously in hostile marriages or distant marriages frequently had improved health (Hetherington & Kelly, 2002).

Adolescents may need clear role boundaries and stability to promote adjustment after divorce. Definite boundaries result in lower levels of cohesion and adaptability, but in the long term give youth a sense of security in the face of profound family changes (Dreman & Ronen-Eliav, 1997). Mediation or counseling helps parents to work out their differences and lessen the stress on children. Many partners experience ambivalent feelings of love and hate in the divorce process. Children sense this, and talking about this conflict helps to sort out the entangled feelings. Children also can blame one parent or the other and take sides unfairly. Joint custody arrangements have been rapidly increasing. Both parents and children in joint custody arrangements report higher levels of satisfaction and fewer problems in parenting.

Although it is impossible in a divorce to remove all the negative aspects of stress on children and their communication, parents can certainly reduce the stress. If neither parent uses the child as a go-between, nor encourages "tattletale" behavior, opportunities for conflict are reduced. If each supports the other's discipline, the child cannot play one against the other. When dads depart, there is evidence that boys suffer more than girls. They display more behavior and school problems (Mott, Kowaleski-Jones, & Menaghan, 1997). A 12-year survey reveals "evidence that divorce and low parental marital quality have long-term negative consequences for child-parents relations" (Booth & Amato, 1994, p. 32). In addition, when marital quality, including communication, deteriorates, children have difficulty in maintaining relationships with both parents, and, as a result, develop closer ties to one parent. When parents begin to date, children have questions, and in the beginning do not readily approve (Mott et al., 1997). Children dislike the amount of dating time their parents spend away from them and prefer that their mothers not bring dates to school functions (Ferguson, 1997). However, most children will go through this parent-dating stress, because within five years after divorce, 25 percent of African American women, 30 percent of Hispanic women, and 53 percent of white women are remarried (Hines, 1997).

Maintaining good communication between children of divorce and their parents may be important to society, in general, as Wallerstein and colleagues (2000) note that aging, divorced parents are less likely to get care from their children than are aging, nondivorced parents. For all involved, divorce involves a sense of loss, especially for those who have lost their support systems as well as their current sense of family.

Support and Communication

Throughout any of these crises—death, illness, disability, or divorce—the family's capacity for open communication, reflective of its levels of cohesion and adaptation and its images, themes, boundaries, and biosocial beliefs, determines how the system will weather the strain. A family with low cohesion may fragment under pressure, unless such pressure can link the unconnected members. A family with limited adaptability faces a painful time, since such crises force change on the system and the lives of each member. A family whose images and themes allow outside involvement in family affairs may use its flexible boundaries to find institutional and social support. A family with rigid biosocial beliefs faces difficult challenges if key family figures are lost or injured and others are not permitted to assume some of the role responsibilities. How much social support family members receive in crises depends on how much support they have given one another prior to the crises. Couples who had given more to their children over the years in the form of nurturing received more help later when they were old (Lee, Netzer, & Coward, 1994).

Family support can lead to positive health outcomes for those who are ill. Among women with HIV, family support is more important to the women's mental health than support from friends. This may be because family support has a higher value than support from friends (Serovich, 2001). Additionally, family support has a positive effect on stroke sufferers' functional status, depression, and social status. Family support is especially important to those who are severely impaired (Tsouna-Hadjis, Vemmos, Zakopoulos, & Stamatelopoulos, 2000). Family support can also have positive outcomes for the family member caring for a stroke survivor (Mant, Carter, Wade, & Winner, 2000). Throughout this process, communication among family members either facilitates or hinders the revising of the system to meet the demands of the crisis.

Coping Strategies Every family undergoes periods of unpredictable stress. Many of these stresses are not as immediately critical as death, illness, or divorce, but they do eat away at members' resources and affect coping strategies.

Burr, Klein, and Associates (1994) view stress as a multifaceted phenomenon with multiple causes and coping strategies. Their research indicates that families deal with stress in a sequential process, trying Level I coping strategies first and if these fail, moving on to Level II and III strategies (see Table 11.1).

When a stress occurs, a family will first try to use a Level I process by perhaps changing the family rules or role expectations, modifying a family member's responsibilities, securing additional household help, trying to discipline a stubborn child differently, or agreeing to not use credit cards. If any of these changes work, the family proceeds into a period of recovery and "has no need to try coping strategies that develop into Level II or III changes" (Burr, Klein, and Associates, 1994, p. 45). If changing the rules and more superficial aspects of the family's operation fails, then the family seeks more basic or metalevel changes at Level II.

Level II changes involve a middle level of abstraction, ones that alter the system in fundamentally different ways. For example, at Level II, the family may need to change metarules about how their rules are made and by whom. Level II strategies include talking about decision making in the family, changing the way Mom as a single parent directs the family now that Dad has left, modifying the way the family makes and changes rules, and replacing competitive strategies with cooperative ones. If the family has a parent who gambles excessively, a Level II change would be giving up gambling and setting the money aside for a special family trip.

If Level II strategies fail to reduce the stresses to a comfortable point for the family's well-being, the need arises for more abstract Level III coping strategies—ones that entail attempts to change the fundamental values or philosophies of life that govern the family (Burr, Klein, and Associates, 1994, p. 179). Changes at this level require communication about what being a member in a particular family means and how members can enhance one another's lives by participating more effectively or efficiently

TABLE 11.1   Coping Strategies Sequence

Level	Strategy
I	Change or adapt existing rules, ways of doing things, rearranging responsibilities to address the stress.
II	Change metarules (rules about rules) so that new areas of rules are created to address the stress.
III	Change the basic assumptions about life; reorder value structure to address stress.

within the system they have created. Level III changes are the hardest to make, and desertion, divorce, and even violence happen when individual family members refuse to consider significant changes.

Level III refers to highly abstract processes that seek to make changes in the family beliefs, paradigms, and values to reduce stress. For example, an aged couple with strong views in their earlier years about their gay son using drugs discovers when he returns home dying from AIDS that he sometimes uses marijuana to relieve some of the symptoms, especially eye problems and side effects from powerful drugs. At first they question their son's drug use, but when it seemed to relieve his pain and fears of dying, they relent and just ignore the drug use.

At Level III, the family will question its basic beliefs and try to decide if members can change in any ways to accommodate the negative effects of stress. Examples of Level III changes might be a family changing religions or connecting to kinship networks after ignoring them for years.

Many of the predictable and unpredictable stresses will be handled easily by families with Level I coping strategies. Some significant stresses will force the family system to adopt new, creative, and possibly painful ways. Members have less experience in creating new coping strategies, and thus creating Levels II and III strategies is difficult and requires trial and error.

A family's established patterns of cohesion and adaptability have great bearing on its ability to cope with external stresses. A family with a high capacity for adaptation and above-average cohesion is likely to weather stressor events more easily than families who are rigid and fragmented. More adaptable families have the capacity to find alternative ways of relating and can adjust their communication behaviors to cope with a tragic or difficult situation.

Support Groups   Negative stresses—such as alcoholism, drug abuse, child abuse, economic reversals, job transfers, and suicides—take their toll on a family's emotional resources (Shreve & Kunkel, 1991). A stress, such as divorce, reduces the family's support systems at the same time that the family's pain is increasing. Without a strong communication network, the individuals—forced to rely on themselves—may become alienated or severely depressed. Even such seemingly positive experiences as raising a gifted child, getting a high-powered position, adopting a child, or receiving large sums of money can stress the system. In order to understand a family's coping capacity, a family's immediate and postcrisis resources, especially support networks, must be understood.

Self-help support groups have become increasingly large and visible (Wuthernow, 1994). In a society characterized by mobility and smaller families, persons are finding interpersonal support from others who share similar experiences and pain. Chapters of groups such as Alcoholics

Anonymous, Parents Without Partners, Candlelighters, Overeaters Anonymous, or groups for families with members who have AIDS, Alzheimer's, leukemia, multiple sclerosis, and so on are found within driving distance in most larger communities. The 12-step program developed by AA has been adopted by related groups such as Al-Anon, Alateen, and CODA for co-dependent family members. In all cases, the self-help groups rely on members' communication as a healing process because "speech is a way for support group members to heal their wounds, to prepare for living and for death, to vent emotion and to change society" (Cawyer & Smith-Dupre, 1995, p. 254). Crises illustrate how little control individuals have over life and death. Communication becomes an important way to share and receive comfort.

Most importantly, support groups can help keep primary caregivers from "burning out." Today, family members without medical competence or training often take more care of the seriously ill, especially impacting families with limited financial needs or no insurance. As illnesses progress, care partners "become increasingly involved in daily care activities and in related decisions" (Miller & Zook, 1997).

Conclusion

This chapter examined communication and unpredictable life stresses. Specifically, it focused on (1) the process of dealing with unpredictable stresses and (2) communication during certain major stressful life events, such as death, illness, disability, and divorce. Over the years, every family system encounters external stress from crisis situations as well as stress from developmental change. The system's ability to cope effectively with stress depends on a number of factors, such as the number of recent stresses, role changes, and social and institutional support. The Double *ABCX* model provides an effective explanation of family coping, because it focuses on precrisis and postcrisis variables. Death, illness, and divorce necessarily alter family systems over long periods of time. Communication may facilitate or restrict a family's coping procedures. In most families, sharing of information and feelings can lower the stress level. The family with flexible boundaries has the capacity to accept support and the potential for surviving crises more effectively than families who close themselves off from others. Many family members find support through membership in self-help organizations.

In Review

1. Using a real or fictional family, analyze the effects on the family of a severe stress that impacted one member (e.g., drug problem, serious car accident, or severe illness).
2. Using the same example of family stress, compare and contrast an analysis of the problem according to the *ABCX* model and the Double *ABCX* model.

3. Describe how a "happy event" has brought high levels of stress to a family with which you are familiar.

4. How do different cultural and/or religious attitudes toward death aid or restrict the mourning process for surviving family members?

5. What guidelines for communication would you recommend to spouses who have children and are about to separate?

6. Using Baxter's concepts of dialectical tensions in relationships, discuss with examples how you think crises affect openness–closedness, predictability–novelty, and autonomy–connectedness in a family system.

7. Give examples of Level I, II, and III coping strategies that reflect how families cope with crises.

CONTEXTUAL DIMENSIONS *of* FAMILY COMMUNICATION

12

Our efforts to construct and maintain the families we live by take a multitude of forms, many of them astonishingly elaborate. Our desire to represent ourselves has turned our living rooms into family portrait galleries and our attics into archives. Our residences are mini-museums, filled with heirlooms, mementos, and souvenirs of family.

John R. Gillis, *A World of Their Own Making*

Family interaction occurs within social, physical, and cultural contexts. More concretely, family interaction occurs in a particular place, at a particular time, and within a particular social setting. Context and temporality are two dimensions that can be used to define and organize family communication behavior (Vangelisti, 1993). Just as it is important to understand the individual within the family's context, so too, families must be understood within their environmental and social contexts. The home world in which a family functions must be considered in order to fully understand family interaction. This implies exploring family relationships through the dual lenses of space and time within the physical and psychological context of home. Such a perspective is clear from the following example.

We have always been part of a strong extended family and lived with my parents since the divorce four years ago. Although my children are 8 and 5, we have, until now, been connected with the overall family, so we adapted to that household and acted as they did. This week we moved into our own apart-

343

ment and realized that a lot had changed. We looked at each other around the small kitchen table, which seemed so incomplete with just the three of us. Here we were, alone, in our own space, and a little scared. We sat in uneasy silence for a while before we began the tentative discussion about how we would live in this new world.

The following questions may stimulate your initial thinking about family relationships as they are affected by environmental context:

1. What was the best place and time to talk to a parent about personal problems when you were younger?
2. What was your family's pattern for eating dinner?
3. How could you gain privacy in your family? Did family members have any spaces that were theirs?
4. How were holidays celebrated in your home? To what extent were holidays shared with your neighborhood or community?
5. How did the cultural, regional, or religious nature of your community affect your family's interaction? Did your family reflect the surrounding community or differ from the community?

These issues will be explored further in an investigation of the interaction between environmental factors and the interpersonal relationships within a family.

Advances in environmental psychology have led architects, designers, and social scientists to focus more directly on the environment as a context for, as well as a type of, communication. The environmental context creates a system of communication that is learned and socially understood. Persons learn to act appropriately within particular dimensions of space and time by interpreting messages from the physical and social environment, which provide cues about appropriate behavior. In addition, the environment reflects cultural expectations for interaction. Such a position suggests that, although the environment does not determine how persons will interact, it strongly influences interpersonal interaction.

Relationships and context are inseparable. Relationships cannot be understood outside the cultural norms and psychological processes that bind people together (Werner, Altman, & Brown, 1992). Hierarchical levels of social relationships, including parent-child and family relationships, are organized both spatially and temporally. Reiss (1981) refers to space and time as two fundamental resources a family requires for conducting its day-to-day life, proposing that families are "strikingly different in their management of these two resources," and that these differences are crucial in how a family defines itself (p. 233).

Contextual features create boundaries that affect and define a family's experience and, hence, communication. Places, objects, routines, and cultural traditions are as embedded in the relationship as are feelings and other aspects of relationships (Brown, Werner, & Altman, 1994). Structural design, arrangement of furniture and objects within the structure, and time can influence who interacts with whom, where, and when, for how long, the tone of the interaction, and the topics about which they can communicate. Certain family members are more likely to have greater interactions because they share a room, play basketball in the backyard, e-mail each other, or drink an evening cup of coffee together. Basketball games do not foster intense, deep conversations but they do provide ongoing interactions; talking at the kitchen table may lead to conversations that address issues. Ritualistic patterns of behavior, past encounters, and cultural norms influence the style of interaction.

Although spatial or temporal factors do not *determine* the kinds of family interactions that take place, they do *influence* interactions that occur both within and outside the home. Thus, a transactional viewpoint recognizes the mutual influence of context and family interaction through the process of place making. This is the lifelong process of constructing, altering, embellishing, and assigning meaning to places or contexts (Brown, Werner, & Altman, 1994).

FACTORS OF FAMILY CONTEXT

The environment and the people in it combine to form a communication system. This section will examine the environmetal factors of space and time from physical and psychological perspectives and then demonstrate how these interrelate with each other and affect communication within family systems.

Space

Space may be viewed from the perspective of distance regulation, affecting the processes of coming together or separating. Space may also be understood as physical (an actual place) or as psychological (the sense of intimacy or separateness).

Proxemics The study of distances as a function of communication is based on an understanding of how people use space. Anthropologist Hall (1966) coined the term *proxemics* to refer to the interrelated observations and theories of human use of space within culture. He conceptualized the way humans use space as fixed feature space, semi-fixed feature space, and informal space (pp. 103–112).

Fixed feature space refers to that physical space organized by unmoving boundaries, such as walls in a room or the invisible line dividing space that is recognized by those who use it. The latter may be called a nonphysical, or psychological, boundary. Each type serves as a "real" boundary to which inhabitants must adapt. The physical wall between the kitchen and the dining room may keep the cook out of conversations. Such boundaries are obvious and often culturally designed. For example, according to Brown, Werner, and Altman:

> In the U.S. . . . the walls of a household help to create what we think of as natural separation between the household and the larger community. Inside the home the separate bedrooms for parents and children correspond to our way of thinking of these relationships as having a certain degree of separation. (1994, p. 350)

Yet, if you shared a room with siblings, you may remember the times when parts of the room became separate territories, and you did not cross the imaginary lines or the psychological boundary.

Semi-fixed feature space refers to flexible space created by the arrangement of furniture and/or other moveable objects over which the inhabitants have control. You probably remember helping rearrange the living room when your parent wanted to encourage conversation at a party.

Informal space refers to the way people position their bodies as they relate to others. Hall (1966) has divided the distances at which a person relates into four major levels: *intimate space,* ranging from 0 to 18 inches; *personal space,* ranging from 18 inches to 4 feet; *social space,* including 4 to 12 feet; and *public space,* which encompasses interaction at distances over 12 feet.

Whereas intimate space encourages the nonverbal expression of such emotions and behaviors as hugging, kissing, tickling, lovemaking, wrestling, hitting, and whispering, personal space supports interpersonal discussion, decision making, and the sharing of emotions with limited physical contact. Within social space, small groups may engage in social or business conversations. Public space encourages short discussions or waves and greetings from a distance. Touch is not possible, but unique communication signs, such as a wink or a disapproving look, may travel between persons who know each other well. The area of proxemics has yielded some interesting and consistent variations across age, gender, and culture (McGoldrick, Anderson, & Walsh, 1989).

Territory   *Territoriality,* a basic concept in the study of animal behavior, refers to behavior by which an animal lays claim to an area and defends it against members of its own species. Human territoriality is concerned with claiming places for functional purposes: places to learn, places to play, or safe places to hide.

Family territory may be understood as an area that members of a close-knit group in joint tenancy claims and will "defend." Individual family members may claim territory within the system. In other words, a family or a person stakes out real or imagined space and lays personal claim to it.

Those who claim or recognize territory behave in particular ways as they approach the boundary, even if it is not marked by fences, walls, or other barriers. Small territories may be marked by gestures, such as an arm that defends a space, or by the placement of a possession. People defend their territory through verbal and nonverbal communication strategies, such as aggression or dominance.

Household territory may be as real as "my parents' room," or as nonphysical as "Mike's part of the yard." Places may be recognized as belonging to someone by decrees ("This is my chair"), by tenure ("I always sat there"), by markers ("I left my magazine here because I was coming back"), or by agreement ("We each have two drawers"). Yet, without mutual agreement among those who believe the territory is "theirs" and other potential users, the concept of limited use may eventually disappear or conflicts about the use will arise.

One area of growing discord is the placement of a home computer. Although computers may be used for fun, school work, or staying in touch, the territory affects its use. In her analysis of women's roles and home computers, Cassidy (2001) suggests, "Misplaced in the bedroom, the den, the home office, the kitchen, the living room, and the family room, a woman's home computer for the 1990's failed to settle tranquilly into the American family home" (p. 58). Issues of gender and parenting impact this territorial decision.

Privacy   *Privacy* may be viewed as the "claims of individuals, groups, or institutions to determine for themselves when, how, and to what extent information about them is communicated to others" (Westin, 1967, p. 10). Privacy maintains an individual's need for personal autonomy, through which he or she can control the environment, including the ability to choose to be alone or to have private communication with another. Privacy regulation refers to how people manage the psychological and physical boundaries between themselves and others (Werner, Altman, & Brown, 1992). Often this regulation involves implicit or explicit rules, a concept explored here.

In our family, there seems to be a careful balance between allowing someone to have total personal control of space, and allowing everyone to go wherever they please. A rule is that when a door is shut, a person wants to be left alone and nobody should enter the room without knocking and getting permission first. Friends frequently enter our home at various hours and often unan-nounced without disruption or question. The only exceptions to this rule occur when family members have set aside time to be home alone together, and such visits seem to be intrusions. Then we try to cut the visit short so we can enjoy our time alone with each other.

Some dwellings encourage such privacy, whereas others cannot or do not. The ability to regulate privacy varies with socioeconomic status, since low-income families frequently live in crowded dwellings. If you share a home with nine others and a bedroom with three others, privacy may be attained only outside the home. Yet, in certain households with ample physical space, privacy is restricted by family rules or one's own perceptions. Privacy and territory interrelate to provide the means for protective communication, such as the sharing of confidences, problems, and affection.

Fences contribute to setting family boundaries.

As with spatial distance, territory and privacy are relative. In certain cultures, personal places and possessions are held in high regard, whereas in others, total sharing is the norm. In some cultures, one gains privacy by isolation, but in other cultures, psychological withdrawal permits privacy within a group. In many urban African American communities, intergenerational extended-family networks increase familiarity within the neighborhood and provide a feeling of connectedness, but privacy is hard to find (Patillo-McCoy, 1999).

Time

Familial relationships, influenced by cultural and historical patterns, unfold in temporal routines and rhythms involving mundane daily events and occasional important ceremonies (Werner & Baxter, 1994). The way in which a family lives in time interacts with how it lives in space. In their study of family typologies, Kantor and Lehr (1976) discuss families' use of time as orientation, clocking, and synchronization. Families or individuals may experience an *orientation* toward the past or future, which supersedes life in the present. Each individual also has a time orientation. Some people live in the "good old days" and their communication reflects a focus on yesterday. A present orientation reflects a concern for the "here and now." Less time is spent reminiscing or planning than is spent on immediate concerns. A future orientation emphasizes what is to come. Planning, dreaming, or scheming characterize such a mind set, typified by many immigrant families sacrificing for their children's future. Such orientations may be reflected in household furnishings, contacts with kin, patterns of friendship, attitudes toward money, and career planning (Reiss, 1981). Time is a commodity, the use of which indicates much about a family's view of the world.

Clocking refers to the daily use of time. It regulates the order, frequency, length, and pace of immediate events. Certain family rules, such as who talks first in certain situations or who gets the last word, may be part of a subtle sequencing pattern. On a more obvious level, some families must establish functional rituals for moving into a day.

In our attempt to maintain a two-career family with two small children, we have become very organized with specific morning patterns so we can get out of the house on time and in a good frame of mind. I get up and start to make coffee. My wife then gets out of bed, dresses, and starts to wake our daughters. When they come into the kitchen, I dress while Helen fixes the rest of breakfast. During the week, no one eats breakfast until they are dressed and ready to go. This way we can have a semi-peaceful morning, talk a little, and minimize the conflict.

Families clock how often and for how long things may be done, such as talking with friends or length of disagreements, and the pace with which a day is lived. Do you do 52 things and call it a "good day," or do you like to maintain a slower pace? Pacing varies with age, health, and mental state.

Synchronization is the process of maintaining a program for regulating the overall and day-to-day life of a family. Often, this is done through discussing how things are going and setting or reaffirming plans and priorities. Family members integrate individual schedules to create an overall approach to spending time. A spouse may turn down a position that requires extensive travel because it would take time away from the family. As an example of role-cycling, a couple may agree to a commuter marriage, which would establish each partner's career. Werner and Baxter (1994) suggest that *synchrony* refers to "the willingness and ability of two partners to coordinate their individual cycles into an overall rhythm" (p. 333). Family members are most satisfied when there is a "fit" in rhythms. Family discontent may lead to a reorganization of original priorities. Some families may establish respect for individual "clocks," whereas others may dictate a "family clock" to which everyone must adhere. The use of time varies according to culture; northern European families may stress punctuality, whereas Latin American families may not value punctuality as highly.

Space and time are synchronized in families as members go about the patterned routines of their lives. There may be appropriate times for being alone and times when togetherness is important. Children may be allowed to play in adult space until an adult indicates that the space is taken. Holidays may require the presence of all family members in a particular space for a specified time, particularly if their themes stress togetherness. Gender beliefs influence how males and females may spend time "legitimately." The degree of synchronization often distinguishes well-functioning families from those experiencing conflict and/or change. Underlying beliefs about time are played out in family discussions and in the messages members receive about "using" time.

Many families today struggle to claim leisure time, although historically there have been positive relationships between leisure and marital satisfaction. The interactive nature of family leisure helps develop and strengthen family communication because "communication between family members in a leisure context is often less threatening and demanding and more open and relaxed than in other family contexts" (Zabriskie & McCormick, 2001, p. 282). Space and time are important dimensions of a family's communication context influencing their sense of home and their relations with each other.

THE HOME WORLD: OUTSIDE AND INSIDE

Not all dwellings qualify as "homes." Many environment scholars believe that a "person's concept of home is better understood as a *relationship* to such an environment, rather than the environment itself" (Horwitz & Tognoli, 1982, p. 335). Creating a home is a type of place making involving place-making activities, including particular patterns of teritoriality, privacy regulations, rituals, use of objects, and ongoing maintenance that contribute to a sense of identity and meaning in the world (Brown, Werner, & Altman, 1994). Such place making can create great stress, especially for a couple establishing their first home (Meyer, 1987). The physical dwelling contributes to developing a sense of home, which must be examined in conjunction with related community factors. Thus, we will examine the home environment to understand how it influences the family.

A home influences the interactions that occur within it and around it, since its structure, design, and location affect the development of relationships with oneself and between family members, friends, and strangers (Werner, 1987). In his ground-breaking work on environment and interaction, psychologist Osmond (1970) distinguished between sociofugal and sociopetal space. *Sociofugal space* discourages human interaction; *sociopetal space* supports it. "Sociopetality is that quality which encourages, fosters, and even enforces the development of stable interpersonal relationships and which may be found in small face-to-face groups, in home or circular wards" (p. 576). Both the exterior and interior of a house contributes to the creation of relational experiences for the family members. In addition, the design and use of home interiors and their external appearance reflect cultural and social values. As more adults work from home on a part-time or full-time basis, there is increasing interest in home/employment "boundary work" (Nippert-Eng, 1996).

Exterior Arrangements

A dwelling's exterior may affect the interactions of family members with the community at large and specifically with neighbors. Some studies of homogeneous populations indicate that housing planned for easy social interaction (such as doors opening on a common court or homes built around a cul-de-sac) promote neighborliness. Yet, some homogeneous populations are living in neighborhoods where the external environment reflects continual danger and homes serve as fortresses. The exterior of a dwelling may be understood by examining its placement, the surrounding community, and the management of boundaries.

Housing Placement   Housing placement influences with whom an individual interacts and therefore, to some extent, with whom he or she develops friendships. In a classic study, Festinger, Schachter, and Back (1950) examined the development of friendships in a new housing project for married students. They were able to demonstrate that the distance between apartments and the direction in which an apartment faced affected friendships. Friendships developed more frequently between next-door neighbors and less frequently between persons who lived in apartments separated by more than four or five other apartments. If a person's front or back door leads into a heavily trafficked area, he or she has a greater chance of developing neighborhood relationships and becoming a central part of the communication network. Yet, perception of similarity with neighbors also affects contacts. In a study of a multicultural urban apartment housing community, Silverman (1992) found that when neighbors were of different cultures, jurisdictional problems, such as shared patio space or noise levels, were magnified. Residents who were afraid to voice complaints over minor issues remained frustrated by them. They did not know how to disagree with diverse neighbors and resolve problems.

The Neighborhood   The surrounding territory partially dictates a family's way of relating to the outside world. A planned community may expect certain social responses from its individual households; those who choose to live another lifestyle may find themselves ostracized. Particular communities may set expectations for attendance at social events or participation in the local Fourth of July parade—activities that require space and time commitments. As families move from one home to another, a new community influences their interactions with each other and with the neighbors. In the 1990s, at least one in four Americans moved; this issue of population mobility challenges a sense of neighborhood.

Planned communities continue to expand, ranging from such highly structured communities as Reston, Virginia, or Disney's town in Florida named Celebration, to more informal communities developed by an individual planner. The town of Celebration is designed to provide residents with the sense of community, which is missing in many locations. Some individuals and families are establishing long-term commitments to build community and occupy close spaces, believing that activity and strong friendships will make aging more productive (Russo, 2002). Co-housing communities are homes and neighborhoods created by a group who agree to share tasks such as cooking, child care, and yard maintenance (Dreyfous, 1994). These may be an oversized home, a small neighborhood, or a set of apartments as an assisted living facility. Such lifestyles imply that boundaries and expectation must be negotiated through regular discussion. Even some high-rise buildings attempt to foster a sense of community through the integration of stores, athletic facilities, and movie theaters into their overall construction plans. The current aging of the U.S. population points toward continued growth of retirement communities and assisted living facilities. For example, San Francisco's Rainbow Adult Community Housing Association is planning a 250-unit senior facility for gay and lesbian seniors (Quittner, 2002).

In contrast, certain communities may prevent attempts at socialization or communication because the territory is "unsafe."

Sometimes I feel like a prisoner in the low-rise building where I live with my mother, because she will not let me use the back stairs or go to the park two blocks away. I can go to the store across the street because she stands at the window and watches me. Our neighborhood is supposed to be safe but there are drug dealers and gang members on our corner. You can't ride your bike without worrying someone will rip it off.

Life in "unsafe" territory is accompanied by many rules about whom not to talk to in order to be safe. The architecture reflects this fear. Gonzalez (1993) suggests that fear affects a range of the less well-off neighborhoods, from working class to the most hard pressed, saying,

> The architecture of fear has transformed the landscape with urban fortifications along bunkerlike blocks where a frontier mentality guides the daily routine. Front porches once used for socializing have given way to caged-in entry ways; bricked up windows keep out both intruders and sunlight; and miles of razor ribbon lace more and more gates. (pp. 2, 18)

Life in such an environment creates a mental state captured by one resident who reported, "When I come home I feel like I'm entering a jail, and psychologically I am." Children in urban inner-city areas may encounter violence regularly and randomly. Studies of Cleveland and Denver reported large numbers of adolescents witnessed knife attacks, stabbings, and shootings (Goldberg, 1994).

Severe economic pressures, usually accompanied by concerns for physical space and safety, can undermine family members' interactions because family strategies interact with neighborhood options (Patillo-McCoy, 1999). Children living in poverty are more likely to suffer depression, social withdrawal, and low self-esteem, all of which affect family interaction (Seccombe, 2000). In a study of neighborhood socioeconomic status and divorce, South (2001) found no direct influence on marital instability but suggested that the high number of single-parent families resulted from pregnancy outside marriage in those communities.

Certain territories encourage or permit particular behaviors. For example, a single-family home may not encourage romantic behavior in teenagers due to the presence of other family members, but the car or a secluded hallway may provide the environment for such behavior.

I observed a difference in the socialization process in my housing complex and the project building. My peers in the project stayed out much later and had more freedom to go places than those in the housing complex. They began to have sexual intercourse and children at an earlier age. I observed intimate behavior when I visited my friends, while on the elevator or walking up the stairs. The parents knew what their kids were doing and acknowledged the fact by trying to get them to use some type of birth control. They had boyfriends before my friends from the housing complex and I did, and they began kissing early in grammar school.

The growing multiculturalism of United States society is reflected in changing neighborhoods, yet such change may be difficult. In some cases, communities are slow to support members who represent differences. For example, African American families in suburbia often found themselves rejected and isolated by their new neighbors. They also felt estranged from the friends, relations, and associates they left behind in the city (Billingsley, 1988). Many Hispanics believe that their neighborhoods or towns are very important to them, and they indicate that their homes are what "says the most about them" (Roper Reports, 2001).

An increasing architectural concern is the development of appropriate housing for the aged. Nearly 50,000 complexes in the United States provide food, shelter, and some assistance to the elderly (Nordheimer, 1996). Such services range from in-house medical care to communal dining rooms. A growing awareness exists of the need for elder housing that encourages interaction and stimulates participation in new activities. Thus, buildings designed for senior citizens may have carefully designed eating or recreation areas and programs ranging from drama and exercise classes to intergenerational day-care experiences. Many communities are developing day-care centers for elderly citizens in order to expand their communication networks.

Boundary Management   One purpose of home design is to distinguish between public and private domains (Lawrence, 1987). Each family engages in "bounding," or managing its boundaries to regulate physical traffic across its borders. Essentially, a family sets a perimeter and defends its territory. It says, "This is ours; we are safe here." Today, millions of Americans live in gated communities or in housing regulated by a community association. Family members defend their territorial borders through the use of devices to regulate entrance to the home. Buzzers, shades, peepholes, bushes, and double locks all provide some privacy and control. At the extreme, razor ribbon or high fences are used. Children may experience a designated territory, which is permitted for safe exploration. In housing projects, there may be no safety beyond the front door, so the boundary may be synonymous with the apartment doorway. In other areas, a neighbor's yard or the road in front may be the limits. A family can create boundaries by turning off the phone, establishing rules or hours for visiting, and appearing not to have the time for interaction. Lack of availability sends a temporal message about the desire for limited interaction.

A family with flexible boundaries in a safe territory may indicate a desire for interaction by using the openings of a house to invite in the outside world. Neighborhood children run through unlocked doors, or folding chairs extend the living room to the sidewalk. A less-scheduled, flexible family can make time for these distractions more easily than a family who runs on a tight clock.

Technology serves to transverse physical boundaries as family members of all ages engage in e-mail interactions with each other, especially with their college students. Research suggests that over 90 percent of college students have access to personal computers and over six million students send and receive e-mail messages daily (E-mail, 1997). Many of these messages involve family members. Yet, recent research indicates that "greater use of the Internet was associated with subsequent declines in family communication" in general (Kraut, Patterson, Lundmark, Kiesler, Mukopadhyay, & Scherlis, 1998, p. 1025).

Interior Arrangements

Home interiors are organized spatially and temporally. The fixed and semi-fixed feature spaces stand as supports for, or as barriers to, interpersonal communication. The interior design influences how much privacy can be attained and how easily members can come together, whereas the furnishings and decor contain messages about how to relate and what is valued. Each of these factors reflect cultural values.

Rooms and Floor Plan In contrast to the "bigger is better" move in home-building, some builders are now moving toward understated homes on smaller lots in towns and cities (Barta, 2001). One way to view a house spatially is to start with the floor plan and determine the possible relationships that may or may not occur based on space arrangement. Interpersonal communication and general living activities may be seen in relation to the public and private zones of a home (Kennedy, 1953; Werner, 1987). The public zones provide greater possibilities for social interaction, whereas the private zones exclude persons from some or all interpersonal contact. Different areas of the home may be associated with specific family functions and, hence, with the system and subsystem boundaries. Various levels and types of interactions are acceptable in different spaces, reflected in the range of highly interpersonal to highly private spaces. As one moves through a home, the spaces may become more highly private to members, whereas persons outside the system or subsystem may be excluded from certain spaces. In many homes, there are spaces for interpersonal interactions with guests, close friends, and other family members. For example, in one family, visitors may have access to living, dining, and kitchen areas but may not enter the bedrooms. In another family, all home space may be open to nonfamily members. Some families establish clear spatial boundaries for nonmembers; others do not.

If I have friends I'm close with over, we don't go into the dining room. We sit in the kitchen, talk, and drink coffee. If it's someone I don't know well, we go into the living room.

Member boundaries may vary. Some families set rigid standards for privacy. In such cases, bathrooms and bedrooms are locked, and special possessions are concealed. On the other hand, you may come from a family in which one brother may be showering, the next brushing his teeth, and another urinating in the same small bathroom. Such variables as age, gender, culture, and family size all interact with the spatial dimension.

The actual floor plan can dictate which persons will have the greatest contact and, potentially, the greatest communication. If you share adjoining territories with your sister, you are more likely to communicate with her than with some other family members, as in the following example.

When my mother remarried, she married a widower with 8 children, which meant that our family suddenly had 12 children, 10 of whom lived at home. This led Mom and Grant to remodel the attic as a dormitory, while they created more bedrooms on the second floor. This really determined the way relationships developed in the family. I didn't see much of the boys who stayed upstairs or who were out playing sports. Because we were on the same floor and always were in and out of each other's rooms, all the girls became really close, and some of us would sit up until 2:00 in the morning talking about people and things.

Many families view home as a "nesting ground" or place of refuge that brings people together. Becker (1994) suggests that family fragmentation can be prevented by a "communications system of architecture," which opens up living areas so people cannot retreat from each other.

The size of a dwelling affects the distances between the people in it. Small apartments force greater contact than do larger houses. Yet, even when space is held constant, families differ in their use of informal space. Crane, Dollahite, Griffin, and Taylor (1987) report that spatial distance is an indicator of conflicted marital relationships because distressed couples tended to converse at greater distances than nondistressed ones. A study of their daily experiences showed that happy couples spent more time together at home, especially for leisure activities, than unhappy couples (Kirchler, 1988).

In some houses, space may discourage communication among family members. Although in previous generations, children shared beds and rooms, many children today have separate rooms equipped for autonomous living leading to limited experience in certain interpersonal encounters and use of problem-solving skills. Thus, two children who do not have to share anything miss opportunities to negotiate. One's room then becomes an escape hatch when personal relationships falter.

Yet, in many cases, small, cramped quarters result in difficulties or pressure. For example, a study of 200 families suggests that there is a marked difference in stress levels between families with one bathroom and families with a small half-bath in addition to the bathroom (Guenther, 1984). A new set of stresses befalls a divorced parent when children visit, and the space, adequate for one or two adults, does not comfortably hold four or five persons. Families experiencing the "refilling nest" syndrome report stress as adult children return to live at home. Many of today's families are attempting to integrate home and occupational spheres. The new rise of cottage industries and part-time work at home adds stress to family interaction. The rise in telecommuting has forced many families to renegotiate the use of space and time since Mom or Dad are "there but really not there." Currently, 79 percent of employees who are allowed to work occasionally at home choose to do so (Gerson & Jacobs, 2001). Families are confronted with managing an ever-present work/home boundary issue.

Countless immigrant and poor families experience severe family stress due to crowding. Many immigrants choose to sacrifice short-term needs for adequate shelter in hopes of providing professional education for their children. Yet, the self-sacrifices can be great. The loss of familiar environmental and social support networks makes the family's functioning more difficult. Major cities, such as New York, are filled with illegal homes in which large families are sharing rooms or cubicles, and where members find privacy by staying outside or closing their eyes (Sontag, 1996). Large families in Scheflen's (1971) East Tremont study lived in small apartments, and most of the time, everyone functioned in the living room. African American women attempted to keep the living room as a parlor, although children usually had to be allowed access to it. If company arrived, the children were likely to be sent to play in a bedroom. Conversations were more likely to be separated for "appropriate ears." Often, an overlapping of space occurred in these cramped quarters so that space was scheduled to be used according to the time of day. As Scheflen states:

> In one Puerto Rican family, breakfast occurred at a fixed time every day. Then Father went to work, the children settled down to watch television, and Mother began a highly regular schedule of chores. In the afternoon, a single visitor came, sat in a particular chair and talked with the mother. At noon each day, the older children were allowed to go out for an hour. [These observations were made in the summer when school was not in session.] Then at a fixed time, the mother cooked dinner, and the children ate in the living room. An hour later the father came home from work, sat at a small table in an alcove and had his supper served to him. Then mother cleaned up and the family settled down for an evening in the living room before the television set. In this case the same sites were used by the same people each day, according to a regular schedule of household activities. (p. 444)

Personal and cultural traditions for spatial use also support connections and separations between people and help define relationships. Rules suggest what types of people have what types of access to each other (Brown, Werner, & Altman, 1994). Individuals or subsystems may have to plan for time and space to be alone. Sometimes it may be very structured, or sometimes it seems to occur naturally, as noted in the following contrasting situations.

Growing up, there was a rule in our house that no one bothered our parents before 11:00 A.M. on Saturday. Their bedroom door was locked, and it was understood they were not to be disturbed.

My parents still manage to have some privacy, although I don't know how, because their bedroom door has always been open to us day and night, and many times it serves as a place to go if you cannot sleep.

In some suburban communities, cultural differences are affecting the size of families living in a home. Hispanic immigrants are more likely to bring three generations of extended relatives into a home, whereas the Anglo neighbors have two generations—parents and children (Kaufman, 2002).

In each family, rules evolve for having visitors, locking doors, opening drawers, reading mail, or using another's things. Frequently repeated statements such as "Always knock," "Call before you visit," or "Never open another's mail" evolve into operating rules. Sometimes status or liking can be conveyed through rule functioning. Parents may have the right to invade privacy; babies may have access to places that are off-limits to teenagers or vice versa; a favorite sibling may be able to use a special place.

For many families, mealtime has specific rituals and is a communication event that takes place in a very specific spatial and temporal setting. An early study of dinner time in middle-class families with small children revealed that dinner occurred in a dining room, dining area, or kitchen at a dinner table that was almost always rectangular. The formal eating territories were distinct. Patterns guided the interaction, as persons sat at the same place (Dreyer & Dreyer, 1984). Many of today's families do not sit at the dinner table together regularly due to conflicting schedules. By the mid-1990s only one-third of families with children sat down together to eat dinner every night (Gillis, 1996). More people are spending time eating in the car (Hamlin, 1995). Yet, a national survey of more than 1,000 married men and women reveals that the daily ritual of eating dinner together is still viewed as the most important way to strengthen family ties (Bowman, 1999). In different socioeconomic settings, things are done differently. For example, many low-income families cannot eat together due to cramped space.

Home life shifts as families undergo unpredictable changes such as divorce. For example, these changes are likely to involve negotiation between new partners and children about the design and management of spaces (Brown, Werner, & Altman, 1994). A key stepfamily issue involves creating a space that adequately supports the newly configured system. Divorce may force a woman and her children to move to a lower income area or to smaller quarters.

Finally, the home interior serves to bring people together or separate them appropriately. Kantor and Lehr capture the regulation of distance within a house with their concept of "linking." For example, a large dining room table may encourage people to come together and may set up some interaction networks. Or, because an apartment is so small that everyone needs to eat and interact in the living room, members may retreat to their rooms to study or to gain some privacy. At a family party, teenagers may be sent to the yard and basement while adults converse. Everyone may interact together, or a variety of patterns may develop. Homes are traditionally sites of family or cultural celebrations that serve to support identity and create identification. Even though U.S. homes may be increasing in size, Sherrod (2001) found that family members tend to congregate in a common area to do individual things, such as reading or hobbies, rather than remain isolated. Through the linking process, family members regulate their contact within the home environment.

Furnishings and Decor   A home's furniture and decorations carry strong messages about how persons should communicate within that space. Some homes contain arrangements of chairs or couches in the family room conducive to relaxed conversations. Perhaps you and your best friend are allowed the privacy and time to talk for hours in your bedroom. A study of interpersonal discussions in living rooms found that "both the topic and the indicated relationship of the person in the other chair were significantly related to distance between chosen chairs" (Scott, 1984, p. 35). Thus, distance may not determine, but it does affect, communication.

Additionally, the quality of communication in a home may be enhanced by artifacts that either stimulate conversation or represent an integral part of the family, and that allow one to understand the inhabitants and talk about appropriate topics. Throughout the home the artifacts may reflect both individual and communal aspects of identify (Brown, Werner, & Altman, 1994). Past memories, present experiences, and future dreams of each person are linked to the objects in the environment (Csikszentmihalyi & Rochberg-Halton, 1981). Intriguing pieces of art, rock collections, matchbooks, family pictures, hunting rifles, or plants may provide the stimulus for good interaction. Symbols of religion, ethnic heritage, hobbies, and family life may indicate what is important. In their study of the meaning of things to people, Csikszentmihalyi and Rochberg-Halton found that objects such as furniture, visual art, and photographs carried special meaning reflecting ties to past events, family members, and other people (p. 61). Eighty-two percent of the respondents cherished at least one object because it reminded them of a close relation. For example, photographs were valued as the prime vehicle for preserving the memory of family members. Women were more likely to decorate with objects that symbolize relationships and treasure those objects that serve as a stimulus for family stories. The childhood photographs, an old farm implement, or an elegant vase may be the repository of powerful memories.

In some cases, prized possessions become the "spoils of war" because "in the last gasp of a marriage two people who failed to save a relationship may try to salvage their belongings instead" (Landis, 1988). Many divorce proceedings have been delayed for months or years over key household objects or family photographs.

Families engage in "centering" behavior, or regulating space according to its values and beliefs reflecting the family's view of itself and its values. There are specific ways of using things to keep the family in touch with each other, such as chalkboards, memo boards, and notes. Objects that remind a family of its identity and values, such as crucifixes, travel posters, or trophies, serve a centering function. Celebrations are essentially centering functions because they weave together particular artifacts and practices to draw kin together.

More and more families are creating some version of an entertainment center. Almost every U.S. home has one or more TVs, 30 percent have DVD players (Hafner, 2002), and some have home theatres. Since September 11, 2001, a larger number of Americans report a desire to spend more time at home interacting with each other (Fetto, 2002). Ninety-four percent of Hispanics view their homes as "retreats" and have main meals together over the weekends (Roper Reports, 2001). Mealtimes tend to be increasingly important. Although high percentages of Americans eat out regularly, this trend is beginning to reverse as being home is increasingly valued. Highly cohesive families may have stronger rules about family togetherness and how to achieve it within the home than families characterized by low cohesion. Family place-making activities impact the ability of members to relate to each other and to persons in the surrounding community. Such experiences directly tie to ethnicity, gender, and socioeconomic status, giving meaning to a family's everyday life.

Although we have been talking about home space, it is important to note another physical space in which family members relate—the car. For rushed parents and children, the dashboard is becoming the family hearth (Shellenbarger, 2002), as important conversations occur while family members spend hours in the car traveling to school, activities, and shopping areas.

FAMILY FIT AND ENVIRONMENT

An ecological approach to group interaction focuses on the way human beings and their environment accommodate each other. "Goodness of fit" is reflected in mutual interaction, negotiation, and compromise (deHoyos, 1989). The concept of "fit" has been applied to people and their home environments. Lennard and Lennard (1977) describe the "fit" between the style of family interaction and the home environment as: the isomorphic fit, the complementary fit, and the non-fit (p. 58).

Isomorphic fit implies congruence between the family and its environment. It occurs when aspects of the environment are clear expressions of the family's identity, how members relate, and their worldview. For example, the Camerons could be characterized as a generally cohesive and highly adaptable family with few intrafamily boundaries, who live by such themes as "We work hard and play hard" and "We stick together." The Camerons (mother, father, four boys, and one girl) bought a large, old farmhouse and tore down some of the walls on the first floor to create more open space. The Camerons are highly affectionate while exhibiting an open conflictual style of interpersonal interaction. The large kitchen provides a place where the family can congregate when someone is cooking, or a number of people can cook at once. The family room is a place that invites occasional wrestling matches and storytelling sessions. The bedrooms are small, but no one seems to spend time alone. The Camerons and their home are well matched.

Complementary fit implies a balance of opposites among two or more aspects of a family's interaction and home environment. This kind of fit reflects the contrasting elements that exist within the family, or it can be consciously selected by a family in order to balance or counteract a special feature of family life. For example, the Muellers are a blended family with four teenagers (two from each spouse) who tried avoiding one another when they began to live together. At that point, the family was characterized by low cohesion and limited adaptability. In their previous homes, each child had a large, well-equipped room to which he or she retreated whenever discomfort arose. When the families merged, the parents purposefully invested in a townhouse with fewer, smaller bedrooms, forcing the two boys to room together and all four young people to spend time in common areas, such as the family room. The parents

Eventually, generational reversals occur as children display highly developed computer skills.

consciously selected a home style complementary to the lifestyle that the children would have preferred.

The *non-fit* category includes those homes that are unsuited to the family's interaction pattern. Obviously, most low-income housing falls into this category. Yet, this style need not apply solely to families economically unable to afford larger housing. When the Morrisons married, they decided to remain child-free. During their early thirties, they built their "dream house," a wood and glass structure with cathedral ceilings, open walkways and staircases, a small kitchen, and two loft bedrooms. Their life was characterized by a belief that "We are complete as a couple"; their energies were directed toward cultural and educational pursuits. Eventually, their plans changed and, at age 39, the Morrisons adopted twins. Soon thereafter, the Morrison family experienced a non-fit situation based on their new lifestyle.

The concept of fit also applies to how families use time. An isomorphic fit characterizes a family that functions according to a particular orientation and clocking pattern, reflecting their values. The Breznehan family consists of Gus and his three school-aged children. Their world involves swimming, baseball, and soccer, along with orthodontist visits and newspaper routes. This is a present- and future-oriented group of people who can adapt to tight schedules and fast pacing. Gus Breznehan's work schedule is flexible, and he can adjust it relatively easily. Since family priorities include getting ahead and self-improvement, this lifestyle is consistent with group goals.

Grant and Jean Foster are partners whose fast-paced jobs take them to exciting places. They place great priority on their relationship and value a connected interpersonal relationship, believing that "Together we can cope with whatever life deals us." Yet, they worried that this hectic, work-orientated lifestyle could destroy their relationship unless they created a retreat for being together. They bought an old farmhouse and dedicated themselves to redoing the home in precise historic fashion and to cultivating large flower and vegetable gardens. Except when Jean travels, they spend most of their personal time at a slower pace and in a past-orientation to consciously counteract the hectic, present-oriented pace of daily life. Thus, they created a complementary style of living.

Charmaine has thrown the McConnell family into a temporary non-fit situation. As a two-career, sociable couple, they had planned a lifestyle in which they would take equal responsibility for the baby, whom they expected to take many places. Five months into parenthood, they became totally frustrated trying to share responsibilities, because Frank's job requires that he stay late for meetings and Myra's real estate position requires her to drop everything when a potential buyer wants to talk. Although Charmaine is a healthy baby, she gets fussy and sleeps fitfully; therefore she cannot be taken easily into adult situations. Thus, each parent needs more ability to live in the present and according to the baby's schedule.

Although the examples of spatial and temporal fit have been developed separately, you can see the need for an integration of the spatial and temporal needs of a family with each other. Some people can integrate these with their levels of cohesion and adaptability for a comfortable fit, while others have real difficulty. No matter how carefully families plan, an unforseen crisis may affect their living arrangements.

We had both looked forward to buying our first home. What we could afford was a two-bedroom townhouse. This was big enough for us and for a first child when the time came. Very quickly I started to use the second bedroom as a home office and the closet filled up with computer stuff. Then my wife's mother began to suffer from Alzheimer's so we took her into our home. She goes to a day-care center but at night the space is tight. We try to share the room but it gets complicated. Our starter home isn't large enough and now we are saving to buy more room.

Sometimes, people have to make significant changes in order to overcome their spatial and temporal situations. A big new house may lessen but not solve a family's conflictual problems unless new negotiating behaviors also accompany the move. Slowing down the pace by eliminating activities may have a limited effect unless the new lifestyle includes exchanging positive interpersonal messages within the less frantic world. Large families in small apartments have the capacity to develop strong nurturing relationships, just as a co-parenting situation does not mean that the quality of a parent-child relationship is cut by 50 percent. Unlimited time together has the potential to enhance a relationship, but the quality of the interactions will finally determine the nature of the relationship. For example, in his study of geographically separated premarital partners, Stephen (1986) found that such couples could overcome the separation and the restricted verbal/vocal means of communication via the telephone. Members of these couples worked to overcome the handicap, perhaps by focusing their talk on topics significant to the relationship or by de-emphasizing the importance of talk. Lennard and Lennard explain this issue as one of choice and control: "To the extent that the interrelationships between a family and the environment are made explicit, the family's area of freedom and control is enlarged" (pp. 49–50).

Finally, a family's living experience is tied to identity and values. Csikszentmihalyi and Rochberg-Halton (1981) capture this point, stating, "Although we live in physical environments we create cultural environments within them. Persons continually personalize and humanize the given environment as a way of both adapting to it and creating order and significance. Thus, the importance that the home has . . . also depends on values" (p. 122). Spatial and temporal factors can only create an atmosphere conducive to nurturing family communication. The rest is up to the family members.

Conclusion

This chapter examined the family environment as a context for communication. Each family's use of space and time affects who interacts with whom, where, when, for how long, about what, and in what way. A consideration of family environment indicated that a relationship exists between family members' communication and the spatial/temporal world in which the family functions.

To understand the family context, you must examine spatial issues, including spatial distance, territory and privacy, and the issue of time. A family's physical dwelling must be considered within the context of its exterior arrangements, including its community and the actual physical surroundings as well as its interior arrangements. The room arrangements, furnishings, and decor play a role in establishing a communication context. Finally, the "fit" between the family and the dimensions of time and space was explored. This chapter is based on the assumption that a way of life and its context are interdependent; environmental patterns do not determine but they do influence family interaction.

In Review

1. Take a position and discuss: How significantly does the physical environment affect family interaction patterns?
2. Describe how the cultural dimensions of space and/or time has affected the communication patterns in a real or fictional family.
3. Using the floor plan of a home found in a magazine or newspaper ad, predict how this floor plan might affect the interaction patterns of a family who lives there.
4. Using a real or fictional family, describe the spatial and temporal "fit" between the family and its environment. If possible, cite implications for the family's communication patterns.
5. Take a position and discuss: To what extent should communities support the development of restrictive housing, such as housing excluding children, designed for senior citizens only, or gated communities? What are the communication implications of such decisions?
6. Interview a parent who works at home about the communication challenges involved in this lifestyle.

IMPROVING FAMILY COMMUNICATION

13

Optimal family members can switch hit, flexibly identifying with the larger world at times and then becoming quite clear as to being a particular individual. We have much to learn about how this is taught, how children can keep a part of their birthright of timelessness and still develop the needed boundaries of self.

W. Robert Beavers, *The Boundary Wisdom of Healthy Families*

How do members of well-functioning families live, grow, and relate to each other year after year? How do they cope with problems and changes? To what extent can family members create new communication patterns, develop different ways of loving, fighting, or making decisions?

Many people believe that life happens *to* them, giving them no sense of control or ability to improve on human relationships. Thus, these people become *reactors,* taking no responsibility for their part in the problem or for change in relationships. Other persons serve as *actors,* believing they can make personal changes and co-create constructive changes within their relationships. The differences between a reactor and an actor are captured in the following example.

"That's the way I am. Take me or leave me" was the common comment of my first husband. He believed that if you had to work on a relationship there was something wrong with it. Needless to say, after a few years we dissolved the marriage. Now I am engaged to a man who wants to talk and think about how to keep a relationship growing over a lifetime. We have even had some

premarital counseling to explore important issues before the marriage. Life is very different when both people are open to change.

As human systems, families have the potential to grow in chosen directions, although such growth may require great risk, effort, and pain. The systems perspective implies that whenever change is attempted by some members, it may be resisted by the other members who want to keep their system in balance no matter how painful that balance is. It is difficult, although not impossible, for an individual to initiate change in the system; change is more easily accomplished when most or all members are committed to an alternative way of relating. Also, it is difficult for members of the system to recognize certain patterns in which they are caught. It may take a third party or clearheaded objective analysis to recognize a destructive pattern. Change depends on one's ability to understand the other and to discover the meanings underlying one's own actions and that of other family members. Or, according to Gottman's "Sound Marital House Theory," it is a process of creating shared, symbolic

A couple often gains insight into their problems when a third party helps to clarify issues.

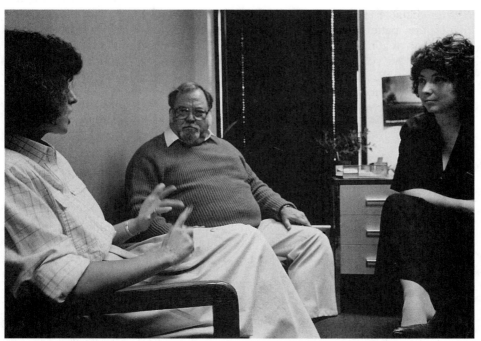

meaning through dreams, narratives, myths, and metaphors (Gottman, Ryan, Carrère, & Erley, 2002).

There is no "one right way" for all families to behave—the members of each family have to continually rediscover what works well for their system. A family's unique membership, family-of-origin patterns, ethnic heritage, and developmental stage influence this process. Communication may be considered a significant factor in changing family systems but the outcome is that functional communication will appear different across families.

This book has focused primarily on functional families, rather than severely troubled ones, recognizing that every functional family experiences alternating periods of ease and stress. Yet, families may be considered on a continuum ranging from severely dysfunctional to optimally functional.

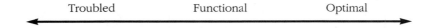

An as you might imagine, few families remain at the optimally functional point indefinitely, because of tension caused by developmental or unpredictable stress, yet many do remain within the functional to optional range over long periods of time. The question is: How do they do it? This chapter will attempt to answer that question by exploring (1) factors that characterize well-functioning families with an emphasis on communication patterns and (2) personal, instructional, and therapeutic approaches for creating and maintaining effective communication within families.

As you experienced families over the years, you must have found some that appeared to work well. In these families, members probably seemed to "have it all together." Yet, each family shares the systems characteristic of equifinality or demonstrating many ways to achieve the same end. Therefore, well-functioning families exhibit both similarities and differences in all areas of living, including their communication.

PERSPECTIVES ON WELL-FUNCTIONING FAMILIES

In recent years, much attention has been given to family strengths and well-functioning families both in professional circles and through the popular media. The following sections highlight representative views of academic and therapeutic experts as well as more popular advice. As you read these, consider the decade in which some of the views were expressed and remember most experts were not taking family structures or cultural variations into consideration. Thus, you may recognize limitations of the perspectives.

Academic/Therapeutic Views

Just as there is no one right way to be a family, there is no one family scholar who has all the answers. Each reflects his or her own professional and personal orientation to family life, as evidenced by the emphasis given to varied areas of concern. Henry (1973), in his classic work on family functioning, studied five dysfunctional families intensively identifying seven characteristic of family psychopathology. By reversing Henry's findings, we may hypothesize that functional families may exhibit the following characteristics: (1) interactions are patterned and meaningful, (2) there is more compassion and less cruelty, (3) persons are not scapegoats because problems are identified with the appropriate persons, (4) members exhibit appropriate self restraint, (5) boundaries are clear, (6) life includes joy, and (7) humor misperceptions are minimal.

Virginia Satir (1988) maintains that untroubled and nurturing families demonstrate the following patterns: "Self-worth is high; communication is direct, clear, specific, and honest; rules are flexible, human, appropriate, and subject to change; and the linking to society is open and hopeful" (p. 4). Walsh (1993) echoes these ideas, maintaining clarity, consistency, and predictability in patterns of interaction, open communication, effective problem solving and conflict resolution processes are important in family functioning. Walsh and Satir's ideas may need to be adapted across cultures, since such open communication may not be possible or desirable for every family, as noted here.

My family struggles with the concept of openness because although my two siblings and I were born in China, our parents moved to Michigan when we were young. We grew up in a Western culture surrounded by families who talked about everything and expressed differences directly. My parents were raised to honor the wishes of their elders and not to question or argue about adult decisions. It has been very hard for them to adjust to open and direct communication patterns. We all struggle between the "new" way and the "old" way.

In his early research on family competence, Beavers (1976) asserts that families with adaptive, well-functioning offspring have a structure of shared power, great appreciation and encouragement of individuation, and the ability to accept separation and loss realistically. He describes healthy families as "skillful interpersonally," with members who can participate in and enjoy negotiation, respect views of others, share openly about themselves, see anger as symptomatic of necessary changes, view

Couples may form groups to share concerns and learn from each other.

sexual interest as positive, and establish meaningful encounters outside the family system. Effective families more readily recognize their conflicts, deal with them promptly, and find solutions quickly.

In his later work, Beavers (1982) holds that well-functioning families consciously operate from a systems orientation, characterized by a flexible position on human behavior. Family members intuitively adopt a systems perspective. Beavers describes the four basic intuitive assumptions of families with a flexible orientation as follows:

1. An individual needs a group, a human system, for identity and satisfaction.
2. Causes and effects are interchangeable.
3. Any human behavior is the result of many variables rather than one "cause." Therefore, simplistic solutions are questioned.
4. Human beings are limited and finite. No one is absolutely helpless or absolutely powerful in a relationship. (p. 45)

In families holding the first assumption, members presume that people do not exist in vacuums but that human needs are met through relationships. Even after children from these families are grown, they seek a sense of human community in new family systems or social networks. Holding the second assumption reflects an understanding of mutual influence. Family members see actions as both responses and as stimuli to other actions. For example, anger in one person promotes withdrawal in another and that withdrawal promotes anger and so on.

The third assumption recognizes that human behavior reflects many influences. Beavers describes this clearly by listing some possible familial explanations for why a 3-year-old spilled his or her milk. Possible explanations include (1) accident—no motive, (2) interpersonal meaning—child is angry with mother, (3) child is tired, (4) glass is too heavy or large for child's hand (p. 145). Whereas a dysfunctional family may always attribute spilled milk to one set explanation, for example, child is angry, an optimally functioning family's responses vary according to each situation. Holding the final assumption implies an awareness that humans are fallible and that self-esteem comes from relative competence. Striving for goals in a realistic way is desirable. In the following description of a stepparent, the speaker captures Beavers's ideas.

My stepfather represents the kind of parent I would like to become. He seems to operate from a basic belief of optimism and faith in people. He usually can see both sides of an issue, can see both parties' points of view, and tries to create solutions without dumping blame on one person. He says, "You do your best and go on."

In their summary of work on family process, Bochner and Eisenberg (1987) summarize the following features as characteristic of optimal family functioning: (1) Strong sense of *trust;* members rarely take oppositional attitudes and avoid blaming each other. (2) *Enjoyment;* optimal families are spontaneous, witty, and humorous. (3) *Lack of preoccupation* with themselves; they do not overanalyze their problems looking for hidden motives; life is not taken too seriously. (4) *Maintenance of conventional boundaries* reflecting a strong parental coalition, and clear sense of hierarchy (p. 559).

Gottman (1994b) notes the importance of a relatively constant five to one ratio of positive to negative interactions; marriages thrive on positivity. Such a ratio concept could well be applied to entire families. Based on his research of well-functioning families, Gottman developed the concept of Emotion-Coaching, a process for parents to encourage children to express and manage emotions (Gottman & DeClaire, 1997).

Almost all experts speak to the centrality of effective communication in well-functioning family systems. Fitzpatrick (1987) suggests the strong correlations between marital satisfaction and self-reports of communication behavior may constitute evidence for strongly held beliefs about the role of communication in marriage; that is, the happily married believe that they have remarkably good communication with their spouses. The same beliefs may be held by those in well-functioning family systems. Well-functioning families must be understood within their cultural and structural contexts. Communication in a well-functioning Hispanic stepfamily may differ from that in an African American single-parent family system.

Popular Advice

Enter any bookstore, video store, or shopping mall and you will be surrounded by books, magazines, audiotapes, and videotapes, all addressing the issues of "How to Have a Healthy Marriage" and "How to Create a Happy Family." Most of the more popular advice literature, based on expert opinion and research, supports the positions of academic researchers but presents the ideas in more readable and prescriptive language. Some popular material directly reflects particular religious or moral positions.

In addition to many journalistic views, key family counselors and researchers have produced more popular works for a general audience. In a survey of professionals in family-related areas, Curran (1983) found that "the ability to communicate and listen" was selected most frequently as an indicator of family health. She lists these communication-related hallmarks of healthy families. Family members can listen and respond, recognize and value nonverbal messages, respect individual feelings and independent thinking, avoid turn-off and put-down phrases, interrupt, but equally, and process disputes into reconciliation (p. 55).

In her ground-breaking book *Families,* journalist Howard (1978) presented another conception of functioning families. She listed the general characteristics of what she calls "good" families (pp. 241–245). These include a founder or significant leader, a central network person who keeps others connected, a sense of affection and attitude of hospitality, connections to older and younger members, a valuing of rituals and place, and an ability to confront problems.

After studying more than 3,000 families, family researchers DeFrain and Stinnett (1985) listed six crucial traits of strong families: (1) family members are committed to each other; (2) family members spend quality time together; (3) family members show appreciation for each other; (4) family members have good communication skills and spend a lot of time talking to each other; (5) family members view crises and stresses as opportunities for growth; and (6) family members reflect spiritual wellness, a sense of greater power that gives them strength or purpose. The following statement represents such involvement.

I have come to realize the importance of traditions and rituals in families. When my father married my stepmother, she spent a great deal of time and energy creating ways to celebrate holidays. We had celebrations for Valentine's Day, Halloween, as well as the usual big ones. At first it seemed rather silly, but over the years I have come to look forward to seeing the decorations and participating in the preparations, since these events seem to bind us together. They are part of our identity as a family and give me a sense of place and belonging.

In their work on family functioning, Kelly and Sequeira (1997) examine themes of family functioning, comparing them to DeFrain and Stinnett's work. They found overlaps in appreciation, communication, family rituals, and togetherness and stability. In a more specifically directed work on stepfamilies, Olson (2000) suggests that communication, as included in the circumplex model, includes listening skills, speaking skills, self-disclosure, clarity, and continuity tracking, as well as respect and regard. Bray and Kelly (1998) discuss issues common to remarriage and suggest family tasks. These include integrating the stepfather, creating a satisfying marriage separate from the first, managing change, and managing boundaries with former spouses. Pipher (1996) develops extensive descriptions of healthy families that include encouraging self-definition, establishing core values, managing pain, and finding joy while appreciating everyday life. Finally, Covey's (1997) seven habits of highly effective families includes communication such as empathic listening, win/win negotiation, and bonding times.

As you remember from earlier chapters, Gottman and his colleagues identified three different styles of functional couples—validating, volatile, and conflict-avoidant—all of which exhibited a high positivity to negativity ratio. In recent writings, Gottman, Ryan, Carrère, and Erley (2002) conclude that positive affect predicted marital stability in newlyweds as well as marital satisfaction in stable relationships.

In their overview of characteristics of successful marriages, synthesized from academic and popular literature, DeGenova and Rice (2002) identify the following 12 qualities: (1) commitment, (2) trust, (3) responsibility, (4) adaptability, (5) unselfishness, (6) communication, (7) empathy, (8) respect, (9) affection, (10) companionship, (11) ability to deal with crises and stress, and (12) spirituality values (p. 221).

A person can find thousands of pages of prose detailing how happy or functional families live, or how they should live. Yet, what is good for a relationship cannot be considered apart from what people *think* is good for a relationship. These creative relational standards emerge from member negotiation and values. As you read these descriptive and prescriptive views on well-family functioning, what is your personal reaction? Are these views too idealistic? Too culture specific? What characteristics would you defend as critical to well-family functioning according to your personal relational standard?

Our Views

We, your authors, hold strong beliefs about the healthy family, based on our concern for communication within such a system reflecting many of the issues introduced in earlier chapters. Our beliefs may be stated as follows:

> A healthy family recognizes the interdependence of all members of the system and attempts to provide for growth of the system as a whole, as well as the individual members involved. Such families develop a capacity for adaptation and cohesion that avoids the extremes of the continuum; it welcomes each life stage, tries to find some joy in the present, and creates a personal network to provide support. Such families exhibit levels of cohesion that allow members to feel cared for but not smothered. Family members make an effort to understand the underlying meanings of messages expressed by other members and attempt to support and care for other members. All members find a sense of connections in the family's stories and rituals and their lives reflect their cultural heritages.

We have been influenced by our counseling and teaching experiences where we repeatedly hear of families who lack the necessary communication skills to negotiate their difficulties and an inability to understand another member's perspective. Recurring themes, boundaries, and rules from partners' family-of-origin interfere with present relationships. Basic parenting skills may be missing.

Family systems need constant and consistent nurturing. In most families, day-to-day routines overwhelm members' lives, resulting in primarily functional rather than nurturing communication patterns. Families profit from taking time to ask, "How are we doing as a family?" and "How can we improve our communication?" Well-functioning families are able to engage in metacommunication—able to talk about how members relate to each other and how, if necessary, the current communication patterns could be strengthened.

We happen to appreciate the jazz ensemble metaphor (Wilkinson, 1999), which captures the dynamics of well-functioning family.

> I like to think of the family as a jazz ensemble, where members move with the flow of what's happening around them, looking

for a harmony of sorts, playing off one another, going solo at times, always respecting the talents and surprises surrounding them. Standards, yes. Expectations, always. But everyone moving with the "feel" of the moment and one another. Anyone at any-time can say or shout, "This isn't working!" and can challenge other members toward a different beat or movement or settle into a silence that regenerates spontaneous creativity and energy. We do know "family" isn't a lonely drum in the distance or a plain-tive flute on an empty stage. Family is found in the creative en-ergy and interplay of its members.

Strong families have learned the values of communication, commit-ment, caring, and change. The following section will describe some specific strategies couples and families have used to strengthen their relationship.

APPROACHES FOR IMPROVING FAMILY COMMUNICATION

If you believe that communication in your family should be improved, what would you do about it? Would you be willing to talk about the diffi-culties with other family members or to participate in a structured im-provement program? As you saw in the recent chapters, a family goes through predictable developmental stresses as well as unpredictable stresses that affect the system's well-being, but often members do not know how to help themselves deal with the difficulties.

Approaches to family change may be viewed on a continuum ranging from personal through instructional to therapeutic approaches. Most of the personal and instructional approaches are designed for functional couples or families who wish to change some aspect of their relationship or wish to find ways to deal with a particular stressful situation. Some instructional and most therapeutic approaches are designed to aid a couple or a family cope with a particular problem or repair a troubled relationship.

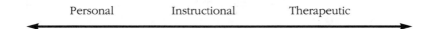

| Personal | Instructional | Therapeutic |

In their analyses of family interventions, Pinsof and Hambright (2002) use a medical analogy. They suggest epidemiologists differentiate among three levels of prevention—primary, secondary, and tertiary—each re-flecting the point of intervention in the disease process. *Primary*-level prevention stops disease from occurring by removing the causes; *secondary*-level prevention detects disease in early stages when treatment can impact it; *tertiary*-level prevention occurs at a point of crisis. Whereas personal approaches reflect nonprofessional efforts, primary, secondary, and tertiary levels of psychological intervention involve professional support.

Personal Approaches

Do you believe that a couple or family can deal with their communication problems on their own? Many individuals, couples, or whole family systems have tried to change relational communication patterns. Frequently, these endeavors reflect a personal effort in which system members embark on the process without significant active outside support. Personal approaches include (1) seeking personal education, such as that found through books or the media; (2) engaging in conscious negotiation with partners or family members; (3) creating ongoing meetings for the family members; and (4) obtaining support from friends or members of a connected network.

Personal Education   Glancing through bookstores, video stores, or web pages reveals countless resources for improving your family relationships and parenting skills, and adjusting to relational change. There are checklists, rules, and prescriptions for family meetings, sexual relations, and constructive conflict. Most resources contain some directives for improving communication among family members.

Family-related self-help resources continue to expand with materials developed for every type of family form. Readers or viewers find relief in discovering that their problems are predictable for a family or couple in a particular situation, such as new stepfamily members.

The "checkup" stands as a cornerstone concept in a personal approach to improving marital or family communication. In their classic work, *The Mirages of Marriage,* Lederer and Jackson (1968) created the concept of marital checkups, suggesting that marriages deserve the same care and attention given to bodies and automobiles. Couples or families may call for a conversation on the question: "How are we doing?"

Personal Negotiation   Family members may discuss and plan new ways to communicate or to solve problems. Based on information or instruction, partners attempt to identify recurring "trouble spots" in their relationship and plan how to avoid them. They may learn to recognize times when intimacy or conflict is too threatening and find ways to acknowledge this. Other couples create and practice their own rules for fair fighting. They may agree to avoid gunnysacking and physical abuse, or attempt to restate the other's position, find areas of compromise, or provide positive feedback.

Parents may consciously attempt to defuse high-anxiety moments by engaging in emotion coaching—trying to listen empathically or helping a child verbally label emotions (Gottman & DeClaire, 1997). Parents and children may try to share feelings when silence or sulking would be more comfortable but less effective. Such negotiations involve a process. One discussion seldom results in permanent change, as demonstrated in the following example.

In my own marriage, my wife and I have been using two mechanisms to serve as a kind of checkup on our marital relations. First, we have learned to communicate both the negative and the positive feelings we have. Second, we sit down together with no outside distractions and, while maintaining eye contact, express our inner-most feelings or our current concerns. We each try very hard to listen rather than judge the other. This ritual is a special part of our relationship.

Members may create quality time together to eat, sing, ride bikes, or just talk. A couple may attempt a second honeymoon. Father and son may try to find a mutual hobby or topic of mutual interest. Sometimes members wish for changes that are impossible due to lack of money, difficult schedules, or illness.

You may wonder, How do these conversations actually start? In some families, one or more members have nagging feelings that things could be better. They compare themselves to other families and see something lacking. They may encounter new ideas or models for relationships through the media, friends, or religious and educational experiences. Then, they take the risk of trying out new behaviors and evaluating their effectiveness. Such approaches take mutual cooperation. If only one member attempts to make the efforts, changes will occur more slowly and may be met with strong resistance.

Ongoing Time Commitments   Long-term patterned approaches involve family experiences such as "couple time," or "family meetings." Couple time or family meetings occur when persons come together regularly to anticipate or solve problems or improve relationships. This can be done at set times or as part of other family rituals, as described here.

Sunday morning breakfasts are our sacred family time to check in and see how everyone is doing. Sometimes we eat in and other times we head for a local coffee shop, but all times we talk about family concerns. We may check practical things, like member's schedules, or we may air gripes, fears, or joys. Without these breakfasts, our family conflicts might have been much greater.

Many couples find that their fast-paced lives provide few obvious interludes for personal exploration and discussion unless that time is built into their weekly schedules. Partners, at all stages of family development and representing varied types of family forms, are carving out predictable times to be together and to "really talk." Some find their topics emerge easily and directly, such as during regular debriefing conversations; others prefer to use a guidebook that prescribes topics or provides questions or evaluation material.

Family meetings or family councils provide opportunities for all family members to address mutual concerns. Rudolf Dreikurs (1964), founder of the family council movement, recommends that councils be established formally as an ongoing part of family life. A definite hour on a definite day of the week should be set aside for this purpose; it should become part of family routine. Every member is expected to be present.

Such experiences provide children with practice in discussion and decision making, which may prove extremely valuable in later family life. This approach undergirds the ideas of the *STEP Program*, or *Systematic Training for Effective Parenting Program*, and the *Stepping Ahead Program*.

Many religious groups recommend set meetings. The Family Home Evening program developed by The Church of Jesus Christ of Latter-day Saints is probably the most well-known family meeting program. Church members are encouraged to set aside one night a week to be together as a family, spending time in religious study and family activities. Many of the ideas suggested for sharing require the family to use positive modes of communication. Other religious and community groups operate similar programs.

Support Networks   In an era when the extended family is increasingly inaccessible, individuals, couples, and families are creating informal or formal support systems to help them face family problems. Informal support networks, such as friends and neighbors, provide adequate support for some persons. Talking may help put things into perspective or just serve as a point of emotional release. Sometimes the support groups become a kind of extended network of friends to provide the caring their biological families cannot or will not provide (Weston, 1993). In other cases, a more structured support system has advantages. Four out of ten Americans belong to a small group that meets regularly and provides caring and support for its members (Wuthernow, 1994). Some of these take the form of an ongoing couples group in which problems are discussed and solutions shared within a context of privacy and confirmation. Many persons, such as the following speaker, attest to the importance of such groups in their lives.

For eight months I have participated in a divorce recovery group through our church and it has helped me with parenting my three sons and with coping with my ex-husband's remarriage. This group has saved my sanity more than once and I have reached some important insights about loss and change.

Sometimes the network is assembled to celebrate, yet such events as renewing marriage vows appear to maintain rather than repair marital bonds (Braithwaite & Baxter, 1995).

The previously discussed approaches are only a few of the many ways of involving individuals, families, and groups of families in enriching their relationships. In addition to personal approaches, partners or individuals may attempt to improve family communication through direct instruction.

Instructional Approaches

My husband and I are team leaders for the Jewish Marriage Encounter, and we keep trying to tell our friends that every marriage should have an "annual checkup." People spend thousands of dollars on "preventive maintenance" for their cars, teeth, bodies, and homes, but how much do we spend either in dollars, effort, or time to have a marital examination? Too often in attempting to get couples to attend on Encounter weekend, I am told, "Our marriage is OK" or "We don't need to go on any weekend, as we have no problems." I am both angry and sad at such blindness, stupidity, and fear. There is not a marriage existing that does not have some problems, and if they are not attended to, they will get bigger.

The above statement captures the underlying philosophy of one instructional approach. The past five decades witnessed a tremendous growth in marital and family enrichment programs designed to instruct individuals, couples, and whole family systems. Generally their purposes are educational, not intensive counseling. Frequently, they are referred to as psychoeducational approaches (Lebow, 1997) or primary- and secondary-level intervention processes.

Cole and Cole (1993) define *marriage and family enrichment programs* as:

> The process of assisting couples and families who have relatively healthy relationships in the development of interpersonal skills that will enable them to enhance and add to individual couple and family strengths, develop more effective strategies for dealing with difficulties, and learn to view their relationships as growing and changing rather than static. (p. 525)

Morgaine (1992) sees instructional programs as "inoculating" functional families with facts, skills, and information to help prevent disasters.

Marital Enrichment Programs Multiple national organizations offer marriage enrichment programs. Such programs, which began in the 1930s and 1940s, are designed to enhance couple growth. Family change may result in an extension of change in the marital pair. Most programs insist that the couple attend together in order to impact the system. Communication skills appear as the core of most of these marital enrichment programs (Arcus, 1995). These programs break the "intermarital taboo," or the strong reluctance of married people to talk about their relationships (Mace, 1985).

Most persons who attend enrichment programs are self-referred and self-screened. Potential participants receive the message: "If your marriage is in serious trouble, our program is not for you. We are designed to help good relationships become better."

Although there are numerous systems-oriented marital and family enrichment programs that stress communication, only a few representative ones will be noted. The most well-known and frequently attended marital enrichment programs include the religion-based Marriage Encounter programs and the privately developed Couples Communication Program, PAIRS (Practical Application of Intimate Relationship Skills), Relationship Enhancement (RE), and the Prevention and Relationship Enhancement Program (PREP). Each places a heavy emphasis on communication. As you read the following brief descriptions, remember that there may be some variations depending on sponsoring groups and specific leaders. There are specialty programs for premarital couples (Engaged Encounter), for newlyweds (Saving Marriages Before They Start), and for troubled couples (Retrouvaille). Programs may focus on sexuality (Passionate Marriage) or remarriage (Personal Reflections).

Marriage Encounter is a weekend program conducted by three couples and a religious leader. The format follows a simple pattern. Each husband and wife "give" each other the Encounter, with the team members merely providing the information and modeling to facilitate each couple's private dialogue. Through a series of nine talks, team members reveal personal and intimate information to encourage participants to do the same when alone. After the talks, each husband and wife separate and write individual responses to the issues raised in each talk. Specific questions to be considered may be provided, or the individual may write his or her feelings about the topic. The couple then comes together for private dialogue using each other's written responses as a starting point. Although the program began within the Catholic faith, almost all religious traditions offer a version. This is the most widely attended program; thousands participate annually (Monsma & Monsma, 1996).

The Couples Communication program involves a small group experience with five to seven couples meeting one night a week for four consecutive weeks with an instructor. This program serves as an educational experience in which couples identify, practice, and experiment with communication skills around topics of their choice. Each couple receives feedback on their skills from the leader and other couples. The focus remains solely on skills accomplishment. Practice sessions are held with nonpartners, but the final demonstration of skills occurs with one's partner. The Prevention and Relationship Enhancement Program (PREP) is an empirically based approach to prevention and treatment of marital distress. The program may take place over a weekend or over 12 sessions. This has a strong communication component.

The IMAGO therapeutic approach has a psychoeducational arm, which is represented as a starting point for realizing one's transformational potential (Sandmaier, 1997). This program, called Reality Love, includes teaching couples to mirror, validate, and empathize. Marital researcher John Gottman has developed a program based on his research entitled "The Marriage Survival Kit," involving a weekend workshop for couples. Some programs focus on a type or stage of marriage.

Personal Reflections is a program uniquely focused on remarried partners (Kaplan & Hennon, 1992). The program focuses on role expectation and role strain as partners bring scripts from earlier marriages into the new one. There is a strong communication component focusing on self-disclosure, sharing differences, and negotiation. Marriage Moments reaches out to couples who are expecting their first child (Hawkins, Gilliland, & Carroll, 2002).

Finally, the PREPARE/ENRICH materials and programs should be noted because they serve as a bridge between instructional and therapeutic approaches. Developed by Olson and colleagues, the PREPARE/ENRICH program is grounded in the circumplex model of family functioning and consists of three inventories and guidelines for counselor/leader training. PREPARE and PREPARE-MC (Married with Children) are designed for couples entering marriage either as two adults or adults with children. ENRICH is designed for use in marriage enrichment programs or marriage counseling. After couples complete the inventories and receive their computerized results, they may discuss the findings with a religious leader as part of a premarital program, within a marriage enrichment program or with a therapist.

A number of the programs have variations for engaged couples, although, according to Mace (1985), giving information to engaged pairs is like "pouring water on a duck's back" since emotionally they cannot imagine being headed for trouble. However, Marriage Encounter does offer Engaged Encounter for premarital couples, and the PREP program is offered by many clergy and lay leaders as a premarital program. In his case for such premarital education, Stanley (2001) presents four benefits: (1) fostering couple deliberation, (2) sending a message that marriage matters, (3) helping couples learn about supports they may use later, and (4) lowering the risk of disasters or divorce for some couples. Although historically most programs address the needs of early marriage, recently programs for later life marriages have been developed (Arcus, 1995).

Descriptions of these major marital enrichment programs indicate that communication plays a central place within each. Desirable interpersonal skills may be taught differently through modeling, role playing, lecture, guided feedback, and readings, but it is incorporated into each program. The unique feature of such programs is the learning context— you learn and practice communications skills with people with whom you have a relationship. Almost every national program has a communication component. Many churches and private organizations run unique marital communication programs for their own congregations or specific constituents such as remarried couples, engaged couples, or senior couples.

Family Enrichment Programs Although programs for families have developed more slowly, many marital programs have fostered familial counterparts, encouraging entire families to examine and improve their relationships. The Marriage Encounter Program offers the Family Weekend Experience. As in Marriage Encounter, the family members "give" each other the weekend. Parents and school-aged children spend their waking weekend hours examining their everyday lives, as background for discussing nine "blocks" to family relationships, such as fighting, criticism, or indifference, and the skills for overcoming such blocks, including listening, acceptance, and respect. Family members experience personal reconciliation with each other and plan ways to maintain the newfound feelings of closeness.

Another widely known program is STEP, Systematic Training for Effective Parenting, developed by the American Guidance Service (AGS). Based on Adlerian psychology, STEP focuses on the goals of children's behavior, the natural and logical consequence of the behavior, and good versus responsible parenting. The program stresses active listening, I-messages, and family meetings.

Relationship Enhancement, or RE (Guerney, 1977), includes a skills approach that can be taught to all family members. In describing her experience with this model, Kirk (1989) declares that RE is based on a family systems perspective, focusing on the improvement of interpersonal communication and problem-solving skills. The skills are implemented through a set of specific techniques such as the expresser mode, the empathic responder mode, the problem/conflict resolution mode, and the generalization/maintenance mode. Kirk describes how a family learned to share feelings and resolve conflicts:

> The parents had originally felt uncomfortable when they disciplined their stepchildren, and the children felt resentful when they adhered to their stepparents. Their communication climate eventually become one of silence and hostility until they were able to communicate in a skilled manner. (pp. 20–21)

In recent years, specialized programs for stepfamilies have emerged that are aimed at normalizing the stepfamily experience and developing communication skills to enhance stepfamily life. The Stepfamily Association of America promotes local support groups and educational programs for stepfamily members, particularly the Stepping Ahead Program. Another established program is Stepping Together, a six-session course for stepfamily couples. There are even programs for divorcing parents designed to help families manage the stresses of separation and family dissolution (Buehler, Betz, Ryan, & Trotter, 1992).

This is a time when government and educational institutions have entered the family enrichment area in response to divorce rates and child neglect or abuse. Some counties and states are providing incentives for couples enrolling in premarital education classes, and others are requiring the teaching of marital and family skills curricula (Belluck, 2000). Arizona, Arkansas, and Louisiana provide marrying couples with the option to choose a "covenant marriage." Those who choose this option are allowed to divorce only in certain cases, such as adultery, abuse, abandonment, imprisonment of a spouse, and long marital separation, although the laws vary from state to state. However, covenant marriage does not seem to be a popular choice. Less than 3 percent of couples in Louisiana and Arizona marry under this law (Schemco, 2001).

Many high schools are developing courses or offering programs such as Partners, developed by a lawyer, Gold-Biken, to avoid divorce (Lewin, 1998). Most of these programs stress communication skills. More communities are sites for parent management training programs (PMT) with communication components (Webster-Stratton, 1997).

Secondary prevention efforts are increasing as more schools, communities, and therapists respond to perceived needs. Frequently, these are directed at disruptive behavior problems. For example, the Fast-Track multisite demonstration project focuses on school children at risk for conduct disorder by engaging families in programs designed to improve parenting and parent-teacher interaction (Pinsof & Hambright, 2002). Programs are developing to aid family members dealing with medical crises such as AIDS, Alzheimer's disease, or chronic illness. Research on family-focused prevention targeted for families with children who are medically ill frequently address issues such as parental coping and retaining needed social support (Tolan, 2002).

Many self-help groups are oriented toward specific topics that also provide a family or relational focus and formal or informal instruction in communication skills for their members. Such groups include Al-Anon, Parents Anonymous, Families Anonymous, Parents Without Partners, Parents of Gay, Lesbian, and Transgendered Children, Families Who Have Adopted Children of Every Skin, Compassionate Friends, and Candlelighters. Such groups are part of a cultural realignment and a source of American cultural transformation.

Appraisal of Enrichment Programs Although these programs sound intriguing, one must raise some questions in considering their effectiveness, focusing primarily on the marital programs. There are difficulties in attempting to teach communication principles and skills without the mutual commitment of both partners. If such mutual commitment does not exist, the results may be contrary to the expected outcomes.

Selection of content and skills may be controversial, although many programs teach similar concepts. A skill as seemingly foundational as active listening is emphasized by certain program such as PREP, whereas Gottman and colleagues (1998) report that active listening occurs infrequently in the resolution of marital conflict. Even these researchers indicate surprise, since they recommended this listening skill in their earlier writings. Currently there is significant debate among enrichment experts on this supposedly critical skill (Cole & Cole 1999, Gottman, Ryan, Carrère, & Erley, 2002, Silliman et al., 2002).

Related research suggests that "the relationship between communication skills and marital satisfaction is not simple and straightforward" (Burleson & Denton, 1997, p. 884). In this research, skills and satisfaction were positively associated in nondistressed couples; the reverse was not the case. Additionally, the skills must be combined with a desire or spirit of good will to motivate partners to use them appropriately (Renick, Blumberg, & Markman, 1992). Concerns include long-range effects, skill maintenance, and nature of participants.

The research on these programs does not attribute undisputed success to their efforts. Although the programs are designed to help couples with satisfactory marriages, many couples enter such workshops because they feel a need for help. There is a need for more stringent controls and measures to determine each partner's commitment to the enrichment experience and also examinations of the makeup of the control groups. Witteman and Fitzpatrick (1987) examined marital enrichment programs and compared them unfavorably to therapy, particularly due to lack of skills orientation. A content analysis of interview and essay data from couples who attended Marriage Encounter revealed that those who were highly positive or highly negative about the experience were likely to report experiencing serious marital distress prior to the weekend (Doherty, Lester, & Leigh, 1986). Lebow (1997) summarizes some of the research findings related to communication that undergird the marital programs, saying, "Satisfied couples are better able to speak clearly with each other and listen empathetically, have more positive than negative exchanges, and have better problem-solving skills" (p. 81).

Couple Communication initially was a highly documented instructional program. The findings based on 31 studies indicate (1) an extremely positive impact on behavior immediately after the program with most studies finding partial decline at follow-up, (2) increases in relationship satisfaction with some decline at follow-up, and (3) no documented negative effects ("Thirty-one studies," 1988). A 1990 review of studies (Wampler, 1990) indicated strong gains in couple communication quality but noted that the effects tend to diminish over time.

The primary concern is the long-term maintenance of skills. PREP remains the most intensively studied program. In their research on PREP program, Renick, Blumberg, and Markman (1992) report on a 10-year longitudinal study involving 83 of the original 135 couples. Couples showed increases in overall positive communication as well as problem solving and support validation. Gender differences appeared on several measures, including higher male dedication to the relationship. At the five-year follow-up, PREP husbands showed greater relationship satisfaction than control-group husbands. Nineteen percent of control group couples divorced or separated; 8 percent of PREP couples had done so. In her summary of evaluation research, Arcus (1995) singles out PREP creators because they "used longitudinal studies to demonstrate both short-term and long-term effectiveness of relationship education programs" (p. 339). Ongoing research reveals program successes as well as a need for "booster sessions" (Stanley, Markman, & Leber, 1997). Currently, a number of studies are underway, including an examination of the effect of different types of leaders (Silliman et al., 2002).

Generally speaking, marital enrichment programs remain understudied. Most research examines outcome criteria of marital satisfaction, relationship skill development, and individual personality variables. A key consideration in evaluating enrichment programs lies in the extent of skill training provided. Witteman and Fitzpatrick (1987) maintain that behavior changes in marital communication are tied to some type of skills training and not the discussion of communication, an approach frequently found in enrichment programs. Information without skills training does not provide enough basis for change.

In their review of parenting programs, Noller and Fitzpatrick (1993) conclude there has been little systematic research that has evaluated the effectiveness of parenting program. They report that studies that compare one parent-training program with another had far from conclusive results. Many of the individual program evaluation programs are methodologically weak. There are significant difficulties in balancing the desire for certain types of measurement with understanding the clientele who choose to enroll in certain family programs (Buehler, Gottman, & Katz, 1992).

A review of family education programs (Thomas, Schvaneveldt, & Young, 1993, p. 122) concludes, "Most program evaluation efforts to date are narrow in scope, limited in methodology and confined to a concern with measuring program outcomes in relation to program objectives." Additional critiques of programs note positive and negative effects (Witteman & Fitzpatrick, 1987; Renick, Blumberg, & Markman, 1992). The growing care with which professional recommend such programs is reflected in the following example.

As a minister I used to suggest to all couples I worked with that they become involved in a marriage enrichment program. It seemed like a cure-all for my congregation members because of the emphasis on communication skills. Yet, over time, I've learned more about the program and am more discriminating in my recommendations since I no longer see them as a panacea but as a valuable resource for many couples. I no longer refer severely troubled couples to this resource because the time is too limited and they do not have a high enough trust level to practice the communication skills effectively.

Research on the long-term effectiveness of marital and family enrichment programs is too limited to draw secure conclusions. Factors such as the history of parental divorce for one partner influence program effects (Widenfelt, Hosman, Schaap, & van der Staak, 1996). Yet, new approaches to marital enrichment have been developed to reflect recent research and to include a research component, thus ensuring a more systematic approach to evaluation (Cleaver, 1987; Renick, Blumberg, & Markman, 1992; Arcus, 1995).

With the exception of the PREP program, developed by Markham and his colleagues, systematic theory testing and program evaluation have not advanced at the same rates as the development of theory and new programs (Giblin, 1996). Stanley (2001), a PREP developer, argues that "there are clear advantages in terms of interaction quality for couples taking the more empirically-based, skills-oriented training" (p. 278).

Scholars have called for, and contributed to, studies of enrichment program effectiveness but there is much work left to do. There is need for sophisticated and well-research programs in family interaction across the lifespan that addresses the issues of many familial forms. Family communication scholars may develop primary intervention programs and partner with therapists to create secondary intervention-level programs.

The important questions about the impact of such programs include: For whom is it effective? For how long? Which programs result in changes in communication that last for a reasonable period of time? And in positive changes relationships? Do the marriage programs result in changes that affect the ways parents relate with children? How does evaluation reflect a balance of external and internal validity, especially in community-based settings? What are the major factors in these programs that create the impacts that occur, such as skills or format and design? (Buehler, Betz, Ryan, & Trotter, 1992; Arcus, 1995).

A key question currently being raised is: To what extent does communication skill level determine marital satisfaction? In the past decade, studies indicate that low-skilled couples are just as happy and satisfied with their marriages as high-skilled couples (Burleson, 1998). Burleson speculates on possible explanations, ranging from ethnic differences to lack of awareness of such skills. Burelson and Denton (1997) demonstrate the difficulty of a naïve assumption that the cause of many marital communication problems is deficient communication skills. They identify moderating factors—skill type, marital distress, gender, and analytical unit (self, couple)—that support a positive association between skill levels and marital satisfaction for nondistressed couples but a negative association among distressed couples. The distressed couple mantra, "We just can't communicate," cannot be addressed by simplistic skill training.

Therapeutic Approaches

The families in relational pain or crisis are most effectively served by direct therapeutic approaches. Because this text is concerned with communication issues of functional families, marital and family therapy is presented only to extend the continuum of options for improving relationships. There is a vast body of literature that explores these approaches in detail (Gurman & Kniskern, 1991; Pinsof & Wynne, 1995); this section highlights only some relevant issues. Individual therapy has long been an established approach to dealing with personal problems or illnesses. This counselor-client situation remains one valid therapeutic approach for certain issues; in other cases, this is not the most appropriate approach.

For those families experiencing a severe crisis or living in long-term dysfunctional patterns, therapeutic interventions may be warranted. In contrast to previous eras when the "identified patient" or "problem person" was shipped off to be "fixed" by a counselor, many family-related problems are addressed through family therapy, sometimes called systems therapy; over five million couples a year seek family therapy. Exactly what does family therapy entail? Family therapy is a psychotherapeutic approach that focuses on altering interactions between a couple, within a nuclear (biological) family or extended family, or between a family and other interpersonal systems, with the goal of alleviating problems presented by individual family members, family subsystems, the family as a whole or other referral sources (Wynne, 1988, p. 9). Family therapists look at system patterns, as this comment indicates.

Two years ago, my family went into therapy because my younger brother was flunking school and shoplifting and his treatment center required the entire family to become involved in the treatment program. Over about a year we were able to understand the patterns of family interaction that "fed" Chris's problem. The therapist kept stressing that Chris's acting out was a family problem, not just Chris's problem. The therapy forced my mother and stepfather to deal with some problems in their marriage that they had been ignoring and allowed us to make enough changes that Chris could return to high school and control the shoplifting.

The family therapy movement's roots are found in the research and clinical developments of the 1950s, including hospital psychiatry, group dynamics, interpersonal psychiatry, the child guidance movement, research in communication and schizophrenia, and marriage counseling. Persons such as Nathan Ackerman, Gregory Bateson, John Bell, Ivan Boszormenyinagy, Murray Bowen, James Framo, Jay Haley, Don Jackson, Christian Midelfort, Salvador Minuchin, Virginia Satir, Carl Whitaker, Theodore Widz, Lyman Wynne, and Gerald Zuk were significant pioneers in the "first wave" family treatment (Broderick & Schrader, 1991; Barker, 1998).

Communication issues emerged as a key feature of the family therapy movement because many of these pioneers, most notably Satir, focused explicit attention on communication patterns. In his description of the roots of the family therapy movement, Nichols (1984) noted how communication was an integral part of early methods. Family therapy as a treatment method began when clinicians first brought families together for observation; doing so forced a shift in focus from intrapsychic content to interpersonal process. Instead of trying to understand what goes on inside individuals, family therapists began to examine what goes on between them. Clarifying communication and issuing tasks and directives were the first methods used to outwit resistance and to help families change. Even in the early days of family therapy, however, different practitioners developed alternate strategies and tactics of change.

Early family therapy is rooted in a systems perspective, reflecting assumptions about change and context reflecting systems theory. In many cases, once therapists examined a whole family system, they realized that the "problem" member, or symptom bearer, reflected the rest of the system's dynamics. Olson (2000) captures this approach in describing a problem family with an enmeshed mother-adolescent coalition and disengaged father. "In this case, the marital dyad would not be emotionally close. Increasing their marital/parental collaboration is an effective strategy for breaking up the strong parent-child coalition" (p. 163). Thus, events in families must be examined in the context in which they happen and attention given to how communication among family members affects connections and relationships (Papp, 1983).

After explaining the overlap of systems theory and family therapy, Doherty and Baptiste (1993) list the six core working assumptions: (1) family relationships are a principal source of mental health and psychopathology for individuals, (2) family interaction patterns tend to repeat across generations, (3) family health requires a balance of conviction and individuation, (4) family flexibility is a core trait that prevents family dysfunction, (5) the triad is the minimum unit for a complex understanding of family interactions, and (6) individuals' symptoms frequently have meaning within the family's interaction patterns or worldview (pp. 511–512).

After interviewing counselors about couples' communication problems, Vangelisti (1994a) reported the most frequently voted communication problems involved failing to take the other's perspective when listening, blaming the other for negative occurrences and criticizing the other. Counselors felt communication problems were the result of patterns taught to individuals by their family of origin. A majority of counselors saw communication frequently as a manifestation of more fundamental difficulties. Only one-quarter saw communication as a central issue. Olson (2000) argues that although increasing positive communication skills of couples and families can facilitate change, it is a necessary but not sufficient condition to alter a family's cohesion and adaptability. He believes one therapeutic goal is to provide members with skills to negotiate system change over time.

A primary goal of family therapy is to affect changes in family members' interpersonal relationships but there are many schools of thought regarding the most effective ways to alter family systems. Gurman and Kniskern (1991) address 12 models of family therapy. Barker (1998) discusses eight approaches. In the metaframework approach, Breunlin, Schwartz, and Kune-Karrer (1997) present an overarching model that transcends multiple, narrow approaches and provides a comprehensive view of family patterns. Most therapists move strategically among approaches and focus on whole systems, subgroups, or individuals at particular points.

Family therapists may work with individuals, couples, families, or entire social networks—a therapeutic range that necessitates flexibility. Although one therapist may value an examination of family history to uncover family-of-origin or transgenerational patterns, another may focus exclusively on the "here-and now" interaction patterns. Recently, many therapists are focusing on narratives and meanings with the belief that therapy can be described as the process of transforming a family's dominant stories to include new meanings (White & Epston, 1990; Yerby, 1995). Over time, a family's needs and issues may change as indicated in the following statement.

Over the 16 years of our marriage we have experienced marital or family therapy two times, each a very different experience. Early in our marriage we had trouble separating from my original family, so we worked a lot on couple identity and family-of-origin issues using genograms. During our daughter's lengthy hospitalization for kidney disease, the other four of us went into therapy to keep us functioning and to release our feelings. Now I would be comfortable going again if an issue arose that we could not handle.

Family therapy has influenced approaches to treatment for drug and alcohol abuse, eating disorders, major illness, sexual abuse, and related areas. Currently, family therapy is being extended by focusing on the central question: "What prevents the patient system from solving the presenting problem?" (Pinsof, 1995, p. 7). Such problem-centered therapy is an alternative to value-centered therapy, which is organized around a definition of health, normality, or ideal functioning. The integration problem-solving approach encompasses the contexts of family-community, couple, and individual. It relies on a range of orientations involving behavioral, biobehavioral, experiential, family origin, psychodynamic, and self-psychology (Pinsof, 1995).

American family therapists are grappling with critical issues of culture and gender and their effect on the treatment process. The growing number of culturally diverse families who need the services of family therapists has led to extensive interest in cross-cultural family norms and treatment approaches (McGoldrick, Garcia-Preto, Hines, & Lee, 1991; Breunlin, Schwartz, & Kune-Karrer, 1997). Research investigating communication in intercultural marriages reveals the continuing salience of cultural background of the partners and the unique problems encountered in these relationships (Martin, Hecht, & Larkey, 1994). Cross-cultural family relationships encounter differences in areas of attitudes toward marriage, male-female roles, and the significance of extended family. Although few therapists can demonstrate expertise in communication patterns of multiple cultures, it is essential for therapists to be open to cultural variability and the relativity of their own values (McGoldrick et al., 1991).

Gender concerns have raised questions of equity and justice; therapists are encouraged to examine myths such as women need to be taken care of; women are nurturers, men are not; men must be instrumental, women must be expressive; and women should meet men's sexual needs but not reveal their own. Rampage (1992) clearly depicts difficulty with systems theory in certain circular problems such as wife beating, rape, and incest, saying,

> Circular causality subtly removes responsibility for his behavior from the man, while implying the woman is co-responsible and in some way "asks for it" by participating in the interactional patterns which results in violence and abuse. (p. 4)

The past decades witnessed an increase in research addressing the overall effectiveness of family therapy and specific issues of unique approaches (Pinsof & Wynne, 1995; Lebow & Gurman, 1996; Gottman, Ryan, Carrère, & Erley, 2002). The effectiveness of family therapy has been investigated primarily through an analysis of family improvement through treatment, treatment results compared to no treatment, and comparison of family treatment to other forms. Behavioral marital therapy appears effective for mildly or moderately distressed couples (Hahlweg & Markman, 1988). In a review of research, Lebow and Gurman (1996) include the following points. Family therapy is at least as helpful as more traditional, individual approaches; troubled couples relationships is the area in which a wide range of systemic approaches have been validated as effective; and family therapy engages the difficult to engage. They conclude that although there are many positive findings, some of the treatment effects lose hold over time and there are many underresearched areas.

Even as researchers uncover some answers to key questions, there is more to be examined, since current issues in family therapy research are the relationship between clinical approaches and psychoeducational approaches (Lebow, 1997). Gottman and colleagues (2002) argue that marital therapy remains relatively uninformed by empirical research relying instead on clinical history. Researchers demonstrate that although marital therapy creates significant short-term effects, there is a high relapse factor over time. Those who show improvement are likely to be less distressed, be more emotionally engaged, and show less negative affect. As part of building his Sound Marital House Theory, Gottman argues that marital satisfaction is related to high levels of everyday positivity and low levels of negative affect and calls for therapeutic approaches designed to achieve that marital state. The need continues for longitudinal, large sample, well-controlled studies.

As you change the current communication patterns within your family system, many options are open to you, ranging from individual approaches to efforts on the part of the system. The most exciting aspect is the possibility of change. Communication can be improved; families can grow through effort, time, and struggle. Relationships take work to maintain, and communication stands at the core of that process. The effort is worth it since, according to Wallerstein and Blakeslee (1995), ultimately it is loving connections that give life meaning. Through intimate relationships people enlarge their visions of life and diminish their preoccupation with self. We are at our most considerate, most loving, and most selfless within the orbit of a good family.

A FINAL WORD

As authors, we have grown from the process of writing this book and hope that you have developed new insights about families in general, and your family in particular. We close with our belief, shared with Beavers (1976), that a healthy family may be viewed as a "phoenix." It grows in an atmosphere of flexibility and intimacy. It accepts conflicts, change, and loss. It declines—to rise again in another well-functioning generation, which, in turn, produces well-functioning family members.

Conclusion

This chapter explored the factors that characterize functional to optimally functional families, with an emphasis on communication, and discussed the approaches for creating and maintaining effective communication within families. Historically, academic and therapeutic experts have emphasized effective communication as a central factor in a well-functioning family. Although there is no absolute agreement on definitions and terminology, one may hypothesize that functional families may exhibit some or all of the following characteristics:

1. Interactions are patterned and meaningful.
2. There is more compassion and less cruelty.
3. Persons are not scapegoated as problems are identified with the appropriate persons.
4. Family members exhibit appropriate self-restraint.
5. Boundaries are clear.
6. Life includes joy and humor.

7. Misperceptions are minimal.

8. Positive interactions outweigh negative ones.

Popular literature espouses similar ideas in a prescriptive mode.

Approaches to improving marital and family communication include personal actions, instructional programs, and therapeutic interventions. Such approaches can be helpful because they require a level of commitment and openness to change, they force the participants to move beyond the daily maintenance issues, and they provide a chance to reflect on family experience. These opportunities present a chance for individual and system self-examination. Each approach reflects a strong communication component. More research is needed to establish the effectiveness of these approaches.

In Review

1. How would you describe communication in a well-functioning family? Answer within a context of a specific developmental stage, culture, and family form.

2. Analyze the prescriptions for marital or parent-child communication found in a popular book or magazine article and evaluate their effectiveness based on your understanding of family systems and communication patterns.

3. What goals and criteria would you establish for a successful marriage or family enrichment program with a communication focus?

4. Take a position: To what extent should couples or parents be required by religious or civic institutions to engage in workshops or therapy?

5. In what ways would you predict that family therapy would differ across two ethnic groups?

BIBLIOGRAPHY

Abe, J. A. A., & Izard, C. E. (1999). Compliance, noncompliance strategies, and the correlates of compliance in 5-year-old Japanese and American children. *Social Development, 8*(1), 1–20.

Ackerman, N. J. (1980). The family with adolescents. In E. Carter & M. McGoldrick (Eds.), *The family life cycle: A framework for family therapy*. New York: Gardner Press.

Adams, R. J., & Parrott, R. (1994). Pediatric nurses' communication of role expectations to parents of hospitalized children. *Journal of Applied Communication Research, 22,* 36–47.

Adelman, A., Chadwick, K., & Baerger, D. (1996). Marital quality of black and white adults over the life course. *Journal of Social and Personal Relationships, 13,* 361–384.

Adelman, M. (1988, November). *Sustaining passion: Eroticism and safe sex talk.* Paper presented at the meeting of the Speech Communication Association, New Orleans, LA.

Ahlander, N. R., & Bahr, K. S. (1995). Beyond drudgery, power, and equity: Toward an expanded discourse on the moral dimensions of housework in families. *Journal of Marriage and the Family, 57,* 54–68.

Ahmeduzzaman, M., & Roopnaine, J. L. (1992). Sociodemographic factors, functioning style, social support, and fathers' involvement with preschoolers in African-American families. *Journal of Marriage & Family, 54,* 699–707.

Ahrons, O., & Rodgers, R. (1987). *Divorced families.* New York: W. W. Norton.

Aida, Y., & Falbo, T. (1991). Relationships between marital satisfaction, resources & power strategies. *Sex Roles, 41,* 43–50.

Alba, R. (1990). *Ethnic identity: The transformation of white America.* New Haven, CT: Yale University Press.

Alberts, J. K. (1988). An analysis of couples' conversational complaints. *Communication Monographs, 55,* 184–196.

Aldous, J. (1990). Family development and the life course: Two perspectives on family change. *Journal of Marriage and the Family, 52,* 571–583.

Aldous, J. (1995). New views of grandparents in intergenerational context. *Journal of Family Issues, 16,* 104–122.

Aldous, J. (1996). *Family careers: Rethinking the developmental perspective.* Thousand Oaks, CA: Sage.

Aldous, J., & Klein, D. (1991). Sentiment and services: Models of intergenerational relationships in mid-life. *Journal of Marriage and the Family, 53,* 585–608.

Aldridge, H. (1994, April). *Adrift in a sea of words: An examination of the connection between gender, audiences, and argument.* Paper presented at the meeting of the Central States Communication Association, St. Paul, MN.

Allen, K. R., & Demo, D. H. (1995). The families of lesbians and gay men: A new frontier in family research. *Journal of Marriage and the Family, 57,* 111–127.

Allen, K. R., & Wilcox, K. L. (2000). Gay/lesbian families over the life course. In S. J. Price, P. C. McKenry, & M. J. Murphy (Eds.), *Families across time: A life course perspective* (pp. 51–63). Los Angeles: Roxbury.

Allen, M., & Burrell, N. (1996). Comparing the impact of homosexual and heterosexual parents on children: Meta-analysis of existing research. *Journal of Homosexuality, 32,* 19–35.

Almeida, D. M., Wethington, E., & Chandler, A. L. (1999). Daily transmission of tensions between marital dyads and parent-child dyads. *Journal of Marriage and the Family, 61,* 49–61.

Altman, I., & Taylor, D. (1973). *Social penetration.* New York: Holt, Rinehart & Winston.

Amato, P. R. (1996). Explaining the intergenerational transmission of divorce. *Journal of Marriage and the Family, 58,* 628–640.

Amato, P. R., & Booth, A. (1996). A prospective study of divorce and parent-child relationships. *Journal of Marriage and the Family, 59,* 356–365.

Amato, P. R., & Rezacs, S. (1994). Contact with nonresident parents, interpersonal conflict, and children's behavior. *Journal of Family Issues, 15,* 191–207.

Amato, P. R., & Rogers, S. L. (1997). A longitudinal study of marital problems and subsequent divorce. *Journal of Marriage and the Family, 59,* 612–624.

Ambry, M. K. (1993). Receipts from marriage. *American Demographics, 15,* 30–38.

America's Children: Key National Indicators of Well-Being 2002. www.childstats.gov/ac2002/pdf/econ.pdf. Accessed 2/28/03.

Andersen, P. A., Eloy, S. V., Guerrero, L. K., & Spitzberg, B. H. (l995). Romantic jealousy and relational satisfaction: A look at the impact of jealousy experience and expression. *Communication Reports, 8,* 77–85.

Anderson, K. L. (1997). Gender status, and domestic violence: An integration of feminist and family violence approaches. *Journal of Marriage and the Family, 59,* 655–669.

Aquilino, W. S. (1997). From adolescent to young adult: A prospective study of parent-child relations during the transition to adulthood. *Journal of Marriage and the Family, 60,* 678–686.

Aquilino, W. S., & Supple, K. R. (1991). Parent-child relations and parents' satisfaction with living arrangements when adult children live at home. *Journal of Marriage and the Family, 53,* 13–27.

Arcus, M. E. (1995). Advances in family life education: Past, present, and future. *Family Relations, 44,* 336–344.

Arendell, T. (1998). Best case scenario: Fathers, children and divorce. In K. V. Hansen & A. I. Garey (Eds.), *Families in the U.S.* (pp. 388–401). Philadelphia: Temple University Press.

Attridge, M. (1994). Barriers to dissolution of romantic relationships. In D. J. Canary & L. Stafford (Eds.), *Communication and relational maintenance* (pp. 141–164). San Diego: Academic Press.

Avery, C. (1989). How do you build intimacy in an age of divorce? *Psychology Today, 23,* 27–31.

Aylmer, R. (1988). The launching of the single young adult. In B. Carter & M. McGoldrick (Eds.), *The changing family life cycle: A framework for family therapy* (2nd ed., pp. 191–208). New York: Gardner Press.

Bain, A. (1978). The capacity of families to cope with transitions: A theoretical essay. *Human Relations, 31,* 675–688.

Ballard-Reish, D., Elton, M., & Weigel, D. (1993, November). *Marital communication patterns and discussion making: A comparison of third party assessments and couple self reports.* Paper presented at the meeting of the Speech Communication Association, Miami, FL.

Barbato, C. A., Graham, E. E., & Perse, E. M. (2001, April). *Communicating in the family: An examination of the relationship of family communication climate and interpersonal communication motives.* Paper presented at the meeting of the Central States Communication Association, Atlanta, GA.

Barber, B. K. (1994). Cultural, family, and personal contexts of parent-adolescent conflict. *Journal of Marriage and the Family, 56,* 375–386.

Barber, B. K., Chadwick, B., & Oerter, R. (1992). Parental behaviors and adolescent self-esteem in the U.S. & Germany. *Journal of Marriage and the Family, 54,* 128–141.

Barker, P. (1998). *Basic family therapy* (4th ed.), Oxford: Blackwell Science.

Barnett, R., Kibria, N., Baruch, G. K., & Pleck, J. H. (1991). Adult daughter-parent relationships and their associations with daughters: Subjective well-being and psychological distress. *Journal of Marriage and the Family, 53,* 29–42.

Barnett, R., Marshall, N., & Pleck, J. (1992). Men's multiple roles and their relationship to men's psychological distress. *Journal of Marriage and the Family, 54,* 358–367.

Barranti-Ramirez, C. (1985). The grandparent/grandchildren relationship: Family resource in an era of voluntary bonds. *Family Relations, 34*(3), 343–355.

Barta, P. (2001). New American home is smaller, near city. *The Wall Street Journal,* pp. A2, A6.

Bartholet, E. (1993). *Family bonds: Adoption and the practice of parenting.* New York: Houghton Mifflin.

Bavelas, J., & Segal, L. (1982). Family systems theory: Background and implications. *Journal of Communication, 32,* 99–107.

Baxter, C., Cummins, R. A., & Yiolitis, L. (2000). Parental stress attributed to family members with and without disability: A longitudinal study. *Journal of Intellectual & Developmental Disability, 25*(2), 105–118.

Baxter, L. A. (1990). Dialectical contradictions in relationship development. *Journal of Social and Personal Relationships, 7,* 69–88.

Baxter, L. A. (1991, November). *Bakhtin's ghost: Dialectical communication in relationships.* Paper presented at the meeting of the Speech Communication Association, Atlanta, GA.

Baxter, L. A., & Braithwaite, D. O. (2002). Performing marriage: Marriage renewal rituals as cultural performance. *Southern Communication Journal, 67,* 94–109.

Baxter, L. A., Braithwaite, D. O., & Nicholson, J. H. (1999). Turning points in the development of blended families. *Journal of Personal and Social Relationships, 16,* 291–313.

Baxter, L. A., & Bylund, C. L. (in press). Social influence in close relationships. In J. Seiter & R. Gass (Eds.), *Readings in persuasion, social influence, and compliance gaining.* Boston: Allyn and Bacon.

Baxter, L. A., & Dindia, K. (1990). Marital partners' perceptions of marital maintenance strategies. *Journal of Social and Personal Relationships, 7,* 187–208.

Baxter, L. A., & Montgomery, B. M. (1996). *Relating: Dialogues and dialectics.* New York: Guilford Press.

Bay, C. R., & Braver, S. L. (1990). Perceived control of the divorce settlement process and intraparental conflict. *Family Relations, 39,* 362–387.

Beatty, M. J., & McCroskey, J. C. (1998). Interpersonal communication as temperamental expression: A communibiological paradigm. In J. C. McCroskey, J. A. Daly, M. M. Martin, & M. J. Beatty (Eds.), *Communication and personality: Trait perspectives.* Cresskill, NJ: Hampton Press.

Beatty, M. J., McCroskey, J. C., & Heisel, A. D. (1998). Communication apprehension as temperamental expression: A communibiological paradigm. *Communication Monographs, 64,* 197–219.

Beatty, M. J., McCroskey, J. C., & Valencic, K. M. (2001). *The biology of communication: A communibiological perspective.* Cresskill, NJ: Hampton Press.

Beavers, R. W. (1976). A theoretical basis for family evaluation. In J. M. Lewis, W. R. Beavers, J. T. Grossett, & V. A. Philips (Eds.), *No single thread: Psychological health in family systems* (pp. 46–82). New York: Brunner/Mazel.

Beavers, R. W. (1982). Healthy midrange, and severely dysfunctional families. In F. Walsh (Ed.), *Normal family processes.* New York: Guilford Press.

Beavers, R. W., & Voeller, M. (1983). Family models: Comparing and contrasting the Olson circumplex model with the Beavers systems model. *Family Process, 22,* 85–97.

Becker, T. J. (1994, February 19). 90's homes try to match the way we really live. *Chicago Tribune,* sec. 4, pp. 1–2.

Bedford, V. H., & Blieszner, R. (1997). Personal relationships in later-life families. In S. Duck (Ed.), *Handbook of personal relationships* (2nd ed., pp. 523–539). New York: John Wiley & Sons.

Bell, R., Buerkel-Rothfuss, N. L., & Gore, K. E. (1987). Did you bring the yarmulke for the cabbage patch kid?: The idiomatic communication of young lovers. *Human Communication Research, 14,* 47–67.

Belluck P. (2000, April 11). States declare war on divorce rates before any 'I Dos.' *The New York Times,* pp. 1, 14.

Belsky, J., Youngblade, L., Rovine, M., & Volling, B. (1991). Patterns of marital change and parent-child interaction. *Journal of Marriage and the Family, 53,* 488–497.

Bengston, V. L. (2001). Beyond the nuclear family: The increasing importance of multigenerational bonds. *Journal of Marriage and the Family, 63,* 1–16.

Benoit, P. J. (1997, November). *Remembering when: Family stories and the story telling event.* Paper presented at the meeting of the National Communication Association, Chicago, IL.

Benoit, P. J., Kennedy, K. A., Waters, R., Hinton, S., Drew, S., & Daniels, F. (1996, November). *Food, football, and family talk: Thanksgiving rituals in families.* Paper presented at the meeting of the Speech Communication Association, San Diego, CA.

Berger, C. R. (1980). Power and the family. In M. Roloff & G. Miller (Eds.), *Persuasion: New direction in theory and research* (pp. 174–224). Beverly Hills: Sage.

Berger, C. R., & Bradac, J. J. (1982). *Language and social knowledge.* London: Edward Arnold.

Berger, P., & Kellner, H. (1964). Marriage and the construction of reality: An exercise in the microconstruction of knowledge. *Diogenes, 46,* 1–25.

Beutler, I., Burr, W., Bahr, K., & Herrin, D. (1988). The family realm: Theoretical contributions for understanding its uniqueness.

Journal of Marriage and the Family, 51(3), 805–815.

Bielski, V. (1996, March–April). Our magnificent obsession. *The Family Therapy Networker,* 22–35.

Bigbee, J. L. (1992). Family stress, hardiness and illness: A pilot study. *Family Relations, 41,* 212–217.

Billingsley, A. (1988). The impact of technology on Afro-American families. *Family Relations, 37,* 420–425.

Black, C. (1981). *It will never happen to me.* New York: Ballantine Books.

Blau, F. D., Ferber, M. A., & Winkler, A. E. (1997). *The economics of women, men and work* (3rd ed.). Upper Saddle River, NJ: Prentice-Hall.

Blee, K. M., & Tickamyer, A. T. (1995). Racial differences in men's attitudes about women's gender roles. *Journal of Marriage and the Family, 57,* 21–30.

Blieszner, R. (1994). Close relationship over time. In A. Weber & J. Harvey (Eds.), *Perspectives on close relationships* (pp. 1–17). Boston: Allyn and Bacon.

Blum-Kulka, S. (1993). "You gotta know how to tell a story": Telling, tales and tellers in American and Israeli narrative events at dinner. *Language in Society, 22,* 361–402.

Blumenthal, A. (1990/91). Scrambled eggs and seed daddies: Conversations with my son. *Empathy: Gay and Lesbian Advocacy Research Project, 2,* 2.

Blumstein, P., & Schwartz, P. (1983). *American couples.* New York: William Morrow.

Bochner, A. P., & Eisenberg, E. (1987). Family process: System perspectives. In C. Berger & S. Chaffee (Eds.), *Handbook of communication science* (pp. 540–563). Beverly Hills: Sage.

Bok, J. (1983). *Secrets: On the ethics of concealment and revelation.* New York: Vintage Books.

Bollis-Pecci, T. S., & Webb, L. M. (1997, November). *The Memphis family perceptions instrument: Tests for validity and reliability.* Paper presented at the meeting of the National Communication Association, Chicago.

Bonnell, K. H., & Caillovet, L. M. (1991, April). *Partners and communication barriers between teenagers and parents about sex related topics: A survey of teenagers in sex education classes.* Paper presented at the meeting of the Central States Communication Association, Chicago.

Booth, A., & Amato, P. R. (1994). Parental marital quality, parental divorce. *Journal of Marriage and the Family, 56,* 21–34.

Booth, A., Carver, K., & Granger, D. (2000). Biosocial perspectives on the family. *Journal of Marriage and the Family, 62,* 1018–1034.

Bowman, K. (1999, August 25). The family dinner is alive and well. *The New York Times,* p. A27.

Bozett, F. (Ed.). (1987). *Gay and lesbian parents.* New York: Praeger.

Bradt, J. (1988). Becoming parents: Families with young children. In B. Carter & M. McGoldrick (Eds.), *The changing family life cycle: A framework for family therapy* (2nd ed., pp. 237–253). New York: Gardner Press.

Braithwaite, D. O. (1991). Just how much did that wheelchair cost? Management of privacy boundaries by persons with disabilities. *Western Journal of Speech Communication, 55,* 254–274.

Braithwaite, D. O., & Baxter, L. A. (1995). "I do" again: The relational dialectics of renewing marriage vows. *Journal of Social and Personal Relationships, 12,* 177–198.

Braithwaite, D. O., & Thompson, T. L. (2000). Communication and disability reseach: A productive past and a bright future. In D. O. Braithwaite & T. L. Thompson (Eds.), *Handbook of communication and people with disabilities* (pp. 507–515). Mahwah, NJ: Lawrence Erlbaum.

Bray, J. H., & Kelly, J. (1998). *Stepfamilies: Love, marriage and parenting in the first decade.* New York: Broadway Books.

Breunlin, D. C., Schwartz R. C., & Kune-Karrer, B. M. (1997). *Metaframeworks: Transcending the models of family therapy.* San Francisco: Jossey-Bass.

Brighton-Cleghorn, J. (1987). Formulations of self and family systems. *Family Process, 26,* 198–201.

Brock, L., & Jennings, G. (1993). What daughters in their 30s wish their mothers had told them. *Family Relations, 42,* 61–65.

Broderick, C. (1975). Power in the governance of families. In R. E. Cromwell & D. H. Olson (Eds.), *Power in families* (pp. 117–128). New York: Halsted Press.

Broderick, C. (1993). *Understanding family process.* Newbury Park, CA: Sage.

Broderick, C., & Schrader, S. (1991). A history of professional marriage and family therapy. In A. Gurman & D. Kriskern (Eds.), *Handbook of family therapy* (Vol. II). New York: Brunner/Mazel.

Brodzinsky, D. M., Smith, D. W., & Bordzinsky, A. B. (1998). *Children's adjustment to adoption.* Thousand Oaks, CA: Sage.

Brommel, B. J. (1992, November). *Teaching about death and dying in family communication.* Paper presented at the meeting of the Central States Communication Association, Chicago.

Bronstein, P., Clauson, J., Stoll, M. F., & Abrams, C. L. (1993). Parenting behavior and children's social, psychological and academic adjustment in diverse family structures. *Family Relations, 42,* 268–276.

Brothers, J. (1998, June). Are you caught in the middle? *Parade,* pp. 4–7.

Brown, B., Werner, C., & Altman, I. (1994). Close relationships in environmental context. In A. Weber & J. Harvey (Eds.), *Perspectives on close relationships* (pp. 340–358). Boston: Allyn and Bacon.

Brown, J. C. (1990). Loss and grief: An overview & guided imagery intervention model. *Journal of Mental Health Counseling, 12,* 434–445.

Brown, J. E., & Mann, L. (1990). The relationship between family structure and process variables and adolescent decision making. *Journal of Adolescence, 13,* 25–37.

Brubaker, T., & Roberto, K. (1993). Family life education for the later years. *Family Relations, 42,* 212–221.

Bruess, C. J. (1994). *Bare-chested hugs and tough guy nights: Examining the form and function of interpersonal rituals in marriage and friendship.* Unpublished doctoral dissertation, Ohio University.

Bruess, C. J. (1997). *Interview in family communication.* Teleclass, available from PBS Adult Learning Satellite Service, 1320 Braddock Pl., Alexandria, VA.

Bruess, C. J., & Pearson, J. C. (1995, November). *Like sands through the hourglass: Rituals in day to day marriage.* Paper presented at the meeting of the Speech Communication Association, San Antonio, TX.

Bruess, C. J., & Pearson, J. C. (1997). Interpersonal rituals in marriage and adult friendship. *Communication Monographs, 66,* 25–46.

Bryant, C. M., Conger, R. D., & Meehan, J. M. (2001). The influence of in-laws on change in marital success. *Journal of Marriage and the Family, 63,* 614–626.

Bryant, W. K., & Zick, C. D. (1996). An examination of parent-child shared time. *Journal of Marriage and the Family, 58,* 227–237.

Buehler, C., Betz, P., Ryan, C., & Trotter, B. (1992). Description and evaluation of the orientation for divorcing parents: Implications for past divorce prevention programs. *Family Relations, 41*(2), 154–162.

Buehler, K., Gottman, J. M., & Katz, L. (1992). How a couple views their past predicts their future: Predicting divorce from an oral history interview. *Journal of Family Psychology, 5,* 295–318.

Buerkel-Rothfuss, N., Fink, D. S., & Buerkel, R. A. (1995). Communication in the father-child dyad: The intergenerational transmission process. In T. J. Socha & G. H. Stamp (Eds.), *Parents, children and communication* (pp. 63–85). Mahwah, NJ: Lawrence Erlbaum.

Buller, D. B., & Burgoon, J. K. (1994). Deception: Strategic and nonstrategic communication. In J. Daly & J. M. Wiemann (Eds.), *Strategic interpersonal communication* (pp. 191–223). Hillsdale, NJ: Lawrence Erlbaum.

Bullock, C., & Foegen, A. (2002). Constructive conflict resolution for students with behavioral disorders. *Behavioral Disorders, 27*(3), 289–295.

Bumpass, L., Raley, L. K., & Sweet, J. (1995). The changing character of stepfamilies: Implications of cohabitation and nonmarital childbearing. *Demography, 32,* 425–436.

Burger, E., & Milardo, R. M. (1995). Marital interdependence and social networks. *Journal of Social and Personal Relationships, 12*(3), 403–416.

Burleson, B. R. (1998). Similarities in social skills: Interpersonal attraction and the development of personal relationships. In J. S. Trent (Ed.), *Communication: Views from the helm for the 21st century* (pp. 77–84). Boston: Allyn and Bacon.

Burleson, B. R., Delia, J., & Applegate, J. (1992). Effects of maternal communication and children's social-cognitive and communication skills on children's acceptance by the peer group. *Family Relations, 41,* 264–272.

Burleson, B. R., & Denton, W. H. (1997). The relationship between communication skill and marital satisfaction: Some moderating effects. *Journal of Marriage and the Family, 59,* 884–902.

Burleson, B. R., Kunkel, A. W., Samter, W., & Werking, K. J. (1996). Men's and women's evaluations of communication skills in personal relationships: When sex differences make a difference. *Journal of Social and Personal Relationships, 13,* 201–224.

Burr, W. R., Klein, S., & Associates. (1994). *Reexamining family stress.* Thousand Oaks, CA: Sage.

Buzzanell, P. M., & Burrell, N. A. (1997). Family and workplace conflicts: Examining metaphorical conflict schemas and expressions across context and sex. *Human Communication Research, 24*(1), 109–146.

Byers, L. A., Shue, C. K., & Marshall, L. L. (2001, November). *The interplay of violence, relationship quality, commitment, and communication in relationships: An examination of the dyad and the family.* Paper presented at the meeting of the National Communication Association, Atlanta, GA.

Bylund, C. L. (in press). Ethnic diversity and the functions of family stories. *Journal of Family Communication.*

Cahn, D. D. (1992). *Conflict in intimate relationships.* New York: Guilford Press.

Cahn, D. D., & Lloyd, S. A. (1996). *Family violence from a communication perspective.* Thousand Oaks, CA: Sage.

Cain, B. (1990, February 18). Older children and divorce. *New York Times Magazine, 26,* 50–55.

Canary, D. J., Cody, M. J., & Manusov. V. L. (2000). *Interpersonal communication: A goals-based approach* (2nd ed.). Boston: Bedford/St. Martin's.

Canary, D. J., & Stafford, L. (1992). Relational maintenance strategies and equity in marriage. *Communication Monographs, 3,* 243–267.

Canary, D. J., & Stafford, L. (1994). Maintaining relationships through strategic and routine interaction. In D. J. Canary & L. Stafford (Eds.), *Communication and relational maintenance* (pp. 3–22). San Diego, CA: Academic Press.

Canary, D. J., Stafford, L., & Semic, B. A. (2002). A panel study of the associations between maintenance strategies and relational characteristics. *Journal of Marriage and the Family, 64,* 395–406.

Canary, D. J., Weger, H., & Stafford, L. (1991). Couples' argument sequences and their associations with relational characteristics. *Western Journal of Speech Communication, 55,* 159–179.

Cappella, J. N. (1991). The biological origins of automated patterns on human interaction. *Communication Theory, 1,* 4–35.

Cardarelli, A. (1997). *Violence between intimate partners: Patterns, causes and effects.* Boston: Allyn and Bacon.

Carnes, P. (1989). *Contrary to love.* Center City, MN: Hazelden.

Carp, E. W. (1998). *Family matters: Secrecy and disclosure in the history of adoption.* Cambridge, MA: Harvard University Press.

Carter, B. (1999). Becoming parents: The family with young children. In B. Carter & M. McGoldrick (Eds.), *The expanded family life cycle* (pp. 249–273). Boston: Allyn and Bacon.

Carter, B., & McGoldrick, M. (1988). Overview, the changing family life cycle: A framework for family therapy. In B. Carter & M. McGoldrick (Eds.), *The changing family life cycle* (2nd ed., pp. 3–28). New York: Gardner Press.

Carter, B., & McGoldrick, M. (1999). Overview: The expanded family life cycle. In B. Carter & M. McGoldrick (Eds.), *The expanded family life cycle* (pp. 1–26). Boston: Allyn and Bacon.

Caruthers, S. C. (1998). Catching sense: Learning from our mothers to be black and female. In K. V. Hansen & A. I. Garey (Eds.), *Families in the U.S.* (3rd ed., pp. 315–327). Philadelphia: Temple University Press.

Cassidy, M. F. (2001). Cyberspace meets domestic space: Personal computers, women's work, and the gendered territories of the family home. *Critical Studies in Media Communication, 18,* 44–65.

Cate, R. M., Levin L. A., & Richmond, L. S. (2002). Premarital relationship stability: A review of recent research. *Journal of Social and Personal Relationships, 19,* 261–284.

Caughlin, J. P. (2002). The demand/withdraw pattern of communication as a predictor of marital satisfaction over time. *Human Communication Research, 28*(1), 49–85.

Caughlin, J. P., Golish, T. D., Olson, L. N., Sargent, J. E., Cook, J. S., & Petronio, S. (2000). Intrafamily secrets in various family configurations: A communication boundary management perspective. *Communication Studies, 51,* 116–134.

Caughlin, J. P., & Vangelisti, A. L. (2000). An individual difference explanation of why married couples engage in the demand/withdraw pattern of conflict. *Journal of Social and Personal Relationships, 17*(4–5), 523–551.

Cawyer, C. S., & Smith-Dupre, A. (1995). Communicating social support: Identifying supportive episodes in an HIV/AIDS support group. *Communication Quarterly, 43,* 243–358.

Cetron, M. J., & Davies, O. (2001, January/February). Trends now changing the world: Technology, the workplace, management, and institutions. *The Futurist,* 30–43.

Chaitin, J. (2002). Issues and interpersonal values among three generations in families of Holocaust survivors. *Journal of Social and Personal Relationships, 19,* 379–402.

Chen, Z., & Kaplan, H. B. (2001). Intergenerational transmission of constructive parenting. *Journal of Marriage and the Family, 63,* 17–31.

Chung, D. K. (1992). Asian cultural commonalities: A comparison with mainstream American culture. In S. M. Furuto, R. Biswas, K. Murase, & F. Ross-Sheriff (Eds.), *Social work practice with Asian Americans.* Newbury Park, CA: Sage.

Cissna, K. H., Cox, D. E., & Bochner, A. P. (1990). The dialectic of marital and parental relationships within the stepfamily. *Communication Monographs, 57,* 45–61.

Clark, M. S. (1999). The double ABCX model of family crisis as a representation of family functioning after rehabilitation from stroke. *Psychology, Health & Medicine, 4*(2), 203–220.

Cleaver, G. (1987). Marriage enrichment by means of a structured communication program. *Family Relations, 36,* 49–54.

Clements, P. T., & Burgess, A. W. (2002). Children's responses to family member homicide. *Family & Community Health, 25*(1), 32–42.

Cline, K. (1989). The politics of intimacy: Costs and benefits determining disclosure intimacy in male-female dyads. *Journal of Social and Personal Relationships, 6,* 5–20.

Cloven, D. H., & Roloff, M. I. (1993). The chilling effect of aggressive potential on the expression of complaints in intimate relationships. *Communication Monograph, 60*(660), 199–219.

Cole, C., & Cole, A. (1993). Family therapy theory implications for marriage and family enrichment. In P. Boss et al. (Eds.), *Sourcebook for family theories and methods* (pp. 525–529). New York: Plenum Press.

Cole, C. L., & Cole, A. L. (1999). Marriage enrichment and prevention really works: Interpersonal competence training to maintain and enhance relationships. *Family Relations, 48,* 273–276.

Coleman, D. (1992, December 2). Gay parents called no disadvantage. *The New York Times* (Health), p. 31.

Coleman, M., Fine, M. A., Ganong, L. H., Downs, K. J. M., & Pauk, N. (2001). When you're not the Brady Bunch: Identifying perceived conflicts and resolution strategies in stepfamilies. *Personal Relationships, 8,* 55–73.

Coleman, M., Ganong, L., & Fine, M. (2000). Reinvestigating remarriage: Another decade of progress. *Journal of Marriage and the Family, 62,* 1288–1307.

Collins, R. (1997). *Interview in family communication.* Teleclass, available from PBS Adult Learning Satellite Service, 1320 Braddock Pl., Alexandria, VA.

Conger, R. D., & Conger, K. J. (2002). Resilience in midwestern families: Selected findings from the first decade of a prospective longitudinal study. *Journal of Marriage and the Family, 64,* 361–373.

Constantine, L. (1986). *Family paradigms: The practice of theory in family therapy.* New York: Guilford Press.

Cooney, T. M. (1997). Parent-child relations across adulthood. In S. Duck (Ed.), *Handbook of personal relationships: Theory, research and interventions* (pp. 451–468). New York: John Wiley & Sons.

Cooney, T. M., Pedersen, F., Indelicato, S., & Palkovitz, R. (1993). Timing of fatherhood: Is "on time" optimal? *Journal of Marriage and the Family, 55,* 205–215.

Coontz, S. (1992). *The way we never were: American families and the nostalgia trap.* New York: HarperCollins.

Coontz, S. (1996, May–June). Where are the good old days? *Modern Maturity,* 36–43.

Coontz, S. (1999). Introduction. In S. Coontz, M. Parson, & G. Raley (Eds.), *American families: A multicultural reader* (pp. ix–xxxiii). New York: Routledge.

Coontz, S., & Folbre, N. (2002, April 26–28). *Marriage, poverty, and public policy: A discussion paper from the council on contemporary families.* Paper prepared for the Fifth Annual CCF Conference. http://www.contemporaryfamilies.org/briefing.html.

Corden, A., Sloper, P., & Sainsbury, R. (2002). Financial effects for families after the death of a disabled or chronically ill child: A neglected dimension of bereavement. *Child: Care, Health & Development, 28*(3), 199–204.

Courtright, J. A., Millar, F. E., & Rogers-Millar, L. E. (1979). Domineeringness and dominance: Replication and expansion. *Communication Monographs, 46*, 179–192.

Covey, S. R. (1997). *The 7 habits of highly effective families*. New York: Golden Books.

Cowan, C. P., & Cowan, P. A. (1997). Working with couples during stressful transitions. In S. Dreman (Ed.), *The family on the threshold of the 21st century*. Mahwah, NJ: Lawrence Erlbaum.

Cowan, C. P., Cowan, P. A., Heming, H., Garrett, E., Coysh, W., Curtis-Boles, H., & Boles, A. J. (1985). Transitions to parenthood: His, hers, theirs. *Journal of Family Issues, 6*, 451–481.

Cox, M. J., & Harter, K. S. M. (2002). The road ahead for research on marital and family dynamics. In J. P. McHale & W. S. Grolnick (Eds.), *Retrospect and prospect in the psychological study of families* (pp. 167–188). Mahwah, NJ: Lawrence Erlbaum.

Cramer, D. (2002). Linking conflict management behaviours and relational satisfaction: The intervening role of conflict outcome satisfaction. *Journal of Social & Personal Relationships, 19*(3), 425–432.

Crane, D. R., Dollahite, D., Griffin, W., & Taylor, K. (1987). Diagnosing relationships with spatial distance: An empirical test of a clinical principle. *Journal of Marital and Family Therapy, 13*, 307–310.

Cronen, V., Pearce, W. B., & Harris, L. (1979). The logic of the coordinated management of meaning: A rules-based approach to the first course in inter-personal communication. *Communication Education, 23*, 22–38.

Crosbie-Burnett, M., & McClintic, K. (2000). Remarried families over the life course. In S. J. Prece, P. C. McKenry, & M. J. Murphy (Eds.), *Families across time: A life course perspective* (pp. 37–50). Los Angeles: Roxbury.

Crowell, N. A., & Burgess, A. W. (1996). *Understanding violence against women*. Washington, DC: National Academy Press.

Csikszentmihalyi, M., & Rochberg-Halton, E. (1981). *The meaning of things: Domestic symbols and the self*. Cambridge, UK: Cambridge University Press.

Curran, D. (1983). *Traits of a healthy family*. Minneapolis: Winston Press.

Current Population Reports. (1998). *Household and family characteristics: March 1997*. Series P-20, No. 509. Washington, DC: U.S. Government Printing Office.

Dainton, M., Stafford, L., & McNeilis, K. S. (1992, October). *The maintenance of relationships through the use of routine behaviors*. Paper presented at the meeting of the Speech Communication Association, Chicago.

Daly, K. J. (1996). Spending time with the kids: Meaning of family time for fathers. *Family Relations 45*, 466–476.

Daniel, J., & Daniel, J. (1999). African-American child rearing: The context of the hot stove. In T. H. Socha & R. C. Diggs (Eds.), *Communication, race and family: Exploring communication in black, white, and biracial families* (pp. 25–43). Mahwah, NJ: Lawrence Erlbaum.

Davies, P. T., Myers, R. L., Cummings, E. M., & Heindel, S. (1999). Adult conflict history and children's subsequent responses to conflict: an experimental test. *Journal of Family Psychology, 13*(4), 610–628.

DeFrain, J., & Stinnett, N. (1985). *Secrets of strong families*. Boston: Little, Brown.

DeGenova, M. K., & Rice, F. P. (2002). *Intimate relationships, marriages, and families* (5th ed.). Boston: McGraw-Hill.

deHoyos, G. (1989). Person in environment: A tri-level practice model. *Social Casework, 70*(3), 131–138.

Dell, P. F. (1982). Beyond homeostasis: Toward a concept of coherence. *Family Process, 21*, 21–42.

DeMaris, A. (2001). The influence of intimate violence on transitions out of cohabitation. *Journal of Marriage and the Family, 63*, 235–246.

Demo, D. (1992). Parent-child relations: Assessing recent changes. *Journal of Marriage and the Family, 54*, 104–117.

Demos, J. (1998). Child abuse in context: An historian's perspective. In K. V. Hansen & A. I. Garey (Eds.), *Families in the U.S.* (pp. 651–667). Philadelphia: Temple University Press.

Denton, W. H., Burleson, B. R., & Sprenkle, D. H. (1994). Motivation in marital communication: Comparison of distressed and nondistressed husbands and wives. *American Journal of Family Therapy, 22*, 17–26.

DeSteno, D. A., & Salovey, P. (1994). Jealousy in close relationships: Multiple perspectives on the green-eyed monster. In A. L. Weber & J. H. Harvey (Eds.), *Perspectives on close relationships* (pp. 217–242). Boston: Allyn and Bacon.

deTurck, M. A., & Miller, G. R. (1983). Adolescent perceptions of parental persuasive message strategies. *Journal of Marriage and the Family, 45*(3), 543–552.

DeVito, J. (1993). *Messages: Building interpersonal communication skills.* New York: HarperCollins

Dickson, F. C. (1988). *Family words.* Reading, MA: Addison-Wesley.

Dickson, F. C. (1995). The best is yet to be: Research on long-lasting marriages. In J. T. Wood & S. Duck (Eds.), *Understudied relationships* (pp. 22–50). Thousand Oaks, CA: Sage.

Dickson, F. C., Hughes, P. C., Manning, L. D., Walker, K., Bollis-Pecci, L., & Gratson, S. (2002). Conflict in later-life, long-term marriages. *Southern Communication Journal, 67,* 110–121.

Dickson, F. C., & Walker, K. L. (2001, Summer). The expression of emotion in later-life married men. *Qualitative Research Reports in Communication,* 66–71.

Dickson, F. C., & Wood, R. V. (1997, November). *Ritual storytelling and the constitution of family.* Paper presented at the meeting of the National Communication Association, Chicago.

Dietz, T. L. (1995). Patterns of intergenerational assistance within the Mexican-American family. *Journal of Family Issues, 16,* 344–356.

Diggs, R. (1994, November). *Parent and peer communication, racial esteem, and support influence on self-esteem among African-American adolescents.* Paper presented at the meeting of the Speech Communication Association, New Orleans, LA.

Diggs, R. C. (2001, November). *Searching for commitment with a radical(izing) method: The experiences of an African-American long-distance married couple.* Paper presented at National Communication Association convention. Atlanta, GA.

DiGiulio, J. F. (1992). Early widowhood: An atypical transition. *Journal of Mental Health Counseling, 14,* 97–109.

Dill, B. (1998). Fictive kin, paper sons, and *compadrazgo:* Women of color and the struggle for family survival. In K. V. Hansen & A. I. Garey (Eds.), *Families in the U.S.* (pp. 431–445). Philadelphia: Temple University Press.

Dilworth-Anderson, P., & Burton, L. M. (1996). Rethinking family development: Critical conceptual issues in the study of diverse groups. *Journal of Social and Personal Relationships, 13,* 325–334.

Dilworth-Anderson, P., & McAdoo, H. P. (1988). The study of ethnic minority families: Implications of practitioners and policymakers. *Family Relations, 37,* 265–267.

Dindia, K., & Canary, D. J. (1993). Definitions and theoretical perspectives on relational maintenance. *Journal of Social and Personal Relationships, 10,* 163–173.

Dindia, K., Fitzpatrick, M. A., & Kenny, D. A. (1997). Self-disclosure in spouse and stranger interaction: A social relations analysis. *Human Communication Research, 23,* 388–412.

Dixson, M. D. (1995). Models and perspectives of parent-child communication. In T. Socha & G. Stamp (Eds.), *Parent, children and communication* (pp. 433–462). Mahwah, NJ: Lawrence Erlbaum.

Doherty, W. J., & Baptiste, J. (1993). Theories emerging from family therapy. In P. Boss et al. (Eds.), *Sourcebook of family theories and methods* (pp. 525–524). New York: Plenum Press.

Doherty, W. J., Lester, M., & Leigh, G. (1986). Marriage encounter weekends: Couples who win and couples who lose. *Journal of Marital and Family Therapy, 12,* 49–62.

Dornbusch, S. M., Ritter, P. L., Mont-Reynaud, R., & Chen, Z.-Y. (1990). Family decision making and academic performance in a diverse high school population. *Journal of Adolescent Research, 5,* 143–160.

Downs, K. J., Coleman, M., & Ganong, L. (2000). Divorced families over the life course. In S. J. Prece, P. C. McKenry, & M. J. Murphy (Eds.), *Families across time: A life course perspective* (pp. 24–36). Los Angeles: Roxbury.

Dreikurs, R. (1964). *Children: The challenge,* New York: Hawthorn Books.

Dreman, S., & Ronen-Eliav, H. (1997). The relation of divorced mothers' perceptios of family cohesion and adaptability to behavior problems in children. *Journal of Marriage and the Family, 59,* 324–331.

Dreyer, C., & Dreyer, A. (1984). Family dinner times as unique behavior habitat. *Family Process, 12,* 291–302.

Dreyfous, L. (1994). Cohousing: A new way of living. *Chicago Tribune,* sec. 16, p. 5.

Duck, S. (1986). *Human relationships: An introduction to social psychology.* London: Sage.

Duck, S. (1994). Steady as (s)he goes: Relational maintenance as a shared meaning system. In D. J. Canary & L. Stafford (Eds.), *Communication and relational maintenance* (pp. 45–60). San Diego: Academic Press.

Duck, S., Miell, D., & Miell, D. (1984). Relationship growth and decline. In H. Sypher & J. Applegate (Eds.), *Communication by children and adults* (pp. 292–312). Beverly Hills: Sage.

Duck, S., & Pond, K. (1989). Friends, Romans and countrymen, send me your retrospectives: Rhetoric and reality in personal relationships. In C. Hendrick (Ed.), *Close relationships* (pp. 17–38). Newbury Park, CA: Sage.

Dumka, L. E., Roosa, M. W., & Jackson, K. M. (1997). Risk, conflict, mothers' parenting, and children's adjustment in low-income, Mexican immigrant, and Mexican American families. *Journal of Marriage and the Family, 59,* 309–323.

Duncan, B. L., & Rock, J. W. (1993, January/February). Saving relationships: The power of the unpredictable. *Psychology Today,* 46–51, 86, 95.

Dunlop, R. (1978). *Helping the bereaved.* Bowie, MD: Charles Press.

Duvall, E. (1988). Family development's first forty years. *Family Relations, 37,* 127–134.

Eckloff, M. (1994, November). *The young adult grandchild's view of grandparent-grandchild interaction in today's family community.* Paper presented at the meeting of the Speech Communication Association, New Orleans, LA.

Eckstein, N. J. (2002). *Adolescent-to-parent abuse: A communicative analysis of conflict processes present in verbal, physical, or emotional abuse of parents.* Unpublished dissertation, University of Nebraska-Lincoln.

Edin, K., Nelson, T., & Paranal, R. (2001). Fatherhood and incarceration as parental E-mail: A hot ticket on college campuses. *PC Week, 14,* 131.

"E-mail: A hot ticket on college campuses." (1997, May 12). *PC Week, 14,* 131.

Emmers, T. M., & Hart, R. D. (1995, April). *Hey, I'm alive, and attractive, and I don't need you: Rituals of moving out on.* Paper presented at the meeting of the Central States Communication Association, Indianapolis, IN.

Endres, T. G. (1997). Father-daughter dramas: A Q-investigation of rhetorical visions. *Journal of Applied Communication Research, 25,* 317–340.

Ennett, S. T., Bauman, K. E., Foshee, V. A., Pemberton, M., & Hicks, K. A. (2001). Parent-child communication about adolescent tobacco and alcohol use: What do parents say and does it affect youth behavior? *Journal of Marriage and the Family, 63,* 48–62.

Epstein, N. B., Bishop, D. S., & Baldwin, L. M. (1982). McMaster model of family functioning. In F. Walsh (Ed.), *Normal family processes* (pp. 115–141). New York: Guilford Press.

Erickson, B. M., & Simon, J. S. (1996). Scandinavian families: Plain and simple. In M. McGoldrick, J. Giordano, & J. K. Pearce (Eds.), *Ethnicity and family therapy* (2nd ed., pp. 595–608). New York: Guilford Press.

Erikson, E. H. (1968). *Identity, youth, and crisis.* New York: W. W. Norton.

Escudero, V., Rogers, L. E., & Gutierrez E. (1997). Patterns of relational control and nonverbal affect in clinic and nonclinic couples. *Journal of Social and Personal Relationship, 14,* 5–29.

Fadiman, A. (1997). *The spirit catches you and you fall down.* New York: Farrar, Straus and Giroux.

Falbo, T., & Peplau, L. A. (1980). Power strategies in intimate relationships. *Journal of Personality and Social Psychology, 38,* 618–628.

Falicov, C. J. (1999). The Latino family life cycle. In B. Carter & M. McGolderick (Eds.), *The expanded family life cycle* (3rd ed., pp. 141–152). Boston: Allyn and Bacon.

Families and Work Institute. (1998, April 15). *1997 National Study of the Changing Workforce: Executive summary.* New York.

"Family chats." (1998, February). *American Demographics,* 37.

Farrell, M. P. (2000). Adolescents' effects on the psychological functioning and adult development of their parents. *Family Science Review, 13,* 10–18.

Farrell, M. P., & Barnes, G. M. (1993). Family systems and social support: A test of the effects of cohesion and adaptability on the functioning of parents and adolescents. *Journal of Marriage and the Family, 55,* 119–132.

Feifel, H. (1977). *New meaning of death.* New York: McGraw-Hill.

Fein, E. B. (1998, October 25). Secrecy and stigma no longer clouding adoptions. *The New York Times,* pp. A1, A18.

Feldman, L. B. (1979). Marital conflict and marital intimacy: An integrative psychodynamic-behavioral systemic model. *Family Process, 18,* 69–78.

Fenigstein, A., & Peltz, R. (2002). Distress over the infidelity of a child's spouse: A crucial test of evolutionary and socialization hypotheses. *Personal Relationships, 9,* 301–312.

Ferguson, I. B. (1999). African-American parent-child communication about racial derogation. In T. J. Socha & R. C. Diggs (Eds.), *Communication, race and family: Exploring communication in Black, White and biracial families* (pp. 45–67). Mahwah, NJ: Lawrence Erlbaum.

Ferguson, S. M. (1996, November). *From nightmares to peace: A case study of sexual abuse recovery using a pre-critical thinking approach.* Paper presented at the meeting of the Speech Communication Association, San Diego, CA.

Ferguson, S. M. (1997, November). *Children's attitudes toward parental dating: An empirical inquiry into contemporary family lifestyles.* Paper presented at the meeting of the National Communication Association, Chicago.

Festinger, L., Schachter, S., & Back, K. (1950). *Social pressure in informal groups: A study of human factors in housing.* New York: Harper & Row.

Fetto, J. (2002). Indicators: Defrosting dinner. *American Demographics, 24,* 22.

Fiese, B. H., Hooker, K. A., Kotary, L., Schagler, J., & Rimmer, M. (1995). Family stories in the early stages of parenthood. *Journal of Marriage and the Family, 57,* 763–770.

Fiese, B. H., Hooker, K. A., Kotary, L., & Schwagen, J. (1993). Family rituals in the early stages of parenthood. *Journal of Marriage and the Family, 55,* 633–642.

Fincham, F. D. (2000). The kiss of the porcupines: From attributing responsibility to forgiving. *Personal Relationships, 7,* 1–23.

Fincham, F. D., & Beach, S. R. (2002). Forgiveness in marriage: Implications for psychological aggression and constructive communication. *Personal Relationships, 9,* 239–251.

Fink, D. S., Buerkel-Rothfuss, N. L., & Buerkel, R. A. (1994, November). *Father-son relational closeness: The role of attribution-making in reducing the impact of bad behavior.* Paper presented at the meeting of the Speech Communication Association, New Orleans, LA.

Finkenauer, C., & Hazam, H. (2000). Disclosure and secrecy in marriage: Do both contribute to marital satisfaction? *Journal of Social and Personal Relationships, 17,* 245–263.

Fisher, T. D. (1986). Parent-child communication about sex and young adolescents' sexual knowledge and attitudes. *Adolescence, 16,* 517–527.

Fitzpatrick, M. A. (1977). A typological approach to communication in relationships. In B. Rubin (Ed.), *Communication yearbook I* (pp. 263–275). New Brunswick, NJ: Transaction Press.

Fitzpatrick, M. A. (1987). Marital interaction. In C. Berger & S. Chaffee (Eds.), *Handbook of communication science* (pp. 564–618). Newbury Park, CA: Sage.

Fitzpatrick, M. A. (1988). *Between husbands and wives.* Beverly Hills: Sage.

Fitzpatrick, M. A. (1998). Interpersonal communication on the Starship Enterprise: Resilience, stability, and change in relationships in the twenty-first century. In J. S. Trent (Ed.), *Communication: Views from the helm for the 21st century* (pp. 41–46). Boston: Allyn and Bacon.

Fitzpatrick, M. A., & Badzinski, D. M. (1994). All in the family: Interpersonal communication in kin relationships. In M. L. Knapp & G. L. Miller (Eds.), *Handbook of interpersonal communication* (2nd ed., pp. 726–771). Thousand Oaks, CA: Sage.

Fitzpatrick, M. A., & Best, P. (1979). Dyadic adjustment in relational types: Consensus, cohesion, affectional expression, and satisfaction in enduring relationships. *Communication Monographs, 46,* 165–178.

Fitzpatrick, M. A., Fallis, S., & Vance, L. (1982). Multifunctional coding of conflict resolution strategies in marital dyads. *Family Relations, 31,* 61–70. Adult Learning Satellite Service, 1320 Braddock Pl., Alexandria, VA.

Fitzpatrick, M. A., & Ritchie, L. D. (1994). Communication schemata within the family: Multiple perspectives on family interaction. *Human Communication Research, 20,* 275–301.

Flanagan, K. M., Clements, M. L., Whitton, S. W., Portney, M. J., Randall, D. W., & Markman, H. J. (2002). Retrospect and prospect in the psychological study of marital and couple relationships. In J. P. McHale & W. S. Grolnick (Eds.), *Retrospect and prospect in the psychological study of families* (pp. 99–128). Mahwah, NJ: Lawrence Erlbaum.

Forehand, R., McCombs, A., Long, N., Brady, G., & Fauber, R. (1988). Early adolescent adjustment to recent parental divorce: The role of interparental conflict and adolescent sex as mediating variables. *Journal of Consulting and Clinical Psychology, 56*(4), 624–627.

Forgatch, M. (1989). Patterns and outcomes in family problem solving: The disrupting effect of negative emotion. *Journal of Marriage and the Family, 51,* 115–124.

Friedman E. H. (1988). Systems and ceremonies: A family view of rites of passage. In B. Carter & M. McGoldrick (Eds.), *The changing family lifecycle* (2nd ed., pp. 119–147). New York: Gardner Press.

Frieze, I. H., & McHugh, M. C. (1992). Power and influence strategies in violent and nonviolent marriages. *Psychology of Women Quarterly, 16,* 449–465.

Fujishin, R. (1998). *Gifts from the heart.* San Francisco: Acada Books.

Fulmer, R. (1999). Becoming an adult. In B. Carter & M. McGoldrick (Eds.), *The expanded family life cycle* (3rd ed., pp. 215–230). Boston: Allyn and Bacon.

Gage, G. M., & Christensen, D. (1991). Parental role socialization and the transition to parenthood. *Family Relations, 40,* 332–337.

Gaines, S. O. (1995). Relationships between members of cultural minorities. In J. Wood & S. Duck (Eds.), *Under-studied relationships* (pp. 51–88). Thousand Oaks, CA: Sage.

Galvin, K. M. (1993). First marriage families: Gender and communication. In L. Arliss & D. Borisoff (Eds.), *Men and women communicating* (pp. 86–101). Fort Worth, TX: Harcourt Brace Jovanovich.

Galvin, K. M. (in press.). It's not all blarney: Intergenerational transmission of communication patterns in Irish-American families. In P. Cooper & R. Hoel (Eds.), *Intercultural communication.* Boston: Allyn and Bacon.

Galvin, K. M., & Cooper, P. (1990). *Development of involuntary relationships: The stepparent/stepchild relationship.* Paper presented at the meeting of the International Communication Association Conference, Dublin, Ireland.

Galvin, K. M., & Wilkinson, C. (2000, November). *That's your family picture?!: Korean adoptees' communication management issues during the transition to college.* Paper presented at the National Communication Association Convention, Seattle, WA.

Gangotena, M. (1997). The rhetoric of *La Familia* among Mexican Americans. In A. Gonzalez, M. Houston & V. Chen (Eds.), *Our voices: Essays in culture, ethnicity, and communication* (2nd ed., pp. 70–83). Los Angeles: Roxbury.

Ganong, L., & Coleman, M. (1994). *Remarried family relationships.* Thousand Oaks, CA: Sage.

Garrett, P., Ferron, J., Ng'Andu, N., Bryant D., & Harbin, G. (1994). A structural model for the developmental status of young children. *Journal of Marriage and the Family, 56,* 147–163.

Gass, R. H., & Seiter, S. J. (1999). *Persuasion, social influence, and compliance-gaining.* Boston: Allyn and Bacon.

Gerson, K., & Jacobs, J. A. (2001). Changing the structure and culture of work. In R. Hertz & N. H. Marshall (Eds.), *Working families: The transformation of the American home* (pp. 207–226). Berkeley: University of California Press.

Giblin, P. (1994). Marital satisfaction. *The Family Journal, 2,* 48–50.

Giblin, P. (1996). Marriage and family enrichment: A process whose time has come (and gone?). *Family Journal, 4,* 143–153.

Gilbar, O., & Refaeli, R. (2000). The relationship between adult cancer patients' adjustment to the illness and that of their parents. *Families, Systems & Health: The Journal of Collaborative Family HealthCare, 18*(1), 5–17.

Gilligan, C. (1982). *In a different voice.* Cambridge, MA: Harvard University Press.

Gillis, J. R. (1996). *A world of their own making: Myth, ritual and the quest for family values.* New York: HarperCollins.

Giordano J., & McGoldrick, M. (1996). Italian families. In M. McGoldrick, J. Giordano, & T. K. Pearce (Eds.), *Ethnicity and family therapy* (2nd ed., pp. 567–582). New York: Guilford Press.

Glick, P. (1989). *American families: As they are and were (realities in fact).* Paper presented at the Florida Conference on Family Development, Jacksonville, FL.

Goldberg, J. (1994, August). Rescuing children and adolescents from the coming crime storm. *Family Theory News,* 14–15, 23–25.

Golden, A. (1997). *Juggling work and family: The effects of modernity on the communicative management of multiple roles.* Paper presented at the meeting of the National Communication Association, Chicago.

Golden, A. G. (2002). Speaking of work and family: Spousal collaboration on defining role-identities and developing shared meanings. *Southern Communication Journal, 67,* 122–141.

Goldner, V. (1989). Generation and gender: Normative and covert hierarchies. In M. Mc-Goldrick, C. Anderson, & F. Walsh (Eds.), *Women in families* (pp. 42–60). New York: W. W. Norton.

Goldner, V., Penn, P., Sheinberg, M., & Walker G. (1990). Love & violence: Gender paradoxes in volatile attachments. *Family Process, 29,* 343–364.

Gonzaga, G. C., Keltner, D., Londahl, E. A., & Smith, M. D. (2001). Love and the commitment problem in romantic relations and friendship. *Journal of Personality and Social Psychology, 81*(2), 247–262.

Gonzalez, D. (1993, January 17). Seeking security, man retreats behind bars and razor wire. *New York Times,* sec. 1, pp. 1, 18.

Goozner, M. (1998, June 2). Are Americans working better or just more? *Chicago Tribune.*

Gotcher, J. M. (1993). The effects of family communication on psychological adjustment of cancer patients. *Journal of Applied Communication Research, 21,* 176–188.

Gottlieb, A. S. (1994). Single mothers of children with developmental disabilities: The impact of multiple roles. *Family Relations, 46,* 5–12.

Gottman, J. M. (1979). *Marital interaction: Experimental investigations.* New York: Academic Press.

Gottman, J. M. (1982). Emotional responsiveness in marital conversations. *Journal of Communication, 32,* 103–120.

Gottman, J. M. (1993). The roles of conflict engagement, escalation of avoidance in marital interaction: A longitudinal view of five types of couples. *Journal of Consulting and Clinical Psychology, 61,* 6–15.

Gottman, J. M. (1994a). *What predicts divorce?* Hillsdale, NJ: Lawrence Erlbaum.

Gottman, J. M. (1994b). *Why marriages succeed or fail.* New York: Simon and Schuster.

Gottman, J. M. (1994c, May/June). Why marriages fail. *The Family Therapy Networker,* 41–48.

Gottman, J. M. (1999). *The marriage clinic: A scientifically based marital therapy.* New York: W. W. Norton.

Gottman, J. M., Coan, J., Carrere, S., & Swanson, C. (1998). Predicting marital happiness and stability from new interactions. *Journal of Marriage and the Family, 60,* 5–22.

Gottman, J. M., & DeClaire, J. (1997). *The heart of parenting.* New York: Simon and Schuster.

Gottman, J. M., & Krokoff, L. J. (1989). Marital interaction and satisfaction: A longitudinal view. *Journal of Consulting and Clinical Psychology, 57,* 47–52.

Gottman, J. M., & Krokoff, L. J. (1990). Complex statistics are not always clearer than simple statistics: A reply to Woody and Costenzo. *Journal of Consulting and Clinical Psychology, 58,* 502–505.

Gottman, J. M., Ryan, K. D., Carrère, S., & Erley, A. M. (2002). Toward a scientifically based marital therapy. In H. A. Liddle, D. A. Santisteban, R. F. Levant, & J. H. Bray (Eds.), *Family psychology: Science-based interventions* (pp. 147–174). Washington, DC: American Psychological Association.

Grady, D. P. (1997, November). *Conversation strategies for detecting deception: An analysis of parent-adolescent child interactions.* Paper presented at the meeting of the National Communication Association, Chicago.

Graham, E. E. (1997). Turning points and commitment in post-divorce relationships. *Communication Monographs, 64,* 350–368.

Graham, E. E., & Edwards, A. P. (2002, November). *Dialectic characteristics and shadow realities in postmarital relationships.* Paper presented at the meeting of the National Communication Association. New Orleans, LA.

Greeff, A. P., & de Bruyne, T. (2000). Conflict management style and marital satisfaction. *Journal of Sex and Marital Therapy, 26,* 221–224.

Green, R., & Elffers, J. (1998). The laws of power. *Utne Reader, 1,* 78–85.

Griffin, E. (1997). *A first look at communication theory* (3rd ed.). New York: McGraw-Hill.

Grimm-Thomas, K., & Perry-Jenkins, M. (1993). All in a day's work: Job experiences, self-esteem and fathering in working-class families. *Family Relations, 42,* 174–181.

Gringlas, M., & Weinraub, M. (1995). The more things change . . . single parenting revisited. *Journal of Family Issues, 16,* 29–52.

Grzywacz, J. G., Almeida, D. M., & McDonald, D. A. (2002). Spillover and daily reports of work and family stress in the adult labor force. *Family Relations, 51,* 28–36.

Gudykunst, W. B., & Lee, C. M. (2001). An agenda for studying ethnicity and family communication. *Journal of Family Communication, 1*(1), 75–86.

Guenther, R. (1984, April 11). Real estate column. *The Wall Street Journal,* p. 1.

Guerney, B. G. (1977). *Relationship enhancement: Skill training programs for therapy, problem prevention, and enrichment.* San Francisco: Jossey-Bass.

Guerrero, L. K., & Afifi, W. (1995). What parents don't know: Topic avoidance in parent-child relationships. In T. J. Socha & G. H. Stamp (Eds.), *Parents, children and communication* (pp. 219–245). Mahwah, NJ: Lawrence Erlbaum.

Guerrero, L. K., & Andersen, P. A. (1998). The dark side of jealousy and envy: Desire, delusion, desperation, and destructive communication. In B. H. Spitzberg & W. R. Cupach (Eds.), *The dark side of close relationships* (pp. 33–40). Mahwah, NJ: Lawrence Erlbaum.

Guerrero, L. K., & Andersen, P. A. (2000). Emotion in close relationships. In C. Hendrick & S. S. Hendrick (Eds.), *Close relationships: A sourcebook* (pp. 171–183). Thousand Oaks, CA: Sage.

Guerrero, L. K., Andersen, P. A., & Afifi, W. A. (2001). *Close encounters: Communicating in relationships.* Mountain View, CA: Mayfield.

Gunter, N., & Gunter, B. G. (1990). Domestic division of labor among working couples. *Psychology of Women Quarterly, 14,* 355–370.

Gurman, A., & Kniskern, D. (Eds.). (1991). *Handbook of family therapy* (Vol. II). New York: Brunner/Mazel.

Haas, S. (2002). Social support as relationship maintenance in gay male couples coping with HIV or AIDS. *Journal of Social and Personal Relationships, 19,* 87–111.

Haas, S. M., & Stafford, L. (1998). An initial examination of maintenance behaviors in gay and lesbian relationships. *Journal of Social and Personal Relationships, 15,* 846–855.

Haefner, P., Notarius, C., & Pellegrini, D. (1991). Determinants of satisfaction with marital discussions. An exploration of husband-wife differences. *Behavioral Assessments, 13,* 67–82.

Hafner, K. (2002, January 24). Drawn to the hearth's electronic glow. *The New York Times,* pp. D1, D7.

Hahlweg, K., & Markman, H. (1988). The effectiveness of behavioral marital therapy: Empirical status of behavioral techniques in preventing and alleviating marital distress. *Journal of Consulting and Clinical Psychology, 56,* 440–447.

Halford, W. K., Sanders, M. R., & Behrens, B. C. (2000). Repeating the errors of our parents? Family-of-origin spouse violence and observed conflict management in enraged couples. *Family Process, 39*(2), 219–235.

Hall, D. L., & Langellier, K. M. (1988). Storytelling strategies in mother-daughter communication. In B. Bate & A. Taylor (Eds.), *Women communicating: Studies of women's talk* (pp. 107–126). Norwood, NJ: Ablex.

Hall, E. T. (1966). *The hidden dimension.* Golden City, NY: Doubleday.

Hamby, S. L., Poindexter, V. C., & Gray-Little, B. (1996). Four measures of partner violence: Construct similarity and classification differences. *Journal of Marriage and the Family, 58,* 127–139.

Hamlin, S. (1995, September 6). Time flies, but where does it go? *The New York Times,* pp. B1, B4.

Hample, D., & Dallinger, J. (1995). A Lewian perspective on taking conflict personally: Revision, refinement, and validation of the instrument. *Communication Quarterly, 43,* 297–319.

Handel, G., & Whitchurch, G. (Eds.). (1994). *The psychological interior of the family.* Hawthorne, NY: Aldine de Gruyter.

Hare-Mustin, R. (1989). The problem of gender in family therapy theory. In M. McGoldrick, C. Anderson, & F. Walsh (Eds.), *Women in families* (pp. 61–77). New York: W. W. Norton.

Hare-Mustin, R. (1994). Discourses in a mirrored room: A postmodern analysis of therapy. *Family Process, 33,* 19–36.

Harevan, T. (1982). American families in transition: Historical perspective on change. In F. Walsh (Ed.), *Normal family processes* (pp. 446–465). New York: Guilford Press.

Harker, C. (1997, Autumn). Life-saving stories. *Iowa Alumni Quarterly,* 32–34.

Harris, J. R. (1998). *The nurture assumption: Why children turn out the way they do; Parents matter less than you think and peers matter more.* Boston: Free Press.

Hatfield, E., & Rapson, R. (1993). *Love, sex and intimacy.* New York: HarperCollins.

Hawkins, A., & Belsky, J. (1989). The role of father involvement in personality change in men across the transition to parenthood. *Family Relations, 38,* 378–383.

Hawkins, A. J. Gilliland, T. T., & Carroll, J. S. (2002, June). Marriage moments: Strengthening your marriage as you become parents. In *Family Focus On . . . Bridging Research and Practice, 14,* F8–F9.

Hayes, R. L. (1994). The legacy of Lawrence Kohlberg: Implications for counseling and human development. *Journal of Counseling/Development, 72,* 261–267.

Heaton, T. B., & Jacobson, C. K. (1994). Race differences in changing family demographics in the 1980s. *Journal of Family Issues, 15,* 290–308.

Henry, J. (1973). *Pathways to madness.* New York: Vintage Books.

Herz, F. (1980). The impact of death and serious illness on the family life cycle. In E. Carter & M. McGoldrick (Eds.), *The family life cycle: A framework for family therapy* (pp. 223–240). New York: Gardner Press.

Herz-Brown, H. (1988). The post divorce family. In B. Carter & M. McGoldrick (Eds.), *The changing family life cycle: A framework for therapy* (2nd ed., pp. 371–398). New York: Gardner Press.

Hess, R., & Handel, G. (1959). *Family worlds.* Chicago: University of Chicago Press.

Hetherington, E. M. (1987). Family relations six years after divorce. In K. Pasley & M. Inhinger-Tallman (Eds.), *Remarriage and stepparenting: Current research* (pp. 185–205). New York: Guilford Press.

Hetherington, E. M., & Kelly, J. (2002). *For better or for worse: Divorce reconsidered.* New York: W. W. Norton.

Hewlett, S. A. (2002). *Creating a life: Professional women and the quest for children.* New York: Talk Mirimax Books.

Hey, R., & Neubeck, G. (1990). Family life education. In D. H. Olson & M. K. Hanson (Eds.), *2001: Preparing families for the future* (pp. 7–25). Hillsdale, NJ: Lawrence Erlbaum.

Hiedemann, B., Suhomlinova, O., & O'Rand, A. M. (1998). Economic independence, economic status, and empty nest in midlife marital disruption. *Journal of Marriage and the Family, 21,* 219–231.

Hill, R. (1949). *Families under stress.* New York: Harper & Brothers.

Hill, R. (1986). Life cycle stages for types of single parent families: Of family development theory. *Family Relations, 35,* 19–29.

Hilton, B. A., Crawford, J. A., & Tarko, M. A. (2000). Men's perspectives on individual and family coping with their wives' breast cancer and chemotherapy. *Western Journal of Nursing Research, 22*(4), 438–459.

Hines, A. M. (1997). Divorce-related transitions, adolescent development, and the role of the parent-child relationship: A review of the literature. *Journal of Marriage and the Family, 59,* 375–388.

Hines, P. M. (1999). The family life cycle of African-American families living in poverty. In B. Carter & M. McGolderick (Eds.), *The expanded family life cycle* (3rd ed., pp. 327–345). Boston: Allyn and Bacon.

Hines, P. M., & Boyd-Franklin, N. (1996). African-American families. In M. McGoldrick, J. Giordano, & T. K. Pearce (Eds.), *Ethnicity and family therapy* (2nd ed., pp. 66–84). New York: Guilford Press.

Ho, D. Y. F. (1989). Continuity of variation in Chinese patterns of socialization. *Journal of Marriage and the Family, 51,* 149–163.

Hochschild, A. (1989). *The second shift.* New York: Avon Books.

Hochschild, A. (1997, April 10). There's no place like work. Americans say they want more time with their families. The truth is, they'd rather be at the office. *New York Times Magazine,* 51–55, 81–84.

Hochschild, A., & Machung, A. (1998). The working wife as urbanizing peasant. In K. Hanson & A. I. Garey (Eds.), *Family in the U.S.* (pp. 789–790). Philadelphia: Temple University Press.

Hocker, J. L, & Wilmot, W. (1998). Interpersonal conflict. Dubuque, IA: Wm. C. Brown.

Hof, L., & Miller, W. R. (1983). *Marriage enrichment.* Bowie, MD: Brady/Prentice-Hall.

Hoffman, L. (1990). Constructing realities: The art of lenses. *Family Process, 29* (1), 1–12.

Hohn, C. (1987). The family life cycle: Needed extension of the concept. In T. K. Burch & K. W. Wachter (Eds.), *Family demography: Methods and their application* (pp. 156–180). New York: Oxford University Press.

Honeycutt, J. M. (1997, November). *Typological differences in predicting marital happiness from oral history behaviors and imagined interactions.* Paper presented at the meeting of the National Communication Association, Chicago.

Hoopes, M. (1987). Multigenerational systems: Basic assumptions. *American Journal of Family Therapy, 15,* 195–205.

Hoppe-Nagao, A., & Ting-Toomey, S. (2002). Relational dialectics and management strategies in marital couples. *Southern Communication Journal, 67*(20), 142–159.

Hoppough, S. K., & Ames, B. (2001). Death as normative in family life. In *Family focus on . . . . Death and dying* (pp. F1-F2). Minneapolis: National Council in Family Relations.

Horwitz, J., & Tognoli, J. (1982). Role of home in adult development: Women and men living alone describe their residential histories. *Family Relations, 31,* 335–341.

Howard, J. (1978). *Families.* New York: Simon & Schuster.

Hutchinson, K. M., & Cooney, T. (1998). Patterns of parent-teen sexual risk communication: Implications for intervention. *Family Relations, 47,* 185–194.

Hutchinson, M. K. (2002). The influence of sexual risk communication between parents and daughters on sexual risk behaviors. *Family Relations, 51,* 238–247.

Imber-Black, E. (1993). Secrets in families and family therapy: An overview. In E. Imber-Black (Ed.), *Secrets in families and family therapy* (pp. 369–386). New York: Guilford Press.

Imber-Black, E. (1996). Idiosyncratic life cycle transitions and therapeutic rituals. In B. Carter & McGoldrick (Eds.), *The changing family lifecycle* (2nd ed., pp. 149–189). New York: Gardner Press.

Imber-Black, E. (1998). *The secret life of families.* New York: Bantam Books.

Imber-Black, E. (1999). Creating meaningful rituals for new life cycle transitions. In B. Carter & M. McGolderick (Eds.), *The expanded family life cycle* (3rd ed., pp. 202–214). Boston: Allyn and Bacon.

Invik, J., & Fitzpatrick, M. A. (1982). If you could read my mind love. . . . Understanding misunderstanding in the marital dyads. *Family Relations, 31,* 43–52.

Ishii-Kuntz, M. (1994). Paternal involvement and perception toward fathers' roles: A comparison. *Journal of Family Issues, 15,* 30–48.

Isler, L., Popper, T., & Ward, S. (1987, October–November). Children's purchase requests and parental responses. *Journal of Advertising Research, 27,* 28–39.

Jacob, A., & Borzi, M. G. (1996, April). *Foster families and the co-construction of shared experiences: A narrative approach.* Paper presented at the meeting of the Central States Communication Association, Chicago.

Jacobson, N. S., & Gottman, J. M. (1998). *When men batter women: New insights into ending abusive relationships.* New York: Simon & Schuster.

Jaramillo, P., & Zapata, J. (1987). Roles and alliances within Mexican-American & Anglo families. *Journal of Marriage and the Family, 49*(4), 727–735.

Johnson, C., & Vinson, L. (1990). Placement and frequency of powerless talk and impression formation. *Communication Quarterly, 28,* 325–333.

Johnson, M. P. (1995). Patriarchal terrorism and common couple violence: Two forms of violence against women. *Journal of Marriage and the Family, 57,* 283–294.

Johnson, M. P., Caughlin, J. P., & Huston, T. L. (1999). The tripartite nature of marital commitment: Personal, moral, and structural reasons to stay married. *Journal of Marriage and the Family, 61,* 160–177.

Jones, E., & Gallois, C. (1989). Spouses impressions of rules for communication in public and private marital conflicts. *Journal of Marriage and the Family, 51,* 957–967.

Jourard, S. (1971). *The transparent self.* New York: Van Nostrand Reinhold.

Julian, T., McKenry, P., & McKelvey, M. W. (1994). Cultural variations in parenting—Perceptions of Caucasian, African-American, and Asian parents. *Family Relations, 43,* 30–37.

Kalmuss, D., Davidson, A., & Cushman, L. (1992). Parenting expectations, experiences and adjustment to parenthood: A test of the violated expectations framework. *Journal of Marriage and the Family, 54,* 516–526.

Kanter, R. M. (1977). *Men and women of the corporation.* New York: Basic Books.

Kantor, D., & Lehr, W. (1976). *Inside the family.* San Francisco: Jossey-Bass.

Kaplan, L. (2001). A couplehood typology for spouses of institutionalized persons with Alzeheimer's disease: Perceptions of "We"–"I". *Family Relations, 50*(1), 87–98.

Kaplan, L., & Hennon, C. (1992). Remarriage education: Reflections program. *Family Relations, 41,* 127–134.

Kaufman, J. (2002, January 2). Whites and Hispanics fall out over quest for suburban dream. *The Wall Street Journal,* pp. A1, A14.

Kelley, D. (1998). The communication of forgiveness. *Communication Studies, 49,* 255– 271.

Kelley, D. (2003). Communicating forgiveness. In K. M. Galvin & P. J. Cooper (Eds.), Making connections: Reading in relational communication. (3rd ed., pp. 222–232). Los Angeles: Roxbury.

Kellogg, T. (1990). *Broken toys, broken dreams: Understanding and healing boundaries codependence, compulsion and family relationships*. Amherst, MA: BRAT Publishing.

Kelly, D., & Sequeira, D. L. (1997). Understanding family functioning in a changed America. *Communication Studies, 48,* 93–108.

Kelly, D., & Warshafsky, L. (1987). *Partner abuse in gay male and lesbian couples*. Paper presented at the Third National Conference for Family Violence Researchers, Durham, NC.

Kennedy, R. W. (1953). *The house and the art of its design*. New York: Reinhold.

Kibria, N. (1998). Household structure and family ideologies: The case of Vietnamese refugees. In K. V. Hansen & A. I. Garey (Eds.), *Families in the U.S.* (pp. 55–68). Philadelphia: Temple University Press.

Kieren, D. K., Maguire, T. O., & Hurlbut, N. (1996). A marker method to test a phasing hypothesis in family problem-solving interaction. *Journal of Marriage and the Family, 58,* 442–455.

Kilmann, R., & Thomas, K. (1975). Interpersonal conflict handling behavior as reflections of Jungian personality dimensions. *Psychological Reports, 37,* 971–980.

Kim, D. S. (1977). How they fared in American homes: A follow-up study of adopted Korean children in the United States. *Children Today, 6,* 2–6, 36.

Kim, M., Shin, H., & Cai, D. (1998). Cultural influences on prepared forms of requesting and re-requesting. *Communication Monograph, 65,* 47–55.

Kirchler, E. (1988). Marital happiness and interaction in everyday surroundings. *Journal of Social and Personal Relationships, 5,* 375–382.

Kirchler, E. (1993). Spouses' joint purchase decisions: Determinants of influence tactics for muddling through the process. *Journal of Economic Psychology, 14*(2), 405–438.

Kirk, L. (1989, November). *Contemporary family scripts and intergenerational communication*. Paper presented at the meeting of the Speech Communication Association, San Francisco.

Kivett, R. V. (1993). Racial comparisons of the grandmother role. *Family Relations, 42,* 165–172.

Kleiman, C. (1998, January 27). A dream come true: A way to figure out fatigue. *Chicago Tribune*.

Klein, D. M., & White, J. M. (1996). *Family theories: An introduction*. Thousand Oaks, CA: Sage.

Klein, K. E. (2002, March 21). When it's all in the family. *Business Week Online*.

Klein, R. C. A., & Johnson, M. J. (1997). Strategies of couple conflict. In S. Duck (Ed.), *Handbook of personal relationships: Theory, research and interventions* (pp. 307–324). New York: John Wiley.

Kline, S. L., & Clinton, B. L. (1998). Developments in children's persuasive message practices. *Communication Education, 47,* 120–136.

Knapp, M., & Taylor, E. (1994). Commitment and its communication in romantic relationships. In A. Weber & J. Harvey (Eds.), *Perspectives on close relationships* (pp. 153, 175). Boston: Allyn and Bacon.

Knapp, M., & Vangelisti, A. L. (1992). *Interpersonal communication and human relationships* (2nd ed.) Boston: Allyn and Bacon.

Knapp, M., & Vangelisti, A. L. (1996). *Interpersonal communication and human relationships* (3rd ed.). Boston: Allyn and Bacon.

Knapp, M. L., & Vangelisti, A. L. (2000). *Interpersonal communication and human relationships* (4th ed.). Boston: Allyn and Bacon.

Koepke, L., Mare, J., & Moran, P. (1992, April). Relationship quality in a sample of lesbian couples with children and child free. *Family Relations, 41,* 224–229.

Koerner, A. F., & Fitzpatrick, M. A. (2002). You never leave your family in a fight: The impact of family of origin on conflict behavior in romantic relationships. *Communication Studies, 53*(3), 234–251.

Koerner, A. K., & Fitzpatrick, M. A. (1997). Family type and conflict: The impact on conversation orientation and conformity orientation on conflict in the family. *Communication Studies, 48,* 59–74.

Kohlberg, L. (1969). Stage and sequence. The cognitive developmental approach to socialization. In D. Goshen (Ed.), *Handbook of socialization theory and research* (pp. 347–480). Chicago: Rand McNally.

Koppen, M. M. (1997). *Exploring the typology of mother-daughter rituals*. Unpublished paper presented at Northwestern University.

Kraemer, S. (1991). The origins of fatherhood: An ancient family process. *Family Process, 30,* 377–390.

Kramer, J. (1985). *Family interfaces: Transgenerational patterns*. New York: Brunner-Mazel.

Kraut, R., Patterson, M., Lundmark, V., Kiesler, S., Mukopadhyay, T., & Scherlis, W. (1998). A social technology that reduces social involvement and psychological well-being? *American Psychologist, 53*(9), 1017–1031.

Krishnakumar, A., & Buehler, C. (2000). Interparental conflict and parenting behaviors: A meta-analytic review. *Family Relations, 49*(1), 25–44.

Krueger, D. L. (1983). Pragmatics of dyadic decision making: A sequential analysis of communication patterns. *Western Journal of Speech Communication, 47,* 99–117.

Krusiewicz, E. S., & Wood, J. T. (2001). "He was our child from the moment we walked in that room": Entrance stories of adoptive parents. *Journal of Social and Personal Relationships, 18,* 785–803.

Kubler-Ross, E. (1970). *On death and dying.* New York: Macmillan.

Kurdek, L. A. (1989). Relationship quality in gay and lesbian cohabiting couples: A 1-year follow-up study. *Journal of Social and Personal Relationships, 6,* 39–60.

Kurdek, L. A. (1991). The relations between reported well-being and divorce history, availability of a proximate adult, and gender. *Journal of Marriage and the Family, 53,* 71–78.

Kurdek, L. A. (1994). Conflict resolution styles in gay, lesbian, heterosexual nonparent and heterosexual parent couples. *Journal of Marriage and the Family, 56*(3), 705–722.

Labrecque, J., & Ricard, L. (2001). Children's influence on family decision-making: A restaurant study. *Journal of Business Research, 54*(2), 173–176.

Laing, R. D. (1972). *The politics of the family.* New York: Vintage Books.

Laird, J. (1993). Lesbian and gay families. In F. Walsh (Ed.), *Normal family processes* (2nd ed., pp. 282–328). New York: Guilford Press.

Laird, J. (1996). Family-centered practice with lesbian and gay families. *Families in Society. The Journal of Contemporary Human Services,* 559–571.

Landis, D. (1988, January 10). Yours, mine, but no longer ours: Dividing the spoils after divorce. *Chicago Tribune,* sec. 15, pp. 1, 5.

Langellier, K. M. (2002). Performing family stories, forming cultural identity: Franco American memere stories. *Communication Studies, 53*(1), 56–73.

Langhinrichsen-Rohling, J., Smutzler, N., & Vivian, D. (1994). Positivity in marriage: The role of discord and physical aggression against wives. *Journal of Marriage and the Family, 56,* 69–79.

LaRossa, R. (1998). The culture and conduct of fatherhood. In K. V. Hansen & A. I. Garey (Eds.), *Family in the U.S.* (pp. 377–385). Philadelphia: Temple University Press.

LaRossa, R., & Reitzes, D. (1993). Symbolic interactionism and family studies. In P. G. Boss, W. J. Doherty, R. La Rossa, W. R. Schumm, and S. K. Steinmetz (Eds.), *Sourcebook of family theory and methods* (pp. 135–163). New York: Plenum Press.

Larson, J. (1992, July). Understanding stepfamilies. *American Demographics, 14*(7), 36–40.

Lavee, L., Sharlin, S., & Katz, R. (1996). The effect of parenting stress on marital quality: An integrated mother-father model. *Journal of Family Issues, 17,* 114–135.

Lavee, Y., & Olson, D. (1991). Family types and response to stress. *Journal of Marriage and the Family, 53,* 786–798.

Lawlor, J. (1998, April 26). For many blue-collar fathers, child care is shift work, too. *The New York Times,* p. 111.

Lawrence, R. (1987). What makes a house a home? *Environment and Behavior, 19*(2), 154–158.

Lebow, J. (1997). Is couples therapy obsolete? *The Family Therapy Networker, 21,* 81–88.

Lebow, J., & Gurman, A. S. (1996). Making a difference: A new research review offers good news to couples and family therapists. *The Family Networker, 20,* 69–76.

Lederer, W., & Jackson, D. D. (1968). *The mirages of marriage.* New York: W. W. Norton.

Lee, C. (1988). Meta-commentary: On synthesis and fractionation in family theory and research. *Family Process, 27,* 93–97.

Lee, G. R., Netzer, J., & Coward, R. T. (1994). Filial responsibility expectations and patterns of intergenerational assistance. *Journal of Marriage and the Family, 56,* 559–565.

Lee, G. R., Peek, C. W., & Coward, R. T. (1998). Race differences in filial responsibility expectations among older parents. *Journal of Marriage and the Family, 60,* 404–412.

Leeds-Hurwitz, W. (2002). *Wedding as text: Communicating cultural identities through ritual.* Mahwah, NJ: Lawrence Erlbaum.

Lennard, S., & Lennard, H. (1977). Architecture: Effect of territory, boundary, and orientation on family functioning. *Family Process, 16,* 49–66.

Lerner, H. (1989). *The dance of intimacy.* New York: Harper and Row.

Levinson, D. (1978). *The seasons of a man's life.* New York: Ballantine Books.

Lewin, T. (1998, October 14). High schools talk marriage skills. *The New York Times,* p. A22.

Lewis, R. (1998). Boomers may spend their retired time working. *AARP Bulletin, 39,* p. 7.

Littlejohn, S. (1992). *Theories of human communication* (4th ed.). Belmont, CA: Wadsworth.

Littlejohn, S. W. (2002). *Theories of human communication* (7th ed.). Belmont CA: Wadsworth/ Thomson Learning.

Lloyd, S., & Emery, B. (1994). Physically aggressive conflict in romantic relationships. In D. Cahn (Ed.), *Conflict in personal relationships* (pp. 27–46). Hillsdale, NJ: Lawrence Erlbaum.

Lohan, J. A., & Murphy, S. A. (2002). Parents' perceptions of adolescent sibling grief responses after an adolescent or young adult child's sudden, violent death. *Omega, 44*(3), 195–213.

Lorenz, F. O., Simons, R. L., Conger, R. D., Elder, R. H., Johnson, C., & Chao, W. (1997). Married and recently divorced mothers' stressful events and distress: Tracing change across time. *Journal of Marriage and the Family, 59,* 219–232.

Lucchetti, A. E., & Roghaar, L. A. (2001, November). *The dark side of families: Communicating favoritism to children.* Paper presented at the meeting of the National Communication Association, Atlanta, GA.

Mace, D. (1985). The coming revolution in human relationships. *Journal of Social and Personal Relationships, 2,* 81–94.

Macias, M. M., Clifford, S. C., Saylor, C. F., & Kreh, S. M. (2001). Predictors of parenting stress in families of children with spina bifida. *Children's Health Care, 30*(1), 57–65.

Mackey, R. A., Diemer, M. A., & O'Brien, B. A. (2000). Conflict-management styles of spouses in lasting marriages. *Psychotherapy, 37*(2), 134–148.

Maddock, J. (1989). Healthy family sexuality: Positive principles for educators and clinicians. *Family Relations, 38,* 130–136.

Magdol, L., Moffitt, T., Capsi, A., & de Silva, P. (1998) Hitting without a license: Testing explanations for differences in partner abuse between young adult daters and cohabitors. *Journal of Marriage and the Family, 60,* 41–55.

Mahoney, A., Pargament, K. I., Tarakeshwar, N., & Swank, A. B. (2001). Religion in the home in the 1980s and 1990s: A meta-analytic review and conceptual analysis of links between religion, marriage, and parenting. *Journal of Family Psychology, 15,* 559–596.

Malone, T., & Malone, P. (1987). *The art of intimacy.* New York: Prentice-Hall.

Manning L. M. (1996, November). *Adolescents communication concerns.* Paper presented at the meeting of the National Communication Association, San Diego, CA.

Mant, J., Carter, J., Wade, D. T., & Winner, S. (2000). Family support for stroke: A randomised controlled trial. *Lancet, 356*(9232), 808–813.

Marano, H. E. (1997, November/December). New focus on family values. *Psychology Today,* 53–55.

March, K., & Miall, C. (2000) Adoption as a family form. *Family Relations, 49,* 359–362.

Markowitz, L. (1994). The cross-currents of multiculturalism. *The Family Therapy Networker, 18*(4), 18–27, 69.

Marks, S. R., Huston, T. L., Johnson, E. M., & MacDermid, S. M. (2001). Role balance among white married couples. *Journal of Marriage and Family, 63,* 1083–1098.

Marshall, L. (1994). Physical psychological abuse. In W. Cupach & B. Spitzberg (Eds.), *The dark side of inter-personal communication* (pp. 281–311). Hillsdale, NJ: Lawrence Erlbaum.

Marshall, L., & Rose, P. (1988). Family-of-origin violence and courtship abuse. *Journal of Counseling and Development, 66,* 414–418.

Marsiglio, W., & Donnelly, D. (1991). Sexual relations in later life: A national study of married persons. *Journal of Gerontology, 46,* 82–90.

Martin, J., Hecht, M., & Larkey, L. (1994). Conversational improvement strategies for interethnic communication: African-American and European American perspectives. *Communication Monographs, 61*(3), 237–255.

Martinez, E. A. (2001). Death: A family event for Mexican-Americans. In *Family focus on . . . Death and dying.* Issue FF12. Minneapolis: National Council on Family Relations.

Marwell, G., & Schmitt, D. R. (1967). Dimensions of compliance-gaining behavior: An empirical analysis. *Sociometry, 30,* 350–364.

Masheter, C. (1997). Former spouses who are friends: Three case studies. *Journal of Social and Personal Relationships, 14*(2), 207–222.

McAdams, D. (1993). *Stories we live by: Personal myths and the making of the self.* New York: William Morrow.

McCroskey, J. C. (1997, November). *Why we communicate the ways we do: A communibiological perspective.* The Carroll C. Arnold Distinguished Lecture presented at the meeting of the National Communication Association, Chicago.

McCubbin, H. I., & Patterson, J. (1983a). The family stress process: The double ABCX model of adjustment and adaptation. In H. McCubbin, M. Sussman, & J. Patterson (Eds.), *Social stress and the family: Advances and developments in family stress theory and research* (pp. 7–37). New York: Haworth Press.

McCubbin, H. I., & Patterson, J. M. (1983b). Family transitions: Adaptation to stress. In H. I. McCubbin & C. R. Figley (Eds.), *Coping with normative transitions* (Vol. I, pp. 5–25). New York: Brunner/Mazel.

McCubbin, H. I., Patterson, J. M., Cauble, A. E., Wilson, W. R., & Warwick, W. (1983). CHIP-coping health inventory for parents: An assessment of parental coping patterns in the case of the chronically ill. *Journal of Marriage and the Family, 45,* 359–370.

McCullough, P. G., & Rutenberg, S. K. (1988). Launching children and moving on. In B. Carter & M. McGoldrick (Eds.), *The changing family life cycle* (2nd ed., pp. 285–309). New York: Gardner Press.

McDonald, G. W. (1980). Family power: The assessment of a decade of theory and research, 1970–1979. *Journal of Marriage and the Family, 42,* 841–852.

McGoldrick, M. (1993, October 12). *You can go home again.* Lecture at Family Institute, Northwestern University, Chicago.

McGoldrick, M. (1994). The ache for home. *The Family Therapy Networker, 18*(4), 38–45.

McGoldrick, M. (1995). *You can go home again: Reconnecting with your family.* New York: W. W. Norton

McGoldrick, M., Anderson, C., & Walsh, F. (Eds.). (1989). *Women in families.* New York: W. W. Norton.

McGoldrick, M., Garcia-Preto, N., Hines, P. M., & Lee, E. (1991). Ethnicity and family therapy.

In A. German & D. Kniskern (Eds.), *Handbook of family therapy* (Vol. II, pp. 546–582). New York: Brunner/Mazel.

McGoldrick, M., & Gerson, R. (1985). *Genograms in family assessment.* New York: W. W. Norton.

McGoldrick, M., & Walsh, F. (1999). Death and the family life cycle. In B. Carter & M. M. Goldrick (Eds.), *The expanded family life cycle* (3rd ed., pp. 185–201). Boston: Allyn and Bacon.

McLaughlin, B. (1983). Child compliance to parental control techniques. *Developmental Psychology, 19*(5), 667–673.

McWhirter, D. P., & Mattison, A. M. (1984). *The male couple.* Englewood Cliffs, NJ: Prentice-Hall.

Mederer, H., & Hill, R. (1983). Cultural transitions over the family span: Theory and research. In H. McCubbin et al. (Eds.), *Social stress and the family* (pp. 39–60). New York: Hayworth Press.

Menees, M. C. (1996, April). *Social support, and family communication: Do they impact the self-esteem of children of alcoholics?* Paper presented at the meeting of the Central States Communication Association.

Meyer, C. (1987). Stress: There's no place like a first home. *Family Relations, 36,* 198–203.

Meyer, D. R., & Bartfeld, J. (1996). Compliance with child support orders in divorce cases. *Journal of Marriage and the Family, 58,* 201–212.

Michall-Johnson, P., & Bowen, S. (1989). AIDS and communication: Matter of influence. *AIDS and Public Policy Journal, 4,* 1–3.

Miller, K., & Zook, E. G. (1997). Care partners for persons with AIDS: Implications for health communication. *Journal of Applied Communication Research, 25,* 57–74.

Minow, M. (1998). Redefining families: Who's in and who's out? In K. V. Hansen & A. I. Garey (Eds.), *Families in the U.S.* (pp. 7–19). Philadelphia: Temple University Press.

Minton, C., & Pasley, K. (1996). Fathers' parenting role identity and father involvement: A comparison of nondivorced and divorced, nonresident fathers. *Journal of Family Issues, 17,* 26–45.

Minuchin, S. (1974). *Families and family therapy.* Cambridge, MA: Harvard University Press.

Minuchin, S. (1984). *Family kaleidoscope.* Cambridge, MA: Harvard University Press.

Mitchell, B. A., & Gee, E. M. (1996). "Boomerang kids" and midlife parental marital satisfaction. *Family Relations, 45,* 442–448.

Monsma, J. W., & Monsma, M. L. (1996, November). *Stability and commitment through ongoing couple mentoring.* Paper presented at the meeting of the Speech Communication Association, San Diego, CA.

Montgomery, B. M. (1992). Communication as the interface between couples and culture. In S. Deeter (Ed.), *Communications Yearbook, 15* (pp. 476–508). Newbury Park, CA: Sage.

Montgomery, B. M. (1994). Communication in close relationships. In A. Weber & J. Harvey (Eds.), *Perspectives on close relationships* (pp. 67–87). Boston: Allyn and Bacon.

Morgaine, C. (1992). Alternative paradigms for helping families change themselves. *Family Relations, 41,* 12–17.

Mott, F. L. (1994). Sons, daughters and fathers' absence: Differentials in father-leaving probabilities and in home environments. *Journal of Family Issues, 15,* 97–128.

Mott, F. L., Kowaleski-Jones, L., & Menaghan, E. G. (1997). Paternal absence and child behavior: Does a child's gender make a difference? *Journal of Marriage and the Family, 59,* 103–118.

Murphy, S. A., Johnson, L. C., Lohan, J., & Tapper, V. J. (2002). Bereaved parents' use of individual, family, and community resources 4 to 60 months after a child's violent death. *Family & Community Health, 25*(1), 71–82.

Myerhoff, B. (1984). Rites and signs of ripening: The intertwining of ritual, time, and growing older. In D. Kertzer & J. Keith (Eds.), *Age and Anthropological Theory* (p. 306). Ithaca, NY: Cornell University Press.

Myers, S. A., and Members of COM 200. (2001). Relational maintenance behaviors in the sibling relationship. *Communication Quarterly, 49,* 19–34.

National Center for Health Statistics. (2001, May 24). *43 percent of first marriages break up within 15 years.* http://www.cdc.gov/nchs/releases/01news/firstmarr.htm.

National Council on Family Relations. (1998). Annual Report. Minneapolis.

Neugarten, B., & Weinstein, K. K. (1964). The changing American grandparent. *Journal of Marriage and the Family, 26,* 199–204.

Newton, D. A., & Burgoon, J. K. (1990). The use and consequences of verbal influence strategies during interpersonal disagreements.

Human Communication Research, 16(4), 477–518.

Nichols, M. (1984). *Family therapy: Concepts and methods.* New York: Gardner Press.

Nicholson, J. H. (1999, November). *Sibling alliance rules.* Paper presented at the annual meeting of the National Communication Association, Chicago.

Niedzwiecki, C. K. (1997, November). *The influence of affect and attribution on the outcome of parent-adolescent communication in decision-making.* Paper presented at the meeting of the National Communication Association, Chicago.

Nippert-Eng, C. E. (1996). *Home and work.* Chicago: University of Chicago Press.

Noller, P. (1995). Parent-adolescent relationships. In M. Fitzpatrick & A. Vangelisti (Eds.), *Explaining family interactions* (pp. 77–111). Thousand Oaks, CA: Sage.

Noller, P., & Fitzpatrick, M. A. (1993). *Communication in family relationships.* Englewood Cliffs, NJ: Prentice-Hall.

Noone, R. (1989). Systems thinking and differentiation of self. *Center for Family Communication Consultation Review, 1*(1).

Nordheimer, J. (1996, May 19). Elderly get a needed assist with hybrid housing. *Chicago Tribune,* sec. 16, pp. 1K, 7K.

Nussbaum, J. F., Pecchioni, L. L., Baringer, D. K., & Kundrat, A. L. (2002). Lifespan communication. In W. B. Gudykinst (Ed.), *Communication Yearbook, 26* (pp. 366–389). Mahwah NJ: Lawrence Erlbaum.

O'Connor, T. G., Hetherington, E. M., & Clingempeel, W. G. (1997). Systems and bidirectional influences in families. *Journal of Social and Personal Relationships, 14,* 491–504.

O'Leary, K. D., Malone, J., & Tyree, A. (1994). Physical aggression in early marriage: Prerelationship and relationship effects. *Journal of Consulting and Clinical Psychology, 62*(3), 594–602.

Ochs, E., & Taylor, C. (1992). Family narrative as political activity. *Discourse and Society, 3*(3), 301–340.

Olson, D., Lavee, Y., & McCubbin, H. (1998). Types of families and family response to stress across the family life cycle. In J. Aldous & D. Klein (Eds.), *Social stress and family development* (pp. 16–43). New York: Guilford Press.

Olson, D. H. (1997). Family stress and coping: A multisystem perspective. In S. Dreman (Ed.),

The family on the threshold of the 21st century (pp. 259–282). Mahwah, NJ: Lawrence Erlbaum.

Olson, D. H. (2000). Circumplex model of marital and family systems. *Journal of Family on . . . Death and dying* (p. F4). Minneapolis: National Council in Family

Olson, D. H., McCubbin, H., & Associates. (1983). *Families: What makes them work.* Beverly Hills: Sage.

Olson, D. H., Russell, C., & Sprenkle, D. (Eds.). (1983). *Circumplex model: Systematic assessment and treatment of families.* New York: Haworth Press.

Olson, D. H., Sprenkle, D., & Russell, C. (1979). Circumplex model of marital and family systems: Cohesion and adaptability dimensions, family types, and clinical applications. *Family Process, 18,* 3–28.

Olson, L. N. (2002). Exploring "Common Couple Violence" in heterosexual romantic relationships. *Western Journal of Communication, 66*(1), 104–128.

Olson, L. N., & Golish, T. D. (2002). Topics of conflict and patterns of aggression in romantic relationships. *Southern Communication Journal, 67*(2), 180–200.

Ono, H. (1998). Husbands' and wives' resources and marital dissolution. *Journal of Marriage and the Family, 60,* 674–689.

Oppenheim, D., Wamboldt, F. S., Gavin, L. A., Renouf, A. G., & Emde, R. N. (1996). Couples' co-construction of the story of their child's birth: Associations with marital adaptation. *Journal of Narrative and Life History, 6*(1), 1–21.

Orbuch, T., Veroff, J., & Holmberg, D. (1993). Becoming a married couple: The emergence of the meaning in the first year of marriage. *Journal of Marriage and the Family, 55,* 815–826.

Orford, J. (2001). Ways of coping and the health of relatives facing drug and alcohol problems in Mexico and England. *Addiction, 96*(5), 761–774.

Osmond, H. (1970). Function as the basis of psychiatric ward design. In H. Proshansky, W. Ittleson, & L. Rivlin (Eds.), *Environmental psychology* (pp. 560–588). New York: Holt, Rinehart & Winston.

Palan, K. M., & Wilkes, R. E. (1997). Adolescent-parent interaction in family decision making. *Journal of Consumer Research, 24*(2), 159–169.

Papernow, P. (1984). The stepfamily cycle: An experiential model of stepfamily development. *Family Relations, 33,* 335–363.

Papernow, P. (1993). *Becoming a stepfamily.* San Francisco: Jossey-Bass.

Papp, P. (1983). *The process of change.* New York: Guilford Press.

Parke, R. D. (2002). Parenting in the new millennium: Prospects, promises, and pitfalls. In J. S. McHale & W. S. Grolnick (Eds.), *Retrospect and prospect in the psychological study of families* (pp. 65–93). Mahwah, NJ: Lawrence Erlbaum.

Pasley, K. (1997). Family boundary ambiguity: Perceptions of adult stepfamily members. In K. Pasley & M. Ihninger-Tallman (Eds.), *Remarriage and stepparenting: Current research* (pp. 206–224). New York: Guilford Press.

Patillo-McCoy, M. (1999). *Black picket fences: Privilege and peril among the Black middle class.* Chicago: University of Chicago Press.

Patterson, C. J. (2000). Family relationships of lesbians and gay men. *Journal of Marriage and the Family, 62,* 1052–1069.

Patterson, D., & Schwartz, P. (1994). The social construction of conflicts in intimate same-sex couples. In D. Cahn (Ed.), *Conflict in personal relationships* (pp. 3–26). Hillsdale, NJ: Lawrence Erlbaum.

Patterson, J. M. (2002). Integrating family resilience and family stress theory. *Journal of Marriage and Family, 64,* 349–360.

Pawlowski, D. R. (1996, April). *Jelly beans and yo-yos: Perceptions of metaphors and dialectical tensions within the family.* Paper presented at the meeting of the Central State Communication Association, Minneapolis, MN.

Pearce, W. B., & Sharp, S. M. (1973). Self-disclosing communication. *Journal of Communication, 23,* 409–425.

Pearson, J. (1989). *Communication in the family.* New York: Harper & Row.

Pearson, J. (1992). *Lasting love.* Dubuque, IA: Wm. Brown.

Pearson, J. C., West, R., & Turner, L. H. (1995). *Gender and communication.* Madison, WI: Brown & Benchmark.

Pecchioni, L. L., & Nussbaum, J. F. (2001). Mother-adult daughter discussions of caregiving prior to dependency: Exploring concepts among European-American women. *Journal of Family Communication, 1,* 133–149.

Peck, J., & Manocherian, J. (1988). Divorce in the changing family life cycle. In B. Carter & M. McGoldrick (Eds.), *The changing family life cycle* (2nd ed., pp. 335–369). New York: Gardner Press.

Peddle, N., & Wang, C.. (2001). Current trends in child abuse prevention, reporting and fatalities: The 1999 fifty state survey. National Center on Child Abuse Prevention Research. ⟨http://www.preventchildabuse.org/learnmore/ research docs/199950 survey. pdf⟩.

Pelias, R. J. (1996). *Naming men: The business of performing manly*. Paper presented at the meeting of the Central States Communication Association, St. Paul, MN.

Pennebaker, J. W. (1990). *Opening up: The healing power of confiding in others*. New York: William Morrow.

Pennington, B. A. (1997, November). *Pecked to death by ducks: Managing dialectical tensions in the mother-adolescent daughter relationship*. Paper presented at the meeting of the National Communication Association, Chicago.

Peplau, L. A., Veniegas, R. C., Campbell, S. M. (1996). Gay and lesbian relationships. In R. C. Savin-Williams & K. M. Cohen (Eds.), *The lives of lesbians, gays, and bisexuals: Children to adults* (pp. 250–273). New York: Harcourt Brace.

Perlmutter, M. (1988). Enchantment of siblings: Effects of birth order on family myth. In M. Kahn & K. Lewis (Eds.), *Siblings in therapy* (pp. 25–45). New York: W. W. Norton.

Peterson, G., Madden-Derdich, D., & Leonard, S. A. (2000). Parent-child relations across the life course. In S. J. Prece, P. C. McKenry, & M. J. Murphy (Eds.), *Families across time: A life course perspective* (pp. 187–203). Los Angeles: Roxbury.

Petronio, S. (1991). Communication boundary management: A theoretical model of managing disclosure of private information between married couples. *Communication Theory, 1,* 311–335.

Petronio, S. (1994). Privacy binds in family interactions: The case of parental privacy invasion. In W. R. Cupach & B. H. Spitzberg (Eds.), *The darkside of interpersonal communication* (pp. 241–257). Mahwah, NJ: Lawrence Erlbaum.

Petronio, S. (2000). The boundaries of privacy: Praxis of everyday life. In S. Petronio (Ed.), *Balancing the secrets of private disclosures* (pp. 37–49). Mahwah, NJ: Lawrence Erlbaum.

Petronio, S. (2002). *Boundaries of privacy: Dialectics of disclosure*. Albany: State University of New York Press.

Petronio, S., & Braithwaite, D. O. (1993). The contributions and challenges of family communication to the field of communication. *Journal of Applied Communication Research, 21*(1), 103–110.

Petronio, S., Jones, S., & Morr, M. C. (1999, November). *Family privacy dilemmas: A communication boundary management perspective*. Paper presented at the meeting of the National Communication Association Convention, Chicago.

Petronio, S., Reeder, H. M., Hecht, M. L., & Mon't Ros-Mendoza, T. (1996). Disclosure of sexual abuse by children and adolescents. *Journal of Applied Communication Research, 24,* 181–199.

Petronio, S. (1991). Communication boundary management: A theoretical model of managing disclosure of private information between married couples. *Communication Theory, 1,* 311–335.

Pickerd, M. (1998). Fatherhood in contemporary society. *Family Relations, 47,* 205–208.

Pilkington, C., & Richardson, D. (1988). Perceptions of risk in intimacy. *Journal of Social and Personal Relationships, 5,* 503–508.

Pinsof, W. M. (1995). *Integrative problem-centered therapy*. New York: Basic Books.

Pinsof, W. M. (1997). *Interview in family communication*. Teleclass, available from PBS Adult Learning Satellite Service, 1320 Braddock Pl., Alexandria, VA.

Pinsof, W. M., & Hambright, A. B. (2002). Toward prevention and clinical relevance: A preventive intervention model for family therapy research and practice. In H. Liddle, D. Santisteban, R. Levant, & J. Bray (Eds.), *Family psychology: Science-based intervention* (pp. 177–195). Washington, D.C.: American Psychological Association.

Pinsof, W. M., & Wynne, L. (Eds.). (1995). *The Journal of Marital and Family Therapy, 21,* 339–610.

Pinson-Millburn, N., Fabrian, E. S., Schlosberg, N., & Pyle, M. (1996). Grandparents raising grandchildren. *Journal of Counseling & Development, 74,* 548–554.

Pipher, M. (1996). *The shelter of each other: Rebuilding our families*. New York: Ballantine Books.

Pistole, M. C. (1994). Adult attachment styles: Some thoughts on closeness-distance struggles. *Family Process, 33*(2), 147–159.

Pleck, J. (1992). Pleck discusses work-family issues. *National Council on Family Relations Report, 37,* 1–4. Minneapolis.

Plunkett, S. W., Henry, C. S., & Knaub, P. K. (1999). Family stressor events, family coping, and adolescent adaption in farm and ranch families. *Adolescence, 34*(133), 147–168.

Pogrebin, L. (1992, November 29). To tell the truth. *New York Times Magazine,* 22–23.

Pollan, M. (1997, December 14). Town-building is no Mickey Mouse operation. *New York Times Magazine,* 56–63, 76–81, 88.

Prager K. J., & Buhrmester, D. (1998). Intimacy and need fulfillment in couple relationships. *Journal of Social and Personal Relationships. 15,* 435–469.

Preto, N. G. (1999). Transformation of the family system during adolescence. In B. Carter & M. McGolderick (Eds.), *The expanded family life cycle* (3rd ed., pp. 274–286). Boston: Allyn and Bacon.

Price, S. J., McKenry, P. C., & Murphy, M. J. (2000). *Families across time: A life course perspective*. Los Angeles: Roxbury.

Quittner, J. (2002, July 9). Where will they live? *Advocate,* 27–25.

Radina, M. E., & Armer, J. M. (2001). Post-breast cancer lymphedema and the family: A qualitative investigation of families coping with chronic illness. *Journal of Family Nursing, 7*(3), 281–299.

Ragsdale, J. D. (1996). Gender, satisfaction level, and the use of relational maintenance strategies in marriage. *Communication Monographs, 63,* 354–369.

Rampage, C. (1992). Family therapy and violence toward women: A feminist perspective. *The Family Institute News, 1*(1), 4–5.

Ratner, P. A. (1998). Modeling acts of aggression and dominance as wife abuse and exploring adverse health effects. *Journal of Marriage and the Family, 60,* 453–465.

Raush, H. L., Barry, W. A., Hertel, R. K., & Swain, M. A. (1974). *Communication conflict and marriage*. San Francisco: Jossey-Bass.

Rawlins, W. K. (1992). *Friendship matters*. New York: Aldine de Gruyter.

Reilly, T., Entwisle, D., & Doering, S. (1987). Socialization into parenthood: A longitudinal study of the development of self-evaluation. *Journal of Marriage and the Family, 49*(2), 295–309.

Reiss, D. (1981). *The family's construction of reality*. Cambridge, MA: Harvard University Press.

Reitz, M., & Watson, K. W. (1992). *Adoption and the family system*. New York: Guilford Press.

Renick, M., Blumberg, S. L., & Markman, H. J. (1992). The prevention and relationship enhancement program (PREP): An empirically based preventive intervention program for couples. *Family Relations, 41,* 141–147.

Renzetti, C. (1989). Building a second closet: Third party responses to victims of lesbian partner abuse. *Family Relations, 38,* 157–163.

Reuter, M. A., & Conger, R. D. (1995). Antecedents of parent adolescent disagreement. *Journal of Marriage and the Family, 57,* 435–448.

Robinson, L., & Blanton, P. (1993). Marital strengths in enduring marriages. *Family Relations, 42,* 38–45.

Rogers, E., Castleton, A., & Lloyd, S. (1996). Relational control and physical aggression in satisfying marital relationships. In D. Cahn & S. Lloyd (Eds.), *Family violence from a communications perspective* (pp. 218–239). Thousand Oaks, CA: Sage.

Rogers, R., & White, J. (1993). Family development theory. In P. Boss, W. Doherty, R. LaRossa, W. Shumm, & S. Steimmetz (Eds.), *Sourcebook of family theories of methods* (pp. 225–254). New York: Plenum Press.

Rogers-Millar, L. E., & Millar, F. E. (1979). Domineeringness and dominance: A transactional view. *Human Communication Research, 5,* 238–246.

Rohlfing, M. E. (1995). "Doesn't anybody stay in one place anymore?" An exploration of the understudied phenomenon of long-distance relationships. In J. T. Wood & S. Duck (Eds.), *Understudied relationships: Off the beaten track* (pp. 173–196). Thousand Oaks, CA: Sage

Roloff, M. (1987). Communication conflict. In C. Berger & S. Chafee (Eds.), *Handbook of communication science* (pp. 484–534). Beverly Hills: Sage.

Roloff, M. (1996). The catalyst hypothesis: Condition under which coercive communication leads to physical aggression. In D. Cahn & S. Floyd (Eds.), *Family violence from a communication perspective* (pp. 20–36). Thousand Oaks, CA: Sage.

Roper Reports. (2001, June). *The changing face of Hispanic culture in America.* New York: Roper Starch Worldwide Inc.

Rosen, E. J., & Weltman, S. F. (1996). Jewish families: An overview. In M. McGoldrick, J. Giordano, & J. K. Pearce (Eds.), *Ethnicity and family therapy* (2nd ed., pp. 611–630). New York: Guilford Press.

Rosenbaum, J. (1995). Beat the clock. *American Health, 14*(10), 70–74.

Rosenfeld, R. (1986). U.S. farm women: Their participation in farm work and decision making. *Work & Occupations,* 13, 179–202.

Ross, C. (1991). Marriage and the sense of control. *Journal of Marriage and the Family, 53,* 831–838.

Rossi, A., & Rossi, P. (1990). *Of human bonding: Parents child relations across the life course.* New York: Aldine de Gruyter.

Roxema, H. J. (1986). Defensive communication climate as a barrier to sex education in the home. *Family Relations, 35,* 531–537.

Rubin, L. (2001). Getting younger while getting older: Building families at midlife. In R. Hertz & N. L. Marshall (Eds.), *Working families* (pp. 58–71). Berkeley: University of California Press.

Rusbult, C. E., Drigotas, S. M., & Verette, J. (1994). An interdependence analysis of commitment processes and relationship maintenance phenomena. In D. J. Canary & L. Stafford (Eds.), *Communication and relational maintenance* (pp. 115–139). San Diego: Academic Press.

Russo, F. (2002, January). Buddy system. *Time,* pp. G1–G3.

Rutter, M. (2002). Family influences on behavior and development: Challenges for the future. In J. P. McHale & W. S. Grolnick (Eds.), *Retrospect and prospect in the psychological study of families* (pp. 321–351). Mahwah, NJ: Lawrence Erlbaum.

Sabourin, T. (1992, November). *Dialectical tensions in family life: A comparison of abusive and nonabusive families.* Paper presented at the meeting of the Speech Communication Association, Chicago.

Sabourin, T. (1994). *The role of negative reciprocity in spouse abuse: A relational control analysis.* Cincinnati, OH: Dept. of Communication, University of Cincinnati.

Sabourin, T. (1996). The role of communication in verbal abuse between spouses. In D. Cahn & S. Lloyd (Eds.), *Family violence from a communication perspective* (pp. 199–217). Thousand Oaks, CA: Sage.

Sabourin, T., Infante, D., & Rudd, J. (1990, November). *Argumentativeness and verbal aggression in interspousal violence: A test of the argumentative skill deficiency model using couple data.* Paper presented at the meeting of the Speech Communication Association, Chicago.

Sanderson, B., & Kurdek, L. A. (1993). Race and gender as moderator variables in predicting relationship satisfaction and relationship commitment in a sample of dating heterosexual couples. *Family Relations, 42,* 263–267.

Sandmaier, M. (1997). Love for the long haul. *Family Therapy Networker, 21,* 22–35.

Saphir, M. N., & Chaffee, S. H. (2002). Adolescents' contributions to family communication patterns. *Human Communication Research, 28*(1), 86–108.

Satir, V. (1988). *The new peoplemaking.* Mountain View, CA: Science and Behavior Books.

Scanzoni, J. (1972). *Sexual bargaining.* Englewood Cliffs, NJ: Prentice-Hall.

Scanzoni, J., & Polonko, K. (1980). A conceptual approach to explicit marital negotiation. *Journal of Marriage and the Family, 42,* 31–44.

Schaeffer, H. R., & Crook, C. K. (1980). Child compliance and maternal control techniques. *Developmental Psychology, 16*(1), 54–61.

Schaninger, C. M., & Buss, W. C. (1986). A longitudinal comparison of consumption and finance handling between happily married and divorced couples. *Journal of Marriage and the Family, 48,* 129–136.

Scheflen, A. (1971). Living space in an urban ghetto. *Family Process, 10,* 429–449.

Schellenbarger, S. (2002, February 13). Americans are spending so much time in cars, living takes a back seat. *The Wall Street Journal,* p. B6.

Schemco, D. J. (November 10, 2001). In covenant marriage, forging ties that bind. North Little Rock, Ark. *The New York Times,* sect. A, p. 10.

Schnarch, C. M. (1991). *Constructing the sexual crucible: An integration of sexual and marital therapy*. New York: W. W. Norton.

Schock, A. M., Gavazzi, S. M., Fristad, M. A., & Goldberg-Arnold, J. S. (2002). The role of father participation in the treatment of childhood mood disorders. *Family Relations, 51,* 230–237.

Schonpflug, U. (2001). Decision-making influence in the family: A comparison of Turkish Families in Germany and in Turkey. *Journal of Comparative Family Studies,* 219–230.

Schrimshaw, E. W., & Siegel, K. (2002). HIV-infected mothers' disclosure to their uninfected children: Rates, reasons, and reactions. *Journal of Social and Personal Relationships, 19,* 19–43.

Schwartz, P. (1994). *Peer marriage*. New York: Free Press.

Schwartz, S. J., & Liddle, H. A. (2001). The transmission of psychopathology from parents to offspring: Development and treatment in context. *Family Relations, 50,* 301–307.

Scoresby, A. L. (1977). *The marriage dialogue*. Reading, MA: Addison-Wesley.

Scott, J. (1984). Comfort and seating distance in living rooms. The relationship of interactants and topic for conversation. *Environment and Behavior, 16,* 35–54.

Scott, J. (2002, February 7). Foreign born in U.S. at record high. *The New York Times,* p. A18.

Seccombe, K. (2000). Families in poverty in the 1990s: Trends, causes, consequences, and lessons learned. *Journal of Marriage and the Family, 62,* 1094–1113.

Seligman, M. (1988). Psychotherapy with siblings of disabled children. In M. Kahn & L. Lewis (Eds.), *Siblings in therapy: Life span and clinical issues* (pp. 167–189). New York: W. W. Norton.

Seltzer, J. (1991). Relationships between father & children who live apart: The father's role after separation. *Journal of Marriage and the Family, 53,* 79–98.

Selzer, J. (2000). Families formed outside of marriage. *Journal of Marriage and the Family, 62,* 1247–1268.

Serovich, J. M. (2001). The role of family and friend social support in reducing emotional distress among HIV-positive women. *AIDS Care, 13*(3), 335–341.

Sexton, C. S., & Perlman, D. S. (1989). Couples' career orientation, gender role orientation, and perceived equity as determinants of marital power. *Journal of Marriage and the Family, 51*(4), 933–941.

Sheehy, G. (1998, April 26). How to age well. *Parade,* pp. 4–5.

Sheehy, M. (1997). *Interview in family communication*. Teleclass, available from PBS Adult Learning Satellite Service, 1320 Braddock Pl., Alexandria, VA.

Sherrod, P. (2001, February 25). Room to grow. *Chicago Tribune,* sec. 15, pp. 1, 6.

Shreve, B., & Kunkel, M. (1991). Self-psychology, shame and adolescent suicide: Theoretical and practical considerations. *Journal of Counseling and Development, 69,* 305–312.

Sieburg, E. (1973). *Interpersonal confirmation: A paradigm for conceptualization and measurement*. Paper presented at the meeting of the International Communication Association, Montreal, Quebec. (ERIC document No. ED 098 634 1975.)

Silber, K., & Dorner, P. M. (1990). *Children of open adoption*. San Antonio, TX: Corona.

Sillars, A., Roberts, L. J., Leonard, K. E., & Dun, T. (2000). Cognition during marital conflict: The relationship of thought and talk. *Journal of Social and Personal Relationships, 17,* 479–502.

Sillars, A. L. (1980). The stranger and the spouse as target persons for compliance-gaining strategies: A subjective expected utility model. *Human Communication Research, 6,* 265–279.

Sillars, A. L. (1995). Communication and family culture. In M. A. Fitzpatrick & A. L. Vangelisti (Eds.), *Explaining family interactions* (pp. 375–399). Thousand Oaks, CA: Sage.

Sillars, A. L., Weisberg, J., Burggraf, C., & Wilson, E. (1987). Content themes in marital conversations. *Human Communication Research, 13,* 495–528.

Sillars, A. L., & Wilmot, W. (1989). Marital communication across the life span. In J. Nussbaum (Ed.), *Life-span communication: Narrative processes* (pp. 225–254). Hillsdale, NJ: Lawrence Erlbaum.

Silliman, B., Stanley, S. M., Coffin, W., Markman, H. J., & Jordan, P. L. (2002). Preventive interventions for couples. In H. A. Liddle, D. A. Santisteban, R. F. Levant, & J. H. Bray (Eds.), *Family psychology: Science-based interventions* (pp. 123–146). Washington, DC: American Psychological Association.

Silverberg, L., & Steinberg, L. (1987). Adolescent autonomy, parent-adolescent conflict and parental well-being. *Journal of Youth and Adolescence, 16,* 293–312.

Silverman, C. (1992). Neighborhood life, communication and the metropolis. *Asia Journal of Communication, 2*(3), 92–105.

Simmons, T., & O'Neill, G. (2001, September). *Households and families: 2000.* Census 2000 Brief. Washington, DC: U.S. Census Bureau, Department of Commerce.

Simon, R., & Alstein, H. (1987). *Transracial adoptees and their families: A study of identity and commitment.* New York: Praeger.

Simons, R. L., Beaman, J., Conger, R. D., & Chao, W. (1993). Stress, support, and antisocial behavior trait as determinants of emotional well-being and parenting practices among single mothers. *Journal of Marrige and the Family, 55,* 385–398.

Simons, R. L., Whitbeck, L. B., Beaman, J., & Conger, R. D. (1994). The impact of mothers' parenting, involvement by nonresidential fathers, and parental conflict on the adjustment of adolescent children. *Journal of Marriage and the Family, 56,* 356–374.

Sluzki, C. (1992). Transformations: A blueprint for narrative changes in therapy. *Family process, 31*(3), 217–230.

Small, S., & Riley, D. (1990). Toward a multidimensional assessment of work spillover into family life. *Journal of Marriage and the Family, 52,* 51–61.

Smith, G. C., Savage-Stevens, S. E., & Fabian E. S. (2002). How caregiving grandparents view support groups for children in their care. *Family Relations, 51,* 274–281.

Smith, T. E. (1983). Adolescent reactions to attempted parental control and influence techniques. *Journal of Marriage and the Family, 45*(3), 533–542.

Smits, J., Ultee, W., & Lammers, J. (1996). Effects of occupational status differences between spouses on the wife's labor force participation and occupational achievement: Findings from 12 European countries. *Journal of Marriage and the Family, 58,* 101–115.

Socha, T. J., Bromley, J., & Kelly, B. (1995). Invisible parents and children: Exploring African-American parent-child communication. In T. J. Socha & G. H. Stamp (Eds.), *Parents, children and communication: Frontiers of theory and research* (pp. 127–145). Mahwah, NJ: Lawrence Erlbaum.

Sontag, D. (1996, October 6). For poor, life "trapped in a cage." *The New York Times,* pp. 1, 10.

Soule, K. (2001). *Persistence in compliance-gaining interactions: The role of nagging behavior.* Unpublished dissertation, Northwestern University, Evanston, IL.

Soule, K. P. (2002). The what, when, who and why of nagging in interpersonal relationships. In K. M. Galvin & P. J. Cooper (Eds.), *Making connections: Readings in relational communication* (3rd ed., pp. 215–221). Los Angeles: Roxbury.

South, S. J. (2001). The geographic context of divorce: Do neighborhoods matter? *Journal of Marriage and the Family, 63,* 755–766.

Spooner, S. (1982). Intimacy in adults: A developmental model for counselors and helpers. *The Personnel and Guidance Journal, 60,* 168–170.

Sprecher, S., & McKinney, K. (1994). Sexuality in close relationships. In A. Weber & J. Harvey (Eds.), *Perspectives in close relationships* (pp. 193–216). Boston: Allyn and Bacon.

Stack, C., & Burton, L. (1998). Kinscripts. In K. V. Hansen & A. I. Garey (Eds.), *Families in the U.S.* (pp. 431–445). Philadelphia: Temple University Press.

Stafford, L., & Canary, D.J. (1991). Maintenance strategies and romance relationship type, gender and relational characteristics. *Journal of Social and Personal Relationships, 8,* 217–242.

Stafford, L., & Dainton, M. (1994). The darkside of "normal" family interaction. In W. R. Cupach & B. H. Spitzberg (Eds.), *The darkside of interpersonal communication* (pp. 259–280). Mahwah, NJ: Lawrence Erlbaum.

Stamp, G. H. (1994). The appropriation of the parental role through communication during the transition to parenthood. *Communication Monographs, 61,* 89–112.

Stanley, S. M. (1998). *The heart of commitment: Compelling research that reveals the secrets of life-long intimate marriage.* Nashville, TN: Nelson.

Stanley, S. M. (2001). Making a case for premarital education. *Family Relations, 50,* 272–280.

Stanley, S. M., Markman, H. J., & Leber, B. D. (1997). Strengthening marriages and preventing divorce. *Family Relations, 44,* 368–376.

Steffenmeier, R. H. (1982). A role model of the transition to parenthood. *Journal of Marriage and the Family, 44,* 319–334.

Steil, J. M., & Weltman, K. (1992). Influence strategies at home and at work: A study of sixty dual-career couples. *Journal of Social and Personal Relationships, 9,* 65–88.

Steier, F. (1989). Toward a radical and ecological constructivist approach to family communication. *Journal of Applied Communication Research, 17,* 1–26.

Steinberg, L., & Silverberg, S. (1987). Influences on marital satisfaction during the middle stages of the family life cycle. *Journal of Marriage and the Family, 49,* 751–761.

Stephen, T. (1984). A symbolic exchange framework for the development of intimate relationships. *Human Relations, 37,* 393–408.

Stephen, T. (1986). Communication and interdependence in geographically separated relationships. *Human Communication Research, 13*(2), 191–210.

Stephen, T. (1994). Communication in the shifting concept of intimacy: Marriage, meaning and modernity. *Communication Theory, 4,* 191–218.

Stephen, T., & Enholm, D. (1987). On linguistic and social forms: Correspondences between metaphoric and intimate relationships. *The Western Journal of Speech Communication, 51,* 329–344.

Stewart, A. J., Copeland, A. P., Chester, N. L., Malley, J. E., & Barenbaum, N. B. (1997). *Separating together: How divorce transforms families.* New York: Guilford Press.

Stinnett, N., & DeFrain, J. (1985). *Secrets of strong families.* Boston: Little, Brown.

Stith, S., & Bischof, G. (1996). Communication patterns in families of adolescent sex offenders. In D. Cahn & S. Lloyd (Eds.), *Family violence from a communication perspective* (pp. 108–126). Thousand Oaks, CA: Sage.

Stone, E. (1988). *Black sheep and kissing cousins.* New York: Penguin.

Straus, M. A. (1979). Measuring intrafamily conflict and violence. The conflict tactics (C. T. Scales). *Journal of Marriage and the Family, 41,* 75–88.

Straus, M. A. (1998). Ten myths that perpetuate corporal punishment. In K. V. Hansen & A. I. Garey (Eds.), *Families in the U.S.* (pp. 641–650). Philadelphia: Temple University Press.

Straus, M. A., & Gelles, R. J. (1986). Societal change and change in family violence from 1975 to 1985 as revealed by two national surveys. *Journal of Marriage and the Family, 48,* 465–479.

Straus, M. A., Hamby, S. L., Finekelhor, D., Moore, D. W., & Runyan, D. (1998). Identification of child maltreatment with the parent-child conflict tactics scales: Development and psychometric data for a national sample of American parents. *Child Abuse & Neglect, 22*(4), 249–270.

Sudarkasa, N. (1998). Interpreting the African heritage in Afro-American family organization. In K. V. Hansen & A. I. Garey (Eds.), *Families in the U.S.* (pp. 91–104). Philadelphia: Temple University Press.

Sulloway, F. J. (1996). *Born to rebel: Birth order, family dynamics, and creative lives.* New York: Pantheon.

Sun, Y., & Li, Y. (2002). Children's well-being during parents' marital disruption process: A pooled time-series analysis. *Journal of Marriage and the Family, 64*(2), 472–488.

Swanson, J. L. (1992). Sexism strikes men. *American Counselor,* 10–13.

Tak, Y. R., & McCubbin, M. (2002). Family stress, perceived social support and coping following the diagnosis of a child's congenital heart disease. *Journal of Advanced Nursing, 39*(2), 190–198.

Tardy, C., Hosman, L., & Bradac, J. (1981). Disclosing self to friends and family: A reexamining of initial questions. *Communication Quarterly, 29,* 263–268.

Taylor, R. J., Chatters, L. M., & Jackson, J. S. (1993). A profile of familial relations among three-generation Black families. *Family Relations, 42,* 332–341.

Terkelsen, K. G. (1980). Towards a theory of the family life cycle. In E. Carter & M. McGoldrick (Eds.), The family life cycle: *A framework for family therapy* (pp. 21–52). New York: Gardner Press.

Tessler, R., Gamache, G., & Liu, L. (1999). *West meets east: Americans adopt Chinese children.* Westport, CT: Bergin & Garvey.

Thilborger, C. (1998, April). *Metaphorical perceptions of familial communication: Where gender differences are really more than skin deep.* Paper presented at the meeting of the Central State Communication Association, Chicago.

"Thirty-one studies published on couple communication." (1989, March). *Relationship Building, 3*(1), 1–5.

Thomas, J., Schvaneveldt, J. D., & Young, M. (1993). Programs in family life education: Development, implementation and evaluation. In M. E. Arens, J. D. Schvanveldt, & J. J. Moss (Eds.), *Handbook of family life education: Vol. 1. Foundations of family life education* (pp. 106–130). Newbury Park, CA: Sage.

Thomas, V., & Olson, D. H. (1994). Circumplex model: Curvilinearity using clinical rating scale (CRS) and FACES III. *Family Journal, 2*, 36–44.

Thompson, D. C., & Dickson, F. (1995, November). *Family rituals as communicative events: A grounded theory.* Paper presented at the annual meeting of the Speech Communication Association, San Antonio, TX.

Thomson, E., McLanahan, S., & Curtin, R. B. (1992). Family structure, gender and parental socialization. *Journal of Marriage and the Family, 54*, 368–378.

Tilden, V. P., Tolle, S. W., Nelson, C. A., & Fields, J. (2001). Family decision-making to withdraw life-sustaining treatments from hospitalized patients. *Nursing Research, 50*(2), 105–115.

"Times will begin reporting gay couples' ceremonies." (2002, August 18). *The New York Times*, p. 23.

Tolan, P. H. (2002). Family-focused prevention research: "Tough but tender." In H. A. Liddle, D. A. Santisteban, R. F. Levant, & J. H. Bray (Eds.), *Family psychology: Science-based interventions* (pp. 197–213). Washington, DC: American Psychological Association.

Tomlinson, P. S., Swiggum, P., & Harbaugh, B. L. (1999). Identification of nurse-family intervention sites to decrease health-related family boundary ambiguity in PICU. *Issues in Comprehensive Pediatric Nursing, 22*, 27–47.

Toro-Morn, M. (1998). Gender, class, family and migration: Puerto Rican woman in Chicago. In K. Hansen & A. Garey (Eds.), *Families in the U.S.* (pp. 190–199). Philadelphia: Temple University Press.

Townsend, N. (1998). Fathers and sons: Men's experience and the reproduction of fatherhood. In K. V. Hansen & A. I. Garey (Eds.), *Families in the U.S.* (pp. 364–376). Philadelphia: Temple University Press.

Trice, H. M., & Beyer, J. M. (1984). Studying organizational cultures through rites and ceremonies. *Academy of Management Review, 9*, 653–669.

Troth, A., & Peterson, C. C. (2000). Factors predicting safe-sex talk and condom use in early sexual relationships. *Health Communication, 12*, 195–218.

Trujillo, N. (1998). In search of Naunny's grave. *Text and Performance Quarterly, 18*(4) 344–368.

Tschann, J. (1988). Self-disclosure in adult friendship: Gender and marital status differences. *Journal of Social and Personal Relationships, 5*, 65–81.

Tsouna-Hadjis, E., Vemmos, K. N., Zakopoulos, N., & Stamatelopoulos, S. (2000). First-stroke recovery process: The role of family social support. *Archives of Physical Medicine & Rehabilitation, 81*(7), 881–887.

Tucker, J. S., & Anders, S. L. (2001). Social control of health behaviors in marriage. *Journal of Applied Social Psychology, 31*(3), 467–485.

Tucker, J. S., & Mueller, J. S. (2000). Spouses' social control of health behaviors: Use and effectiveness of specific strategies. *Personality and Social Psychology Bulletin, 26*(9), 1120–1130.

Turner, R. H. (1970). Conflict and harmony. *Family interaction* (pp. 135–163). New York: John Wiley.

U.S. Census. (1998). Washington, DC: Government Printing Office.

U.S. Census. (2000). Washington, DC: Government Printing Office.

Udry, J. R., & Campbell, B. (Eds.). (1994). *Sexuality across the life course.* Chicago: University of Chicago Press.

Uttal, L. (1998). Racial safety and cultural maintenance: The child care concerns of employed mothers. In K. V. Hansen & A. I. Garey (Eds.), *Families in the U.S.* (pp. 597–618). Philadelphia: Temple University Press.

Vaillant, C. O., & Vaillant, G. E. (1993). Is the U-curve of marital satisfaction an illusion? A 40-year study of marriage. *Journal of Marriage and the Family, 55*, 230–239.

Van Riper, M. (2000). Family variables associated with well-being in siblings of children with down syndrome. *Journal of Family Nursing, 6*(3), 267–286.

Vangelisti, A. L. (1993). Communication in the family: The influence of time, relational prototypes and irrationality. *Communication Monographs, 60*, 42–54.

Vangelisti, A. L. (1994a). Couples' communication problems: The counselor's perspective. *Journal of Applied Communication Research, 22*, 106–126.

Vangelisti, A. L. (1994b). Family secrets: Forms, functions, and correlates. *Journal of Social and Personal Relationships, 11*, 113–135.

Vangelisti, A. L., & Banski, M. A. (1993). Couples debriefing conversations, the impact of gender, occupation and demographic characteristics. *Family Relations, 42,* 149–157.

Vangelisti, A. L., & Caughlin, J. (1997). Revealing family secrets: The influence of topic function and relationships. *Journal of Social and Personal Relationships, 14*(5), 679–705.

Vangelisti, A. L., Caughlin, J. P., & Timmerman, L. (2000, November). *Criteria for revealing family secrets.* Paper presented at the meeting of National Communication Association, Seattle, WA.

Vangelisti, A. L., & Crumley, L. (1998). Reactions to messages that hurt: The influence of relational contexts. *Communication Monographs, 65,* 173–196.

Vangelisti, A. L., Crumley, L. P., & Baker, J. L. (1999). Family portraits: Stories as standards for family relationships. *Journal of Social and Personal Relationships, 3,* 335–368.

Vangelisti, A. L., & Huston, T. L. (1994). Maintaining marital satisfaction and love. In D. J. Canary & L. Stafford (Eds.), *Communication and relational maintenance* (pp. 165–186). San Diego, CA: Academic Press.

Villard, K., & Whipple, L. (1976). *Beginnings in relational communication.* New York: John Wiley.

Vissing, Y., & Baily, W. (1996). Parent-to-child verbal aggression. In D. Cahn & S. Lloyd (Eds.), *Family violence from a communication perspective* (pp. 85–107). Thousand Oaks, CA: Sage.

Vogl-Bauer, S. M., & Kalbfleisch, P. J. (1997, November). *The impact of perceived equity on parent/adolescent communication strategy usage and relational outcomes.* Paper presented at the meeting of the National Communication Association, Chicago.

Vuchinich, S. (1987). Starting and stopping spontaneous family conflicts. *Journal of Marriage and the Family, 49*(3), 591–601.

Vuchinich, S., & DeBaryske, B. D. (1997). Factor structure and predictive validity of questionnaire reports on family problem solving. *Journal of Marriage and the Family, 59,* 915–927.

Vuchinich, S., Ozretich, R. A., Pratt, C. C., & Keeedler, B. (2002). Problem-solving communication in foster families and birth families. *Child Welfare, 81*(4), 571–594.

Vuchinich, S., Teachman, J., & Crosby, L. (1991). Families and hazard rates that change over time: Some methodological issues in analyzing transitions. *Journal of Marriage and the Family, 53,* 898–912.

Waite, L. (1987). Nest-leaving patterns and the transition to marriage for young men and women. *Journal of Marriage and the Family, 49*(3), 507–516.

Waite, L. J., & Gallagher, M. (2000). *The case for marriage.* New York: Doubleday.

Waite, L. J., & Joyner, K. (2001). Emotional satisfaction and physical pleasure in sexual unions: Time horizon, sexual behavior, and sexual exclusivity. *Journal of Marriage and Family, 63,* 247–262.

Walker, A. J. (1993). Teaching about race, gender, and class diversity in U.S. families. *Family Relations, 42,* 342–350.

Wallerstein, J. (1997). Forget the notion divorce won't hurt kids. It will. Interview by J. M. Adams. *Biography,* 79–81.

Wallerstein, J., & Blakeslee, S. (1989). *Second chances.* New York: Ticknor and Fields.

Wallerstein, J., & Blakeslee, S. (1995). *The good marriage.* Boston: Houghton Mifflin.

Wallerstein, J. S., Lewis, J. M., & Blakeslee, S. (2000). *The unexpected legacy of divorce: A 25 year landmark study.* New York: Hyperion.

Walsh, F. (1993). Conceptualization of normal family processes. In F. Walsh (Ed.), *Normal family processes* (2nd ed., pp. 3–69). New York: Guilford Press.

Walsh, F. (1999). Families in later life. In B. Carter & M. McGolderick (Eds.), *The expanded family life cycle* (3rd ed., pp. 307–326). Boston: Allyn and Bacon.

Wamboldt, F., & Reiss, D. (1989). Defining a family heritage and a new relationship identity: Two central tasks in the making of a marriage. *Family Process, 28,* 317–335.

Wampler, K. S. (1990). An update of research on the Couple Communication Program. *Family Science Review, 3,* 21–40.

Warren, C. (1995). Parent-child communication about sex. In T. J. Socha & G. H. Stamp (Eds.), *Parents, children and communication: Frontiers of theory and research* (pp. 173–201). Mahwah, NJ: Lawrence Erlbaum.

Warren, C. (2003). Communicating about sex with parents and partners. In K. M. Galvin & P. J. Cooper (Eds.), *Making connections: Readings in relational communication* (3rd ed., pp. 317–324). Los Angeles: Roxbury.

Waterman, J. (1979). Family patterns of self-disclosure. In G. Chelune & Associates (Eds.), *Self-disclosure* (pp. 225–242). San Francisco: Jossey-Bass.

Watzlawick, P., Beavin, J., & Jackson, D. D. (1967). *Pragmatics of human communication.* New York: W. W. Norton.

Webster-Stratton, C. (1997). From parent training to community building. *Families and Society, 78,* 156–171.

Weigel, D. J., & Ballard-Reisch, D. S. (2001). The impact of relational maintenance behaviors on marital satisfaction: A longitudinal analysis. *Journal of Family Communication, 1,* 265–279.

Weiss, R. (1997, November 10). Aging new answers to old questions. *National Geographic,* 31.

Weiss, R., & Dehle, C. (1994). Cognitive behavioral perspectives on marital conflict. In D. Cahn (Ed.), *Conflict in personal relationships* (pp. 95–116). Hillsdale, NJ: Lawrence Erlbaum.

Weldon, M. (1997a, July 13). Marriage: Men won't budge for wives' careers. *Chicago Tribune,* sec. 13, p. 3.

Weldon, M. (1997b, July 20). Many new moms feel guilt, anger. *Chicago Tribune,* sec. 13, p. 3.

Weldon, M. (1998, January 11). Elderly care usually falls to daughters. *Chicago Tribune,* sec. 13, p. 3.

Wells, B. (1986). *The meaning makers.* Portsmouth, NH: Heineman.

Wenk, D. A., Hardesty, C. L., Morgan, C. S., & Blair, S. L. (1994). The influence of parental involvement on the well-being of sons and daughters. *Journal of Marriage and the Family, 56,* 229–234.

Werner, C. (1987). Home interiors: A time and place for interpersonal relationships. *Environment and behavior, 19*(2), 169–179.

Werner, C., Altman, I., & Brown, B. (1992). A transactional approach to interpersonal relations: Physical environment, social context and temporal qualities. *Journal of Social and Personal Relationships, 9,* 287–323.

Werner, C., & Baxter, L. A. (1994). Temporal qualities of relationships: Organismic, transactional and dialectical. In M. L. Knapp & G. R. Miller (Eds.), *Handbook of interpersonal communication* (pp. 323–379). Thousand Oaks, CA: Sage.

West, R., & Turner, L. H. (1995). Communication in lesbian and gay families: Developing a descriptive base. In T. Socha & G. Stamp (Eds.), *Parents, children and communication* (pp. 147–170). Mahwah, NJ: Lawrence Erlbaum.

West, R., & Turner, L. H. (2000). *Introducing communication theory.* Mountain View, CA: Mayfield.

Westin, A. (1967). *Privacy and freedom.* New York: Atheneum.

Weston, K. (1993). *Families we choose.* New York: Columbia University Press.

"What constitutes a family?" (1992, July–August). *Public Opinion and Demographic Report,* American Enterprise, p. 101.

Whitchurch, G., & Constantine, L. (1993). Systems theory. In P. Boss et al. (Eds.), *Sourcebook of family theories and methods* (pp. 325–352). New York: Plenum Press.

Whitchurch, G., & Dickson, F. C. (1999). Family communication. In M. B. Sussman, S. K. Steinmetz, & G. W. Peterson (Eds.), *Handbook of marriage and the family* (2nd ed., pp. 687–704). New York: Plenum Press.

Whitchurch, G., & Pace, T. (1993). Communication skills & interpersonal violence. *Journal of Applied Communication, 21,* 96–102.

White, J. M., & Klein, D. M. (2002). *Family theories* (2nd ed.). Thousand Oaks, CA: Sage.

White, L. & Rogers, S.J. (2000) Economic circumstances and family outcomes: A review of the 1990's. *Journal of the Marriage and Family, 62,* 1035–1051.

White, M., & Epston, T. D. (1990). *Narrative means to therapeutic ends.* New York: W. W. Norton.

Whiteside, M. F. (1989). Family rituals as a key to kinship connections in remarried families. *Family Relations, 38,* 34–39.

Widenfelt, B. V., Hosman, C., Schaap, C., & van der Staak, C. (1996). The prevention of relationship distress for couples at risk: A controlled evaluation with nine-month and two-year follows. *Family Relations, 45,* 156–165.

Wilder, C., & Collins, S. (1994). Patterns of interactional paradoxes. In W. R. Cupach & B. H. Spitzberg (Eds.), *The darkside of interpersonal communication* (pp. 83–103). Mahwah, NJ: Lawrence Erlbaum.

Wilkie, J. R., Ferree, M. M., & Ratcliff, K. S. (1998). Gender and fairness: Marital satisfaction in two-earner couples. *Journal of Marriage and the Family, 60,* 577–594.

Wilkinson, C. (1989). Family first. *Emphasis, 24,* 1–2. Evanston: Mental Health Association of Evanston.

Wilkinson, C. (2000). Expressing affection: A vocabulary of loving messages. In K. Galvin & P. Cooper (Eds.), *Making connections: Readings in relational communication* (2nd ed., pp. 160–167). Los Angeles: Roxbury.

Wilmot, J., & Wilmot, W. (1981). *Interpersonal conflict.* Dubuque, IA: William C. Brown.

Wilmot, W. W. (1987). *Dyadic communication* (3rd ed.). New York: Random House.

Wilson, S. R., Bylund, C. L., Hayes, J., Morgan, W., & Herman, A. (2002, July). *Mothers' child abuse potential and trait verbal aggressive-*

ness as predictors of their on-line thoughts and feelings during mother-child playtime interactions. Paper presented at the 11th International Conference on Personal Relationships, Halifax, Nova Scotia.

Wilson, S. R., Morgan, W., Hayes, J., Bylund, C., & Herman, A. (2002). Mothers's child abuse potential as a predictor of maternal and child behaviors during playtime interactions. Paper presented at the Center for Disease Control sponsored meeting "Victimization of children and youth: An international research conference," Portsmouth, NH.

Wilson, S. R., & Whipple, E. E. (1995). Communication, discipline, and physical child abuse. In T. Socha & G. Stamp (Eds.), Parents, children, and communication: Frontiers in theory and research (pp. 299–317). Hillsdale, NJ: Lawrence Erlbaum.

"Wired seniors: A fervent few, inspired by family ties." (2001, September 9). The PEW Internet and American Life Project. www.pewinternet.org.

Witteman, H., & Fitzpatrick, M. A. (1986). Compliance-gaining in marital interaction: Power bases, processes, and outcomes. Communication Monographs, 53(2), 130–143.

Witteman, H., & Fitzpatrick, M. A. (1987). A social scientific view of marriage encounter. Journal of Clinical and Social Psychology.

Wolff, L. O. (1993, November). Family narrative: How our stories shape us. Paper presented at the meeting of the Speech Communication Association, Miami, FL.

Wolin, S. J., & Bennett, L. A. (1984). Family rituals. Family Process, 23, 401–420.

Wood B., & Talmon, M. (1983). Family boundaries in transition: A search for alternatives. Family Process, 22, 347–357.

Wood, J. T. (1997). Gendered lives: Communication, gender, and culture (2nd ed.). Belmont, CA: Wadsworth.

Wood, J. T. (1998). But I thought you meant . . . Misunderstandings in human communication. Mountain View, CA: Mayfield.

Wood, J. T. (1999). Everyday encounters: An introduction to interpersonal conversation (2nd ed.). Belmont, CA: Wadsworth.

Wood, J. T. (2000). Relational communication (2nd ed.). Belmont, CA: Wadsworth.

Wood, J. T. (2001). Gendered lives: Communication gender and culture (4th ed.). Belmont, CA: Wadsworth.

Wood, J. T., & Inman, C. C. (1993). In a different mode: Masculine styles of communicating

closeness. Journal of Applied Communication Research, 21, 279–295.

World Population Profile: 1998—Highlights. (2002, January 17), Washington, DC: U.S. Census Bureau. http://www.census.gov/ipc/www/wp98001.html.

Wu, Z., & Penning, M. (1997). Marital instability after midlife. Journal of Family Issues, 21, 191–224.

Wuthernow, R. (1994). Sharing the journey. New York: The Free Press.

Wynne, L. (Ed.). (1988). The state of the art in family therapy research: Controversies and recommendations. New York: Family Process Press.

Xu, X., & Lai, S. (2002). Resources, gender ideologies and marital power. Journal of Family Issues, 23(2), 209–245.

Yerby, J. (1993, November). Co-constructing alternative stories: Narrative approaches in the family therapy literature. Paper presented at the meeting of the Speech Communication Association, Miami, FL.

Yerby, J. (1995). Family systems theory reconsidered: Integrating social construction theory and dialectical processes. Communication Theory, 5, 339–365.

Yerby, J., & Buerkel-Rothfuss, N. L. (1982, November). Communication patterns, contradictions, and family functions. Paper presented at the meeting of the Speech Communication Association, New York.

Yerby, J., Buerkel-Rothfuss, N. L., & Bochner, A. (1990). Understanding family communication. Scottsdale, AZ: Gorsuch Scarisbrick.

Zabriskie, R. B., & McCormick, B. P. (2001). The influences of family leisure patterns on perceptions of family functioning. Family Relations, 50, 281–289.

Zernike, K. (1998, June 21). Feminism has created progress, last man, oh, man, look what else. Chicago Tribune.

Zill, N., & Nord, C. W. (1994). How American families are faring in a changing economy and an individualistic society. Washington, DC: Child Trends, Inc.

Zukow, P. G. (1989). Sibling interaction across cultures: Theoretical and methodological issues. New York: Springer-Verlag.

Zvonkovic, A. M., Schmiege, C. J., & Hall, L. D. (1994). Influence strategies used when couples make work family decisions and their importance for marital satisfaction. Family Relations, 43(2), 182–188.

Name Index

427

SUBJECT INDEX